NMTA 16

History, Geography, Economics, Civics and Government

Teacher Certification Exam

By: Sharon Wynne, M.S
Southern Connecticut State University

XAMonline, INC.
Boston

XAMonline, Inc.
21 Orient Ave.
Melrose, MA 02176
Toll Free 1-800-301-4647
Email: info@xamonline.com
Web www.xamonline.com
Fax: 1-781-662-9268

Library of Congress Cataloging-in-Publication Data

Wynne, Sharon A.
History, Geography, Economics, Civics and Government 16: Teacher Certification / Sharon A. Wynne. -2nd ed. ISBN 978-1-58197-762-2
1. History, Geography, Economics, Civics and Government 16. 2. Study Guides.
3. NMTA 4. Teachers' Certification & Licensure. 5. Careers

Disclaimer:
The opinions expressed in this publication are the sole works of XAMonline and were created independently from the National Education Association,
Educational Testing Service, or any State Department of Education, National Evaluation Systems or other testing affiliates.

Between the time of publication and printing, state specific standards as well as testing formats and website information may change that is not included in part or in whole within this product. Sample test questions are developed by XAMonline and reflect similar content as on real tests; however, they are not former tests. XAMonline assembles content that aligns with state standards but makes no claims nor guarantees teacher candidates a passing score. Numerical scores are determined by testing companies such as NES or ETS and then are compared with individual state standards. A passing score varies from state to state.

Printed in the United States of America

NMTA: History, Geography, Economics, Civics and Government 16
ISBN: 978-1-58197-762-2

About the Subject Assessments

Subject Assessment in the Middle Schools Social Science examination

Purpose: The assessments are designed to test the knowledge and competencies of prospective secondary level teachers. The question bank from which the assessment is drawn is undergoing constant revision. As a result, your test may include questions that will not count towards your score.

Test Version: There are two versions of subject assessments for social science tests in New Mexico. Although both versions of the test emphasize conceptual comprehension, synthesis, and analysis of the principles of the social sciences, the major difference between versions lays in the *degree* to which the examinee's knowledge is tested.

Version 1: **Social Science 7-12 Field 16** This version requires a greater depth of comprehension in history, economics, geography, and civics and government. The social science guide is based on a typical knowledge level of persons who have completed a *bachelor's degree program* in social science.

Version 2: **Social Science K-8 Field 26** This version test the examinee's knowledge level in less detail than the first version of the subject assessments. The degree of knowledge required is typically based on completion of *introductory-level course work* in the same areas mentioned above.

Taking the Correct Version of the Subject Assessment: While some states other than New Mexico offer just one test called a social science secondary test, New Mexico Public Education Department breaks out those topics into two tests. The History is basically what you would take to become a middle school teacher and 7-12 if you plan on teaching at the high school level. However, as New Mexico's licensure requirements change, it's highly recommended that you consult your educational institution's teaching preparation counselor or your state board of education's teacher licensure division, to verify which version of the assessment you should take. If you plan on applying for a position in another state as well as New Mexico consider a History option. XAMonline.com website can inform you what you need to do to become certified in any particular state.

Time Allowance, Format, and Length: The time allowance and format for both versions are identical; you will have up to four hours to complete the test and the questions are presented in a 100 question selected response format. New Mexico does not test using construct essays or other essay formats. Tests are offered throughout the year at selected test sites.

Content Areas: Both versions of the subject assessments share a degree of commonality in that the test content categories are divided into four broad areas that roughly overlap between test versions. However, version (1) has a narrower focus on specific disciplines than does version (2).

Test Taxonomy: Both versions of the subject assessments are constructed on the comprehension, synthesis and analysis levels of Bloom's Taxonomy. In many questions, the candidate must apply knowledge of more than one discipline in order to correctly answer the questions.

Additional Information about the New Mexico Teacher Assessments: The New Mexico series subject assessments are developed by the *Public Education Department of Santa Fe*, New Mexico. They provide additional information on the New Mexico Teacher Assessments, including registration, preparation and testing procedures, study materials such as topical guides that are about 22 pages of information including approximately 10 additional sample questions.

Topical guides versus study guides. The latest topical guide developed by the State of New Mexico is presented below. The topics are in bold face type. The numbers following the competencies represents the interpretation of the major topics by the State of New Mexico test preparation staff.

TABLE OF CONTENTS

SUBAREA III—ECONOMICS

Great Study and Testing Tips!

What to study in order to prepare for the subject assessments are the focus of this study guide but equally important is *how* you study.

You can increase your chances of truly mastering the information by taking some simple, but effective steps.

Study Tips:

1. **Some foods aid the learning process.** Foods such as milk, nuts, seeds, rice, and oats help your study efforts by releasing natural memory enhancers called CCKs (*cholecystokinin*) composed of *tryptophan*, *choline*, and *phenylalanine*. All of these chemicals enhance the neurotransmitters associated with memory. Before studying, try a light, protein-rich meal of eggs, turkey, and fish. All of these foods release the memory enhancing chemicals. The better the connections, the more you comprehend.

Likewise, before you take a test, stick to a light snack of energy boosting and relaxing foods. A glass of milk, a piece of fruit, or some peanuts all release various memory-boosting chemicals and help you to relax and focus on the subject at hand.

2. **Learn to take great notes.** A by-product of our modern culture is that we have grown accustomed to getting our information in short doses (i.e. TV news sound bites or USA Today style newspaper articles.)

Consequently, we've subconsciously trained ourselves to assimilate information better in neat little packages. If your notes are scrawled all over the paper, it fragments the flow of the information. Strive for clarity. Newspapers use a standard format to achieve clarity. Your notes can be much clearer through use of proper formatting. A very effective format is called the *"Cornell Method."*

> Take a sheet of loose-leaf lined notebook paper and draw a line all the way down the paper about 1-2" from the left-hand edge.
>
> Draw another line across the width of the paper about 1-2" up from the bottom. Repeat this process on the reverse side of the page.

Look at the highly effective result. You have ample room for notes, a left hand margin for special emphasis items or inserting supplementary data from the textbook, a large area at the bottom for a brief summary, and a little rectangular space for just about anything you want.

3. **<u>Get the concept then the details.</u>** Too often we focus on the details and don't gather an understanding of the concept. However, if you simply memorize only dates, places, or names, you may well miss the whole point of the subject.

A key way to understand things is to put them in your own words. If you are working from a textbook, automatically summarize each paragraph in your mind. If you are outlining text, don't simply copy the author's words.

Rephrase them in your own words. You remember your own thoughts and words much better than someone else's, and subconsciously tend to associate the important details to the core concepts.

4. **<u>Ask Why?</u>** Pull apart written material paragraph by paragraph and don't forget the captions under the illustrations.

Example: If the heading is "Stream Erosion", flip it around to read "Why do streams erode?" Then answer the questions.

If you train your mind to think in a series of questions and answers, not only will you learn more, but it also helps to lessen the test anxiety because you are used to answering questions.

5. **<u>Read for reinforcement and future needs.</u>** Even if you only have 10 minutes, put your notes or a book in your hand. Your mind is similar to a computer; you have to input data in order to have it processed. *By reading, you are creating the neural connections for future retrieval.* The more times you read something, the more you reinforce the learning of ideas.

Even if you don't fully understand something on the first pass, *your mind stores much of the material for later recall.*

6. **<u>Relax to learn so go into exile.</u>** Our bodies respond to an inner clock called biorhythms. Burning the midnight oil works well for some people, but not everyone.

If possible, set aside a particular place to study that is free of distractions. Shut off the television, cell phone, pager and exile your friends and family during your study period.

If you really are bothered by silence, try background music. Light classical music at a low volume has been shown to aid in concentration over other types.

Music that evokes pleasant emotions without lyrics are highly suggested. Try just about anything by Mozart. It relaxes you.

7. **Use arrows not highlighters.** At best, it's difficult to read a page full of yellow, pink, blue, and green streaks.

Try staring at a neon sign for a while and you'll soon see my point, the horde of colors obscure the message.

A quick note, a brief dash of color, an underline, and an arrow pointing to a particular passage is much clearer than a horde of highlighted words.

8. **Budget your study time**. Although you shouldn't ignore any of the material, ***allocate your available study time in the same ratio that topics may appear on the test.***

Testing Tips:

1. **Get smart, play dumb. Don't read anything into the question.** Don't make an assumption that the test writer is looking for something else than what is asked. Stick to the question as written and don't read extra things into it.

2. **Read the question and all the choices *twice* before answering the question.** You may miss something by not carefully reading, and then re-reading both the question and the answers.

If you really don't have a clue as to the right answer, leave it blank on the first time through. Go on to the other questions, as they may provide a clue as to how to answer the skipped questions.

If later on, you still can't answer the skipped ones . . . ***Guess.***
The only penalty for guessing is that you *might* get it wrong. Only one thing is certain; if you don't put anything down, you will get it wrong!

3. **Turn the question into a statement.** Look at the way the questions are worded. The syntax of the question usually provides a clue. Does it seem more familiar as a statement rather than as a question? Does it sound strange?

By turning a question into a statement, you may be able to spot if an answer sounds right, and it may also trigger memories of material you have read.

4. **Look for hidden clues.** It's actually very difficult to compose multiple-foil (choice) questions without giving away part of the answer in the options presented.

In most multiple-choice questions you can often readily eliminate one or two of the potential answers. This leaves you with only two real possibilities and automatically your odds go to Fifty-Fifty for very little work.

5. **Trust your instincts.** For every fact that you have read, you subconsciously retain something of that knowledge. On questions that you aren't really certain about, go with your basic instincts. **Your first impression on how to answer a question is usually correct.**

6. **Mark your answers directly on the test booklet.** Don't bother trying to fill in the optical scan sheet on the first pass through the test.

Just be very careful not to miss-mark your answers when you eventually transcribe them to the scan sheet.

7. **Watch the clock!** You have a set amount of time to answer the questions. Don't get bogged down trying to answer a single question at the expense of 10 questions you can more readily answer.

SUBAREA I—HISTORY

COMPETENCY 1: Understand key historical terms and concepts and recognize ways in which human beings view themselves and others over time.

Skill 1.1: Apply important conceptual terms to the analysis of general historical phenomena and specific historical events.

HISTORY is the study of the past, especially the aspects of the human past, political and economic events as well as cultural and social conditions. Students study history through textbooks, research, field trips to museums and historical sights, and other methods. Most nations set the requirements in history to study the country's heritage, usually to develop an awareness and feeling of loyalty and patriotism. History is generally divided into the three main divisions: (a) time periods, (b) nations, and (c) specialized topics. Study is accomplished through research, reading, and writing.

History is without doubt an integral part of every other discipline in the social sciences. Knowing historical background on anything and anyone anywhere goes a long way towards explaining that what happened in the past leads up to and explains the present.

Causality: The reason something happens, its cause, is a basic category of human thinking. We want to know the causes of some major event in our lives. Within the study of history, causality is the analysis of the reasons for change. The question we are asking is why and how a particular society or event developed in the particular way it did given the context in which it occurred.

Conflict: Conflict within history is opposition of ideas, principles, values or claims. Conflict may take the form of internal clashes of principles or ideas or claims within a society or group or it may take the form of opposition between groups or societies.

Bias: A prejudice or a predisposition either toward or against something. In the study of history, bias can refer to the persons or groups studied, in terms of a society's bias toward a particular political system, or it can refer to the historian's predisposition to evaluate events in a particular way.

Interdependence: A condition in which two things or groups rely upon one another; as opposed to independence, in which each thing or group relies only upon itself.

Identity: The state or perception of being a particular thing or person. Identity can also refer to the understanding or self-understanding of groups, nations, etc.

Nation-state: A particular type of political entity that provides a sovereign territory for a specific nation in which other factors also unite the citizens (e.g., language, race, ancestry, etc.).

Culture: the civilization, achievements, and customs of the people of a particular time and place.

Skill 1.2: Recognize varying perspectives in historical writing and analyze social and cultural influences on historical inquiry

Varying perspectives on the study of history may be summarized under one of three definitions:

1. History is the study of what persons have done and said and thought in the past.
2. History is a creative attempt to reconstruct the lives and thoughts of particular persons who lived at specific times (biography).
3. History is the study of the social aspects of humans, both past and present.

The first definition essentially applies to the *narrative school of history.* This approach attempts to provide a general account of the most important things people have said, done, written, etc. in the past. Several schools fall within this category:

- The political-institutional school believes that what has occurred in government and law is the most important.
- The school of intellectual history (the history of ideas) finds greatest importance in the emergence of higher thought and feeling (including philosophy, art, science, literature).
- Economic historians are most concerned with the way humans have controlled the environment and made a living.
- Cultural historians focus on the development of ideas within the total context of a social, economic, and political situation.

The second definition above understands history as biography of important persons. These historians fall into one of two schools:

- Psychologizing approaches – historians who believe the motivations and actions of people in the past can be understood and explained in terms of modern psychological theories
- Non-psychologizing approaches – historians who believe it is impossible to psychoanalyze people who are dead and that people of the past must be understood in terms of the theories of personality and motivation that were accepted at the time.

The third definition above essentially equates history with sociology. This approach believes it is possible to study history to observe forms of social change that are relevant to current social problems. This group is also divided:

- One group uses the Marxist doctrine of dialectical materialism to explain social change.
- Another group believes that each society is unique and distinctive Comparative sociological historians study history to identify consistent patterns that run through all or several societies.

Skill 1.3: Use key concepts to identify and explain patterns of historical change and continuity within and across cultures.

Innovation is the introduction of new ways of performing work or organizing societies, and can spur drastic changes in a culture. Prior to the innovation of agriculture, for instance, human cultures were largely nomadic and survived by hunting and gathering their food. Agriculture led directly to the development of permanent settlements and a radical change in social organization. Likewise, technological innovations in the Industrial Revolution of the 19th Century changed the way work was performed and transformed the economic institutions of western cultures. Recent innovations in communications are changing the way cultures interact today.

Cultural diffusion is the movement of cultural ideas or materials between populations independent of the movement of those populations. Cultural diffusion can take place when two populations are close to one another, through direct interaction, or across great distances, through mass media and other routes. American movies are popular all over the world, for instance. Within the US, hockey, traditionally a Canadian pastime, has become a popular sport. These are both examples of cultural diffusion.

Adaptation is the process that individuals and societies go through in changing their behavior and organization to cope with social, economic and environmental pressures.

Acculturation is an exchange or adoption of cultural features when two cultures come into regular direct contact. An example of acculturation is the adoption of Christianity and western dress by many Native Americans in the United States.

Assimilation is the process of a minority ethnic group largely adopting the culture of the larger group it exists within. These groups are typically immigrants moving to a new country, as with the European immigrants who traveled to the United States at the beginning of the 20th Century who assimilated to American culture.

Extinction is the complete disappearance of a culture. Extinction can occur suddenly, from disease, famine or war when the people of a culture are completely destroyed, or slowly over time as a culture adapts, acculturates or assimilates to the point where its original features are lost.

Skill 1.4: Use historical facts and concepts to make informed decisions on public issues with emphasis on the United States.

Political science examines the theory of politics and how it behaves in countries and in international situations. Political science has certain varied aspects, including political history, political philosophy, economics, and international relations. All of these aspects can be used to examine both general and specific political issues today.

For example, a general issue in the United States is the preponderance of the two-party system. American politics is full of political parties, but only the Democrats and Republicans get major funding and large slates of candidates for elections across the country.

- This is due in large part to the political history of the country, which has tended to discourage any other participation. The Reform Party was a major force in America until a few years ago, but it now seems to fading into irrelevance.
- Political philosophy speaks to this issue in that the ideologies of the Democratic and Republican Parties are generally wide enough to cover the views of most Americans. Extreme left- or right-wing parties have their adherents, but they (the adherents and the parties) are few and far between.
- Economics speaks to this in that it is very difficult for parties other than the two big ones to afford any kind of parity-achieving efforts. The two big parties are so much a dichotomous part of American political thinking that any outside forces face an inherently uphill battle just to get dollars and cents to conduct campaigns.
- In international relations as well, the Democratic and Republican Parties are familiar to leaders of and observers from other countries. Again we see the ideologies of these parties, which encompass a wide range of political beliefs, many of which can be found in the leaders of other countries as well.

A specific issue that can be examined in these terms is capital punishment.

- The political history of the United States includes a long history of capital punishment, by both the federal and state governments. (Theoretically, local governments have no such power.) This tradition was handed down from the European countries that spawned the settlers who eventually became the forerunners of Americans today. The Supreme Court has, from time to time, found elements of capital punishment unconstitutional because of the Eighth Amendment prohibition of cruel and unusual punishment; but the general practices of lethal injection remain on the legal books of many governments.

- Political philosophy on this issue generally falls into the two camps of Yes or No. Those in favor of capital punishment usually have their beliefs for a reason, as do those who oppose it. In many cases, those who favor it have been victims of crimes. This is the case for many who oppose it, however, so this issue cannot be classified in just one camp. The U.S. Government doesn't make a habit of executing people. Certain states do, however.
- Economics is definitely a factor in this debate. Those who favor capital punishment point to how much money the state saves by avoiding the expensive legal alternative, life imprisonment. Those who oppose capital punishment, however, point to the legal system in America, which requires exhaustive appeals and seemingly endless amounts of time, to make sure not only that an innocent person is not executed but also that that person is not treated inhumanely in the process.
- International relations can be examined as well. The U.S. is one of a handful of First World countries that have laws providing for capital punishment. This subject is sometimes a sore spot for American diplomats when dealing with countries whose people expressly detest executing criminals.

COMPETENCY 2.0: Understand relationships between science, technology, and society; and analyze these developments from diverse perspectives.

Skill 2.1: Recognize the significance of key scientific discoveries and major technological advances.

Society and culture are very closely related. They are in fact closely intertwined. Together they have influenced every aspect of the human life. Science and technology are no exception to this.

Let us examine **the influence of social and cultural factors on science** first and then we will see their effect on technology.

The influence of social and cultural factors on science is profound. In a way we can say that society has changed the face of science by absorbing the scientific innovations. Science has always been a big part of society. The difference is that in ancient societies, people did not realize that it was science, but took as a part of their lives. In the modern society, everything has a label and a name, so that people are aware of science and other disciplines.

Societies had a very big concern regarding accepting science, especially, when the science proved some of the cultural aspects as myths. There was a big dilemma as to accept the proven facts provided by scientific investigations or cling to cultural norms. This went on for centuries. It took a long time for societies to accept these facts and to leave some of the cultural practices. At the same time, we must give full credit to cultural practices, which are scientifically correct, but are connected to religion so that people would take them more seriously. The ancient cultures did this to protect their societies from infections and deaths. The interesting thing is that

We can conclude that there are two factors - one is **cultural practices** by societies which are scientifically correct and the second one is cultural practices which have no scientific foundation, but which are myths and superstitions. A society's progress depends on distinguishing between these two. Some indigenous societies suffered very badly, when they were not quick enough to move along with times, since their cultures are very ancient and the people very proud to accept new challenges and adapt to new changes.
At the same time, ancient cultures like the Chinese, Egyptian, Greek, Asian Indian had well developed science which was recorded in their writings.

Let's take a look at **the effect of society and culture on technology.**
If we compare science to a volcano, technology is like lava spewing out of the volcano. That was the scenario in the last few centuries in terms of rapid strides in the development of technology. Technology greatly influenced society and culture and at the same time, science and culture exercised their influence on technology. It is like a two way thorough fare.
It became extremely difficult for societies to come to terms with the technological advances. Even today, some cultures are not using modern technology, but at the same time, they are using technology in principle - using simple machines for farming rather than using complex machines like tractors etc. What we notice here is that our lives are intertwined with the modern technology so much so that we are lost without computer, microwave, dishwasher, washing machine, cell phone etc. We have no clue what will happen to us if we do not have TV. It is very surprising and startling to realize that we are enslaved to technology. Those cultures, which are not in tune with modern technology are lagging behind. They may have more peace of mind, serenity and happiness, but when it comes to opportunities in this age of communication, they are lost.

The good things about **technology** are it revolutionized education, medicine, communication, travel etc. The world has shrunk now and we are never far away and we are always connected. It is very comforting to know that we are very close even though we are very far.

As a result of this technology, man is exploring space, to find out what it is like and to learn and gain knowledge, which used to be elusive and as distant as the planets themselves.

When we take a critical look at these facts, we have to commend societies for trying to keep their culture, as culture is a very important aspect of human life. We also need to appreciate cultures which took on new things and moved with times.

The advances in technology come with a price. Sometimes the price tag looks threatening and we get the feeling that we may go bankrupt. That's what will happen to and what is happening to our society now. The indiscriminate use of technology is putting us at risk. We can't afford to ignore technology, but what we need is caution and care, while using it.

Skill 2.2: Examine ways in which science and technology have transformed the physical world and human society.

New technologies have made production faster, easier, and more efficient. People found their skills and their abilities replaced by machines that were faster and more accurate. To some degree, machines and humans have entered an age of competition. Yet these advances have facilitated greater control over nature, lightened the burden of labor, and extended human life span. These advances in science, knowledge and technology have also called into question many of the assumptions and beliefs that have provided meaning for human existence. The myths that provided meaning in the past have been exposed and there are no new structures of belief to replace them. Without the foundational belief structures that have given meaning to life, an emptiness and aimlessness has arisen. Technology and science have extended life and made life easier. They have provided power and knowledge, but not the wisdom to know how to use it effectively. It was not accompanied by self-mastery, or the willingness to prevent class conflicts and prejudice, or to stop war, cruelty and violence.

The extraordinary advances in science and technology opened new frontiers and pushed back an ever-growing number of boundaries. These influences have had a profound effect in shaping modern civilization. Each discovery or machine or insight built upon other new discoveries or insights or machines. By the 20th century the rate of discovery and invention became literally uncontrollable. The results have, in many cases, been beneficial. But others have been horrifying.

Advances in biology and medicine have decreased infant mortality and increased life expectancy dramatically. Antibiotics and new surgical techniques have saved countless lives. Inoculations have essentially erased many dreadful diseases. Yet others have resulted from the careless disposal of by-products and the effects of industrialization upon the environment and the individual.

Tremendous progress in communication and transportation has tied all parts of the earth and drawn them closer. There are still vast areas of the former Soviet Union that have unproductive land, extreme poverty, food shortages, rampant diseases, violent friction between cultures, the ever-present nuclear threat, environmental pollution, rapid reduction of natural resources, urban over-crowding, acceleration in global terrorism and violent crimes, and a diminishing middle class.

New technologies have changed the way of life for many. This is the computer age and in many places, computers are even in the grade schools. Technology makes the world seem a much smaller place. Even children have cell phones today. The existence of television and modern technology has us watching a war while it is in progress. Outsourcing is now popular because of technological advances. Call centers for European, American and other large countries are now located in India, Pakistan, etc. Multinational corporations located plants in foreign countries to lower costs.

In many places technology has resulted in a mobile population. Popular culture has been shaped by mass production and the mass media. Mass production and technology has made electronic goods affordable to most. This is the day of the **cell phone** and the PDA. The **Internet** and email allow people anywhere in the world to be in touch and allows people to learn about world events. In the industrial countries and in many others, the popular culture is oriented towards the electronic era.

Skill 2.3: Analyze the social, political, economic, and cultural factors that have affected scientific discovery and technological innovation throughout human history.

The last century and a half has been a time of rapid and extensive change on almost every front. Notably, there has been a growing concern for human rights and civil rights. The end of imperialism and the liberation of former colonies and territorial holdings have created new nations and increased communication and respect among the nations of the world. Democracy has grown; Communism has risen and almost fallen. Nations are no longer ruled by distant mother countries or their resident governors. But these freedoms have been won at great cost in human lives. Both political and individual freedoms have been won through struggle. Nationalism has risen and created new states and nations have cultivated a national identity. Yet these individual nations have been brought into contact and cooperation in ways never before experienced in human history. Scientific and technological developments, new thinking in religion and philosophy, and new political and economic realities have combined to begin to create a global society that must now learn to define itself and understand how to cooperate and respect diversity in new ways.

After the defeat of Napoleon in 1815, Europe began a 100-year period of relative peace. There were vast changes in agricultural technology, new policies of land tenure, and the rise of both capitalism and mercantilism. Liberal and democratic institutions began to exercise greater influence throughout the world.

The developing technologies of war have moved society from battle with swords and spears to battle with single-shot muskets and cannon; from cannon and muskets came repeating rifles and the gatling gun, from those automatic weapons were developed. Cannon were replaced by missiles and rockets that were able to be propelled farther and farther. Bombs became more and more powerful, culminating in the atomic bomb. And in every development, the act of war became more remote for those engaging in it. The cost of war could be counted, but the fighters were becoming more removed from it.

Developments for war, however, also brought benefits as such things as plastics, alloys, electronic devices and more were perfected for industrial or medical purposes. The development of the radio is a case in point. Developed to a new extent during WWI, new applications were discovered for peacetime communication and entertainment. Throughout the **Cold War** and the **Arms Race,** more attention and more money were devoted to the development of weapons than to the conditions of human existence.

The deeper human problems have been more seriously addressed only since the end of the Cold War and the Arms Race. Only then could attention be given to the growing divide between the rich and the poor. The conditions of life in the cities and in third world countries have only begun to be addressed. The massive relocation from the farm to the city has changed the way people think about the environment, about values, and about other people.

Skill 2.4: Analyze ways in which science and technology influence and are influenced by core values, ethics, beliefs, and social attitudes.

In the last century, the advances in the fields of science and technology were amazing, unimaginable and have changed the lives of human beings for ever. The life style was greatly affected and the society experienced dramatic changes and people stared to take science technology very seriously. In ordinary, lay terms, the advances in these two interrelated fields are no longer the domain of the few elite and sophisticated. The ordinary, average persons started to use the advances in the field of technology in their daily lives. Because of this, the societal structure, the ethos and norms are fast changing to the extent that even young children are using technology.

With any rapid change, there are always good and bad things associated with that. Caution and care are the two words we need to associate with these giant strides in technology. At the same time, we need high tech. in our lives and we can't afford not to make use of these developments and get the benefits for the good of humanity.

Our environment we live, the human biology, society at large and our culture are being affected.

Let us take each point and examine very carefully the effects of science and technology on the above.

1. Environment:
The environment we live in is constantly and rapidly undergoing tremendous changes.

The positive effects are predicting hurricanes, measuring the changes in terms of radioactivity present in our environment, the remedial measures for that problem, predicting the levels of gases like carbon monoxide, carbon dioxide and other harmful gases, various estimates like the green house effect, ozone layer, UV radiation, to name a few. With the help of modern technology, it is possible to know the quantities and to monitor and plan remedial measures and implement them. Even with the most advanced technology available to us, it is impossible to go back to that clean, green earth, since man has made mark on it in a negative way. But at the same time, it is possible to a limited extent to alleviate the problem, but it is impossible to eradicate it.

The negative aspects of the effect of technology on our environment are numerous. The first and foremost is pollution of various kinds - water, air, noise etc. The greenhouse effect, the indiscriminate use of fertilizers, the spraying of pesticides, the use of various additives to our food, the deforestation, unprecedented exploitation of non renewable energy resources, to name a few. As we discussed earlier, it is not possible to solve these problems with money, human resources etc, but educating the society and making them aware of these negative aspects will go a long way.
For example, as teachers we need to educate them about using natural resources cautiously, trying to save them as maniacs and we need to teach them that little steps in the right direction will go a long way e.g., car pooling, not wasting paper, whenever possible, to walk, if it is safe. It is absolutely important to teach the students to have trees, if they have space or at least have house plants, as they change the quality of air we breath.

2. Human biology:
The strides science and technology made have lasting effects on human biology.

A few examples are - organ transplants, in vitro fertilization, cloning, new drugs, new understanding of various diseases using scientific knowledge, cosmetic surgery, reconstructive surgery, use of computers in operations, lasers in medicine, forensic science etc. These and the other changes not mentioned above have made lasting difference to the humanity.

As always there are pros and cons to these changes.

The positive aspects are - organ transplanted people have a new hope now. Their life spans are increased and their quality of life has changed with the high technology gadgets like pace makers etc. Couples who have no hope of having children of their own are having babies now including older women. Corrective and cosmetic surgery is giving new confidence to the clients. Glasses to correct vision problems are being replaced slowly by laser surgery. The list goes on and on. The most important thing is as always caution and when to use it.

The negative aspects are paternity issues arising out of in vitro fertilization, some medical blunders which are expensive and heart wrenching (when a wrong egg is implanted), the indiscriminate use of corrective and cosmetic surgery, older mothers and young orphans, etc.

3. Society:
Society is not the same as it used to be even 25 years ago. The use of technology has changed our patterns of life style, our behavior, our ethical and moral thinking, our economy and career opportunities, to name a few.

The positive effects are the economy booming due to high tech., more career opportunities for people to choose, rising of standard of living, prolonged life with quality, closeness even though we are separated by thousands of kilometers/miles, quicker and faster communication etc. The computer has contributed a lot to these changes. Normal household chores are being done by machines giving relief to women, cost effective and time saving gadgets for kitchen and home.

The negative aspects are too many. The breakdown in family structure could be attributed partly to high tech. The family meals and the family togetherness are vanishing. As a result of this, our young people are becoming insecure. They are lacking confidence and this affects indirectly to their problem solving skills. Young people are becoming increasingly vulnerable due to programs like chat rooms etc., pornography etc. There must be stringent measures to protect our younger generation from these internet predators. Close scrutiny must be done to the sites visited by young people. The effects of various high tech gadgets like the microwave are not entirely positive. Lack of communication is becoming a major problem in this era of communication since each is engrossed in their own world with their cell -hones, computers, I pods and other things. The music that is being made available is a matter of great concern. Children and young people are exposed to a whole new range of undesirable things, which are not at all positive. The games that are played on the game boys are not good for their psyche.

4. Culture:
This is a very sensitive yet very important issue. Those above listed factors are affecting the culture of people. In a way, it is good that we all have almost similar culture which will help us to bond as a nation of diverse cultures.

The positive aspects are technology is uniting us to a certain extent - e.g., it is possible to communicate to a person of any culture when we are not seeing them face to face. It makes it much easier. Some people are not comfortable with communicating with other cultures, since they are closed society, but e-mail has changed that. When we use the same pieces of technology, we understand better and a common ground is established. Internet can definitely boast of some successful marriages, which are cross cultural. Sharing opinions and information across the board has become easy.

With modern technology, travel is changing the way we think and the opportunities we get in careers. It is helping us to know other cultures, different ways of doing the same thing and to learn the positive values of other cultures.

The negative aspects are - the moral and ethical values are making for the new wave of thinking. Care must be exercised how much of our good culture we want to trade for the modern. I think good aspects of any culture must be guarded carefully and passed on to generations to come.

On the whole, we can safely conclude that science and technology are part of our lives and we must always exercise caution and be careful when we are adapting to new ideas and new thinking. It is important that the good values and aspects of different cultures will make us a better nation, which our founding fathers envisaged and dreamed of.

COMPETENCY 3.0: Understand major political, social, economic, and cultural developments that shaped the course of world history through the thirteenth century; and analyze major periods of historical change within and across cultures.

Skill 3.1: Identify preliterate groups and recognize their accomplishments.

Prehistory is defined as the period of man's achievements before the development of writing. In the Stone Age cultures, there were three different periods. They are the **Lower Paleolithic Period** with the use of crude tools. The **Upper Paleolithic Period** exhibiting a greater variety of better-made tools and implements, the wearing of clothing, highly organized group life, and skills in art. And finally the **Neolithic Period** which showed domesticated animals, food production, the arts of knitting, spinning and weaving cloth, starting fires through friction, building houses rather than living in caves, the development of institutions including the family, religion, and a form of government or the origin of the state.

ARCHAEOLOGY is the scientific study of past human cultures by studying the remains they left behind--objects such as pottery, bones, buildings, tools, and artwork. Archaeologists locate and examine any evidence to help explain the way people lived in past times. They use special equipment and techniques to gather the evidence and make special effort to keep detailed records of their findings because a lot of their research results in destruction of the remains being studied. The first step is to locate an archaeological site using various methods. Next, surveying the site takes place starting with a detailed description of the site with notes, maps, photographs, and collecting artifacts from the surface. Excavating follows either by digging for buried objects or by diving and working in submersible decompression chambers, when underwater. They record and preserve the evidence for eventual classification, dating, and evaluating their find.

Sources of knowledge about early humans:

- Fossils derived from burial pits
- Occasional bones found in rock deposits
- Archaeological excavations of tools, pottery, well paintings
- Study of living primitives

Although written records go back about 4,500 years, scientists have pieced together evidence that documents the existence of humans (or "man-apes) as much as 600,000 years ago. The first manlike creatures arose in many parts of the world about 1 million years ago. By slow stages, these creatures developed into types of men who discovered fire and tools. These creatures had human-sized brains and inbred to produce *Cro-Magnon* type creatures (25,000 years ago), from which *homo sapiens* descended.

These primitive humans demonstrated wide behavior patterns and great adaptability. Little is known in the way of details, including when language began to develop. They are believed to have lived in small communities that developed on the basis of the need to hunt. Cave paintings reveal a belief that magic pictures of animals could conjure up real ones. Some figurines seem to indicate belief in fertility gods and goddesses. Belief in some form of afterlife is indicated by burial formalities.

Fire and weapons were in use quite early. Archaeological evidence points to the use of hatchets, awls, needles and cutting tools in the Old Stone Age (one million years ago). Artifacts of the New Stone Age (6,000-8,000 BCE) include indications of polished tools, domesticated animals, the wheel, and some agriculture. Pottery and textiles have been found dating to the end of the New Stone Age (Neolithic period). The discovery of metals in the Bronze Age (3,000 BCE) is concurrent with the establishment of what are believed to be the first civilizations. The Iron Age, followed quickly on the heels of the Bronze Age.

By 4,000 BCE humans lived in villages, engaged in animal husbandry, grew grains, sailed in boats, and practiced religions. Civilizations arose earliest in the fertile river valleys of the Nile, Mesopotamia, the Indus, and the Hwang Ho.

Prerequisites of civilization:

- Use of metals rather than stone for tools and weapons
- A system of writing
- A calendar
- A territorial state organized on the basis of residence in the geographic region

The earliest known civilizations developed in the Tigris-Euphrates valley of Mesopotamia (modern Iraq) and the Nile valley of Egypt between 4000 BCE and 3000 BCE. Because these civilizations arose in river valleys, they are known as *fluvial civilizations*. Geography and the physical environment played a critical role in the rise and the survival of both of these civilizations.

We know the most about the empires of South America, the Aztec, Inca, and Maya. People lived in South America before the advent of these empires, of course. One of the earliest people of record was the Olmecs, who left behind little to prove their existence except a series of huge carved figures.

The Aztecs dominated Mexico and Central America. They weren't the only people living in these areas, just the most powerful ones. The Aztecs had many enemies, some of whom were only too happy to help Hernan Cortes precipitate the downfall of the Aztec society. The Aztecs had access to large numbers of metals and jewels, and they used these metals to make weapons and these jewels to trade for items they didn't already possess. Actually, the Aztecs didn't do a whole lot of trading; rather, they conquered neighboring tribes and demanded tribute from them; this is the source of so much of the Aztec riches. They also believed in a handful of gods and believed that these gods demanded human sacrifice in order to continue to smile on the Aztecs. The center of Aztec society was the great city of Tenochtitlan, which was built on an island so as to be easier to defend and boasted a population of 300,000 at the time of the arrival of the conquistadors. Tenochtitlan was known for its canals and its pyramids, none of which survive today.

The Inca Empire stretched across a vast period of territory down the western coast of South America and was connected by a series of roads. A series of messengers ran along these roads, carrying news and instructions from the capital, Cusco, another large city along the lines of but not as spectacular as Tenochtitlan. The Incas are known for inventing the *quipu*, a string-based device that provided them with a method of keeping records. The Inca Empire, like the Aztec Empire, was very much a centralized state, with all income going to the state coffers and all trade going through the emperor as well. The Incas worshiped the dead, their ancestors, and nature and often took part in what we could consider strange rituals.

The most advanced Native American civilization was the Maya, who lived primarily in Central America. They were the only Native American civilization to develop writing, which consisted of a series of symbols that has still not been deciphered. The Mayas also built huge pyramids and other stone figures and sculptures, mostly of the gods they worshiped. The Mayas are most famous, however, for their calendars and for their mathematics. The Mayan calendars were the most accurate on the planet until the 16th Century. The Mayas also invented the idea of zero, which might sound like a small thing except that no other culture had thought of such a thing. Maya worship resembled the practices of the Aztec and Inca, although human sacrifices were rare. The Mayas also traded heavily with their neighbors.

Skill 3.2: Analyze economic, political, social, and cultural relationships of the ancient civilizations of Africa, Asia, Europe, and the Americas.

Ancient civilizations were those cultures which developed to a greater degree and were considered advanced. These included the following eleven with their major accomplishments.

Egypt made numerous significant contributions including construction of the great pyramids; development of hieroglyphic writing; preservation of bodies after death; making paper from papyrus; contributing to developments in arithmetic and geometry; the invention of the method of counting in groups of 1-10 (the decimal system); completion of a solar calendar; and laying the foundation for science and astronomy.

The ancient civilization of the **Sumerians** invented the wheel; developed irrigation through use of canals, dikes, and devices for raising water; devised the system of cuneiform writing; learned to divide time; and built large boats for trade. The Babylonians devised the famous **Code of Hammurabi**, a code of laws.

The ancient **Assyrians** were warlike and aggressive due to a highly organized military and used horse drawn chariots.

The **Hebrews**, also known as the ancient Israelites instituted "monotheism," which is the worship of one God, Yahweh, and combined the 66 books of the Hebrew and Christian Greek scriptures into the Bible we have today.

The **Minoans** had a system of writing using symbols to represent syllables in words. They built palaces with multiple levels containing many rooms, water and sewage systems with flush toilets, bathtubs, hot and cold running water, and bright paintings on the walls.

The **Mycenaeans** changed the Minoan writing system to aid their own language and used symbols to represent syllables.

The **Phoenicians** were sea traders well known for their manufacturing skills in glass and metals and the development of their famous purple dye. They became so very proficient in the skill of navigation that they were able to sail by the stars at night. Further, they devised an alphabet using symbols to represent single sounds, which was an improved extension of the Egyptian principle and writing system.

In **India**, the caste system was developed, the principle of zero in mathematics was discovered, and the major religion of Hinduism was begun.

China began building the Great Wall; practiced crop rotation and terrace farming; increased the importance of the silk industry, and developed caravan routes across Central Asia for extensive trade. Also, they increased proficiency in rice cultivation and developed a written language based on drawings or pictographs (no alphabet symbolizing sounds as each word or character had a form different from all others).

The ancient **Persians** developed an alphabet; contributed the religions/philosophies of **Zoroastrianism**, **Mithraism**, and **Gnosticism**; and allowed conquered peoples to retain their own customs, laws, and religions.

The classical civilization of **Greece** reached the highest levels in man's achievements based on the foundations already laid by such ancient groups as the Egyptians, Phoenicians, Minoans, and Mycenaeans.

Among the more important contributions of Greece were the Greek alphabet derived from the Phoenician letters which formed the basis for the Roman alphabet and our present-day alphabet. Extensive trading and colonization resulted in the spread of the Greek civilization. The love of sports, with emphasis on a sound body led to the tradition of the Olympic Games. Greece was responsible for the rise of independent, strong city-states. Note the complete contrast between independent, freedom-loving Athens with its practice of pure democracy i.e. direct, personal, active participation in government by qualified citizens and the rigid, totalitarian, militaristic Sparta. Other important areas that the Greeks are credited with influencing include drama, epic and lyric poetry, fables, myths centered on the many gods and goddesses, science, astronomy, medicine, mathematics, philosophy, art, architecture, and recording historical events. The conquests of Alexander the Great spread Greek ideas to the areas he conquered and brought to the Greek world many ideas from Asia. The value of ideas, wisdom, curiosity, and the desire to learn as much about the world as possible was important to Alexander.

In **India**, Hinduism was a continuing influence along with the rise of Buddhism. Industry and commerce developed along with extensive trading with the Near East. Outstanding advances in the fields of science and medicine were made along with being one of the first to be active in navigation and maritime enterprises during this time.

China is considered by some historians to be the oldest, uninterrupted civilization in the world and was in existence around the same time as the ancient civilizations founded in **Egypt**, **Mesopotamia**, and the **Indus Valley**. The Chinese studied nature and weather; stressed the importance of education, family, and a strong central government; followed the religions of Buddhism, Confucianism, and Taoism; and invented such things as gunpowder, paper, printing, and the magnetic compass.

The civilization in **Japan** appeared during this time having borrowed much of their culture from China. It was the last of these classical civilizations to develop. Although they used, accepted, and copied Chinese art, law, architecture, dress, and writing, the Japanese refined these into their own unique way of life, including incorporating the religion of Buddhism into their culture.

The civilizations in **Africa** south of the Sahara were developing the refining and use of iron, especially for farm implements and later for weapons. Trading was overland using camels and at important seaports. The Arab influence was extremely important, as was their later contact with Indians, Christian Nubians, and Persians. In fact, their trading activities were probably the most important factor in the spread of and assimilation of different ideas and stimulation of cultural growth.

The **Vikings** had a lot of influence at this time with spreading their ideas and knowledge of trade routes and sailing, accomplished first through their conquests and later through trade.

The ancient empire of **Ghana** occupied an area that is now known as Northern Senegal and Southern Mauritania. There is no absolute certainty regarding the origin of this empire. Oral history dates the rise of the empire to the 7th century BCE. Most believe, however, that the date should be placed much later. Many believe the nomads who were herding animals in the fringes of the desert posed a threat to the early Soninke people, who were an agricultural community. In times of drought, it is believed the nomads raided the agricultural villages for water and places to pasture their herds. To protect themselves it is believed that these farming communities formed a loose confederation that eventually became the empire of ancient Ghana.

The word "Ghana" means king or war chief. It is believed that the Arabs and Europeans took this reference to the king to be the name of the society. These rulers conquered neighboring communities and thus extended the boundaries of the growing empire. The purpose of expansion was to gain control of trade routes. By the fifth century (some say the 7th century) a kingdom had been established. This kingship was significantly different from most other kingships of the time. First, kingship was matrilineal. The sister of the king provided the heir to the throne. Second, the king ruled in conjunction with a People's Council chosen from all social strata.

The empire's economic vitality was determined by geographical location. It was situated mid-way between the desert, which was the major source of salt, and the gold fields. This location along the trade routes of the camel caravans provided exceptional opportunity for economic development. The caravans brought copper, salt, dried fruit, clothing, manufactured goods, etc. For these goods, the people of Ghana traded kola nuts, leather goods, gold, hides, ivory and slaves. In addition, the empire collected taxes on every trade item that entered the boundaries of the empire.

With the revenue from the trade goods tax, the empire supported a government, an army that protected the trade routes and the borders, the maintenance of the capital, and primary market centers. But it was control of the gold fields that gave the empire political power and economic prosperity. The location of the gold fields was a carefully guarded secret. By the 10th century Ghana was very rich, and controlled an area about the size of the state of Texas. Demand for this gold sharply increased in the 9th and 10th centuries as the Islamic states of Northern Africa began to mint coins. As the gold trade expanded, so did the empire.

The availability of local iron ore enabled the early people of the **Ghana** kingdom to make more efficient farm implements and more effective weapons. But in the 11th century the Berbers attacked the empire in an attempt to gain control of the gold fields and to purify Islam as it was practiced in Ghana. They eventually withdrew, but they left behind a greatly weakened empire. Later invasions and internal rebellions further weakened the empire and made the trade routes quite dangerous. The merchants moved east, and the empire began to crumble. A serious drought compounded the disintegration of the empire through deterioration of the environment and overgrazing. By the middle of the 13th century, the empire was just a memory.

The **Tang Dynasty** extended from 618 to 907. Its capital was the most heavily populated of any city in the world at the time. Buddhism was adopted by the imperial family (Li) and became an integral part of Chinese culture. The emperor, however, feared the monasteries and began to take action against them in the 10th century. Confucianism experienced a rebirth during the time of this dynasty as an instrument of state administration. Following a civil war, the central government lost control of local areas. Warlords arise in 907, and China was divided into north and south. These areas came to be ruled by short-lived minor dynasties. A major political accomplishment of this period was the creation of a class of career government officials, who functioned between the populace and the government. This class of "scholar-officials" continued to fulfill this function in government and society until 1911.

The period of the Tang Dynasty is generally considered a pinnacle of Chinese civilization. Through contact with the Middle East and India, the period of the Tang Dynasty was marked by great creativity in many areas. Block printing was invented, and made much information and literature available to wide audiences.

In science, astronomers calculated the paths of the son and the moon and the movements of the constellations. This facilitated the development of the calendar. In agriculture, such technologies as cultivating the land by setting it on fire, the curved-shaft plow, separate cultivation of seedlings, and sophisticated irrigation system increased productivity. Hybrid breeds of horses and mules were created to strengthen the labor supply. In medicine, there were achievements like the understanding of the circulatory system and the digestive system, and great advances in pharmacology.

Ceramics was another area in which great advances were made. A new type of glazing was invented that gave Tang Dynasty porcelain and earthenware its unique appearance through three-colored glazing.

In literature, the poetry of the period is generally considered the best in the entire history of Chinese literature. The rebirth of Confucianism led to the publication of many commentaries on the classical writings. Encyclopedias on several subjects were produced, as well as histories and philosophical works

Skill 3.3: Demonstrate an understanding of the principal teachings and historical development of Judaism and Christianity

Judaism: Judaism is the oldest of the Western world's three monotheistic religions. It grew out of the ancient religion of the Hebrews or Israelites. This early religion shared a number of common elements and primordial stories with neighboring peoples, especially the Mesopotamian and Babylonian cultures. Judaism's sacred writing, the Hebrew Scripture, is generally referred to as Torah or Tannakh. It consists of 24 books which are divided into three sections: Law (*Torah*), Prophets (*Nevi'im*), and Writings (*Ketuvim*).

The word and law of God were transmitted orally for many generations prior to the writing of the Hebrew Scripture. The *Mishna* is the collection of the oral tradition. The *Gemara* is a collection of commentary by the rabbis (teachers). The tradition of living interpretation and commentary continued through the centuries. *Halakah* is the tradition of interpretation of law, history and practice. *Kabbalah* is a body of Jewish mystical literature. *Kabbalah* arose from a movement in France in the 11th Century that discovered an esoteric system of symbolic interpretation of scripture.

Judaism is centered in belief in a single, all-powerful, all-seeing, and all-knowing God. God chose the Hebrew people from all the people of the earth and entered into a covenant with them. "I will be your God, and you will be my people." This covenant implies special privileges, but it also implies certain obligations of the people. The life of the people is to be structured around the promises and commandments of God. The Law provides the structure of religious practice and daily life. The Law is the guide for making ethical choices that reflect and demonstrate their unique character as the chosen people of God. Failure to act in accordance with God's law is a willful act, called sin. Sin destroys the proper relationship between the person and God. It is, however, possible to return from willful rebellion and restore the broken relationship. Judaism is also marked by a strong sense of communal identity, and sin can be either individual or communal.

The Hebrew people, as the chosen people of God, are to remain separate or apart from other peoples in several ways: first, the Hebrews are to avoid marriage to persons outside the faith; second, they are to observe certain dietary restrictions (The rules for *kosher* (ritually correct) food preparation and consumption are quite detailed, and include prohibitions against eating certain animals, including pork and shellfish, specifications for the slaughter and butchering of meat, and a prohibition against mixing meat and dairy products.); third, they not to marry foreigners (this protects the faith of the community against other influences and conflicting ideas); fourth is the circumcision of all males (This is both an act of obedience to the covenant and an indication of the separateness of the people).

Among devout Jews, special times for prayer are at dawn, noon, dusk and, for some, bedtime. The Jewish Sabbath is observed from sunset on Friday until sunset on Saturday. The Sabbath is a day of rest. Many observant Jews gather on the Sabbath for worship in synagogues, where a Rabbi leads them in readings from the Scriptures, prayer and singing. The Jewish religious calendar is based on a lunar calendar, so the dates of religious holidays vary from year to year. With the exception of the New Year observance and the Day of Atonement, most holidays are based on either seasonal or historical events. The frequent prohibitions against idolatry in Hebrew Scripture reflect a deep and abiding concern that no limited entity or belief be mistaken for the one true God by God's chosen people.

The basic beliefs of Judaism are:

(1) There is one and only one God, with whom each believer has direct personal experience, and to whom prayers may be addressed.

(2) God is the ultimate authority and possesses final dominion over the universe, which God created.

(3) Life is holy.

(4) The *Torah* is a guide to correct living and a source of continued revelation of the word of God

(5) Group worship and prayer are indispensable elements of a righteous life.

(6) Jews share a broad common diversity and a sense of collective purpose and responsibility to one another.

Today, there are three basic branches or schools of Jewish belief and practice.
Orthodox Judaism is the most rigorous and the smallest branch. This group conducts worship in Hebrew and interprets the Law very strictly and literally.
Reform Judaism, which originated in the 18th century, attempted to integrate Judaism into the mainstream European culture. Law, doctrine, and ritual are more liberally interpreted, and dietary laws generally are not observed.
Conservative Judaism combines doctrinal reform with traditional observance. This attempt to retain much of the old orthodoxy while keeping in touch with contemporary culture has made them somewhat slower in embracing most of the changes of Reform Judaism.

Christianity: Christianity grew out of Judaism and its belief that God would send a Messiah ("anointed one") who would establish the Kingdom of God on earth. Jesus of Nazareth appeared in the early years of the first century CE, preaching repentance in preparation for the arrival of the Kingdom of God. His brief (about three years) ministry of teaching, preaching, healing and miracles gathered followers from among the common and the despised of his day, as well as non-Jews and the wealthy. This ministry was confined to the areas of Galilee and northwest Palestine. According to Christian writings, Jesus eschewed the separatism of Judaism and reached out to the poor, the sick, and the social outcasts. He preached a Kingdom of God not of this world, which ran contrary to Jewish expectation of a political Messiah who would establish an earthly kingdom. As the movement grew, the teachings of Jesus were perceived as a danger to the political order by both the Jews and the Roman government. Jesus was handed over to the authorities by one of his closest followers, arrested, tried, and crucified. According to Christian belief, Jesus rose from the dead on the third day, appeared to his disciples and then ascended to heaven.

Christians believe that Jesus was the Son of God who died on the cross as an offering and sacrifice that saved humankind from sin. Those who believe in him will be saved. Christian scripture (the Bible) consists of two major parts: the Old Testament, which is an adoption of the Hebrew Scripture, and the New Testament, which consists of 27 books. As an outgrowth of Judaism, Christianity accepts many of the beliefs, though not the practices of Judaism. Fundamental beliefs of Christianity are: (1) there is one God who is the creator and redeemer of humankind; God is all-knowing, all-powerful, and all-present; (2) Jesus Christ is the unique Son of God who is the savior of humankind. The doctrine of the Trinity teaches that the one God has three natures through/by which God is active in the world: God the Father, the creator and governor of creation, is the judge of humankind, God the Son (Jesus) is God in the flesh, who came among humankind to save them from sin, and God the Holy Spirit is the invisible presence of God in believers to provide strength, faith and guidance.

Christians observe Sunday as the Sabbath because Jesus was believed to have risen from the dead on a Sunday morning. Christian worship consists of the reading of scripture, the proclamation of the word of God, prayer, and the observance of the Sacraments. The Roman Catholic and Eastern Orthodox churches recognize 7 sacraments: baptism, confirmation, marriage, ordination, anointing and absolution of the sick and dying, the confession of sins, and the Eucharist or Holy Communion. Protestant churches recognize only two sacraments: baptism and Holy Communion. Christians believe that each human being has an eternal soul that will be judged by God after death. The soul will then be "rewarded" or punished according to one's faith and actions in life. Roman Catholics and Eastern Orthodox also believe in the existence of a purgatory, which is a state in which some souls are purified for entry to heaven.

Christian ethics are based on the Ten Commandments of the Old Testament and the teachings of Jesus, which include the "Golden Rule" (Do unto others as you would have them do unto you") and a broadening of the application of the commandments.

Until 1054 there was one Christian Church. In 1054 the Eastern Orthodox Church split from the Roman Catholic Church over several issues of belief and practice. In the 16th century, several reformers split from the Roman Catholic church, again over issues of belief and practice, in what is known as the Protestant Reformation.

Skill 3.4: Identify key factors in the rise and decline of the Roman Empire and evaluate major legal, artistic, architectural, technological, and literary achievements of Roman society.

Rome was one of the early Italian cities conquered by the Etruscans, who ruled over Rome until 509 BCE when they were overthrown by the Roman Republic. The Etruscans had absorbed and modified Greek civilization. Such elements of Greek culture as writing, certain religious practices, and engineering skills were passed on to the Italian peoples during their rule.

The period prior to the establishment of the Republic remains somewhat a mystery to modern historians. The following, however, has been reconstructed: Rome was composed of three tribes, each divided into clans. Clans were composed of groups of families. There was apparently a division into a class of nobles and the class of commoners very early. The nobles, called patricians (fathers) appear to have been the privileged class that functioned as an advisory council to the king and had certain political rights. There was no protective function in the government, and thus there was no army. Protection of the citizenry was the responsibility of the father of the family, who was also the priest of the religious cult of the home. The father was also a patron to commoner clients. In exchange for services to the family, these clients were given political and legal protection. The family unit, then, was composed of the family itself, free clients, and slaves (once wars of conquest began). The early kings were elected by the nobles, and ruled with supreme power in legal matters and in time of war. They were advised by the council, or the senate, which was composed of 30 senators (10 to each tribe). The religion of the early Romans was animistic – they believed that every thing was inhabited by a spirit. These were not personified or anthropomorphic until just prior to the birth of the Republic. The religion absorbed a number of Greek and Etruscan elements. The household religion was devoted to household gods, called *lares* and *penates*. They were believed to protect the household. In addition, ancestors were worshiped and their death masks were maintained in an in-house chapel.

The primary factors that led to the overthrow of the last king and the establishment of the Roman Republic appear to be: (1) a desire to be free of the Etruscans, (2) a desire to put an end to the tyranny of the last king, and (3) the kind of political evolution that occurred elsewhere as the noble classes wanted to cast aside the control of the monarch and establish an aristocratic form of government.

The factors that enabled Rome to conquer Italy were:

- Geographical location in the center of the peninsula with no mountain barriers,
- A sturdy citizen army and superior military tactics,
- The disunity of their enemies
- The use of a superior form of imperialism, by which military veterans settled in conquered areas, providing structure and guidance that allowed self-government to local peoples
- A highly disciplined family structure and a very powerful father
- A superior form of government – the republic.

The structure of the early Republic was clearly aristocratic. The nobles subjugated the commoners and dominated both the consuls and the Senate. In 450BC a written law gave new rights to the common people: the right to popular assembly, the creation of *tribunes* to protect the rights of all citizens, the creation of special new officials (judges and treasury officials) who were to make government fairer and more efficient. By 287 BC the *Hortensian law* allowed nobles and commoners to intermarry and permitted commoners to hold public offices.

The next 275 years, approximately, were occupied with expansion. This involved numerous wars of conquest. By 100 BC Rome controlled most of the Hellenistic world. This rapid conquest was one of the factors in the decline of the Republic. The republic did not have the infrastructure to absorb the conquered people. In addition, there was political decay, vast economic and social change, and military failure. In politics, the Senate refused to grant rights to the mass of the populace. A civil war erupted between rival factions. And, lacking adequate infrastructure, Rome was not able to provide good government to conquered territories. Heavy taxation of these territories, oppression by the government, and corrupt resident government officials led to decay. Critical social and economic changes included: the ruin of small farmers by importing slaves from conquered areas, a vast migration of the poor to the city of Rome, a failure to encourage and invest in industry and trade, the dissatisfaction of the new business class, and a general decline in morale among all classes of citizens. At the same time, the republic experienced a vast slave uprising in Southern Italy and faced the first attacks from Germanic invaders.

The end of the Republic was marked by two significant power struggles. The first was the grasp of power by the *First Triumvirate* in 59 BCE. The Triumvirate consisted of Caesar, Pompey and Crassus. Caesar eliminated Pompey and attempted to establish a dictatorship. Caesar made many reforms, including reducing the power of the Senate, but he was killed in the Senate in 44 BCE.
The following year experienced the rise of the *Second Triumvirate*, composed of Octavian, Mark Antony, and Lepidus. Octavian (later called Augustus) emerged victorious from the ensuing power struggle and became ruler of Rome in 31BCE.

Octavian (Augustus) established a "disguised monarchy" in which he appeared to share power with the Senate, though withholding most power. He established the boundaries of Rome on the Rhine and Danube rivers, improved government, and extended citizenship rights to all Roman soldiers. The power of the emperor was gradually enlarged by his successors. The height of the empire was achieved under "the five good emperors" – Nerva, Trajan, Hadrian, Antoninus Pius, and Marcus Aurelius.

The major contributions of the Roman Empire are:

- Peace and prosperity (the *Pax Romana*)
- The codification of Roman law
- A unified empire that allowed much self-government to component city-states
- The introduction of the idea of separation of powers and popular sovereignty
- The development of the "science" of public administration
- Formalized methods of tax collection
- Construction of an extensive civil service program
- Tolerance and the granting of citizenship rights to all inhabitants
- Engineering and construction of excellent roads, bridges, aqueducts and sanitation systems
- Construction of massive buildings – colosseums, public baths, basilicas
- Architectural innovations in the use of vaults and arches
- Preservation of Greek artistic techniques
- Development of education
- Refinement of rhetoric
- Literature: Cicero, Caesar, Lucretius, Virgil, Juvenal, Livy, Plutarch
- Extension of philosophy in the Greek tradition

The reasons for the decline of the Roman Empire are still a matter of debate. Among the reasons cited are the following:

1. Political: a period of anarchy and military emperors led to war and destruction; Diocletian reconstructed the Empire, establishing a "divine-right" absolute monarchy, a new imperial bureaucracy, and new administrative divisions to lessen the burden of ruling; Diocletian also reorganized the army, and established a new efficient, but very oppressive, taxation system. Constantine reunited the Empire, but moved the capital to the East. All of this reform demoralized the city-states.

2. Economic: the rise of large villas owned and controlled by landlords who settled poor people on the land as hereditary tenants who lived under conditions of partial servitude; use of wasteful agricultural methods; a decline of commerce; skilled workers were bound to jobs and were forced to accept government wages and prices; corruption, lack of productivity and inadequate investment of capital; the draining of gold from the western part of the empire through unfavorable trade balances with the East.

2. Biological, ecological and social: deforestation, bad agricultural methods, diseases (particularly malaria), earthquakes, immorality, brutalization of the masses in the cities, demoralization of the upper classes. This was accompanied by the decay of pagan beliefs and Roman ideals with the rise of Christianity.

The beginning of the barbarian infiltrations and invasions further weakened the sense of Roman identity. All of these factors contributed to an empire that was ill equipped to contend with invaders.

Skill 3.5: Explain commonalties and differences among nations and societies and analyze patterns of change within and across cultures.

During this time, the system of **feudalism** became the dominant feature. It was a system of loyalty and protection. The strong protected the weak that returned the service with farm labor, military service, and loyalty. Life was lived out on a vast estate, owned by a nobleman and his family, called a "manor." It was a complete village supporting a few hundred people, mostly peasants. Improved tools and farming methods made life more bearable although most never left the manor or traveled from their village during their lifetime.

In feudal societies a very small number of people (or no one) owned land. Instead, they held it as a hereditary trust from some social or political superior in return for services. The superiors were a small percentage of the people, a fighting and ruling aristocracy. The vast majority of the people were simply workers. One of the largest landowners of the time was the Roman Catholic Church. It was estimated that during the 12th and 13th centuries the Church controlled one third of the useable land in Western Europe.

Also coming into importance at this time was the era of knighthood and its code of chivalry as well as the tremendous influence of the Church (Roman Catholic). Until the period of the Renaissance, the Church was the only place where people could be educated. The Bible and other books were hand-copied by monks in the monasteries. Cathedrals were built and were decorated with art depicting religious subjects.

With the increase in trade and travel, cities sprang up and began to grow. Craft workers in the cities developed their skills to a high degree, eventually organizing guilds to protect the quality of the work and to regulate the buying and selling of their products. City government developed and flourished centered on strong town councils. Active in city government and the town councils were the wealthy businessmen who made up the rising middle class.

The end of the feudal manorial system was sealed by the outbreak and spread of the infamous **Black Death**, which killed over one-third of the total population of Europe. Those who survived and were skilled in any job or occupation were in demand and many serfs or peasants found freedom and, for that time, a decidedly improved standard of living. Strong nation-states became powerful and people developed a renewed interest in life and learning

From its beginnings, Japan morphed into an imperial form of government, with the divine emperor being able to do no wrong and, therefore, serving for life. **Kyoto**, the capital, became one of the largest and most powerful cities in the world. Slowly, though, as in Europe, the rich and powerful landowners, the nobles, grew powerful. Eventually, the nobles had more power than the emperor which required an attitude change in the minds of the Japanese people.

The nobles were lords of great lands and were called **Daimyos**. They were of the highest social class and people of lower social classes worked for them, including the lowly peasants, who had few privileges other than being allowed to work for the great men that the Daimyos told everyone they were. The Daimyos had serving them warriors known as **Shogun**, who were answerable only to the Daimyo. The Shogun code of honor was an exemplification of the overall Japanese belief that every man was a soldier and a gentleman. The contradiction that the emerging social classes identified didn't seem to get noticed much, nor did the needs of women.

The main economic difference between imperial and feudal Japan was that the money that continued to flow into the country from trade with China, Korea, and other Asian countries and from good, old-fashioned plundering on the high seas, made its way into the pockets of the Daimyos rather than the emperor's coffers. Feudalism developed in Japan later than it did in Europe and lasted longer as well. Japan dodged one huge historical bullet when a huge Mongol invasion was driven away by the famed **kamikaze**, or "divine wind," in the 12th Century. Japan was thus free to continue to develop itself as it saw fit and to refrain from interacting with the West, especially. This isolation lasted until the 19th Century.

Skill 3.6: Recognize major characteristics of Byzantine and Moslem cultures, analyze the emergence of Islam, and identify achievements of Islamic empires.

In other parts of the world were the **Byzantine** and **Saracenic** (or Islamic) civilizations, both dominated by religion. The major contributions of the Saracens were in the areas of science and philosophy. Included were accomplishments in astronomy, mathematics, physics, chemistry, medicine, literature, art, trade and manufacturing, agriculture, and a marked influence on the Renaissance period of history.

The **Byzantines** (Christians) made important contributions in art and the preservation of Greek and Roman achievements including architecture (especially in Eastern Europe and Russia), the Code of Justinian and Roman law.

A few years after the death of the Emperor Justinian, Mohammed was born (570 CE) in a small Arabian town near the Red Sea. Before this time, Arabians played only an occasional role in history. Arabia was a vast desert of rock and sand, except the coastal areas on the Red Sea. It was populated by nomadic wanderers called *Bedouin*, who lived in scattered tribes near oases where they watered their herds. Tribal leaders engaged in frequent war with one another. The family or tribe was the social and political unit, under the authority of the head of the family, within which there was cruelty, infanticide, and suppression of women. Their religion was a crude and superstitious paganism and idolatry. Although there was regular contact with Christians and Jews through trading interactions, the idea of monotheism was foreign. What vague unity there was within the religion was based upon common veneration of certain sanctuaries. The most important of these was a small square temple called *the Kaaba* (cube), located in the town of Mecca. Arabs came from all parts of the country in annual pilgrimages to Mecca during the sacred months when warfare was prohibited. For this reason, Mecca was considered the center of Arab religion.

In about 610 a prophet named Mohammed came to some prominence. He called his new religion *Islam* (submission [to the will of God]) and his followers were called Moslems – those who had surrendered themselves. His first converts were members of his family and his friends. As the new faith began to grow, it remained a secret society. But when they began to make their faith public, they met with opposition and persecution from the pagan Arabians who feared the new religion and the possible lose of the profitable trade with the pilgrims who came to the Kaaba every year.

Islam slowly gained ground, and the persecutions became more severe around Mecca. In 622, Mohammed and his close followers fled the city and found refuge in Medina to the North. His flight is called the *Hegira*. This event marks the beginning of the Moslem calendar. Mohammed took advantage of the ongoing feuds between Jews and Arabs in the city and became the rules of Medina, making it the capital of a rapidly growing state.

In the years that followed, Islam changed significantly. It became a fighting religion, and Mohammed became a political leader. The group survived by raiding caravans on the road to Mecca and plundering nearby Jewish tribes. This was a victorious religion that promised plunder and profit in this world and the blessings of paradise after death. It attracted many converts from the Bedouin tribes. By 630, Mohammed was strong enough to conquer Mecca and make it the religious center of Islam, toward which all Moslems turned to pray, and the *Kabba* the most sacred *Mosque* or temple. Medina remained the political capital.

Mohammed left behind a collection of divine revelations (*surahs)* he believed were delivered by the angel Gabriel. These were collected and published in a book called the *Koran* (reading), which has since been the holy scripture of Islam. The revelations were never dated or kept in any kind of chronological order. After the prophet's death they were organized by length (in diminishing order). The *Koran* contains Mohammed's teachings on moral and theological questions, his legislation on political matters, and his comments on current events.

Islam has five basic principles:

1. The oneness and omnipotence of God – *Allah*
   - Mohammed is the prophet of Allah to whom all truth has been revealed by God
   - To each of the previous prophets (Adam, Noah, Abraham, Moses and Jesus) a part of the truth was revealed
2. One should pray five times a day at prescribed intervals, facing Mecca
3. Charity – for the welfare of the community
4. Fasting from sunrise to sunset every day during the holy month of Ramadan to cleanse the spirit
5. Pilgrimage to Mecca should be made if possible and if no one suffers thereby

The moral principles of Islam are:

- The practice of the virtues of charity, humility and patience
- Enemies are to be forgiven
- Avarice, lying and malice are condemned
- Drinking (alcohol), eating pork, and gambling are prohibited.

Mohammed believed that on the Day of Judgment all souls would be judged. The infidel would be condemned to a hell (*gehennem*) of perpetual fire; the good/faithful would go to Paradise, a beautiful place of cool waters, sensual delights, and ease. He emphasized a strong sense of predestination. The *Koran* elevated the level of women. A man could marry as many as four wives, if he loved them equally. Divorce was easy, but the wife had to be given a dowry.

Mohammed drew freely upon Christianity, Judaism, and Arab paganism. His knowledge of the first two was limited to what he learned through casual conversation. The resulting doctrine was a mixture of ideas that is original when taken as a whole. It appealed to both the simple Arab of the prophet's day and to the faith of more civilized people.

Mohammed died without either a political or a religious succession plan. His cousin, Ali, who had married Mohammed's daughter Fatima, believed his kinship and his heroism as a warrior gave him a natural claim to leadership. But Moslems in Medina thought one of their own should succeed Mohammed. *Abu Bakr* was finally chosen. He took the title of *Caliph*. The title was retained throughout the duration of the Moslem Empire.

These Moslem Arabians immediately launched an amazing series of conquests which, in time, extended the empire from the Indus to Spain. It has often been said that these conquests were motivated by religious fanaticism and the determination to force Islam upon the infidel. In fact, however, the motives were economic and political.

During the period of expansion there was a brief civil war that occurred because Ali was proclaimed Caliph at Medina. He was opposed by an aristocratic family of Mecca called the Umayyad. Ali was assassinated in 661, and the Umayyads emerged supreme, handing the caliphate down in their family for nearly a century. Because their strongest support was in Syria, they moved the capital from Medina to Damascus.

There ware significant changed during the century of Umayyad rule.

- There was little effort to convert conquered people. Infidels were taxed, the faithful were not. But taxation encouraged conversion. Conversion brought not only freedom from taxation, but a role in political and other privileges reserved for the faithful. By the end of the Seventh Century, great numbers of conquered people had adopted Islam.

- The Arabs, though still the ruling class, had become scattered and they were mingling with the other peoples and races of the empire.
- Islam, rather than Arab nationalism, was becoming the important factor in Moslem patriotism.

The Umayyads had always represented Arabian rather than broader Moslem interests. More devout Moslems, especially in Persia, were unhappy with their rule. They turned to the *Abbasid* family for leadership. This family was descended from Abbas, the uncle of Mohammed. They relied on their relation to the prophet's family to attract the loyalty of devout Moslems of all races. The Abbasid dynasty began with the overthrow of the Umayyad family in 750, although an Umayyad emir continued to rule in Spain. This group then became separated from the rest of the empire. Persia then replaced Syria as the center of the empire, and the capital was moved from Damascus to Baghdad.

The Arab aristocracy was succeeded by a mixed official aristocracy drawn from all of the Moslem races. The caliphs modeled themselves after the Persian kings. Moslem civilization became a composite of Arab, Persian and Greek who were united by the teachings of Islam and the Arabic language. The Abbasid dynasty ushered in a period of great prosperity and absolute power that lasted for about 75 years. It was during the reign of Haroun al Rashid (786-809) that the caliphate reached its greatest power. Baghdad was one of the richest cities in the world, center of an empire that reached from central Asia to the Atlantic. But the empire was too large and its people too diverse to be held together by a single individual for very long. Shortly after Haroun's reign, the caliph began to lose power and the empire began to disintegrate. This continued through the Tenth Century.

The Umayyed emir in Spain took the title Caliph of Cordova; in Egypt a descendant of Mohammed's daughter (Fatima) founded the caliphate of Cairo, which later came to include Syria. From 945-1055 the caliphs of Baghdad were completely dominated by a Persian dynasty of emirs, until they were conquered by the Seljuk Turks, who had come down from central Asia and adopted Islam with fanatical zeal. The Turkish emirs and sultans ruled for 200 years, reviving the political strength of the empire for a time and recovering Syria. It was the Turkish emirs who dealt with the crusaders.

The converts to Islam, who brought their cultural traditions, probably contributed more to this emerging synthetic civilization than the Arabs. This blending of cultures, facilitated by a common language, a common religion, and a strong economy, created learning, literature, science, technology and art that surpassed anything found in the Western Christian world during the Early Middle Ages. Interestingly, the most brilliant period of Moslem culture was from the eighth century through the eleventh, coinciding with the West's darkest cultural period.

Reading and writing in Arabic, the study of the Koran, arithmetic and other elementary subjects were taught to children in schools attached to the mosques. In larger and wealthier cities, the mosques offered more advanced education in literature, logic, philosophy, law, algebra, astronomy, medicine, science, theology and the tradition of Islam. Books were produced for the large reading public. The wealthy collected private libraries and public libraries arose in large cities.

The most popular subjects were theology and the law. But the more important field of study was philosophy. The works of the Greek and Hellenistic philosophers were translated into Arabic and interpreted with commentaries. These were later passed on to the Western Christian societies and schools in the twelfth and thirteenth centuries. The basis of Moslem philosophy was Aristotelian and Neoplatonic ideas, which was essentially transmitted without creative modification.

The Moslems were also interested in natural science. They translated the works on Galen and Hippocrates into Arabic and added the results of their own experience in medicine. Avicenna was regarded in Western Europe as one of the great masters of medicine. They also adopted the work of the Greeks in the other sciences and modified and supplemented them with their own discoveries. Much of their work in chemistry was focused on alchemy (the attempt to transmute baser metals into gold).

Adopting the heritage of Greek mathematics, the Moslems also borrowed a system of numerals from India. This laid the foundation for modern arithmetic, geometry, trigonometry and algebra.

Moslem art and architecture tended to be mostly uniform in style, allowing for some regional modification. They borrowed from Byzantine, Persian and other sources. The floor plan of the mosques was generally based on Mohammed's house at Medina. The notable unique elements were the tall minarets from which the faithful were called to prayer. Interior decoration was the style now called arabesque. Mohammed had banned paintings or other images of living creatures. These continued to be absent from mosques, although they occasionally appeared in book illustration and secular contexts. But their skilled craftsmen produced the finest art in jewelry, ceramics, carpets, and carved ivory.

The Moslems also produced sophisticated literature in both prose and poetry. The flexibility of the Arabic language was very well adapted to poetry. Little, however, of their poetry or prose was carried down by Western culture. The best-known works of this period are the short stories known as the *Arabian Nights* and the poems of Omar Khayyam.

COMPETENCY 4: Understand major political, social, economic, and cultural developments that shaped the course of world history from 1300 through 1750; and analyze major periods of historical change within and across cultures.

Skill 4.1: Analyze the evolution of medieval European civilization during the late Middle Ages and major developments associated with the Renaissance and Reformation that led to the emergence of modern nation-states.

The word "Renaissance" literally means "rebirth", and signaled the rekindling of interest in the glory of ancient classical Greek and Roman civilizations. It was the period in human history marking the start of many ideas and innovations leading to our modern age.

The Renaissance began in Italy with many of its ideas starting in Florence, controlled by the infamous Medici family. Education, especially for some of the merchants, required reading, writing, math, the study of law, and the writings of classical Greek and Roman writers. Contributions of the Italian Renaissance period were in:

Art - the more important artists were **Giotto** and his development of perspective in paintings; **Leonardo da Vinci** was not only an artist but also a scientist and inventor; **Michelangelo** was a sculptor, painter, and architect; and others including **Raphael**, **Donatello**, **Titian**, and **Tintoretto**

Political philosophy - the writings of **Machiavelli**

Literature - the writings of **Petrarch** and **Boccaccio**

Science - **Galileo**

Medicine - the work of Brussels-born **Andrea Vesalius** earned him the title of "father of anatomy" and had a profound influence on the Spaniard **Michael** Servetus and the Englishman **William Harvey**

In Germany, Gutenberg's invention of the **printing press** with movable type facilitated the rapid spread of Renaissance ideas, writings and innovations, thus ensuring the enlightenment of most of Western Europe. Contributions were also made by Durer and Holbein in art and by Paracelsus in science and medicine.
The effects of the Renaissance in the Low Countries can be seen in the literature and philosophy of Erasmus and the art of van Eyck and Breughel the Elder. Rabelais and de Montaigne in France also contributed to literature and philosophy. In Spain, the art of El Greco and de Morales flourished, as did the writings of Cervantes and De Vega. In England, Sir Thomas More and Sir Francis Bacon wrote and taught philosophy and inspired by Vesalius. William Harvey made important contributions in medicine.
The greatest talent was found in literature and drama and given to mankind by Chaucer, Spenser, Marlowe, Jonson, and the incomparable Shakespeare.

The Reformation period consisted of two phases: the **Protestant Revolution** and the **Catholic Reformation**. The Protestant Revolution came about because of religious, political, and economic reasons. The religious reasons stemmed from abuses in the Catholic Church including fraudulent clergy with their scandalous immoral lifestyles; the sale of religious offices, indulgences, and dispensations; different theologies within the Church; and frauds involving sacred relics.

The political reasons for the Protestant Revolution involved the increase in the power of rulers who were considered "absolute monarchs", who desired all power and control, especially over the Church. The growth of "nationalism" or patriotic pride in one's own country was another contributing factor.

Economic reasons included the greed of ruling monarchs to possess and control all lands and wealth of the Church, the deep animosity against the burdensome papal taxation, the rise of the affluent middle class and its clash with medieval Church ideals, and the increase of an active system of "intense" capitalism.

The Protestant Revolution began in Germany with the revolt of Martin Luther against Church abuses. It spread to Switzerland where it was led by Calvin. It began in England with the efforts of King Henry VIII to have his marriage to Catherine of Aragon annulled so he could wed another and have a male heir. The results were the increasing support given not only by the people but also by nobles and some rulers, and of course, the attempts of the Church to stop it.

The Catholic Reformation was undertaken by the Church to "clean up its act" and to slow or stop the Protestant Revolution. The major efforts to this end were supplied by the Council of Trent and the Jesuits. Six major results of the Reformation included:

- Religious freedom,
- Religious tolerance,
- More opportunities for education,
- Power and control of rulers limited,
- Increase in religious wars, and
- An increase in fanaticism and persecution.

A number of individuals and events led to the time of exploration and discoveries. The Vivaldo brothers and Marco Polo wrote of their travels and experiences, which signaled the early beginnings. From the Crusades, the survivors made their way home to different places in Europe bringing with them fascinating, new information about exotic lands, people, customs, and desired foods and goods such as spices and silks.

The Renaissance ushered in a time of curiosity, learning, and incredible energy sparking the desire for trade to procure these new, exotic products and to find better, faster, cheaper trade routes to get to them. The work of geographers, astronomers and mapmakers made important contributions and many studied and applied the work of such men as Hipparchus of Greece, Ptolemy of Egypt, Tycho Brahe of Denmark, and Fra Mauro of Italy.

Portugal made the start under the encouragement, support, and financing of Prince Henry the Navigator. The better known explorers who sailed under the flag of Portugal included Cabral, Diaz, and Vasco da Gama, who successfully sailed all the way from Portugal, around the southern tip of Africa, to Calcutta, India.

Christopher Columbus, sailing for Spain, is credited with the discovery of America although he never set foot on its soil. Magellan is credited with the first circumnavigation of the earth. Other Spanish explorers made their marks in parts of what are now the United States, Mexico, and South America.

For France, claims to various parts of North America were the result of the efforts of such men as Verrazano, Champlain, Cartier, LaSalle, Father Marquette and Joliet. Dutch claims were based on the work of one Henry Hudson. John Cabot gave England its stake in North America along with John Hawkins, Sir Francis Drake, and the half-brothers Sir Walter Raleigh and Sir Humphrey Gilbert.

Actually the first Europeans in the New World were Norsemen led by Eric the Red and later, his son Leif the Lucky. However, before any of these, the ancestors of today's Native Americans and Latin American Indians crossed the Bering Strait from Asia to Alaska, eventually settling in all parts of the Americas.

Skill 4.2: Analyze major causes and consequences of European expansion and examine economic, political, and cultural relations among peoples of Europe, Africa, Asia, the Pacific (Oceania), and the Americas.

In the century and a half after 1520, European nations began to reap the benefits of the age of exploration and discovery. They began a period of economic and colonial expansion that spread European civilization throughout the world. Europeans invaded the far East and the unknown areas to the West, pillaging, trading, colonizing, and introducing Christianity to native peoples. Capitalism spread to an extent that essentially dominated the economic activities of the nations. Consideration of the rate of expansion of overseas trade, the great increase in the volume and variety of goods transported, and the resulting increase in the wealth of European nations, it seems appropriate to speak of a "commercial revolution." Several factors fueled this desire for expansion: the desire for knowledge, the desire to convert the heathen natives to Christianity, the lust for gold and silver, and the capitalist desire to reap the benefits of trade.

In the early years of expansion, the most active peoples were the Spanish, the Portuguese, and the Dutch. In fact, in 1494, the Pope divided the planet between Spain and Portugal. The French and English did not become active players in the competition for foreign colonies and domination until the 17th century. By 1600 foreign trade was becoming more important to both nations. The English East India Company was typical of the way this expansion was occurring. This was a chartered company, rather than a government effort, that became the agency of expansion.

Competition for trade monopolies in the East led to a struggle between the English and the Dutch. England's first Navigation Act (1651) was directed against the Dutch. There was rivalry with Spain for control of various areas on the part of the Dutch and the English. This was superseded by the *Anglo-Dutch Wars*. There were a number of issues in this conflict: slave trade of Africa, Atlantic fisheries, North American settlements, and trade. The Dutch East India Company had shut off the Spice Islands from the English. The final result was an English trading post in the Spice Islands.

England and France had stood together to evict the Dutch from the North American mainland. Numerous changes were occurring, however, within England, eventually bringing William of Orange to the throne. William and Louis XIV were bitter enemies, and opinion turned toward the view that the true enemy of England was France. This resulted in the Anglo-French Conflict. Both nations had adopted mercantilist policies. Both countries had competing colonies and trading interests in the New World, Asia and the West Indian islands. On the North American Mainland, English settlements essentially controlled the Atlantic coast from Maine to Georgia. These areas were well populated and provided fish, tobacco, and trade. Although less densely populated, the French had claims of a large area of land. The Louisiana Territory was under French control. Competition between England and France for land, sugar, and furs was intense. The English colonies were barred from westward expansion by French territory, which was being protected by strong line of military defenses. India, which was densely populated and in possession of a strong culture, was also highly prized by both nations. By 1689 the English had established outposts at Bombay, Madras, and Calcutta. The French had come to India somewhat later and established their outposts in two areas near Calcutta and Madras. Both nations saw these outposts as entry points for greater penetration of India. These areas were the loci of the conflicts that ensued.

The first struggle was *The War of the League of Augsburg*. This occurred in Acadia. The treaty of Ryswick restored the previous division of territory. The second struggle was *The War of the Spanish Succession*. English and Dutch sea power prevailed over Frensh and Spanish. The treaty of Utrecht gave England clear possession of Acadia (New Scotland), Newfoundland, and Hudson Bay, as well as St. Kitts in the West Indies. The third conflict was *The War of the Austrian Succession*. This was a resumption of the hostilities between England and Spain. It merged into the European War. France and England were at odds again in North America and in India. The treaty of Aix-la-Chapelle restored pre-war territorial holdings.

The French had, however, strengthened their positions in the Louisiana territory. The issue of control of the Ohio Valley led to the French and Indian Wars. Spain tried to intervene on behalf of France, but it was too late. The war in India, at about the same time, ended with the British dominating the east coast of India. Both of these struggles came to be incorporated into the Seven Years War in Europe. The Treaty of Paris (1763) restored peace at a very high cost to France. The treaty essentially ended France's claim to be an imperial power. When the American colonies declared independence thirteen years latter, the assistance of the French was critical to the success of the colonies.

With the decline of French power, England was able to expand her empire and consolidate her interests. By this time, the Dutch, Portuguese and Spanish empires were not a threat to British interests. The naval power of Britain and the extent of the British Empire continued, essentially unchallenged, until the 10th century.

Skill 4.3: Compare the exercise of power by world political leaders.

Louis XIV acceded to the throne shortly before his fifth birthday. His mother and the First Minister, Mazarin, controlled the government until Mazarin's death in 1661, at which time Louis XIV declared that he would rule the country. He has been referred to alternately as Louis the Great, the Great Monarch and as The Sun King. During his reign France attained cultural dominance, as well as military and political superiority. Louis XIV created a centralized government that he ruled with absolute power. He is often considered "the archetype of an absolute monarch." He is quoted as claiming "I am the State." However, many scholars believe this statement was falsely attributed to him by political opponents. It did, however, summarize the absolute power he held.

Mazarin was hated and distrusted in most political circles because he was not French born. The absolute rule exercised by Anne (his mother) and Mazarin was very unpopular among the people. At about the time the Thirty Years' War ended (1648), the *Fronde*, a civil war broke out in France. Mazarin continued the policies of his predecessors in trying to expand the power of the Crown at the expense of the nobles. He tried to impose a tax on the members of the Parliament. Parliament refused to pay the tax and ordered all of his previous financial edicts burned. Mazarin responded by arresting several members of the Parliament. The result was insurrection and rioting in Paris. The royal family fled. When the war ended the French army was available to aid and protect the royal family. By January 1649 the conflict was temporarily ended with the Peace of Rueil.

The second Fronde broke out in 1650. This was a revolt of the nobility and the clergy against the crown. During these times of rebellion the Queen sold jewels to feed her family. Louis XIV emerged from these years of internal rebellion with a strong distrust of both the nobility and the common people.

Louis XIV reigned as an absolute monarch. To be sure, he and his advisors moved France to economic strength and political power and influence in Europe. But the claim of absolute power by divine right combined with his distrust of others led to unique actions to maintain power and to control any who might instigate rebellion against him. One of his tactics to control the nobility was to require them to remain at the palace of Versailles, where he could watch them and prevent them from plotting unrest in their communities. He spent lavishly on parties and distractions to keep the nobility occupied and to strengthen his control over them. He was determined to undercut the power and influence of the nobility. He tried to fill high offices with commoners or members of the new aristocracy because he believed that if commoners got out of hand, they could be dismissed. He knew he could not mitigate the influence of great nobles. By forcing the powerful nobles to remain at court he effectively reduced their power and influence. By appointing commoners and new aristocracy to government functions he increased his control over both the functions and those who held them. He controlled the nobles to such an extent that he was able to ensure that there would never be another Fronde.

Louis also tried to control the Church. He called an assembly of the clergy in 1681. By the time the assembly ended, he had won acceptance of the "Declaration of the Clergy of France," by which the power of the Pope was greatly reduced and his power was greatly enhanced. This Declaration was never accepted by the Pope.

Perhaps the great mistake of Louis' reign was his attitude toward Protestantism and his handling of the Huguenots. In 1685 he revoked the Edict of Nantes. This resulted in the departure from the country of these French Protestants, who were among the wealthiest and most industrious people in the nation. He also alienated the Protestant countries of Europe, particularly England.

Tokugawa *Ieyasu* came to power in Japan in 1600 by defeating a coalition that sought political power in Japan. His rise to power marks the beginning of the Tokugawa shogunate, which held power as military rulers in Japan until 1868. In the 16th century, Japan had absorbed a great deal of European influence. The Portuguese had arrived in 1543 and Francis Xavier, a Jesuit priest, brought a mission to Japan in 1549. By 1600 there were about 300,000 Christians, including a number of the military aristocracy. Hideyoshi began to suppress Christianity as a foreign threat in 1587, and banished the Portuguese missionaries. The Tokugawa shoguns persecuted Christianity more extensively by executing thousands of Christians and driving the Church underground. An uprising in 1637-38 culminated in a massive slaughter. After this event, foreigners were banned from the country, except for a small number of Dutch merchant traders who were strictly confined to an island.

This military dictatorship adopted the existing social class hierarchy that was in place in 1600. The warrior-caste of samurai was at the top of the hierarchy. Next were farmers, artisans, and traders. This very tightly controlled hierarchy eventually led to conflict. The peasants were taxed in fixed amounts. There was no variation in the amount of the tax. As monetary values changed, this resulted in less support for the samurai who collected the taxes. There were a number of confrontations between the samurai, who were growing steadily poorer, and the peasants, who were growing steadily wealthier. None of these conflicts had significant results until the arrival of foreign power and influence.

A rebellion by the "titular Emperor" and several of the powerful nobles resulted in the Boshin War. The war ended in the Meiji Restoration and the overthrow of the Tokugawa shogunate. Foreign travel was banned, as well as foreign books. This permitted a flourishing of local culture. Although the government was stable, the financial situation of the government was slowly declining, resulting in higher taxes. The tax increases caused riots among the farmers and peasants. A number of natural disasters caused years of famine and deepening financial difficulties. The merchant class claimed greater power and many samurai became financially dependent upon them. The second part of the Edo era was marked by corruption, decline of morality, and government incompetence.

The financial difficulties and the inability of the government to respond to the numerous natural disasters and famine produced growing anti-government sentiment. Movements began to arise that tried to limit Western influence and to restore control of the government to the imperial line. Other groups wanted greater openness to Western ideas and technology

Skill 4.4: Evaluate political, economic, and social developments among various cultural groups in the world during this period.

There is strong archaeological evidence supporting the contention that the ancestors of today's Native Americans and Latin American Indians crossed the Bering Strait from Asia to Alaska, eventually settling in all parts of the Americas and there is also some evidence that suggests that some may have arrived from Asia and the Pacific islands via a more southerly transoceanic seafaring route.

Indigenous peoples of North America have been traditionally divided by anthropologists and ethnologists into mutually unintelligible linguistic groups:
Inuit - In the north, from western Arctic Alaska, across Arctic Canada to the Canadian Maritimes
Dineh – From interior Alaska to the Sonoran Desert in Mexico (Athapaskan, Apache, Navajo, etc.)
Anishinabe (Algonquian) – Eastern woodlands United States and Canada (Ojibwe, Mohican, Abenaki)
Siouan – Midwestern and western Great Plains of the United States and Canada (Lakota, Dakota, Nakota)
Iroquoian – Northeastern United States and southeastern Canada woodlands (Seneca, Oneida, Mohawk, Onondaga, Cayuga)

Nahuatl – Central Mexico (Aztec)
Mayan – Southern Mexico and Mesoamerica
Northwest Indian – Southern Alaska Panhandle through Pacific Coastal Canada to the Oregon coast (Tlingit, Haida, Tsimshian, Nitnat)

Native American tribes lived throughout what we now call the United States in varying degrees of togetherness. They adopted different customs, pursued different avenues of agriculture and food gathering, and made slightly different weapons. They fought among themselves and with other peoples. To varying degrees, they had established cultures long before Columbus or any other European explorer arrived on the scene.

Perhaps the most famous of the Native American tribes is the **Algonquians**. We know so much about this tribe because they were one of the first to interact with the newly arrived English settlers in Plymouth, Massachusetts and elsewhere. The Algonquians lived in wigwams and wore clothing made from animal skins. They were proficient hunters, gatherers, and trappers who also knew quite a bit about farming. Beginning with a brave man named Squanto, they shared this agricultural knowledge with the English settlers, including how to plant and cultivate corn, pumpkins, and squash.

Other famous Algonquians included Pocahontas and her father, Powhatan, both of whom are immortalized in English literature, and Tecumseh and Black Hawk, known foremost for their fierce fighting ability. To the overall Native American culture, they contributed wampum and dream catchers.

Another group of tribes who lived in the Northeast were the **Iroquois**, who were fierce fighters but also forward thinkers. They lived in long houses and wore clothes made of buckskin. They, too, were expert farmers, growing the "Three Sisters" (corn, squash, and beans). Five of the Iroquois tribes formed a Confederacy, a shared form of government. The Iroquois also formed the False Face Society, a group of medicine men who shared their medical knowledge with others but kept their identities secret while doing so. These masks are one of the enduring symbols of the Native American era.

Living in the Southeast were the **Seminoles** and **Creeks**, a huge collection of people who lived in chickees (open, bark-covered houses) and wore clothes made from plant fibers. They were expert planters and hunters and were proficient at paddling dugout canoes, which they made. The bead necklaces they created were some of the most beautiful on the continent. They are best known, however, for their struggle against Spanish and English settlers, especially led by the great Osceola.

The **Cherokee** also lived in the Southeast. They were one of the most advanced tribes, living in domed houses and wearing deerskin and rabbit fur. Accomplished hunters, farmers, and fishermen, the Cherokee were known the continent over for their intricate and beautiful basketry and clay pottery. They also played a game called lacrosse, which survives to this day in countries around the world.

In the middle of the continent lived the Plains tribes, such as the **Sioux, Cheyenne, Blackfeet, Comanche, and Pawnee**. These peoples lived in teepees and wore buffalo skins and feather headdresses. (It is this image of the Native American that has made its way into most American movies depicting the period.) They hunted wild animals on the Plains, especially the buffalo. They were well known for their many ceremonies including the Sun Dance and for the peace pipes that they smoked. Famous Plains people include Crazy Horse and Sitting Bull, authors of the Custer Disaster; Sacagawea, leader of the Lewis & Clark expedition; and Chief Joseph, the famous Nez Perce leader.

Dotting the deserts of the Southwest were a handful of tribes, including the famous **Pueblo**, who lived in houses that bear their tribe's name. They wore clothes made of wool and woven cotton, farmed crops in the middle of desert land, created exquisite pottery and Kachina dolls, and had one of the most complex religions of all the tribes. They are perhaps best known for the challenging vista-based villages that they constructed from the sheer faces of cliffs and rocks and for their **adobes**, mud-brick buildings that housed their living and meeting quarters. The Pueblos chose their own chiefs. This was perhaps one of the oldest representative governments in the world.

Another well-known Southwestern tribe was the **Apache**, with their famous leader **Geronimo**. The Apache lived in homes called wickiups, which were made of bark, grass, and branches. They wore cotton clothing and were excellent hunters and gatherers. Adept at basketry, the Apache believed that everything in Nature had special powers and that they were honored just to be part of it all.

The **Navajo**, also residents of the Southwest, lived in hogans (round homes built with forked sticks) and wore clothes of rabbit skin. Their major contribution to the overall culture of the continent was in sand painting, weapon making, silversmithing, and weaving. Navajo hands crafted some of the most beautiful woven rugs.

Living in the Northwest were the **Inuit**, who lived in tents made from animal skins or, in some cases, igloos. They wore clothes made of animal skins, usually seals or caribou. They were excellent fishermen and hunters and crafted efficient kayaks and umiaks to take them through waterways and harpoons with which to hunt animals. The Inuit are perhaps best known for the great carvings that they left behind. Among these are ivory figures and tall totem poles.

Skill 4.5: Identify factors contributing to the scientific revolution of the sixteenth century and analyze the influence of the scientific revolution on the emergence of modern civilization

The **Scientific Revolution** was characterized by a shift in scientific approach and ideas. Near the end of the 16th century Galileo Galilei introduced a radical approach to the study of motion. He moved from attempts to explain why objects move the way they do and began to use experiments to describe precisely how they move. He also used experimentation to describe how forces affect non-moving objects. Other scientists continued in the same approach. Outstanding scientists of the period included Johannes Kepler, Evangelista Torricelli, Blaise Pascal, Isaac Newton and Leibniz. This was the period when experiments dominated scientific study. This method was particularly applied to the study of physics.

Science and technology are often referred to as a "double-edged sword". Although advances in medicine have greatly improved the quality and length of life, certain moral and ethical controversies have arisen. Unforeseen environmental problems may result from technological advances. Advances in science have led to an improved economy through biotechnology as applied to agriculture, yet it has put our health care system at risk and has caused the cost of medical care to skyrocket. Society depends on science, yet is necessary that the public be scientifically literate and informed in order to prevent potentially unethical procedures from occurring. Especially vulnerable are the areas of genetic research and fertility. It is important for science teachers to stay abreast of current research and to involve students in critical thinking and ethics whenever possible.

Skill 4.6: Analyze the emergence of Central Asian empires and their cultural and political influence on other civilizations.

The Mongol Empire, founded by Genghis Khan, included the majority of the territory from Southeast Asia to central Europe during the height of the empire. One of the primary military tactics of conquest was to annihilate any cities that refused to surrender.

Government was by decree on the basis on a code of laws developed by Genghis Khan. It is interesting that one of the tenets of this code was that the nobility and the commoners shared the same hardship. The society, and the opportunity to advance within the society, was based on a system of meritocracy. The carefully structured and controlled society was efficient and safe for the people. Religious tolerance was guaranteed. Theft and vandalism were strictly forbidden. Trade routes and an extensive postal system were created linking the various parts of the empire. Taxes were quite onerous, but teachers, artists and lawyers were exempted from the taxes.

Mongol rule, however, was absolute. The response to all resistance was collective punishment in the form of destruction of cities and slaughter of the inhabitants.

The lasting achievements of the Mongol Empire include:

- Reunification of China and expansions of its borders,
- Unification of the Central Asian Republics that later formed part of the USSR,
- Expansion of Europe's knowledge of the world.

The unique style of architecture of the Mogul Empire was its primary contribution to South Asia. The Taj Mahal was one of many monuments built during this period. The cultural was a blend of Indian, Iranian and Central Asian traditions. Other major accomplishments were:

- Centralized government,
- Blending of traditions in art and culture,
- Development of new trade routs to Arab and Turkish lands,
- A unique style of architecture,
- Landscape gardening,
- A unique cuisine,
- And the creation of to languages (Urdu and Hindi) for the common people.

COMPETENCY 5: Understand major political, social, economic, and cultural developments that shaped the course of world history from 1750 to the present and analyze major periods of historical change within and across cultures.

Skill 5.1: Identify major causes and consequences of the industrial revolution and evaluate its impact on the politics and culture of the modern world

Prior to the Industrial Revolution, most urban centers were either ports or centers of government. With the sudden and rapid growth of industry, which started in England, urban centers began growing based on industrial production and proximity to power resources, such as coal and water power. In the 100 years between 1700 and 1800, the population of England went from a majority living in rural areas to a majority living in cities. As industrialization spread to other countries, a similar pattern of urbanization followed. With the advent of the railroad, moving raw materials over land became easier and less expensive, further fueling urban growth.

The **Industrial Revolution**, which began in Great Britain and spread elsewhere, was the development of power-driven machinery (fueled by coal and steam) leading to the accelerated growth of industry with large factories replacing homes and small workshops as work centers. The lives of people changed drastically and a largely agricultural society changed to an industrial one. In Western Europe, the period of empire and colonialism began. The industrialized nations seized and claimed parts of Africa and Asia in an effort to control and provide the raw materials needed to feed the industries and machines in the "mother country". Later developments included power based on electricity and internal combustion, replacing coal and steam.

The overriding theme of the life in the 18th, 19th, and 20th Centuries was progress. Technological advancements brought great and terrible things in all aspects of life. New theories in economics brought great changes in the way the world does business. New theories in government brought about new nations, uprisings, and wars galore. New theories in art changed the landscape of painting forever.

The use of machines in industry enabled workers to produce a large quantity of goods much faster than by hand. With the increase in business, hundreds of workers were hired, assigned to perform a certain job in the production process. This was a method of organization called "**division of labor**" and by its increasing the rate of production, businesses lowered prices for their products making the products affordable for more people. As a result, sales and businesses were increasingly successful and profitable. A great variety of new products or inventions became available such as: the typewriter, the telephone, barbed wire, the electric light, the phonograph, and the gasoline automobile. From this list, the one that had the greatest effect on America's economy was the automobile.

The increase in business and industry was greatly affected by the many rich natural resources that were found throughout the nation. The industrial machines were powered by the abundant water supply. The construction industry as well as products made from wood depended heavily on lumber from the forests. Coal and iron ore in abundance were needed for the steel industry, which profited and increased from the use of steel in such things as skyscrapers, automobiles, bridges, railroad tracks, and machines. Other minerals such as silver, copper, and petroleum played a large role in industrial growth, especially petroleum, from which gasoline was refined as fuel for the increasingly popular automobile.

Skill 5.2: Examine the diverse views of groups involved in major political revolutions around the globe.

The **American Revolution** resulted in the successful efforts of the English colonists in America to win their freedom from Great Britain. After more than one hundred years of mostly self-government, the colonists resented the increased British meddling and control, they declared their freedom, won the Revolutionary War with aid from France, and formed a new independent nation.

The **French Revolution** was the revolt of the middle and lower classes against the gross political and economic excesses of the rulers and the supporting nobility. It ended with the establishment of the First in a series of French Republics. Conditions leading to revolt included extreme taxation, inflation, lack of food, and the total disregard for the impossible, degrading, and unacceptable condition of the people on the part of the rulers, nobility, and the Church.

Emboldened by the success of the American and French Revolutions, the Spanish and Portuguese colonies in Central and South America grew dissatisfied with their economic and political dependence on Europe, and in the early decades of the 19th Century, several revolutionary movements gained momentum.

In Europe, France had moved into Spain and captured the Spanish King Ferdinand VII in the Napoleonic Wars, effectively weakening Spain's hold over its colonies in the Americas. The royal family of Portugal fled before Napoleon's armies to Brazil, its South American colony. Efforts by the mother countries to suppress the independence movements were thwarted by junta forces led by such figures as Miguel Hidalgo and Simon Bolivar. They were further discouraged by other countries such as the United States and Great Britain which were eager to gain access to South America's natural resources and lucrative markets.

By 1822, Argentina, Chile, Colombia, Mexico, Paraguay, Venezuela, Peru, Ecuador and Brazil had all succeeded in their battles for independence, and looked to the rest of the world for recognition and assistance. In the United States, President James Monroe announced the Monroe Doctrine, which stated that any designs by European countries to take control of the former colonies in the Western Hemisphere would be interpreted as attacks on the United States.

The **Russian Revolution** occurred first in March (or February on the old calendar) 1917 with the abdication of Tsar Nicholas II and the establishment of a democratic government. Those who were the extreme Marxists and had a majority in Russia's Socialist Party, the Bolsheviks, overcame opposition, and in November (October on the old calendar), did away with the provisional democratic government and set up the world's first Marxist state.

The conditions in Russia in previous centuries led up to this. Russia's harsh climate, tremendous size, and physical isolation from the rest of Europe, along with the brutal despotic rule and control of the tsars over enslaved peasants, contributed to the final conditions leading to revolution. Despite the tremendous efforts of Peter the Great to bring his country up to the social, cultural, and economic standards of the rest of Europe, Russia always remained a hundred years or more behind. Autocratic rule, the existence of the system of serfdom or slavery of the peasants, lack of money, defeats in wars, lack of enough food and food production, little, if any, industrialization--all of these contributed to conditions ripe for revolt.

By 1914, Russia's industrial growth was even faster than Germany's and agricultural production was improving, along with better transportation. However, the conditions of poverty were horrendous. The Orthodox Church was steeped in political activities and the absolute rule of the tsar was the order of the day. By the time the nation entered World War I, conditions were just right for revolution. Marxist socialism seemed to be the solution or answer to all the problems. Russia had to stop participation in the war. Industry could not meet the military's needs.

Transportation by rail was severely disrupted and it was most difficult to procure supplies from the Allies. The people had had enough of war, injustice, starvation, poverty, slavery, and cruelty. The support for and strength of the Bolsheviks were mainly in the cities. After two or three years of civil war, fighting foreign invasions, and opposing other revolutionary groups, the Bolsheviks were finally successful in making possible a type of "pre-Utopia" for the workers and the people.

As succeeding Marxist or Communist leaders came to power, the effects of this violent revolution were felt all around the earth. From 1989 until 1991, Communism eventually gave way to various forms of democracies and free enterprise societies in Eastern Europe and the former Soviet Union. The foreign policies of all free Western nations were directly and immensely affected by the Marxist-Communist ideology. Its effect on Eastern Europe and the former Soviet Union was felt politically, economically, socially, culturally, and geographically. The people of ancient Russia simply exchanged one autocratic dictatorial system for another and its impact on all of the people on the earth is still being felt to this day.

World War I 1914 to 1918

In brief, the causes were the surge of nationalism, the increasing strength of military capabilities, massive colonization for raw materials needed for industrialization and manufacturing, and military and diplomatic alliances.
The initial spark, which started the conflagration, was the assassination of Austrian Archduke Francis Ferdinand and his wife in Sarajevo.

There were 28 nations involved in the war, not including colonies and territories. It began July 28, 1914 and ended November 11, 1918 with the signing of the Treaty of Versailles. Economically, the war cost a total of $337 billion; increased inflation and huge war debts; and caused a loss of markets, goods, jobs, and factories. Politically, old empires collapsed; many monarchies disappeared; smaller countries gained temporary independence; Communists seized power in Russia; and, in some cases, nationalism increased. Socially, total populations decreased because of war casualties and low birth rates. There were millions of displaced persons and villages and farms were destroyed. Cities grew while women made significant gains in the work force and the ballot box. There was less social distinction and classes. Attitudes completely changed and old beliefs and values were questioned. The peace settlement established the League of Nations to ensure peace, but it failed to do so.

Fascist movements often had socialist origins. For example, in Italy, where fascism first arose in place of socialism, **Benito Mussolini**, sought to impose what he called "*corporativism*". A fascist "*corporate*" state would, in theory, run the economy for the benefit of the whole country like a corporation. It would be centrally controlled and managed by the elite who would see that its benefits would go to everyone.

World War II 1939 to 1945

Ironically, the Treaty of Paris, the peace treaty ending World War I, ultimately led to the Second World War. Countries that fought in the first war were either dissatisfied over the "spoils" of war, or were punished so harshly that resentment continued building to an eruption twenty years later.

The economic problems of both winners and losers of the first war were never resolved and the worldwide Great Depression of the 1930s dealt the final blow to any immediate rapid recovery. Democratic governments in Europe were severely strained and weakened which in turn gave strength and encouragement to those political movements that were extreme and made promises to end the economic chaos in their countries.

Nationalism, which was a major cause of World War I, grew even stronger and seemed to feed the feelings of discontent, which became increasingly rampant.

Because of unstable economic conditions and political unrest, harsh dictatorships arose in several of the countries, especially where there was no history of experience in democratic government.

Countries such as Germany, Japan, and Italy began to aggressively expand their borders and acquire additional territory.

In all, 59 nations became embroiled in World War II, which began September 1, 1939 and ended September 2, 1945. These dates include both the European and Pacific Theaters of war. The horrible tragic results of this second global conflagration were more deaths and more destruction than in any other armed conflict. It completely uprooted and displaced millions of people. The end of the war brought renewed power struggles, especially in Europe and China, with many Eastern European nations as well as China coming under complete control and domination of the Communists, supported and backed by the Soviet Union. With the development of and two-time deployment of an atomic bomb against two Japanese cities, the world found itself in the nuclear age. The peace settlement established the United Nations Organization, still existing and operating today.

The post WWII years have seen many changes in society. Nations have been involved in a global community since then, partly due to the existence of the United Nations. Governments have been more concerned with the rights of various groups since then, like women and minorities. The role of women has changed throughout the world. Women are now more important to economies. For the most part, they no longer leave the workforce when they have children so they now have a more important role as leaders, consumers and workers. They are also better educated than in the past and have assumed their roles in industry and commerce, as well as politics and government.

Gains have been made in the treatment of minorities and human rights. Much of this is due to the United Nations, which provides a forum for discussion and enforcement by its member nations. International treaties have also come into being to protect the rights of people. The Cold War, of course, also existed during this period.

The Cold War was, more than anything else, an ideological struggle between proponents of democracy and those of communism. The two major players were the United States and the Soviet Union, but other countries were involved as well. It was a "cold" war because no large-scale fighting took place directly between the two big protagonists.

It wasn't just form of government that was driving this war, either. Economics were a main concern as well. A concern in both countries was that the precious resources (such as oil and food) from other like-minded countries wouldn't be allowed to flow to "the other side." These resources didn't much flow between the U.S. and Soviet Union, either.

The Soviet Union kept much more of a tight leash on its supporting countries, including all of Eastern Europe, which made up a military organization called the Warsaw Pact. The Western nations responded with a military organization of their own, NATO. Another prime battleground was Asia, where the Soviet Union had allies in China, North Korea, and North Vietnam and the U.S. had allies in Japan, South Korea, Taiwan, and South Vietnam. The Korean War and Vietnam War were major conflicts in which both big protagonists played big roles but didn't directly fight each other. The main symbol of the Cold War was the arms race, a continual buildup of missiles, tanks, and other weapons that became ever more technologically advanced and increasingly more deadly. The ultimate weapon, which both sides had in abundance, was the nuclear bomb. Spending on weapons and defensive systems eventually occupied great percentages of the budgets of the U.S. and the USSR, and some historians argue that this high level of spending played a large part in the end of the latter.

The war was a cultural struggle as well. Adults brought up their children to hate "the Americans" or "the Communists." Cold War tensions spilled over into many parts of life in countries around the world. The ways of life in countries on either side of the divide were so different that they seemed entirely foreign to outside observers.

The Cold War continued in varying degrees from 1947 to 1991, when the Soviet Union collapsed. Other Eastern European countries had seen their communist governments overthrown by this time as well, marking the shredding of the "Iron Curtain."

The major thrust of U.S. foreign policy from the end of World War II to 1990 was the post-war struggle between non-Communist nations, led by the United States, and the Soviet Union and the Communist nations who were its allies. It was referred to as a "Cold War" because its conflicts did not lead to a major war of fighting, or a "hot war." Both the Soviet Union and the United States embarked on an arsenal buildup of atomic and hydrogen bombs as well as other nuclear weapons. Both nations had the capability of destroying each other but because of the continuous threat of nuclear war and accidents, extreme caution was practiced on both sides. The efforts of both sides to serve and protect their political philosophies and to support and assist their allies resulted in a number of events during this 45-year period.

The problem the world has been dealing with since WWII is population growth, especially in the less developed countries. Economies and the food supply have to expand to accommodate a growing population. This hasn't been the case in many of the less developed countries and as a result they suffer extreme poverty and have a poor quality of life.

Skill 5.3: Recognize major geopolitical developments, social movements, and political/economic initiatives since and evaluate the effect of these developments, movements, and initiatives on the modern world.

During the period of 1823 to the 1890s, the major interests and efforts of the American people were concentrated on expansion, settlement, and development of the continental United States. The Civil War 1861-1865, preserved the Union and eliminated the system of slavery. From 1865 onward, the focus was on taming the West and developing industry. During this period, travel and trade between the United States and Europe were continuous. By the 1890s, American interests turned to areas outside the boundaries of the United States. The West was developing into a major industrial area and people in the United States became very interested in selling their factory and farm surplus to overseas markets. In fact, some Americans desired getting and controlling land outside the U.S. boundaries. Before the 1890s, the U.S. had little, if anything to do with foreign affairs, was not a strong nation militarily, and had inconsequential influence on international political affairs. In fact, the Europeans looked on the American diplomats as inept and bungling in their diplomatic efforts and activities. However, all of this changed and the Spanish-American War of 1898 saw the entry of the United States as a world power.

During the 1890s, Spain controlled such overseas possessions as Puerto Rico, the Philippines, and Cuba. Cubans rebelled against Spanish rule and the U.S. government found itself besieged by demands from Americans to assist the Cubans in their revolt. When the U.S. battleship Maine blew up off the coast of Havana, Cuba, Americans blamed the Spaniards for it and demanded American action against Spain. Two months later, Congress declared war on Spain and the U.S. quickly defeated them. The peace treaty gave the U.S. possession of Puerto Rico, the Philippines, Guam and Hawaii, which was annexed during the war.

This success enlarged and expanded the U.S. role in foreign affairs.

In Europe, Italy and Germany were each totally united into one nation from many smaller states. There were revolutions in Austria and Hungary, the Franco-Prussian War, the dividing of Africa among the strong European nations, interference and intervention of Western nations in Asia, and the breakup of Turkish dominance in the Balkans.

In Africa, France, Great Britain, Italy, Portugal, Spain, Germany, and Belgium controlled the entire continent except Liberia and Ethiopia. In Asia and the Pacific Islands, only China, Japan, and present-day Thailand (Siam) kept their independence. The others were controlled by the strong European nations.

This success enlarged and expanded the U.S. role in foreign affairs. Under the administration of Theodore Roosevelt, the U.S. armed forces were built up, greatly increasing its strength. Roosevelt's foreign policy was summed up in the slogan of "Speak softly and carry a big stick," backing up the efforts in diplomacy with a strong military. During the years before the outbreak of World War I, evidence of U.S. emergence as a world power could be seen in a number of actions. In the spirit of the Monroe Doctrine of non-involvement of Europe in the affairs of the Western Hemisphere, President Roosevelt forced Italy, Germany, and Great Britain to remove their blockade of Venezuela. In addition he gained the rights to construct the Panama Canal by threatening force, assumed the finances of the Dominican Republic to stabilize it and prevent any intervention by Europeans and in 1916 under President Woodrow Wilson, to keep order, U.S. troops were sent to the Dominican Republic.

In Europe, war broke out in 1914, eventually involving nearly 30 nations, and ended in 1918. One of the major causes of the war was the tremendous surge of nationalism during the 1800s and early 1900s. People of the same nationality or ethnic group sharing a common history, language or culture began uniting or demanding the right of unification, especially in the empires of Eastern Europe, such as Russian Ottoman and Austrian-Hungarian Empires. Getting stronger and more intense were the beliefs of these peoples in loyalty to common political, social, and economic goals considered to be before any loyalty to the controlling nation or empire.

Skill 5.4: Relate important developments in the arts, literature, religion, and philosophy to the social, political, and economic history of this period.

The last century and a half has been a time of rapid and extensive change on almost every front. Notably, there has been a growing concern for human rights and civil rights. The end of imperialism and the liberation of former colonies and territorial holdings have created new nations and increased communication and respect among the nations of the world. Democracy has grown; communism has risen and almost fallen; nations are no longer ruled by distant mother-countries and their resident governors. But these freedoms have been won at great cost in human lives. Both political and individual freedoms have been won through struggle. Nationalism has risen and created new states and nations that have cultivated a national identity. Yet these individual nations have been brought into contact and cooperation in ways never before experienced in human history. Scientific and technological developments, new thinking in religion and philosophy, and new political and economic realities have combined to begin to create a global society that must now learn to define itself and understand how to cooperate and respect diversity in new ways.

After the defeat of Napoleon in 1815, Europe began a 100-year period of relative peace. There were vast changes in agricultural technology, new policies of land tenure, and the rise of both capitalism and mercantilism. Liberal and democratic institutions began to exercise greater influence throughout the world.

The late 1800s and early 1900s were a period of the efforts of many to make significant reforms and changes in the areas of politics, society, and the economy. There was a need to reduce the levels of poverty and to improve the living conditions of those affected by it. Regulations of big business, ridding governmental corruption and making it more responsive to the needs of the people were also on the list of reforms to be accomplished. Until 1890, there was very little success, but from 1890 on, the reformers gained increased public support and were able to achieve some influence in government. Since some of these individuals referred to themselves as "**progressives**" the period of 1890 to 1917 is referred to by historians as the Progressive Era.

Things changed in the worlds of literature and art as well. The main development in the 19th Century was **Romanticism**, an emphasis on emotion and the imagination that was a direct reaction to the logic and reason so stressed in the preceding Enlightenment. Famous Romantic authors included John Keats, William Wordsworth, Victor Hugo, and Johann Wolfgang von Goethe. The horrors of the Industrial Revolution gave rise to the very famous realists Charles Dickens, Fyodor Dosteovsky, Leo Tolstoy, and Mark Twain, who described life as they saw it, for better or for worse (and it was usually worse).

The most famous movement of the 1800s, however, was **Impressionism**. The idea was to present an impression of a moment in time one of life's fleeting moments memorialized on canvas. A list of famous impressionists is a who's who of the most famous painters in the world: Monet, Degas, van Gogh, Manet, Cezanne, Renoir, and the list goes on. More than any other time in the history of the arts, Impressionism produced famous faces and famous canvases.
Echoing Dickens's dislike of an industrialized world, 20th Century authors stressed individual action and responsibility. The giants of the 1900s include James Joyce, T.S. Eliot, John Steinbeck, Ernest Hemingway, William Faulkner, and George Orwell, all of whom to varying degrees expressed distrust at the power of machines and weapons and most of modern society.

New technologies have made production faster, easier, and more efficient. People found their skills and their abilities replaced by machines that were faster and more accurate. To some degree, machines and humans have entered an age of competition. Yet these advances have facilitated greater control over nature, lightened the burden of labor, and extended human life span. These advances in science, knowledge and technology have also called into question many of the assumptions and beliefs that have provided meaning for human existence. The myths that provided meaning in the past have been exposed and there are no new structures of belief to replace them. Without the foundational belief structures that have given meaning to life, an emptiness and aimlessness has arisen. Technology and science have extended life and made life easier. They have provided power and knowledge, but not the wisdom to know how to use it effectively. It was not accompanied by self-mastery, or the willingness to prevent class conflicts and prejudice, or to stop war, cruelty and violence.

The extraordinary advances in science and technology opened new frontiers and pushed back an ever-growing number of boundaries. These influences have had a profound effect in shaping modern civilization. Each discovery or machine or insight built upon other new discoveries or insights or machines. By the 20th century the rate of discovery and invention became literally uncontrollable. The results have, in many cases, been beneficial. But others have been horrifying.

Advances in biology and medicine have decreased infant mortality and increased live expectancy dramatically. Antibiotics and new surgical techniques have saved countless lives. Inoculations have essentially erased many dreadful diseases. Yet others have resulted from the careless disposal of byproducts and the effects of industrialization upon the environment and the individual.

The developing technologies of war have moved society from battle with swords and spears to battle with single-shot muskets and cannon; from cannon and muskets came repeating rifles and the gatling gun, from those automatic weapons were developed. Cannon were replaced by missiles and rockets that were able to be propelled farther and farther. Bombs became more and more powerful, culminating in the atomic bomb.

And in every development, the act of war became more remote for those engaging in it. The cost of war could be counted, but the fighters were becoming more removed from it.

Developments for war, however, also brought benefits as such things as plastics, alloys, electronic devices and more were perfected for industrial or medical purposes. The development of the radio is a case in point. Developed to a new extent during WWI, new applications were discovered for peacetime communication and entertainment. Throughout the Cold War and the Arms Race, more attention and more money were devoted to the development of weapons than to the conditions of human existence.

The deeper human problems have been more seriously addressed only since the end of the Cold War and the Arms Race. Only then could attention be given to the growing divide between the rich and the poor. The conditions of life in the cities and in third world countries have only begun to be addressed. The massive relocation from the farm to the city has changed the way people think about the environment, about values, and about other people.

The old adage that art imitates life has certainly been true of the last century and a half. The human struggle for meaning and redefinition has been consistently pursued in all of the arts.

The literature of this period has been an attempt to come to terms with the nature and the cost of war, of the meaning of the human struggle for freedom and the ability to enjoy basic human and civil rights. Literature has cried out against change and it has embraced change. By the beginning of the 20th century literature was reflecting the struggle of the modern individual to find a place and a meaning in a new world that seemed like a jungle. But literature has reflected the observation that not only does the modern human not know how to find meaning, he/she does not actually know what he/she is seeking. It is this crisis of identity that has been the subject of most modern literature. This can be seen is the writings of Joseph Conrad, Sigmund Freud, James Joyce, Eugene O'Neill, Luigi Pirandello, Samuel Beckett, George Bernard Shaw, T.S. Eliot, Kafka, Camus, Pasternak, Graham Greene, Tennessee Williams, and a host of others.

In art and architecture, there has been a search for new forms and for basic symbols that would speak a universal language. This fragmentation and anxiety has found expression in cubism and surrealism. In painting, one need only consider the works of Cezanne and Picasso and Dali. In Sculpture, artists took one of two directions: either looking back and preserving the conventional ideals of beauty, or experimenting with distortion and the abstract concepts of time and force. Architecture tended to move toward more functional lines and expressions.

In Religion and Philosophy there has been great change as well. For much of the period, religious interpretation tended to swing like a pendulum between the liberal and the conservative. By the end of the 21st century, however, the struggle for meaning and identity had resulted in a generalized conservative trend. This tendency can be seen in most religions yet today. Religion and philosophy are, to be sure, the means of self-definition and the understanding of one's place in the universe. Recent conservative trends, however, have had a polarizing effect. Issues of the relationship of Church and State have arisen and been resolved in most countries during this period. Yet, at the same time there has been an increasing effort to understand the religious beliefs of others, either to create new ways to define one's religion over and against other religions, or as the basis of new attacks on the values and teachings of other religions. This same struggle resulted in the rise of the philosophical movement known as existentialism, as seen in the writings of Soren Kierkegaard, Karl Jaspers, and Jean-Paul Sartre.

Skill 5.5: Analyze the causes and consequences of major international conflicts of the nineteenth and twentieth centuries.

The **Mexican Revolution** was a response to Mexico's long history under Spanish control which placed power, control, wealth and land in the hands of a small minority, leaving the majority in poverty. Under General Diaz, the distinction grew between rich and poor, and with this growing divide the lower classes were losing any voice in politics. Opposition to Diaz began when Francisco I. Madero led a series of strikes throughout Mexico. Madero gained a following and brought pressure to bear on Diaz until an election was held in 1910. Madero won a large number of votes. Diaz had Madero imprisoned and claimed that the Mexican people were not prepared for democracy.

As soon as Madero was released from prison, he began an attempt to have Diaz overthrown. At about this time two other local heroes emerged – Pancho Villa and Emiliano Zapata. Villa and Zapata harassed the Mexican army and eventually won control of regions in the north and in the south. Unable to control the spread of the insurgence, Diaz resigned in 1911. Madero and Zapata ran for president of Mexico; Madero won. Madero had a plan of land reform that was too slow in Zapata's opinion. Within a matter of months, Zapata denounced Madero and claimed the presidency. With control of the state of Morelos, he deported the wealthy land owners and divided their lands among the peasants. He was assassinated in 1919.

Many factions began to arise and guerilla units roamed the country pillaging and destroying large haciendas and ranchos. Madero was executed, leaving the country in disarray for several years, allowing Pancho Villa free reign in the north. Various factions vied for control of the government until Venustiano Carranza emerged and became president. He called a constitutional convention resulting in the 1917 Constitution (still in effect). One of the provisions of the Constitution was land reform. The Constitution created the *ejido*, a farm cooperative program that redistributed much of the land among the peasants.

The **Russian Revolution** The Russian Revolution occurred first in March (or February on the old calendar) 1917 with the abdication of Tsar Nicholas II and the establishment of a democratic government. Those who were the extreme Marxists and had a majority in Russia's Socialist Party, the Bolsheviks, overcame opposition, and in November (October on the old calendar), did away with the provisional democratic government and set up the world's first Marxist state

The **Iranian Revolution** in 1979 transformed a constitutional monarchy, led by the Shah, into an Islamic populist theocratic republic. The new ruler was Ayatollah Ruhollah Khomeini. This revolution occurred in two essential stages. In the first, religious, liberal and leftist groups cooperated to oust the Shah (king). In the second stage, the Ayatollah rose to power and created an Islamic state.

The Shah had faced intermittent opposition from the middle classes in the cities and from Islamic figures. These groups sought a limitation of the Shah's power and a constitutional democracy. The Shah enforced censorship laws and imprisoned political enemies. At the same time, living conditions of the people improved greatly and several important democratic rights were given to the people. Giving women the right to vote was fiercely opposed by the Islamic Mullahs. The Shah was said by his opponents to be a puppet of the U.S. government.

A series of protests in 1978 was sparked by a libelous story about the Ayatollah Khomeini that was published in the official press. The protests escalated until December of that year when more than 2 million people gathered in Tehran in protest against the Shah. On the advice of Prime Minister Shapour Bakhtiar, who was an opposition leader, the Shah and the empress left Iran. Bakhtiar freed the political prisoners, permitted Khomeini to return from exile, and asked Khomeini to create a state modeled on the Vatican. Bakhtiar promised free elections and called for the preservation of the Constitution. Khomeini rejected Bakhtiar's demands and appointed an interim government. In a very short period of time, Khomeini gathered his revolutionaries and completed the overthrow of the monarchy.

The revolution accomplished certain goals: reduction of foreign influence and a more even distribution of the nation's wealth. It did not, however, change repressive policies or levels of government brutality. It reversed policies toward women, restoring ancient policies of repression. Religious repression became rife, particularly against members of the Bahai Faith. The revolution has also isolated Iran from the rest of the world, being rejected by both capitalist and communist nations. This isolation, however, allowed the country to develop its own internal political system, rather than having a system imposed by foreign powers.

The **Chinese Revolution** was a response to imperial rule under the Qing Dynasty. Numerous internal rebellions caused widespread oppression and death. Conflicts with foreign nations had tended to end with treaties that humiliated China and required the payment of reparations that amounted to massive cost. In addition, there were popular feelings that political power should be restored from the Manchus to the Han Chinese. There was some attempt at reform, but it was undercut by the conservative supporters of the dynasty. The failures in modernization and liberalization and the violent repression of dissidents moved the reformers toward revolution.

The most popular of the numerous revolutionary groups was led by Sun Yat-sen. His movement was supported by Chinese who were living outside China and by students in Japan. He won the support of regional military officers. Sun's political philosophy consisted of "three principles of the people": (1) nationalism, which called for ousting of the Manchus and putting an end to foreign hegemony; (2) democracy, to establish a popularly elected government; and (3) people's livelihood, or socialism, which was designed to help the common people by equalizing the ownership of land and the tools of production.

Revolution began with the discontented army units. This was called the Wuchang Uprising. The uprising spread to other parts of China. It was put down by the Qing Court within 50 days. During this time, however, a number of other provinces declared independence of the Qing Dynasty. A month later Sun Yat-sen was elected the first Provisional President of the new Republic of China. Yuan Shikai, who had control of the Army tried to prevent civil war and possible intervention by foreign governments. He claimed power in Beijing. Sun agreed to unite China under a government headed by Yuan, who became the second provisional president of the Chinese republic.

Yuan quickly gathered more power than was controlled by the Parliament. He revised the constitution and became a dictator. In the national elections of 1912, Sung Jiaoren led the new Nationalist Party in winning the majority of seats in the parliament. A month later, Yuan had Sung assassinated. This increased Yuan's unpopularity. Several leadership missteps of a dictatorial nature aroused greater discontent. A second revolution began in 1913. This resulted in the flight to Japan of Sun and his followers. While Yuan pursued an imperialistic policy, Sun gathered more followers. Yuan alienated the parliament and the military. When WWI broke out, Japan issued the "Twenty-one Demands." Yuan agreed to many of the demands, further alienating the people of China. Several southern provinces declared independence. In 1916, Yuan repudiated monarchy and stepped down as emperor.

A period of struggle between rival warlords followed. By the end of WWI, Duan Qirui had emerged as the most powerful Chinese leader. He declared war on Germany and Austria-Hungary in 1917 in the hope of getting loans from Japan. His disregard for the constitution led Sun Yat-sen and others to establish a new government and the Constitutional Protection Army. Sun established a military government. The Constitutional Protection War continued through 1918. The result was a divided China, divided along the north-south border.

By 1921, Sun had become president of a unified group of southern provinces. He was unable to obtain assistance from Western nations, and turned to the Soviet Union in 1920. The Soviets supported both Sun and the newly established Communist Party in China. This set off a power struggle between the Communists and the Nationalists. In 1923, Sun and a Soviet representative promised Soviet support for the re-unification of China. The soviet advisers sent Chiang Kai-shek to Moscow to be trained in propaganda and mass mobilization. Sun died in 1925.

Chiang was commander of the National Revolutionary Army, and began to take back the Northern provinces from the warlords. By 1928 all of China was under Chiang's control and his government was recognized internationally.

Skill 5.6: Analyze relationships and tensions between national sovereignty and international interests in such matters as territorial boundaries, economic development, use of natural resources, deployment of weapons systems, and concerns about human rights.

Individuals and societies have divided the earth's surface through conflict for a number of reasons:

- The domination of peoples or societies, e.g., colonialism
- The control of valuable resources, e.g., oil
- The control of strategic routes, e.g., the Panama Canal

Religion, political ideology, national origin, language, and race can spur conflicts. Conflicts can result from disagreement over how land, ocean or natural resources will be developed, shared, and used. Conflicts have resulted from trade, migration, and settlement rights. Conflicts can occur between small groups of people, between cities, between nations, between religious groups, and between multi-national alliances.

Today, the world is primarily divided by political/administrative interests into state sovereignties. A particular region is recognized to be controlled by a particular government, including its territory, population and natural resources. The only area of the earth's surface that today is not defined by state or national sovereignty is Antarctica.

Alliances are developed among nations on the basis of political philosophy, economic concerns, cultural similarities, religious interests, or for military defense. Some of the most notable alliances today are:

- The United Nations
- The North Atlantic Treaty Organization
- The Caribbean Community
- The Common Market
- The Council of Arab Economic Unity
- The European Union

Throughout human history there have been conflicts on virtually every scale over the right to divide the Earth according to differing perceptions, needs and values. These conflicts have ranged from tribal conflicts to urban riots, to civil wars, to regional wars, to world wars. While these conflicts have traditionally centered on control of land surfaces, new disputes are beginning to arise over the resources of the oceans and space. International organizations such as the UN and the World Bank have programs to assist developing nations with loans and education so they might join the international economy. Many countries are taking steps to regulate immigration.

COMPETENCY 6: Understand major political, social, economic, and cultural developments in U.S. history to 1815.

Skill 6.1: Demonstrate knowledge of Native American societies and cultures before European settlement

Though not greatly differing from each other in degree of civilization, the Native peoples north of Mexico varied widely in customs, housing, dress, and religion. Among the native peoples of North America there were at least 200 languages and 1500 dialects. Each of the hundreds of tribes was somewhat influenced by its neighbors. Communication between tribes that spoke different language was conducted primarily through a very elaborate system of sign language. Several groups of tribes can be distinguished.

The Woods Peoples occupied the area from the Atlantic to the Western plains and prairies. They cultivated corn and tobacco, fished and hunted.

The Plains Peoples, who populated the area from the Mississippi River to the Rocky Mountains, were largely wandering and warlike, hunting buffalo and other game for food. After the arrival of Europeans and the re-introduction of the horse they became great horsemen.

The Southwestern Tribes of New Mexico and Arizona included Pueblos, who lived in villages constructed of *adobe* (sun-dried brick), cliff dwellers, and nomadic tribes. These tribes had the most advanced civilizations.

The California Tribes were separated from the influence of other tribes by the mountains. They lived primarily on acorns, seeds and fish, and were probably the least advanced civilizations.

The Northwest Coast Peoples of Washington, British Columbia and Southern Alaska were not acquainted with farming, but built large wooden houses and traveled in huge cedar canoes.

The Plateau Peoples who lived between the plains and the Pacific coast were simple people lived in underground houses or brush huts and subsisted primarily on fish.

The native peoples of America, like other peoples of the same stage of development, believed that all objects, both animate and inanimate, were endowed with certain spiritual powers. They were intensely religious, and lived every aspect of their lives as their religion prescribed. They believed a soul inhabited every living thing. Certain birds and animals were considered more powerful and intelligent than humans and capable of influence for good or evil.

Most of the tribes were divided into clans of close blood relations, whose *totem* was a particular animal from which they were often believed to have descended. The sun and the four principal directions were often objects of worship. The *shaman*, a sort of priest, was often the *medicine-man* of a tribe. Sickness was often supposed to be the result of displeasing some spirit and was treated with incantations and prayer. Many of the traditional stories resemble those of other peoples in providing answers to primordial questions and guidance for life. The highest virtue was self-control. Hiding emotions and enduring pain or torture unflinchingly was required of each. Honesty was also a primary virtue, and promises were always honored no matter what the personal cost.

The communities did not have any strict form of government, for the most part. Each individual was responsible for governing himself or herself, particularly with regard to the rights of other members of the community. The chiefs generally carried out the will of the tribe. Each tribe was a discrete unit, with its own lands. Boundaries of tribal territories were determined by treaties with neighbors. There was an organized confederation among certain tribes, often called a nation. The Iroquois confederation was often referred to as The Five Nations (later The Six Nations).

Customs varied from tribe to tribe. One consistent cultural element was the smoking of the calumet, a stone pipe, at the beginning and end of a war. In Native American communities, no individual owned land. The plots of land that were cultivated were, however, respected. Wealth was sometimes an honor, but generosity was more highly valued. Agriculture was quite advanced, and irrigation was practiced in some locations. Most tribes practiced unique styles of basket work, pottery and weaving, either in terms of shape or decoration.

Skill 6.2: Examine major events related to European exploration and settlement of North America from various perspectives.

The Age of Exploration actually had its beginnings centuries before exploration actually took place. The rise and spread of Islam in the seventh century and its subsequent control over the holy city of Jerusalem led to the European so-called Holy Wars, the Crusades, to free Jerusalem and the Holy Land from this control. Even though the Crusades were not a success, those who survived and returned to their homes and countries in Western Europe brought back with them new products such as silks, spices, perfumes, new and different foods. Luxuries that were unheard of that gave new meaning to colorless, drab, dull lives.

New ideas, new inventions, and new methods also went to Western Europe with the returning Crusaders and from these new influences was the intellectual stimulation which led to the period known as the Renaissance. The revival of interest in classical Greek art, architecture, literature, science, astronomy, medicine and increased trade between Europe and Asia and the invention of the printing press helped to push the spread of knowledge and start exploring.

For many centuries, various mapmakers made many maps and charts, which in turn stimulated curiosity and the seeking of more knowledge. At the same time, the Chinese were using the magnetic compass in their ships. Pacific islanders were going from island to island, covering thousands of miles in open canoes navigating by sun and stars. Arab traders were sailing all over the Indian Ocean in their **dhows**. The trade routes between Europe and Asia were slow, difficult, dangerous, and very expensive. Between sea voyages on the Indian Ocean and Mediterranean Sea and the camel caravans in central Asia and the Arabian Desert, the trade was still controlled by the Italian merchants in Genoa and Venice. It would take months and even years for the exotic luxuries of Asia to reach the markets of Western Europe. A faster, cheaper way had to be found. A way had to be found which would bypass traditional routes and end the control of the Italian merchants.

Prince Henry of Portugal (also called the Navigator) encouraged, supported, and financed the Portuguese seamen who led in the search for an all-water route to Asia. A shipyard was built along with a school teaching navigation. New types of sailing ships were built which would carry the seamen safely through the ocean waters. Experiments were conducted in newer maps, newer navigational methods, and newer instruments. These included the astrolabe and the compass enabling sailors to determine direction as well as latitude and longitude for exact location. Although Prince Henry died in 1460, the Portuguese kept on, sailing along and exploring Africa's west coastline. In 1488, Bartholomew Diaz and his men sailed around Africa's southern tip and headed toward Asia. Diaz wanted to push on but turned back because his men were discouraged and weary from the long months at sea, extremely fearful of the unknown, and just refusing to travel any further.

However, the Portuguese were finally successful ten years later in 1498 when **Vasco da Gama** and his men, continuing the route of Diaz, rounded Africa's Cape of Good Hope, sailing across the Indian Ocean, reaching India's port of Calicut (Calcutta). Although, six years earlier, Columbus had reached the New World and an entire hemisphere, da Gama had proved Asia could be reached from Europe by sea.

Of course, everyone knows that Columbus' first Trans-Atlantic voyage was to try to prove his theory or idea that Asia could be reached by sailing west. To a certain extent, his idea was true. It could be done but only after figuring how to go around or across or through the landmass in between. Long after Spain dispatched explorers and her famed conquistadors to gather the wealth for the Spanish monarchs and their coffers, the British were searching valiantly for the "Northwest Passage," a land-sea route across North America and open sea to the wealth of Asia. It wasn't until after the Lewis and Clark Expedition when Captains Meriwether Lewis and William Clark proved conclusively that there simply was no Northwest Passage. It did not exist.

However, this did not deter exploration and settlement. Spain, France, and England along with some participation by the Dutch led the way with expanding Western

European civilization in the New World. These three nations had strong monarchial governments and were struggling for dominance and power in Europe. With the defeat of Spain's mighty Armada in 1588, England became undisputed mistress of the seas. Spain lost its power and influence in Europe and it was left to France and England to carry on the rivalry, leading to eventual British control in Asia as well.

Spain's influence was in Florida, the Gulf Coast from Texas all the way west to California and south to the tip of South America and some of the islands of the West Indies. French control centered from New Orleans north to what is now northern Canada including the entire Mississippi Valley, the St. Lawrence Valley, the Great Lakes, and the land that was part of the Louisiana Territory. A few West Indies islands were also part of France's empire. England settled the eastern seaboard of North America, including parts of Canada and from Maine to Georgia. Some West Indies islands also came under British control. The Dutch had New Amsterdam for a period but later ceded it into British hands. One interesting aspect of this was each of these three nations, especially England, the land claims extended partly or all the way across the continent, regardless of the fact that the others claimed the same land. The wars for dominance and control of power and influence in Europe would undoubtedly and eventually extend to the Americas, especially North America.

The importance of the Age of Exploration was not just the discovery and colonization of the New World, but better maps and charts, newer, more accurate navigational instruments, increased knowledge, and great wealth. Furthermore, new and different foods and items unknown in Europe and a new hemisphere as a refuge from poverty, persecution, and a place to start a new and better life. The proof that Asia could be reached by sea and that the earth was round; ships and sailors would not sail off the edge of a flat earth and disappear forever into nothingness.

The part of North America claimed by France was called New France and consisted of the land west of the Appalachian Mountains. This area of claims and settlement included the St. Lawrence Valley, the Great Lakes, the Mississippi Valley, and the entire region of land westward to the Rocky Mountains. They established the permanent settlements of Montreal and New Orleans, thus giving them control of the two major gateways into the heart of North America, the vast, rich interior. The St. Lawrence River, the Great Lakes, and the Mississippi River along with its tributaries made it possible for the French explorers and traders to roam at will, virtually unhindered in exploring, trapping, trading, and furthering the interests of France.

Most of the French settlements were in Canada along the St. Lawrence River. Only scattered forts and trading posts were found in the upper Mississippi Valley and Great Lakes region. The rulers of France originally intended New France to have vast estates owned by nobles and worked by peasants who would live on the estates in compact farming villages--the New World version of the Old World's medieval system of feudalism. However, it didn't work out that way. Each of the nobles wanted his estate to be on the river for ease of transportation. The peasants working the estates wanted the prime waterfront location, also. The result of all this real estate squabbling was that New France's settled areas wound up mostly as a string of farmhouses stretching from Quebec to Montreal along the St. Lawrence and Richelieu Rivers.

In the non-settled areas in the interior were the French fur traders. They made friends with the friendly tribes of Indians, spending the winters with them getting the furs needed for trade. In the spring, they would return to Montreal in time to take advantage of trading their furs for the products brought by the cargo ships from France, which usually arrived at about the same time. Most of the wealth for New France and its "Mother Country" was from the fur trade, which provided a livelihood for many, many people. Manufacturers and workmen back in France, ship-owners and merchants, as well as the fur traders and their Indian allies all benefited. However, the freedom of roaming and trapping in the interior was a strong enticement for the younger, stronger men and resulted in the French not strengthening the areas settled along the St. Lawrence.

Into the 18th century, the rivalry with the British was getting stronger and stronger. New France was united under a single government and enjoyed the support of many Indian allies. The French traders were very diligent in not destroying the forests and driving away game upon which the Indians depended for life. It was difficult for the French to defend all of their settlements as they were scattered over half of the continent. However, by the early 1750s, in Western Europe, France was the most powerful nation. Its armies were superior to all others and its navy was giving the British stiff competition for control of the seas. The stage was set for confrontation in both Europe and America.

Spanish settlement had its beginnings in the Caribbean with the establishment of colonies on Hispaniola (at Santo Domingo which became the capital of the West Indies), Puerto Rico, and Cuba. There were a number of reasons for Spanish involvement in the Americas, to name just a few:

- the spirit of adventure
- the desire for land
- expansion of Spanish power, influence, and empire
- the desire for great wealth
- expansion of Roman Catholic influence and conversion of native peoples

The first permanent settlement in what is now the United States was in 1565 at St. Augustine, Florida. A later permanent settlement in the southwestern United States was in 1609 at Santa Fe, New Mexico. At the peak of Spanish power, the area in the United States claimed, settled, and controlled by Spain included Florida and all land west of the Mississippi River--quite a piece of choice real estate. Of course, France and England also lay claim to the same areas. Nonetheless, ranches and missions were built and the Indians who came in contact with the Spaniards were introduced to animals, plants, and seeds from the Old World that they had never seen before. Animals brought in included:
horses, cattle, donkeys, pigs, sheep, goats, and poultry.

Spain's control over her New World colonies lasted more than 300 years, longer than England or France. To this day, Spanish influence remains in names of places, art, architecture, music, literature, law, and cuisine. The Spanish settlements in North America were not commercial enterprises but were for protection and defense of the trading and wealth from their colonies in Mexico and South America. The Russians hunting seals came down the Pacific coast, the English moved into Florida and west into and beyond the Appalachians, and the French traders and trappers were making their way from Louisiana and other parts of New France into Spanish territory. The Spanish never realized or understood that self-sustaining economic development and colonial trade was so important. Consequently, the Spanish settlements in the U.S. never really prospered.

The nation had only itself to blame for this. The treasure and wealth found in Spanish New World colonies went back to Spain to be used to buy whatever goods and products were needed instead of setting up industries to make what was needed. As the amount of gold and silver was depleted, Spain could not pay for the goods needed and was unable to produce goods for themselves. Also, at the same time, Spanish treasure ships at sea were being seized by English and Dutch "pirates" taking the wealth to the coffers of their own countries.

Before 1763, when England was rapidly on the way to becoming the most powerful of the three major Western European powers, its thirteen colonies, located between the Atlantic and the Appalachians, physically occupied the least amount of land. Moreover, it is interesting that even before the Spanish Armada was defeated, two Englishmen, Sir Humphrey Gilbert and his half-brother Sir Walter Raleigh were unsuccessful in their attempts to build successful permanent colonies in the New World. Nonetheless, the thirteen English colonies were successful and, by the time they had gained their independence from Britain, were more than able to govern themselves. They had a rich historical heritage of law, tradition, and documents leading the way to constitutional government conducted according to laws and customs. The settlers in the British colonies highly valued individual freedom, democratic government, and getting ahead through hard work.

The English colonies, with only a few exceptions, were considered commercial ventures to make a profit for the crown or the company or whoever financed its beginnings. One was strictly a philanthropic enterprise and three others were primarily for religious reasons but the other nine were started for economic reasons. Settlers in these unique colonies came for different reasons:

a) religious freedom
b) political freedom
c) economic prosperity
d) land ownership

The colonies were divided generally into the three regions of **New England**, **Middle Atlantic, and Southern**. The culture of each was distinct and affected attitudes, ideas towards politics, religion, and economic activities. The geography of each region also contributed to its unique characteristics.

The **New England colonies** consisted of Massachusetts, Rhode Island, Connecticut, and New Hampshire. Life in these colonies was centered on the towns. What farming was done was by each family on its own plot of land but a short summer growing season and limited amount of good soil gave rise to other economic activities such as manufacturing, fishing, shipbuilding, and trade. The vast majority of the settlers shared similar origins, coming from England and Scotland. Towns were carefully planned and laid out the same way. The form of government was the town meeting where all adult males met to make the laws. The legislative body, the General Court, consisted of an Upper and Lower House.

The **Middle or Middle Atlantic colonies** included New York, New Jersey, Pennsylvania, Delaware, and Maryland. New York and New Jersey were at one time the Dutch colony of New Netherlands and Delaware at one time was New Sweden. These five colonies, from their beginnings were considered "melting pots" with settlers from many different nations and backgrounds. The main economic activity was farming with the settlers scattered over the countryside cultivating rather large farms. The Indians were not as much of a threat as in New England so they did not have to settle in small farming villages. The soil was very fertile, the land was gently rolling, and a milder climate provided a longer growing season.

These farms produced a large surplus of food, not only for the colonists themselves but also for sale. This colonial region became known as the "breadbasket" of the New World and the New York and Philadelphia seaports were constantly filled with ships being loaded with meat, flour, and other foodstuffs for the West Indies and England. There were other economic activities such as shipbuilding, iron mines, and factories producing paper, glass, and textiles. The legislative body in Pennsylvania was unicameral or consisted of one house. In the other four colonies, the legislative body had two houses. Also units of local government were in counties and towns.

The **Southern colonies** were Virginia, North and South Carolina, and Georgia. Virginia was the first permanent successful English colony and Georgia was the last. The year 1619 was a very important year in the history of Virginia and the United States with three very significant events. First, sixty women were sent to Virginia to marry and establish families, Second, twenty Africans, the first of thousands, arrived, Third, most importantly, the Virginia colonists were granted the right to self-government and they began by electing their own representatives to the House of Burgesses, their own legislative body.

The major economic activity in this region was farming. Here the soil was very fertile and the climate was very mild with an even longer growing season. The large plantations eventually requiring large numbers of slaves were found in the coastal or tidewater areas. Although the wealthy slave-owning planters set the pattern of life in this region, most of the people lived inland away from coastal areas. They were small farmers and very few, if any, owned slaves.

The settlers in these four colonies came from diverse backgrounds and cultures. Virginia was colonized mostly by people from England while Georgia was started as a haven for debtors from English prisons. Pioneers from Virginia settled in North Carolina while South Carolina welcomed people from England and Scotland, French Protestants, Germans, and emigrants from islands in the West Indies. Products from farms and plantations included rice, tobacco, indigo, cotton, some corn and wheat. Other economic activities included lumber and naval stores (tar, pitch, rosin, and turpentine) from the pine forests and fur trade on the frontier. Cities such as Savannah and Charleston were important seaports and trading centers.

In the colonies, the daily life of the colonists differed greatly between the coastal settlements and the inland or interior. The Southern planters and the people living in the coastal cities and towns had a way of life similar to that in towns in England. The influence was seen and heard in how people dressed and talked. The architectural styles of houses and public buildings, and the social divisions or levels of society mimicked that of England. Both the planters and city dwellers enjoyed an active social life and had strong emotional ties to England.

On the other hand, life inland on the frontier had marked differences. All facets of daily living--clothing, food, housing, economic and social activities--were all connected to what was needed to sustain life and survive in the wilderness. Everything was produced practically themselves. They were self-sufficient and extremely individualistic and independent. There were little, if any, levels of society or class distinctions as they considered themselves to be the equal to all others, regardless of station in life. The roots of equality, independence, individual rights and freedoms were extremely strong and well developed. People were not judged by their fancy dress, expensive house, eloquent language, or titles following their names.

The colonies had from 1607 to 1763 to develop, refine, practice, experiment, and experience life in a rugged, uncivilized land. The Mother Country had virtually left them on their own to take care of themselves all that time. When in 1763, Britain decided she needed to regulate and "mother" the "little ones," to her surprise she had a losing fight on her hands.

By the 1750s in Europe, Spain was "out of the picture," no longer the most powerful nation and not even a contender. The remaining rivalry was between Britain and France. For nearly 25 years, between 1689 and 1748, a series of "armed conflicts" involving these two powers had been taking place. These conflicts had spilled over into North America. The War of the League of Augsburg in Europe, 1689 to 1697, had been King William's War. The War of the Spanish Succession, 1702 to 1713, had been Queen Anne's War. The War of the Austrian Succession, 1740 to 1748, was called King George's War in the colonies. The two nations fought for possession of colonies, especially in Asia and North America, and for control of the seas, but none of these conflicts was decisive.

The final conflict, which decided once and for all who was the most powerful, began in North America in 1754, in the Ohio River Valley. It was known in America as the French and Indian War and in Europe as the Seven Years War, since it began there in 1756. In America, both sides had advantages and disadvantages. The British colonies were well established and consolidated in a smaller area. British colonists outnumbered French colonists 23 to 1. Except for a small area in Canada, French settlements were scattered over a much larger area (roughly half of the continent) and were smaller. However, the French settlements were united under one government and were quick to act and cooperate when necessary. In addition, the French had many more Indian allies than the British. The British colonies had separate, individual governments and very seldom cooperated, even when needed. In Europe, at that time, France was the more powerful of the two nations.

Both sides had stunning victories and humiliating defeats. If there was one person who could be given the credit for British victory, it would have to be William Pitt. He was a strong leader, enormously energetic, supremely self-confident, and determined on a complete British victory. Despite the advantages and military victories of the French, Pitt succeeded. In the army he got rid of the incompetents and replaced them with men who could do the job. He sent more troops to America, strengthened the British navy, gave to the officers of the colonial militias equal rank to the British officers - in short, he saw to it that Britain took the offensive and kept it to victory. Of all the British victories, perhaps the most crucial and important was winning Canada.

The French depended on the St. Lawrence River for transporting supplies, soldiers, and messages-the link between New France and the Mother Country. Tied into this waterway system was the connecting links of the Great Lakes, Mississippi River and its tributaries along which were scattered French forts, trading posts, and small settlements.

In 1758, the British captured Louisburg on Cape Breton Island, New France was doomed. Louisburg gave the British navy a base of operations preventing French reinforcements and supplies getting to their troops. Other forts fell to the British: Frontenac, Duquesne, Crown Point, Ticonderoga, Niagara, those in the upper Ohio Valley, and, most importantly, Quebec and finally Montreal. Spain entered the war in 1762 to aid France but it was too late. British victories occurred all around the world: in India, in the Mediterranean, and in Europe.

In 1763 in Paris, Spain, France, and Britain met to draw up the Treaty. Great Britain got most of India and all of North America east of the Mississippi River, except for New Orleans. Britain received from Spain control of Florida and returned to Spain Cuba and the islands of the Philippines, taken during the war. France lost nearly all of its possessions in America. India and was allowed to keep four islands: Guadeloupe, Martinique, Haiti on Hispaniola, and Miquelon and St. Pierre. France gave Spain New Orleans and the vast territory of Louisiana, west of the Mississippi River. Britain was now the most powerful nation--period.

Where did all of this leave the British colonies? Their colonial militias had fought with the British and they too benefited. The militias and their officers gained much experience in fighting which was very valuable later. The thirteen colonies began to realize that cooperating with each other was the only way to defend themselves. They didn't really understand that, until the war for independence and setting up a national government, but a start had been made. At the start of the war in 1754, Benjamin Franklin proposed to the thirteen colonies that they unite permanently to be able to defend themselves. This was after the French and their Indian allies had defeated Major George Washington and his militia at Fort Necessity. This left the entire northern frontier of the British colonies vulnerable and open to attack.

Delegates from seven of the thirteen colonies met at Albany, New York, along with the representatives from the Iroquois Confederation and British officials. Franklin's proposal, known as the Albany Plan of Union, was totally rejected by the colonists, along with a similar proposal from the British. They simply did not want each of the colonies to lose its right to act independently. However, the seed was planted.

Skill 6.3: Analyze major causes and key events of the movement for American independence.

The War for Independence occurred due to a number of changes, the two most important ones being economic and political. By the end of the French and Indian War in 1763, Britain's American colonies were thirteen out of a total of thirty-three scattered around the earth. Like all other countries, Britain strove for having a strong economy and a favorable balance of trade. To have that delicate balance a nation needs wealth, self-sufficiency, and a powerful army and navy. This is where the overseas colonies appeared. They would provide raw materials for the industries in the Mother Country, be a market for the finished products by buying them and assist the Mother Country in becoming powerful and strong (as in the case of Great Britain). By having a strong merchant fleet, it would be a school for training for the Royal Navy and provide places as bases of operation for the Royal Navy.

The foregoing explained the major reason for British encouragement and support of colonization, especially in North America. So between 1607 and 1763, at various times for various reasons, the British Parliament enacted different laws to assist the government in getting and keeping this trade balance. One series of laws required that most of the manufacturing be done only in England, such as: prohibition of exporting any wool or woolen cloth from the colonies, no manufacture of beaver hats or iron products. The colonists weren't concerned as they had no money and no highly skilled labor to set up any industries, anyway.

The Navigation Acts of 1651 put restrictions on shipping and trade within the British Empire by requiring that it was allowed only on British ships. This increased the strength of the British merchant fleet and greatly benefited the American colonists. Since they were British citizens, they could have their own vessels, building and operating them as well. By the end of the war in 1763, the shipyards in the colonies were building one third of the merchant ships under the British flag. There were quite a number of wealthy, American, colonial merchants.

The Navigation Act of 1660 restricted the shipment and sale of colonial products to England only. In 1663 another Navigation Act stipulated that the colonies had to buy manufactured products only from England and that any European goods going to the colonies had to go to England first. These acts were a protection from enemy ships and pirates and from competition from European rivals.

The New England and Middle Atlantic colonies felt threatened by these laws as they had started producing many of the products already being produced in Britain. They soon found new markets for their goods and began what was known as a “triangular trade." Colonial vessels started the first part of the triangle by sailing for Africa loaded with kegs of rum from colonial distilleries. On Africa's West Coast, the rum was traded for either gold or slaves. The second part of the triangle was from Africa to the West Indies where slaves were traded for molasses, sugar, or money. The third part of the triangle was home, bringing sugar or molasses (to make more rum), gold, and silver.

The major concern of the British government was that the trade violated the 1733 Molasses Act. Planters had wanted the colonists to buy all of their molasses in the British West Indies but these islands could give the traders only about one eighth of the amount of molasses needed for distilling the rum. The colonists were forced to buy the rest of what they needed from the French, Dutch, and Spanish islands, thus evading the law by not paying the high duty on the molasses bought from these islands. If Britain had enforced the Molasses Act, economic and financial chaos and ruin would have occurred. Nevertheless, for this act and all the other mercantile laws, the government followed the policy of "salutary neglect," deliberately failing to enforce the laws.

In 1763, after the war, money was needed to pay the British war debt, for the defense of the empire, and to pay for the governing of 33 colonies scattered around the earth. It was decided to adopt a new colonial policy and pass laws to raise revenue. It was reasoned that the colonists were subjects of the king and since the king and his ministers had spent a great deal of money defending and protecting them (this especially for the American colonists), it was only right and fair that the colonists should help pay the costs of defense, especially theirs. The earlier laws passed had been for the purposes of regulating production and trade which generally put money into colonial pockets. These new laws would take some of that rather hard-earned money out of their pockets and it would be done, in colonial eyes, unjustly and illegally.

Before 1763, except for trade and supplying raw materials, the colonies had been left pretty much to themselves. England looked on them merely as part of an economic or commercial empire. Little consideration was given as to how they were to conduct their daily affairs, so the colonists became very independent, self-reliant, and extremely skillful at handling those daily affairs. This, in turn, gave rise to leadership, initiative, achievement, and vast experience. In fact, there was a far greater degree of independence and self-government in the British colonies in America than could be found in Britain or the major countries on the Continent or any other colonies anywhere.

There were a number of reasons for this:

1. The religious and scriptural teachings of previous centuries put forth the worth of the individual and equality in God's sight. Keep in mind that freedom of worship and freedom from religious persecution were major reasons to live in the New World.

2. European Protestants, especially Calvinists, believed and taught the idea that government originates from those governed, that rulers are required to protect individual rights and that the governed have the right and privilege to choose their rulers.

3. Trading companies put into practice the principle that their members had the right to make the decisions and shape the policies affecting their lives.

4. The colonists believed and supported the idea that a person's property should not be taken without his consent, based on that treasured English document, Magna Carta, and English common law.

5. From about 1700 to 1750, population increases in America came about through immigration and generations of descendants of the original settlers. The immigrants were mainly Scots-Irish who hated the English, Germans who cared nothing about England, and black slaves who knew nothing about England. The descendants of the original settlers had never been out of America at any time.

6. In America, as new towns and counties were formed, there began the practice' of representation in government. Representatives to the colonial legislative assemblies were elected from the district in which they lived, chosen by qualified property-owning male voters, and representing the interests of the political district from which they were elected. One thing to remember: each of the 13 colonies had a royal governor appointed by the king, representing his interests in the colonies. Nevertheless, the colonial legislative assemblies controlled the purse strings having the power to vote on all issues involving money to be spent by the colonial governments.

Contrary to this was the governmental set-up in England. Members of Parliament were not elected to represent their own districts. They were considered representative of classes, not individuals. If some members of a professional or commercial class or some landed interests were able to elect representatives, then those classes or special interests were represented. It had nothing at all to do with numbers or territories. Some large population centers had no direct representation at all, yet the people there considered themselves represented by men elected from their particular class or interest somewhere else. Consequently, it was extremely difficult for the English to understand why the American merchants and landowners claimed they were not represented because they themselves did not vote for a member of Parliament.

The colonists' protest of "no taxation without representation" was meaningless to the English. Parliament represented the entire nation, was completely unlimited in legislation, and had become supreme; and the colonists were incensed at the English attitude of "of course you have representation--everyone does." The colonists considered their colonial legislative assemblies equal to Parliament, totally unacceptable in England, of course. There were two different environments of the older traditional British system in the Mother Country and in America new ideas and different ways of doing things. In a new country, a new environment has little or no tradition, institutions or vested interests. New ideas and traditions grew extremely fast pushing aside what was left of the old ideas and old traditions. By 1763, Britain had changed its perception of its American colonies to their being a "territorial" empire. The stage was set and the conditions were right for a showdown.

It all began in 1763 when Parliament decided to have a standing army in North America to reinforce British control. In 1765, the Quartering Act was passed requiring the colonists to provide supplies and living quarters for the British troops. In addition, efforts by the British were made to keep the peace by establishing good relations with the Indians. Consequently, a proclamation was issued which prohibited any American colonists from making any settlements west of the Appalachians until provided for through treaties with the Indians.

The Sugar Act of 1764 required efficient collection of taxes on any molasses that were brought into the colonies. It also gave British officials free license to conduct searches of the premises of anyone suspected of violating the law. The colonists were taxed on newspapers, legal documents, and other printed matter under the Stamp Act of 1765. Although a stamp tax was already in use in England, the colonists would have none of it and after the ensuing uproar of rioting and mob violence, Parliament repealed the tax.

Of course, great exultation, jubilance, and wild joy resulted when news of the repeal reached America. However, what no one noticed was the small, quiet Declaratory Act attached to the repeal. This act plainly and unequivocally stated that Parliament still had the right to make all laws for the colonies. It denied their right to be taxed only by their own colonial legislatures--a very crucial, important piece of legislation but virtually overlooked and unnoticed at the time. Other acts leading up to armed conflict included the Townshend Acts passed in 1767 taxing lead, paint, paper, and tea brought into the colonies. This really increased anger and tension resulting in the British sending troops to New York City and Boston.

In Boston, mob violence provoked retaliation by the troops thus bringing about the deaths of five people and the wounding of eight others. The so-called Boston Massacre shocked Americans and British alike. Subsequently, in 1770, Parliament voted to repeal all the provisions of the Townshend Acts with the exception of the tea tax. In 1773, the tax on tea sold by the British East India Company was substantially reduced, fueling colonial anger once more. This gave the company an unfair trade advantage and forcibly reminded the colonists of the British right to tax them. Merchants refused to sell the tea; colonists refused to buy and drink it; and a shipload of it was dumped into Boston Harbor--a most violent Tea Party.

In 1774, the passage of the Quebec Act extended the limits of that Canadian colony's boundary southward to include territory located north of the Ohio River. However, the punishment for Boston's Tea Party came in the same year with the Intolerable Acts. Boston's port was closed; the royal governor of the colony of Massachusetts was given increased power, and the colonists were compelled to house and feed the British soldiers. The propaganda activities of the patriot organizations Sons of Liberty and Committees of Correspondence kept the opposition and resistance before everyone. Delegates from twelve colonies met in Philadelphia September 5, 1774, in the First Continental Congress. They definitely opposed acts of lawlessness and wanted some form of peaceful settlement with Britain. They maintained American loyalty to the Mother Country and affirmed Parliament's power over colonial foreign affairs.

They insisted on repeal of the Intolerable Acts and demanded ending all trade with Britain until this took place. The reply from King George III, the last king of America, was an insistence of colonial submission to British rule or be crushed. With the start of the Revolutionary War April 19, 1775, the Second Continental Congress began meeting in Philadelphia May 10 that year to conduct the business of war and government for the next six years.

One historian explained that the British were interested only in raising money to pay war debts, regulate the trade and commerce of the colonies, and look after business and financial interests between the Mother Country and the rest of her empire. The establishment of overseas colonies was first, and foremost, a commercial enterprise, not a political one. The political aspect was secondary and assumed. The British took it for granted that Parliament was supreme, was recognized so by the colonists, and were very resentful of the colonial challenge to Parliament's authority. They were contemptuously indifferent to politics in America and had no wish to exert any control over it. As resistance and disobedience swelled and increased in America, the British increased their efforts to punish them and put them in their place.

The British had been extremely lax and totally inconsistent in enforcement of the mercantile or trade laws passed in the years before 1754. The government itself was not particularly stable so actions against the colonies occurred in anger and their attitude was one of a moral superiority, that they knew how to manage America better than the Americans did themselves. This of course points to a lack of sufficient knowledge of conditions and opinions in America. The colonists had been left on their own for nearly 150 years and by the time the Revolutionary War began, they were quite adept at self-government and adequately handling the affairs of their daily lives. The Americans equated ownership of land or property with the right to vote. Property was considered the foundation of life and liberty and, in the colonial mind and tradition, these went together.

Therefore when an indirect tax on tea was made, the British felt that since it wasn't a direct tax, there should be no objection to it. The colonists viewed any tax, direct or indirect, as an attack on their property. They felt that as a representative body, the British Parliament should protect British citizens, including the colonists, from arbitrary taxation. Since they felt they were not represented, Parliament, in their eyes, gave them no protection. So, war began. August 23, 1775, George III declared that the colonies were in rebellion and warned them to stop or else.

By 1776, the colonists and their representatives in the Second Continental Congress realized that things were past the point of no return. The Declaration of Independence was drafted and declared July 4, 1776. George Washington labored against tremendous odds to wage a victorious war. The turning point in the Americans' favor occurred in 1777 with the American victory at Saratoga. This victory decided for the French to align themselves with the Americans against the British. With the aid of Admiral deGrasse and French warships blocking the entrance to Chesapeake Bay, British General Cornwallis trapped at Yorktown, Virginia, surrendered in 1781 and the war was over. The Treaty of Paris officially ending the war was signed in 1783.

Skill 6.4: Evaluate the strengths and weaknesses of the Articles of Confederation and analyze issues related to the creation and ratification of the U.S. Constitution.

During the war, and after independence was declared, the former colonies now found themselves independent states. The Second Continental Congress was conducting a war with representation by delegates from thirteen separate states. The Congress had no power to act for the states or to require them to accept and follow its wishes. A permanent united government was desperately needed. On November 15, 1777, the Articles of Confederation were adopted, creating a league of free and independent states.

The central government of the new United States of America consisted of a Congress of two to seven delegates from each state with each state having just one vote. The government under the Articles solved some of the postwar problems but had serious weaknesses. Some of its powers included: borrowing and coining money, directing foreign affairs, declaring war and making peace, building and equipping a navy, regulating weights and measures, asking the states to supply men and money for an army. The delegates to Congress had no real authority as each state carefully and jealously guarded its own interests and limited powers under the Articles. Also, the delegates to Congress were paid by their states and had to vote as directed by their state legislatures. The serious weaknesses were the lack of power: to regulate finances, over interstate trade, over foreign trade, to enforce treaties, and military power. Something better and more efficient was needed. In May of 1787, delegates from all states except Rhode Island began meeting in Philadelphia. At first, they met to revise the Articles of Confederation as instructed by Congress; but they soon realized that much more was needed. Abandoning the instructions, they set out to write a new Constitution, a new document, the foundation of all government in the United States and a model for representative government throughout the world.

The first order of business was the agreement among all the delegates that the convention would be kept secret. No discussion of the convention outside of the meeting room would be allowed. They wanted to be able to discuss, argue, and agree among themselves before presenting the completed document to the American people.

The delegates were afraid that if the people were aware of what was taking place before it was completed the entire country would be plunged into argument and dissension. It would be extremely difficult, if not impossible, to settle differences and come to an agreement. Between the official notes kept and the complete notes of future President James Madison, an accurate picture of the events of the Convention is part of the historical record.

The delegates went to Philadelphia representing different areas and different interests. They all agreed on a strong central government but not one with unlimited powers. They also agreed that no one part of government could control the rest. It would be a republican form of government (sometimes referred to as representative democracy) in which the supreme power was in the hands of the voters who would elect the men who would govern for them.

One of the first serious controversies involved the small states versus the large states over representation in Congress. Virginia's Governor Edmund Randolph proposed that state population determine the number of representatives sent to Congress, also known as the Virginia Plan. New Jersey delegate William Paterson countered with what is known as the New Jersey Plan, each state having equal representation.

After much argument and debate, the Great Compromise was devised, known also as the Connecticut Compromise, as proposed by Roger Sherman. It was agreed that Congress would have two houses. The Senate would have two Senators, giving equal powers in the Senate. The House of Representatives would have its members elected based on each state's population. Both houses could draft bills to debate and vote on with the exception of bills pertaining to money, which must originate in the House of Representatives.

Another major controversy involved economic differences between North and South. One concerned the counting of the African slaves for determining representation in the House of Representatives. The southern delegates wanted this but didn't want it to apply to determining taxes to be paid. The northern delegates argued the opposite: count the slaves for taxes but not for representation. The resulting agreement was known as the "three-fifths" compromise. Three-fifths of the slaves would be counted for both taxes and determining representation in the House.

The last major compromise, also between North and South, was the Commerce Compromise. The economic interests of the northern part of the country were ones of industry and business whereas the south's economic interests were primarily in farming. The Northern merchants wanted the government to regulate and control commerce with foreign nations and with the states. Of course, Southern planters opposed this idea as they felt that any tariff laws passed would be unfavorable to them. The acceptable compromise to this dispute was that Congress was given the power to regulate commerce with other nations and the states, including levying tariffs on imports. However, Congress did not have the power to levy tariffs on any exports. This increased Southern concern about the effect it would have on the slave trade. The delegates finally agreed that the importation of slaves would continue for 20 more years with no interference from Congress. Any import tax could not exceed 10 dollars per person. After 1808, Congress would be able to decide whether to prohibit or regulate any further importation of slaves.

Of course, when work was completed and the document was presented, nine states needed to approve for it to go into effect. There was no little amount of discussion, arguing, debating, and haranguing. The opposition had three major objections:

1) The states seemed as if they were being asked to surrender too much power to the national government.
2) The voters did not have enough control and influence over the men who would be elected by them to run the government.
3) A lack of a "bill of rights" guaranteeing hard-won individual freedoms and liberties.

Eleven states finally ratified the document and the new national government went into effect. It was no small feat that the delegates were able to produce a workable document that satisfied all opinions, feelings, and viewpoints. The separation of powers of the three branches of government and the built-in system of checks and balances to keep power balanced were a stroke of genius. It provided for the individuals and the states as well as an organized central authority to keep a new inexperienced young nation on track. They created a system of government so flexible that it had continued in its basic form to this day. In 1789, the Electoral College unanimously elected George Washington as the first President and the new nation was on its way.

Skill 6.5: Know the role of outside influences on early political development of the United States.

Rousseau's most direct influence was upon the **French Revolution** (1789-1815). In the ***Declaration of the Rights of Man and The Citizen*** (1789), it explicitly recognized the sovereignty of the general will as expressed in the law. In contrast to the American **Declaration of Independence**, it contains explicit mention of the obligations and duties of the citizen, such as assenting to taxes in support of the military or police forces for the common good. In modern times, ideas such as Rousseau's have often been used to justify the ideas of authoritarian and totalitarian systems.

The confederacy of Iroquois tribes was known as the **Haudenosaunee**, the League of Peace and Power. They are often called the people of the Long House. Their original homeland was in upstate New York between the Adirondack Mountains and Niagara Falls. As a result of migration and conquest, they controlled most of the northeastern United States and Eastern Canada by the time of the first European contact. The confederacy had a constitution prior to the arrival of Europeans. It was known as the Gayanashagowa ("Great Law of Peace"). This was recorded in memory using a device in the form of special beads called wampum. There is no consensus among historians about the date of the origin of this constitution. Dating has ranged from 1142 to the early 1600s. The confederacy consisted of five nations, later six.

Slavery began in the Western Hemisphere in 1619 and ended in 1865. During that time, thousands and thousands of African people were brought against their will from their homes to America and elsewhere, as property of other people. The practice of slavery in America ended only after the South's final defeat in the Civil War and the passage of the Thirteenth Amendment, which outlawed slavery. America's Caribbean neighbor, Haiti, had ended slavery a half-century before, thanks to the heroics of Toussaint L'Ouverture.

For the details of the Declaration of the Rights of Man see Skill 22.4.

Skill 6.6: Recognize major accomplishments of early presidential administrations and examine factors that influenced the emergence of political parties.

George Washington (1789-1797) faced a number of challenges during his two terms as President. There were boundary disputes with Spain over the Southeast and wars with the Indians on the western frontier. The French Revolution and the ensuing war between France and England created great turmoil within the new nation. Thomas Jefferson, Secretary of State, was pro-French and believed the U.S. should enter the fray. Alexander Hamilton, Secretary of the Treasury, was pro-British and wanted to support England. Washington took a neutral course, believing the U.S. was not strong enough to be engaged in a war. Washington did not interfere with the powers of the Congress in establishing foreign policy. Two political parties were beginning to form by the end of his first term. In his farewell address he encouraged Americans to put an end to regional differences and exuberant party spirit. He also warned the nation against long-term alliances with foreign nations.

John Adams, of the Federalist Party, was elected President in 1796. When he assumed office the war between England and France was in full swing. The British were seizing American ships that were engaging in trade with France. France, however, was refusing to receive the American envoy and had suspended economic relationships. The people were divided in their loyalties to either France or England. Adams focused on France and the diplomatic crisis known as the XYZ Affair. During his administration, Congress appropriated money to build three new frigates and additional ships, authorized the creation of a provisional army, and passed the Alien and Sedition Acts which were intended to drive foreign agents from the country and to maintain dominance over the Republican Party. When the war ended, Adams sent a peace mission to France. This angered the Republicans. The election of 1800 pitted a unified and effective Republican Party against a divided and ineffective Federalist party.

Thomas Jefferson won the election of 1800. Jefferson opposed a strong centralized government as a champion of States Rights. He supported a strict interpretation of the Constitution. He reduced military expenditures, made budget cuts, and eliminated a tax on whiskey. At the same time, he reduced the national debt by 1/3. The Louisiana Purchase doubled the size of the nation. During his second term, the administration focused on keeping the U.S. out of the Napoleonic wars. Both the French and the British were seizing American ships and trying to deny the other access to trade with the U.S. Jefferson's solution was to impose an embargo on all foreign commerce. The cost to the northeast was great, and the embargo was both ineffective and unpopular.

James Madison won the election of 1808 and inherited the foreign policy issues with England. During the first year of his administration, trade was prohibited with both Britain and France. In 1810, Congress authorized trade with both England and France. The directed the President that, if either nation would accept America's view of neutrality, he was to forbid trade with the other nation. Napoleon pretended to comply. Madison thus banned trade with Great Britain. The British were continuing to harass American shipping and to capture sailors and forcibly make them members of the British navy. In June of 1812, Madison asked Congress to declare war on Great Britain. The nation was really not prepared to fight a war, especially with the strong British army. The British were successful in blockading U.S. ports and troops entered Washington and burned the White House and the Capitol. There were some notable American victories in the war, particularly Andrew Jackson victory at New Orleans. This victory encouraged Americans to believe the war had been successful. The result was a tremendous rise in nationalism. The war ended with the Treaty of Ghent, in which Britain finally accepted U.S. independence. The war had been strenuously opposed by the Federalist Party, which even began to speak of secession. By the time the war was over, the party had been so deeply embarrassed and discredited that it was no longer a national political party.

The political party system in the U.S. has five main objects or lines of action:
(1) to influence government policy
(2) to form or shape public opinion
(3) to win elections
(4) to choose between candidates for office
(5) to procure salaried posts for party leaders and workers

Skill 6.7: Analyze the causes and consequences of the War of 1812.

United States' unintentional and accidental involvement in what was known as the War of 1812 came about due to the political and economic struggles between France and Great Britain. Napoleon's goal was complete conquest and control of Europe, including and especially Great Britain. Although British troops were temporarily driven off the mainland of Europe, the navy still controlled the seas, the seas across which France had to bring the products needed. America traded with both nations, especially with France and its colonies. The British decided to destroy the American trade with France, mainly for two reasons: (a) Products and goods from the U.S. gave Napoleon what he needed to keep up his struggle with Britain. He and France was the enemy and it was felt that the Americans were aiding the Mother Country's enemy. (b) Britain felt threatened by the increasing strength and success of the U.S. merchant fleet. They were becoming major competitors with the ship owners and merchants in Britain.

The British issued the Orders in Council which were a series of measures prohibiting American ships from entering any French ports, not only in Europe but also in India and the West Indies. At the same time, Napoleon began efforts for a coastal blockade of the British Isles. He issued a series of Orders prohibiting all nations, including the United States, from trading with the British. And he didn't stop there. He threatened seizure of every ship entering any French ports after they stopped at any British port or British colony, even threatening to seize every ship inspected by British cruisers or that paid any duties to their government. Adding to all of this, the British were stopping American ships and seizing, or impressing, American seamen to service on British ships. Americans were outraged.

In 1807, Congress passed the Embargo Act, forbidding American ships from sailing to foreign ports. It couldn't be completely enforced and it really hurt business and trade in America so, in 1809, it was repealed. Two additional acts passed by Congress after James Madison became president attempted to regulate trade with other nations and to get Britain and France to remove all the restrictions they had put on American shipping. The catch was that whichever nation removed restrictions, the U.S. agreed not to trade with the other one. Clever Napoleon was the first to do this, prompting Madison to issue orders prohibiting trade with Britain, ignoring warnings from the British not to do so. Of course, this didn't work either and although Britain eventually rescinded the Orders in Council, war came in June of 1812 and ended Christmas Eve, 1814, with the signing of the Treaty of Ghent

During the war, Americans were divided over not only whether or not it was necessary to even fight but also over what territories should be fought for and taken. The nation was still young and just not prepared for war. The primary American objective was to conquer Canada but it failed. Two naval victories and one military victory stand out for the United States. Oliver Perry gained control of Lake Erie and Thomas MacDonough fought on Lake Champlain. Both of these naval battles successfully prevented the British invasion of the United States from Canada.

Nevertheless, the troops did land below Washington on the Potomac, marched into the city, and burned the public buildings, including the White House. Andrew Jackson's victory at New Orleans was a great morale booster to Americans, giving them the impression the U.S. had won the war. The battle actually took place after Britain and the United States had reached an agreement and it had no impact on the war's outcome. The peace treaty did little for the United States other than bringing peace, releasing prisoners of war, restoring all occupied territory, and setting up a commission to settle boundary disputes with Canada. Interestingly, the war proved to be a turning point in American history. European events had profoundly shaped U.S. policies, especially foreign policies.

COMPETENCY 7: Understand major political, social, economic, and cultural developments in U.S. history from 1815 to 1900.

Skill 7.1: Analyze issues and events related to the emergence of the second U.S. party system and evaluate the presidential administration of Andrew Jackson

During the colonial period, political parties, as the term is now understood, did not exist. The issues which divided the people were centered around the relations of the colonies to the mother country. There was initially little difference of opinion on these issues. About the middle of the 18th century, after England began to develop a harsher colonial policy, two factions arose in America. One favored the attitude of home government, and the other declined to obey and demanded a constantly increasing level of self-government. The former came to be known as Tories, the latter as Whigs. During the course of the American Revolution a large number of Tories left the country either to return to England or to move into Canada.

From the beginning of the Confederation, there were differences of opinion about the new government. One faction favored a loose confederacy in which the individual state would retain all powers of sovereignty except the absolute minimum required for the limited cooperation of all the states. (This approach was tried under the Articles of Confederation.) The other faction, that steadily gained influence, demanded that the central government be granted all the essential powers of sovereignty and the what should be left to the states was only the powers of local self-government. The inadequacy and inefficiency of the Confederation demonstrated that the latter were promoting a more effective point of view.

The first real party organization developed soon after the inauguration of Washington as President. His cabinet included people of both factions. Hamilton was the leader of the Nationalists – the Federalist Party – and Jefferson was the spokesman for the Anti-Federalists, later known as Republicans, Democratic-Republicans, and finally Democrats.

Skill 7.2: Analyze factors encouraging the expansion of the United States west of the Mississippi.

Territorial expansion began in 1783 with the signing of the Treaty of Paris ending the Revolutionary War. According to the terms of the treaty, the land gained by the Americans was all of the land between the Appalachian Mountains and the Mississippi River; from the Great Lakes to the Florida boundary. Nine additional states were formed from this area alone.

The next large territorial gain was under President Thomas Jefferson in 1803. In 1800, Napoleon Bonaparte of France secured the Louisiana Territory from Spain, who had held it since 1792. The vast area stretched westward from the Mississippi River to the Rocky Mountains as well as northward to Canada. An effort was made to keep the transaction a secret but the news reached the U.S. State Department. The U.S. didn't have any particular problem with Spanish control of the territory since Spain was weak and did not pose a threat. However, it was different with France. Though not the world power that Great Britain was, nonetheless France was still strong and, under Napoleon's leadership, was again acquiring an empire. President Jefferson had three major reasons for concern:

a. With the French controlling New Orleans at the mouth of the Mississippi River, as well as the Gulf of Mexico, Westerners would lose their "right of deposit" which would greatly affect their ability to trade. This was very important to the Americans who were living in the area between the river and the Appalachians. They were unable to get heavy products to eastern markets but had to float them on rafts down the Ohio and Mississippi Rivers to New Orleans to ships heading to Europe or the Atlantic coast ports. If France prohibited this; it would be a financial disaster.

b. President Jefferson also worried that if the French possessed the Louisiana Territory; America would be extremely limited in its expansion into its interior.

c. Under Napoleon Bonaparte, France was becoming more powerful and aggressive and this would be a constant worry and threat to the western border of the U.S. President Jefferson was very interested in the western part of the country and firmly believed that it was both necessary and desirable to strengthen western lands. So Jefferson wrote to the American minister to Paris, Robert R. Livingston, to make an offer to Napoleon for New Orleans and West Florida, as much as $10 million for the two. Napoleon countered the offer with the question of how much the U.S. would be willing to pay for all of Louisiana. After some discussion, it was agreed to pay $15 million and the largest land transaction in history was negotiated in 1803, resulting in the eventual formation of 15 states.

In 1804, the United States engaged in the first of a series of armed conflicts with the Barbary pirates of North Africa. The Moslem rulers of Morocco, Algiers, Tunis, and Tripoli, the Barbary States of North Africa, had long been seizing ships of nations that were Christian and demanding ransoms for the crews. The Christian nations of Europe decided it was cheaper and easier to pay annually a tribute or bribe. The U.S. had been doing this since 1783 with the beginnings of trade between the Mediterranean countries and the newly independent nation. When the rulers in Tripoli demanded a ridiculously exorbitant bribe and chopped down the flagpole of the American consulate there, Jefferson had had enough. The first skirmish against Tripoli in 1804 and 1805 was successful. In 1815, the payment of bribes to the rulers ceased after the War of 1812 ended. The Americans could trade and sail freely in the Mediterranean.

Westward expansion occurred for a number of reasons, most important being economic. Cotton had become most important to most of the people who lived in the southern states. The effects of the Industrial Revolution, which began in England, were now being felt in the United States. With the invention of power-driven machines, the demand for cotton fiber greatly increased for the yarn needed in spinning and weaving. Eli Whitney's cotton gin made the separation of the seeds from the cotton much more efficient and faster. This, in turn, increased the demand and more and more farmers became involved in the raising and selling of cotton.

The innovations and developments of better methods of long-distance transportation moved the cotton in greater quantities to textile mills in England as well as the areas of New England and Middle Atlantic States in the U.S. As prices increased along with increased demand, southern farmers began expanding by clearing increasingly more land to grow more cotton. Movement, settlement, and farming headed west to utilize the fertile soils. This, in turn, demanded increased need for a large supply of cheap labor. The system of slavery expanded, both in numbers and in the movement to lands "west" of the South.

Cotton farmers and slave owners were not the only ones heading west. Many, in other fields of economic endeavor, began the migration: trappers, miners, merchants, ranchers, and others were all seeking their fortunes. The Lewis and Clark expedition stimulated the westward push. Fur companies hired men, known as "Mountain Men", to go westward, searching for the animal pelts to supply the market and meet the demands of the East and Europe. These men in their own way explored and discovered the many passes and trails that would eventually be used by settlers in their trek to the west. The California gold rush also had a very large influence on the movement west.

There were also religious reasons for westward expansion. Increased settlement was encouraged by missionaries who traveled west with the fur traders. They sent word back east for more settlers and the results were tremendous. By the 1840s, the population increases in the Oregon country alone were at a rate of about a thousand people a year. People of many different religions and cultures as well as Southerners with black slaves made their way west which leads to a third reason: political.

It was the belief of many that the United States was destined to control all of the land between the two oceans or as one newspaper editor termed it, "**Manifest Destiny**." This mass migration westward put the U.S. government on a collision course with the Indians, Great Britain, Spain, and Mexico. The fur traders and missionaries ran up against the Indians in the northwest and the claims of Great Britain for the Oregon country.

The U.S. and Britain had shared the Oregon country. By the 1840s, with the increase in the free and slave populations and the demand of the settlers for control and government by the U.S., the conflict had to be resolved. In a treaty, signed in 1846, by both nations, a peaceful resolution occurred with Britain giving up its claims south of the 49th parallel.

In the American southwest, the results were exactly the opposite. Spain had claimed this area since the 1540s, had spread northward from Mexico City, and, in the 1700s, had established missions, forts, villages, towns, and very large ranches. After the purchase of the Louisiana Territory in 1803, Americans began moving into Spanish territory. A few hundred American families in what is now Texas were allowed to live there but had to agree to become loyal subjects to Spain. In 1821, Mexico successfully revolted against Spanish rule, won independence, and chose to be more tolerant towards the American settlers and traders. The Mexican government encouraged and allowed extensive trade and settlement, especially in Texas. Many of the new settlers were southerners and brought with them their slaves. Slavery was outlawed in Mexico and technically illegal in Texas, although the Mexican government rather looked the other way.

With the influx of so many Americans and the liberal policies of the Mexican government, there came to be concern over the possible growth and development of an American state within Mexico. Settlement restrictions, cancellation of land grants, the forbidding of slavery and increased military activity brought everything to a head. The order of events included the fight for Texas independence, the brief Republic of Texas, eventual annexation of Texas, statehood, and finally war with Mexico. The Texas controversy was not the sole reason for war. Since American settlers had begun, pouring into the Southwest the cultural differences played a prominent part. Language, religion, law, customs, and government were totally different and opposite between the two groups. A clash was bound to occur.

Skill 7.3: Analyze the origins, key events, and major consequences of the Civil War and Reconstruction.

It is ironic that South Carolina was the first state to secede from the Union and the first shots of the war were fired on Fort Sumter in Charleston Harbor. Both sides quickly prepared for war. The North had more in its favor: a larger population; superiority in finances and transportation facilities; manufacturing, agricultural, and natural resources. The North possessed most of the nation's gold, had about 92% of all industries, and almost all known supplies of copper, coal, iron, and various other minerals. Most of the nation's railroads were in the North and mid-West, men and supplies could be moved wherever needed; food could be transported from the farms of the mid-West to workers in the East and to soldiers on the battlefields. Trade with nations overseas could go on as usual due to control of the navy and the merchant fleet. The Northern states numbered 24 and included western (California and Oregon) and border (Maryland, Delaware, Kentucky, Missouri, and West Virginia) states.

The Southern states numbered 11 and included South Carolina, Georgia, Florida, Alabama, Mississippi, Louisiana, Texas, Virginia, North Carolina, Tennessee, and Arkansas, making up the Confederacy. Although outnumbered in population, the South was completely confident of victory. They knew that all they had to do was fight a defensive war and protect their own territory. The North had to invade and defeat an area almost the size of Western Europe. They figured the North would tire of the struggle and gave up. Another advantage of the South was that a number of its best officers had graduated from the U.S. Military Academy at West Point and had had long years of army experience. Many had exercised varying degrees of command in the Indian wars and the war with Mexico. Men from the South were conditioned to living outdoors and were more familiar with horses and firearms than many men from northeastern cities. Since cotton was such an important crop, Southerners felt that British and French textile mills were so dependent on raw cotton that they would be forced to help the Confederacy in the war.

The South had specific reasons and goals for fighting the war, more so than the North. The major aim of the Confederacy never wavered: to win independence, the right to govern themselves as they wished, and to preserve slavery. The Northerners were not as clear in their reasons for conducting war. At the beginning, most believed, along with Lincoln, that preservation of the Union was paramount. Only a few extremely fanatical abolitionists looked on the war as a way to end slavery. However, by war's end, more and more northerners had come to believe that freeing the slaves was just as important as restoring the Union.

The war strategies for both sides were relatively clear and simple. The South planned a defensive war, wearing down the North until it agreed to peace on Southern terms. The only exception was to gain control of Washington, D.C., go North through the Shenandoah Valley into Maryland and Pennsylvania in order to drive a wedge between the Northeast and mid-West, interrupt the lines of communication, and end the war quickly. The North had three basic strategies:

1. blockade the Confederate coastline in order to cripple the South;
2. seize control of the Mississippi River and interior railroad lines to split the Confederacy in two;
3. seize the Confederate capital of Richmond, Virginia, driving southward joining up with Union forces coming east from the Mississippi Valley.

The South won decisively until the Battle of Gettysburg, July 1 - 3, 1863. Until Gettysburg, Lincoln's commanders, McDowell and McClellan, were less than desirable, Burnside and Hooker, not what was needed. Lee, on the other hand, had many able officers, Jackson and Stuart depended on heavily by him. Jackson died at Chancellorsville and was replaced by Longstreet. Lee decided to invade the North and depended on J.E.B. Stuart and his cavalry to keep him informed of the location of Union troops and their strengths. Four things worked against Lee at Gettysburg:

1) The Union troops gained the best positions and the best ground first, making it easier to make a stand there.

2) Lee's move into Northern territory put him and his army a long way from food and supply lines. They were more or less on their own.

3) Lee thought that his Army of Northern Virginia was invincible and could fight and win under any conditions or circumstances.

4) Stuart and his men did not arrive at Gettysburg until the end of the second day of fighting and by then, it was too little too late. He and the men had had to detour around Union soldiers and he was delayed getting the information Lee needed.

Consequently, he made the mistake of failing to listen to Longstreet and following the strategy of regrouping back into Southern territory to the supply lines. Lee felt that regrouping was retreating and almost an admission of defeat. He was convinced the army would be victorious. Longstreet was concerned about the Union troops occupying the best positions and felt that regrouping to a better position would be an advantage. He was also very concerned about the distance from supply lines.

It was not the intention of either side to fight there but the fighting began when a Confederate brigade, who were looking for shoes, stumbled into a unit of Union cavalry. The third and last day Lee launched the final attempt to break Union lines. General George Pickett sent his division of three brigades under Generals Garnet, Kemper, and Armistead against Union troops on Cemetery Ridge under command of General Winfield Scott Hancock. Union lines held and Lee and the defeated Army of Northern Virginia made their way back to Virginia. Although Lincoln's commander George Meade successfully turned back a Confederate charge, he and the Union troops failed to pursue Lee and the Confederates. This battle was the turning point for the North. After this, Lee never again had the troop strength to launch a major offensive.

The day after Gettysburg, on July 4, Vicksburg, Mississippi surrendered to Union General Ulysses Grant, thus severing the western Confederacy from the eastern part. In September 1863, the Confederacy won its last important victory at Chickamauga. In November, the Union victory at Chattanooga made it possible for Union troops to go into Alabama and Georgia, splitting the eastern Confederacy in two. Lincoln gave Grant command of all Northern armies in March of 1864. Grant led his armies into battles in Virginia while Phil Sheridan and his cavalry did as much damage as possible. In a skirmish at a place called Yellow Tavern, Virginia, Sheridan's and Stuart's forces met, with Stuart being fatally wounded. The Union won the Battle of Mobile Bay and in May 1864, William Tecumseh Sherman began his march to successfully demolish Atlanta, then on to Savannah. He and his troops turned northward through the Carolinas to Grant in Virginia. On April 9, 1865, Lee formally surrendered to Grant at Appamattox Courthouse, Virginia.

The Civil War took more American lives than any other war in history, the South losing one-third of its' soldiers in battle compared to about one-sixth for the North. More than half of the total deaths were caused by disease and the horrendous conditions of field hospitals. Both sides paid a tremendous economic price but the South suffered more severely from direct damages. Destruction was pervasive with towns, farms, trade, industry, lives and homes of men, women, children all destroyed and an entire Southern way of life was lost. The deep resentment, bitterness, and hatred that remained for generations gradually lessened as the years went by but legacies of it surface and remain to this day. The South had no voice in the political, social, and cultural affairs of the nation, lessening to a great degree the influence of the more traditional Southern ideals. The Northern Yankee Protestant ideals of hard work, education, and economic freedom became the standard of the United States and helped influence the development of the nation into a modem, industrial power.

The effects of the Civil War were tremendous. It changed the methods of waging war and has been called the first modern war. It introduced weapons and tactics that, when improved later, were used extensively in wars of the late 1800s and 1900s. Civil War soldiers were the first to fight in trenches, first to fight under a unified command, first to wage a defense called "major cordon defense", a strategy of advance on all fronts.

They were also the first to use repeating and breech loading weapons. Observation balloons were first used during the war along with submarines, ironclad ships, and mines. Telegraphy and railroads were put to use first in the Civil War. It was considered a modern war because of the vast destruction and was "total war", involving the use of all resources of the opposing sides. There was probably no *way* it could have ended other than total defeat and unconditional surrender of one side or the other.

By executive proclamation and constitutional amendment, slavery was officially ended, although there remained deep prejudice and racism, still raising its ugly head today. Also, the Union was preserved and the states were finally truly united. Sectionalism, especially in the area of politics, remained strong for another 100 years but not to the degree and with the violence as existed before 1861. It has been noted that the Civil War may have been American democracy's greatest failure for, from 1861 to 1865, calm reason, basic to democracy, fell to human passion. Yet, democracy did survive. The victory of the North established that no state has the right to end or leave the Union. Because of unity, the U.S. became a major global power. Lincoln never proposed to punish the South. He was most concerned with restoring the South to the Union in a program that was flexible and practical rather than rigid and unbending. In fact he never really felt that the states had succeeded in leaving the Union but that they had left the 'family circle" for a short time. His plans consisted of two major steps:

All Southerners taking an oath of allegiance to the Union promising to accept all federal laws and proclamations dealing with slavery would receive a full pardon. The only ones excluded from this were men who had resigned from civil and military positions in the federal government to serve in the Confederacy, those who were part of the Confederate government, those in the Confederate army above the rank of lieutenant, and Confederates who were guilty of mistreating prisoners of war and blacks.

A state would be able to write a new constitution, elect new officials, and return to the Union fully equal to all other states on certain conditions: a minimum number of persons (at least 10% of those who were qualified voters in their states before secession from the Union who had voted in the 1860 election) must take an oath of allegiance.

As the war dragged on to its bloody and destructive conclusion, Lincoln was very concerned and anxious to get the states restored to the Union. He showed flexibility in his thinking as he made changes to his Reconstruction program to make it as easy and painless as possible. Congress had final approval of many actions. It would be interesting to know how differently things might have turned out if Lincoln had lived to see some or all of his kind policies supported by fellow moderates, put into action. Unfortunately, it didn't turn out that way. After Andrew Johnson became President and the radical Republicans gained control of Congress, the harsh measures of radical Reconstruction were implemented.

The economic and social chaos in the South after the war was unbelievable with starvation and disease rampant, especially in the cities. The U.S. Army provided some relief of food and clothing for both white and blacks but the major responsibility fell to the Freedmen's Bureau. Though the bureau agents to a certain extent helped southern whites, their main responsibility was to the freed slaves. They were to assist the freedmen to become self-supporting and protect them from being taken advantage of by others. Northerners looked on it as a real, honest effort to help the South out of the chaos it was in. Most white Southerners charged the bureau with causing racial friction, deliberately encouraging the freedmen to consider former owners as enemies.

As a result, as southern leaders began to be able to restore life as it had once been, they adopted a set of laws known as "black codes", containing many of the provisions of the prewar "slave codes." There were certain improvements in the lives of freedmen, but the codes denied the freedmen their basic civil rights. In short, except for the condition of freedom and a few civil rights, white Southerners made every effort to keep the freedmen in a way of life subordinate to theirs.

Radicals in Congress pointed out these illegal actions by white Southerners as evidence that they were unwilling to recognize, accept, and support the complete freedom of black Americans and could not be trusted. Therefore, Congress drafted its own program of Reconstruction, including laws that would protect and further the rights of blacks. Three amendments were added to the Constitution: the 13th Amendment of 1865 outlawed slavery throughout the entire United States. The 14th Amendment of 1868 made blacks American citizens. The 15th Amendment of 1870 gave black Americans the right to vote and made it illegal to deny anyone the right to vote based on race.

Federal troops were stationed throughout the South and protected Republicans who took control of Southern governments. Bitterly resentful, white Southerners fought the new political system by joining a secret society called the Ku Klux Klan, using violence to keep black Americans from voting and getting equality. However, before being allowed to rejoin the Union, the Confederate states were required to agree to all federal laws. Between 1866 and 1870, all of them had returned to the Union, but Northern interest in Reconstruction was fading. Reconstruction officially ended when the last Federal troops left the South in 1877. It can be said that Reconstruction had a limited success as it set up public school systems and expanded legal rights of black Americans. Nevertheless, white supremacy came to be in control again and its bitter fruitage is still with us today.

Lincoln and Johnson had considered the conflict of Civil War as a "rebellion of individuals". Congressional Radicals, such as Charles Sumner in the Senate, considered the Southern states as complete political organizations and were now in the same position as any unorganized Territory and should be treated as such. Radical House leader Thaddeus Stevens considered the Confederate States, not as Territories, but as conquered provinces and felt they should be treated that way. President Johnson refused to work with Congressional moderates, insisting on having his own way. As a result, the Radicals gained control of both houses of Congress and when Johnson opposed their harsh measures they came within one vote of impeaching him. General Grant was elected President in 1868, serving two scandal-ridden terms. He was himself an honest, upright person but he greatly lacked political experience and his greatest weakness was a blind loyalty to his friends. He absolutely refused to believe that his friends were not honest and stubbornly would not admit to their using him to further their own interests. One of the sad results of the war was the rapid growth of business and industry with large corporations controlled by unscrupulous men. However, after 1877, some degree of normalcy returned and there was time for rebuilding, expansion, and growth.

Skill 7.4: Examine causes and consequences of immigration to the United States.

Most students of American history are aware of the tremendous influx of immigrants to America during the 19th century. It is also a known fact that the majority settled in the ethnic neighborhoods and communities of the large cities, close to friends, relatives, and the work they were able to find. After the U.S. Congress passed the 1862 Homestead Act after the Civil War ended, the West began to open up for settlement. One interesting fact that some are not aware of is that more than half of the hardy pioneers who went to homestead and farm western lands were European immigrants: Swedes, Norwegians, Czechs, Germans, Danes, Finns, and Russians.

By far, the nation's immigrants were an important reason for America's phenomenal industrial growth from 1865 to 1900. They came seeking work and better opportunities for themselves and their families than what life in their native country could give them. What they found in America was suspicion and distrust because they were competitors with Americans for jobs, housing, and decent wages. Their languages, customs, and ways of living were different, especially between the different national and ethnic groups. Until the early 1880s, most immigrants were from the parts of northwestern Europe such as Germany, Scandinavia, the Netherlands, Ireland, and Great Britain.

After 1890, the new arrivals increasingly came from eastern and southern Europe. Chinese immigrants on the Pacific coast, so crucial to the construction of the western part of the first transcontinental railroad, were the first to experience this increasing distrust which eventually erupted into violence and bloodshed. From about 1879 to the present time, the U.S. Congress made, repealed, and amended numerous pieces of legislation concerning quotas, restrictions, and other requirements pertaining to immigrants. The immigrant laborers, both skilled and unskilled, were the foundation of the modern labor union movement as a means of gaining recognition, support, respect, rights, fair wages, and better working conditions.

The historical record of African-Americans is known to all. Sold into slavery by rival tribes, they were brought against their will to the West Indies and southern America to slave on the plantations in a life-long condition of servitude and bondage. The 13th Constitutional Amendment abolished slavery; the 14th gave them U.S. citizenship; and the 15th gave them the right to vote. Efforts of well-known African-Americans resulted in some improvements although the struggle was continuous without let-up. Many were outspoken and urged and led protests against the continued onslaught of discrimination and inequality.

Skill 7.5: Recognize the origins of the industrial revolution in the United States and assess the significance of the economic developments, social changes, and political movements produced by the industrial experience.

There was a marked degree of industrialization before and during the Civil War, but at war's end, industry in America was small. After the war, dramatic changes took place. Machines replaced hand labor, extensive nationwide railroad service made possible the wider distribution of goods, invention of new products made available in large quantities, and large amounts of money from bankers and investors for expansion of business operations. American life was definitely affected by this phenomenal industrial growth. Cities became the centers of this new business activity resulting in mass population movements there and tremendous growth. This new boom in business resulted in huge fortunes for some Americans and extreme poverty for many others. The discontent this caused resulted in a number of new reform movements from which came measures controlling the power and size of big business and helping the poor.

Of course, industry before, during, and after the Civil War was centered mainly in the North, especially the tremendous industrial growth after. The late 1800s and early 1900s saw the increasing buildup of military strength and the U.S. becoming a world power.

The use of machines in industry enabled workers to produce a large quantity of goods much faster than by hand. With the increase in business, hundreds of workers were hired, assigned to perform a certain job in the production process. This was a method of organization called "division of labor" and by its increasing the rate of production, businesses lowered prices for their products making the products affordable for more people. As a result, sales and businesses were increasingly successful and profitable.

A great variety of new products or inventions became available such as: the typewriter, the telephone, barbed wire, the electric light, the phonograph, and the gasoline automobile. From this list, the one that had the greatest effect on America's economy was the automobile.

The increase in business and industry was greatly affected by the many rich natural resources that were found throughout the nation. The industrial machines were powered by the abundant water supply. The construction industry as well as products made from wood depended heavily on lumber from the forests. Coal and iron ore in abundance were needed for the steel industry, which profited and increased from the use of steel in such things as skyscrapers, automobiles, bridges, railroad tracks, and machines. Other minerals such as silver, copper, and petroleum played a large role in industrial growth, especially petroleum, from which gasoline was refined as fuel for the increasingly popular automobile.

Between 1870 and 1916, more than 25 million immigrants came into the United States adding to the phenomenal population growth taking place. This tremendous growth aided business and industry in two ways: (1) The number of consumers increased creating a greater demand for products thus enlarging the markets for the products. (2) with increased production and expanding business, more workers were available for newly created jobs. The completion of the nation's transcontinental railroad in 1869 contributed greatly to the nation's economic and industrial growth. Some examples of the benefits of using the railroads include raw materials were shipped quickly by the mining companies and finished products were sent to all parts of the country. Many wealthy industrialists and railroad owners saw tremendous profits steadily increasing due to this improved method of transportation.

As business grew, methods of sales and promotion were developed. Salespersons went to all parts of the country promoting the various products, opening large department stores in the growing cities, offering the varied products at reasonable affordable prices. People who lived too far from the cities, making it impossible to shop there, had the advantage of using a mail order service, buying what they needed from catalogs furnished by the companies. The developments in communication, such as the telephone and telegraph, increased the efficiency and prosperity of big business.

Investments in corporate stocks and bonds resulted from business prosperity. As individuals began investing heavily in an eager desire to share in the profits, their investments made available the needed capital for companies to expand their operations. From this, banks increased in number throughout the country, making loans to businesses and significant contributions to economic growth. At the same time, during the 1880s, government made little effort to regulate businesses. This gave rise to monopolies where larger businesses were rid of their smaller competitors and assumed complete control of their industries.

Some owners in the same business would join or merge to form one company. Others formed what were called "trusts," a type of monopoly in which rival businesses were controlled but not formally owned. Monopolies had some good effects on the economy. Out of them grew the large, efficient corporations, which made important contributions to the growth of the nation's economy. Also, the monopolies enabled businesses to keep their sales steady and avoid sharp fluctuations in price and production. At the same time, the downside of monopolies was the unfair business practices of the business leaders. Some acquired so much power that they took unfair advantage of others. Those who had little or no competition would require their suppliers to supply goods at a low cost, sell the finished products at high prices, and reduce the quality of the product to save money.

The late 1800s and early 1900s were a period of the efforts of many to make significant reforms and changes in the areas of politics, society, and the economy. There was a need to reduce the levels of poverty and to improve the living conditions of those affected by it. Regulations of big business, ridding governmental corruption and making it more responsive to the needs of the people were also on the list of reforms to be accomplished. Until 1890, there was very little success, but from 1890 on, the reformers gained increased public support and were able to achieve some influence in government. Since some of these individuals referred to themselves as "progressives," the period of 1890 to 1917 is referred to by historians as the Progressive Era.

Skilled laborers were organized into a labor union called the American Federation of Labor, in an effort to gain better working conditions and wages for its members. Farmers joined organizations such as the National Grange and Farmers Alliances. Farmers were producing more food than people could afford to buy. This was the result of (1) new farmlands rapidly sprouting on the plains and prairies, and (2) development and availability of new farm machinery and newer and better methods of farming. They tried selling their surplus abroad but faced stiff competition from other nations selling the same farm products. Other problems contributed significantly to their situation. Items they needed for daily life were priced exorbitantly high. Having to borrow money to carry on fanning activities kept them constantly in debt.

Higher interest rates, shortage of money, falling farm prices, dealing with the so-called middlemen, and the increasingly high charges by the railroads to haul farm products to large markets all contributed to the desperate need for reform to relieve the plight of American farmers.

American women began actively campaigning for the right to vote. Elizabeth Cady Stanton and Susan B. Anthony in 1869 founded the organization called National Women Suffrage Association, the same year the Wyoming Territory gave women the right to vote. Soon after, a few states followed by giving women the right to vote, limited to local elections only.

Governmental reform began with the passage of the Civil Service Act, also known as the Pendleton Act. It provided for the Civil Service Commission, a federal agency responsible for giving jobs based on merit rather than as political rewards or favors. Another successful reform was the adoption of the secret ballot in voting, as were such measures as the direct primary, referendum, recall, and direct election of U.S. Senators by the people rather than by their state legislatures. Following the success of reforms made at the national level, the progressives were successful in gaining reforms in government at state and local levels.

After 1890, more and more attention was called to needs and problems through the efforts of social workers and clergy and the writings of people such as Lincoln Steffans, Ida M. Tarbell, and Upton Sinclair.

Presidents Theodore Roosevelt, William Howard Taft, and Woodrow Wilson supported many of the reform laws after 1890 and in 1884, President Grover Cleveland did much to see that the Civil Service Act was enforced. After 1880, a number of political or "third" parties were formed and although unsuccessful in getting their Presidential candidates elected, significant reform legislation, including Constitutional amendments, were passed by Congress and became law due to their efforts.

Such legislative acts included the Sherman Antitrust Act of 1890, the Clayton Antitrust Act of 1914, the Underwood Tariff of 1913, and the establishment of the Federal Trade Commission in 1914. By the 1890s and early 1900s, the United States had become a world power and began a leading role in international affairs. War loomed on the horizon again and the stage was set for increased activity in world affairs, which had been avoided since the end of the Civil War.

Skill 7.6: Analyze U.S. imperialism and evaluate the experience of the United States as a colonial power.

During the period of 1823 to the 1890s, the major interests and efforts of the American people were concentrated on expansion, settlement, and development of the continental United States. The Civil War 1861-1865, preserved the Union and eliminated the system of slavery. From 1865 onward, the focus was on taming the West and developing industry. During this period, travel and trade between the United States and Europe were continuous. By the 1890s, American interests turned to areas outside the boundaries of the United States. The West was developing into a major industrial area and people in the United States became very interested in selling their factory and farm surplus to overseas markets. In fact, some Americans desired getting and controlling land outside the U.S. boundaries. Before the 1890s, the U.S. had little, if anything to do with foreign affairs, was not a strong nation militarily, and had inconsequential influence on international political affairs. In fact, the Europeans looked on the American diplomats as inept and bungling in their diplomatic efforts and activities. However, all of this changed and the Spanish-American War of 1898 saw the entry of the United States as a world power.

During the 1890s, Spain controlled such overseas possessions as Puerto Rico, the Philippines, and Cuba. Cubans rebelled against Spanish rule and the U.S. government found itself besieged by demands from Americans to assist the Cubans in their revolt. When the U.S. battleship Maine blew up off the coast of Havana, Cuba, Americans blamed the Spaniards for it and demanded American action against Spain. Two months later, Congress declared war on Spain and the U.S. quickly defeated them. The peace treaty gave the U.S. possession of Puerto Rico, the Philippines, Guam and Hawaii, which was annexed during the war.

COMPETENCY 8: Understand major political, social, economic, and cultural developments in U.S. history from 1900 to the present.

Skill 8.1 Analyze factors related to the rise of the Progressive movement and assess its influence.

Populism is the philosophy that is concerned with the common sense needs of average people. Populism often finds expression as a reaction against perceived oppression of the average people by the wealthy elite in society. The prevalent claim of populist movements is that they will put the people first. Populism is often connected with religious fundamentalism, racism, or nationalism. Populist movements claim to represent the majority of the people and call them to stand up to institutions or practices that seem detrimental to their well being.

Populism flourished in the late 19th and early 20th centuries. Several political parties were formed out of this philosophy, including: the Greenback Party, the Populist Party, the Farmer-Labor Party, the Single Tax movement of Henry George, the Share Our Wealth movement of Huey Long, the Progressive Party, and the Union Party.

In the 1890s, the People's Party won the support of millions of farmers and other working people. This party challenged the social ills of the monopolists of the "Gilded Age."

The tremendous change that resulted from the industrial revolution led to a demand for reform that would control the power wielded by big corporations. The gap between the industrial moguls and the working people was growing. This disparity between rich and poor resulted in a public outcry for reform at the same time that there was an outcry for governmental reform that would end the political corruption and elitism of the day.

This fire was fueled by the writings on investigative journalists – the "muckrakers" – who published scathing exposes of political and business wrongdoing and corruption. The result was the rise of a group of politicians and reformers who supported a wide array of populist causes. The period 1900 to 1917 came to be known as the Progressive Era. Although these leaders came from many different backgrounds and were driven by different ideologies, they shared a common fundamental belief that government should be eradicating social ills and promoting the common good and the equality guaranteed by the Constitution.

The reforms initiated by these leaders and the spirit of **Progressivism** were far-reaching. Politically, many states enacted the initiative and the referendum. The adoption of the recall occurred in many states. Several states enacted legislation that would undermine the power of political machines. On a national level the two most significant political changes were (1) the ratification of the 19th Amendment, which required that all U.S. Senators be chosen by popular election, and (2) the ratification of the 19th Amendment, which granted women the right to vote.

Major economic reforms of the period included aggressive enforcement of the Sherman Antitrust Act; passage of the Elkins Act and the Hepburn Act, which gave the Interstate Commerce Commission greater power to regulate the railroads; the Pure Food and Drug Act prohibited the use of harmful chemicals in food; The Meat Inspection Act regulated the meat industry to protect the public against tainted meat; over 2/3 of the states passed laws prohibiting child labor; workmen's compensation was mandated; and the Department of Commerce and Labor was created.

Responding to concern over the environmental effects of the timber, ranching, and mining industries, Roosevelt set aside 238 million acres of federal lands to protect them from development. Wildlife preserves were established, the national park system was expanded, and the National Conservation Commission was created. The Newlands Reclamation Act also provided federal funding for the construction of irrigation projects and dams in semi-arid areas of the country.

The Wilson Administration carried out additional reforms. The Federal Reserve Act created a national banking system, providing a stable money supply. The Sherman Act and the Clayton Antitrust Act defined unfair competition, made corporate officers liable for the illegal actions of employees, and exempted labor unions from antitrust lawsuits. The Federal Trade Commission was established to enforce these measures. Finally, the 16th amendment was ratified, establishing an income tax. This measure was designed to relieve the poor of a disproportionate burden in funding the federal government and make the wealthy pay a greater share of the nation's tax burden.

Skill 8.2: Identify major developments in literature and the arts during the twentieth century.

Music. The 20th century experienced a revolution in music. In keeping with the exceptionally high value of individuality and unique personal expression, there was a quest for new and unique forms of musical expression.

The major forms inspired by classical music have continued, though with certain modifications. The symphony has continued in form, but with greater dissonance and great experimentation in rhythm. Major symphonic composers of the century include: Gustav Mahler, Jean Sibelius, Dmitry Shostakovich, Serge Prokofiev and Sergey Rachmaninov, as well as Leonard Bernstein. Opera began to change after WWII as composers began to incorporate other musical forms that were emerging during the century.

Notable operatic composers include Benjamin Britten, Karlheinz Stockhausen, Virgil Thomson, Douglas Moore, Philip Glass and John Adams. Ballet tended to focus on music written specifically for its needs. This trend included such composers as Claude Debussy, Maruice Ravel and R. Strauss. Igor Stravinsky's *The Rite of Spring*, however was internationally recognized for its violent rhythms and dissonance. The second half of the century was marked by the tendency to re-stage ballets with existing music. The exceptions were Aaron Copland Has Werner Henze and Benjamin Britten.

Musical Theater was an evolution from the operettas of the Romantic period and the traditions of the European music hall and American vaudeville. Most notable in this form are Leonard Bernstein and Steven Sondheim. Film Music also developed during this century. The soundtracks for films were either adaptations of classical music or new compositions from composers like Elmer Bernstein, Bernard Herrman, Max Steiner and Dmitri Tiomkin.

American Popular music evolved from folk music. This was the music of the first half of the century, characterized by a consistent structure of two verses, a chorus, and a repetition of the chorus. The songs were written to be sung by average persons, and the tunes were usually harmonized. Much of this music originated in New York's Tin Pan Alley. Particularly notable during this period were Irving Berlin, George and Ira Gershwin, and a host of others. After WWII, teen music began to dominate. New forms emerged from various ethnic and regional groups including Blues, Rhythm and Blues and Rap from the African American community; Country music from the south and the southwest, folk music, jazz, rock and roll, and rock.

In art, the primary expression of the first half of the decade was Modernism. The avant garde perspective encouraged all types of innovation and experiementation. Key elements of this movement have been abstraction, cubism, surrealism, realism, and abstract expressionism. Notable among the artists of this period for the birth or perfection of particular styles are Henri Matisse, Pablo Picasso, George Rouault, Gustav Klimt, George Braque, Salvator Dali, Hans Arp, Rene Magrite, and Marcel Duchamp. In the U.S. realism tended to find regional expressions including the Ashcan School and Robert Henri, Midwestern Regionalism and Grant Wood. Other particularly notable painters are Edward Hopper and Georgia O'Keeffe. The New York School came to be known for a style known as Abstract Expressionism and included such artists as Jackson Pollock, Willem de Kooning, Larry Rivers. Other painters of the period were Mark Rothko, Clement Greenberg, Ellsworth Kelly and the Op Art Movement.

In sculpture, many of the same patterns and trends were applied. Innovations included the exploration of empty space (Henry Moore), the effort to incorporate cubism in three dimensions (Marcel Duchamp), the use of welded metal to create kinetic sculpture (Alexander Calder).

Postmodernism has been the description of the expansion of forms and the valuing of innovation since 1950. This has included Minimalism, Figurative Styles, Pop Art, Conceptual Art and Installation Art. Photography has developed as an art form, as well, during the 20th century.

The literature of this period has been an attempt to come to terms with the nature and the cost of war, of the meaning of the human struggle for freedom and the ability to enjoy basic human and civil rights. Literature has cried out against change and it has embraced change. By the beginning of the 20th century literature was reflecting the struggle of the modern individual to find a place and a meaning in a new world that seemed like a jungle. But literature has reflected the observation that not only does the modern human not know how to find meaning, he/she does not actually know what he/she is seeking. It is this crisis of identity that has been the subject of most modern literature. This can be seen is the writings of Joseph Conrad, Sigmund Freud, James Joyce, Eugene O'Neill, Luigi Pirandello, Samuel Beckett, George Bernard Shaw, T.S. Eliot, Kafka, Camus, Pasternak, Graham Greene, Tennessee Williams, and a host of others.

In art and architecture, there has been a search for new forms and for basic symbols that would speak a universal language. This fragmentation and anxiety has found expression in cubism and surrealism. In painting, one need only consider the works of Cezanne and Picasso and Dali. In Sculpture, artists took one of two directions: either looking back and preserving the conventional ideals of beauty, or experimenting with distortion and the abstract concepts of time and force. Architecture tended to move toward more functional lines and expressions.

In Religion and Philosophy there has been great change as well. For much of the period, religious interpretation tended to swing like a pendulum between the liberal and the conservative. By the end of the 21st century, however, the struggle for meaning and identity had resulted in a generalized conservative trend. This tendency can be seen in most religions yet today. Religion and philosophy are, to be sure, the means of self-definition and the understanding of one's place in the universe. Recent conservative trends, however, have had a polarizing effect. Issues of the relationship of Church and State have arisen and been resolved in most countries during this period. Yet, at the same time there has been an increasing effort to understand the religious beliefs of others, either to create new ways to define one's religion over and against other religions, or as the basis of new attacks on the values and teachings of other religions. This same struggle resulted in the rise of the philosophical movement known as existentialism, as seen in the writings of Soren Kierkegaard, Karl Jaspers, and Jean-Paul Sartre.

Skill 8.3: Analyze the causes of the Great Depression, its effects on U.S. society, and the impact of the New Deal on American life.

The 1929 Stock Market crash was the powerful event that is generally interpreted as the beginning of the Great Depression in America. Although the crash of the Stock Market was unexpected, it was not without identifiable causes. The 1920s had been a decade of social and economic growth and hope. But the attitudes and actions of the 1920s regarding wealth, production, and investment created several trends that quietly set the stage for the 1929 disaster.
The legislative and executive branches of the Coolidge administration tended to favor business and the wealthy. The Revenue Act of 1926 reduced income taxes for the wealthy very significantly. This bill lowered taxes such that a person with a million-dollar income saw his/her taxes reduced from $600,000 to $200,000. Despite the rise of labor unions, even the Supreme Court ruled in ways that further widened the gap between the rich and the middle class. In the case of Adkins v. Children's Hospital (1923), the Court ruled that minimum wage legislation was unconstitutional.

This kind of disparity in the distribution of wealth weakens the economy. Demand was unable to equal supply. The surplus of manufactured goods was beyond the reach of the poor and the middle class. The wealthy, however, could purchase all they wanted with a smaller and smaller portion of their income. This meant that in order for the economy to remain stable, the wealthy must invest their money and spend money on luxury items and others must buy on credit.

The majority of the population did not have enough money to buy what was necessary to meet their needs. The concept of buying on credit caught on very quickly. Buying on credit, however, creates artificial demand for products people cannot ordinarily afford. This has two effects: first, at some point there is less need to purchase products (because they have already been bought), and second, at some point paying for previous purchases makes it impossible to purchase new products. This exacerbated the problem of a surplus of goods.

The economy also relied on investment and luxury spending by the rich in the 1920s. Luxury spending, however, only occurs when people are confident with regard to the economy and the future. Should these people lose confidence, that luxury spending would come to an abrupt halt. This is precisely what happened when the stock market crashed in 1929. Investing in business produces returns for the investor. During the 1920s, investing was very healthy. Investors, however, began to expect greater returns on their investments. This led many to make speculative investments in risky opportunities.

The disproportionate distribution of wealth between the rich and the middle-class mirrors the uneven distribution of wealth between industries. In 1929, half of all corporate wealth was controlled by just 200 companies. The automotive industry was growing exceptionally quickly, but agriculture was steadily declining. In fact, in 1921 food prices dropped about 70% due to surplus. The average income in agriculture was only about one-third of the national average across all industries.

Two industries, automotive and radio, drove the economy in the 1920s. During this decade, the government tended to support new industries rather than agriculture. During WWI, the government had subsidized farms and paid ridiculously high prices for grains. Farmers had been encouraged to buy and farm more land and to use new technology to increase production. The nation was feeding much of Europe during and in the aftermath of the war. But when the war ended, these farm policies were cut off. Prices plummeted, farmers fell into debt, and farm prices declined. The agriculture industry was on the brink of ruin before the stock market crash.

The concentration of production and economic stability in the automotive industry and the production and sale of radios was expected to last forever. But there comes a point when the growth of an industry slows due to market saturation. When these two industries declined, due to decreased demand, they caused the collapse of other industries upon which they were dependent (e.g., rubber tires, glass, fuel, construction, etc.).

The other factor contributing to the Great Depression was the economic condition of Europe. The U.S. was lending money to European nations to rebuild. Many of these countries used this money to purchase U.S. food and manufactured goods. But they were not able to pay off their debts. While the U.S. was providing money, food, and goods to Europe, however, it was not willing to buy European goods. Trade barriers were enacted to maintain a favorable trade balance.

Risky speculative investments in the stock market was the second major factor contributing to the stock market crash of 1929 and the ensuing depression. Stock market speculation was spectacular throughout the 1920s. In 1929, shares traded on the New York Stock Exchange reached 1,124,800,410. In 1928 and 1929 stock prices doubled and tripled (RCA stock prices rose from 85 to 420 within one year). The opportunity to achieve such profits was irresistible. In much the same way that buying goods on credit became popular, buying stock on margin allowed people to invest a very small amount of money in the hope of receiving exceptional profit. This created an investing craze that drove the market higher and higher. But brokers were also charging higher interest rates on their margin loans (nearly 20%). If, however, the price of the stock dropped, the investor owed the broker the amount borrowed plus interest.

Several other factors are cited by some scholars as contributing to the Great Depression. First, in 1929, the Federal Reserve increased interest rates.

Second, some believe that as interest rates rose and the stock market began to decline, people began to hoard money. This was certainly the case after the crash. There is a question that it was a cause of the crash.

In September 1929, stock prices began to slip somewhat, yet people remained optimistic. On Monday, October 21, prices began to fall quickly. The volume traded was so high that the tickers were unable to keep up. Investors were frightened, and they started selling very quickly. This caused further collapse. For the next two days prices stabilized somewhat. On **Black Thursday**, October 24, prices plummeted again. By this time investors had lost confidence. On Friday and Saturday an attempt to stop the crash was made by some leading bankers. But on Monday the 28th, prices began to fall again, declining by 13% in one day. The next day, **Black Tuesday, October 29**, saw 16.4 million shares traded. Stock prices fell so far, that at many times no one was willing to buy at any price.

Hoover's bid for re-election in 1932 failed. The new president, Franklin D. Roosevelt won the White House on his promise to the American people of a "new deal." Upon assuming the office, Roosevelt and his advisers immediately launched a massive program of innovation and experimentation to try to bring the Depression to an end and get the nation back on track. Congress gave the President unprecedented power to act to save the nation. During the next eight years, the most extensive and broadly-based legislation in the nation's history was enacted. The legislation was intended to accomplish three goals: relief, recovery, and reform.

The first step in the "**New Deal"** was to relieve suffering. This was accomplished through a number of job-creation projects. The second step, the recovery aspect, was to stimulate the economy. The third step was to create social and economic change through innovative legislation.

The National Recovery Administration attempted to accomplish several goals:

- Restore employment
- Increase general purchasing power
- Provide character-building activity for unemployed youth
- Encourage decentralization of industry and thus divert population from crowded cities to rural or semi-rural communities
- To develop river resources in the interest of navigation and cheap power and light
- To complete flood control on a permanent basis
- To enlarge the national program of forest protection and to develop forest resources
- To control farm production and improve farm prices
- To assist home builders and home owners
- To restore public faith in banking and trust operations

- To recapture the value of physical assets, whether in real property, securities, or other investments.

These objectives and their accomplishment implied a restoration of public confidence and courage.

Among the "alphabet organizations" set up to work out the details of the recovery plan, the most prominent were:

- **Agricultural Adjustment Administration** (AAA), designed to readjust agricultural production and prices thereby boosting farm income
- **Civilian Conservation Corps** (CCC), designed to give wholesome, useful activity in the forestry service to unemployed young men
- **Civil Works Administration** (CWA) and the **Public Works Administ**ration (PWA), designed to give employment in the construction and repair of public buildings, parks, and highways
- **Works Progress Administration** (WPA), whose task was to move individuals from relief rolls to work projects or private employment

The **Tennessee Valley Authority** (TVA) was of a more permanent nature, designed to improve the navigability of the Tennessee River and increase productivity of the timber and farm lands in its valley, this program built 16 dams that provided water control and hydroelectric generation.

The Public Works Administration employed Americans on over 34,000 public works projects at a cost of more than $4 billion. Among these projects was the construction of a highway that linked the Florida Keys and Miami, the Boulder Dam (now the Hoover Dam) and numerous highway projects.

To provide economic stability and prevent another crash, Congress passed the **Glass-Steagall Act**, which separated banking and investing. The Securities and Exchange Commission was created to regulate dangerous speculative practices on Wall Street. The Wagner Act guaranteed a number of rights to workers and unions in an effort to improve worker-employer relations. The **Social Security Act of 1935** established pensions for the aged and infirm as well as a system of unemployment insurance.

Many of the steps taken by the Roosevelt administration have had far-reaching effects. They alleviated the economic disaster of the Great Depression, they enacted controls that would mitigate the risk of another stock market crash, and they provided greater security for workers. The nation's economy, however, did not fully recover until America entered World War II.

Unemployment quickly reached 25% nation-wide. People thrown out of their homes created makeshift domiciles of cardboard, scraps of wood and tents. With unmasked reference to President Hoover, who was quite obviously overwhelmed by the situation and incompetent to deal with it, these communities were called "**Hoovervilles**." Families stood in bread lines, rural workers left the dust bowl of the plains to search for work in California, and banks failed. More than 100,000 businesses failed between 1929 and 1932. The despair that swept the nation left an indelible scar on all who endured the Depression.

When the stock market crashed, businesses collapsed. Without demand for products other businesses and industries collapsed. This set in motion a domino effect, bringing down the businesses and industries that provided raw materials or components to these industries. Hundreds of thousands became jobless. Then the jobless often became homeless. Desperation prevailed. Little has been done to assess the toll hunger, inadequate nutrition, or starvation took on the health of those who were children during this time. Indeed, food was cheap, relatively speaking, but there was little money to buy it.

Everyone who lived through the Great Depression was permanently affected in some way. Many never trusted banks again. Many people of this generation later hoarded cash so they would not risk losing everything again. Some permanently rejected the use of credit.

In several parts of the country, economic disaster was exacerbated by natural disaster. The Florida Keys were hit by the "**Labor Day Hurricane**" in 1935. This was one of only three hurricanes in history to make landfall as a Category 5 storm. More than 400 died in the storm, including 200 WWI veterans who were building bridges for a public works project. In the Northeast, The **Great Hurricane of 1938** struck Long Island, causing more than 600 fatalities, decimating Long Island, and resulting in millions of dollars in damage to the coast from New York City to Boston.

By far the worst natural disaster of the decade came to be known as the **Dust Bowl.** Due to severe and prolonged drought in the Great Plains and previous reliance on inappropriate farming techniques, a series of devastating dust storms occurred in the 1930s that resulted in destruction, economic ruin for many, and dramatic ecological change.

Plowing the plains for agriculture removed the grass and exposed the soil. When the drought occurred, the soil dried out and became dust. Wind blew away the dust. Between 1934 and 1939 winds blew the soil to the east, all the way to the Atlantic Ocean. The dust storms, called "black blizzards" created huge clouds of dust that were visible all the way to Chicago. Topsoil was stripped from millions of acres.

In Texas, Arkansas, Oklahoma, New Mexico, Kansas and Colorado over half a million people were homeless. Many of these people journeyed west in the hope of making a new life in California.

Crops were ruined, the land was destroyed, and people either lost or abandoned homes and farms. Fifteen percent of Oklahoma's population left. Because so many of the migrants were from Oklahoma, the migrants came to be called "**Okies**" no matter where they came from. Estimates of the number of people displaced by this disaster range from 300,000 or 400,000 to 2.5 million.

During the first 100 days in office, the Roosevelt Administration responded to this crisis with programs designed to restore the ecological balance. One action was the formation of the **Soil Conservation Service** (now the Natural Resources Conservation Service). The story of this natural disaster and its toll in human suffering is poignantly preserved in the photographs of Dorothea Lange.

To be sure, there were negative reactions to some of the measures taken to pull the country out of the depression. There was a major reaction to the deaths of the WWI veterans in the Labor Day Hurricane, ultimately resulting in a Congressional investigation into possible negligence. The Central Valley Project ruffled feathers of farmers who lost tillable land and some water supply to the construction of the aqueduct and the Hoover Dam. Tennesseans were initially unhappy with the changes in river flow and navigation when the Tennessee Valley Authority began its construction of dams and the directing of water to form reservoirs and to power hydroelectric plants. Some businesses and business leaders were not happy with the introduction of minimum wage laws and restrictions and controls on working conditions and limitations of work hours for laborers. The numerous import/export tariffs of the period were the subject of controversy.

In the long view, however, much that was accomplished under the New Deal had positive long-term effects on economic, ecological, social and political issues for the next several decades. The Tennessee Valley Authority and the Central Valley Project in California provided a reliable source and supply of water to major cities, as well as electrical power to meet the needs of an increasingly electricity-dependent society. For the middle class and the poor, the labor regulations, the establishment of the Social Security Administration, and the separation of investment and banking have served the nation admirably for more than six decades.

Skill 8.4: Evaluate the effects of World Wars I and II on U.S. politics and society and examine the changing role of the United States in world affairs during the twentieth century

World War I saw the introduction of such warfare as use of tanks, airplanes, machine guns, submarines, poison gas, and flame throwers. Fighting on the Western front was characterized by a series of trenches that were used throughout the war until 1918. U.S. involvement in the war did not occur until 1916. When it began in 1914, President Woodrow Wilson declared that the U.S. was neutral and most Americans were opposed to any involvement anyway. In 1916, Wilson was reelected to a second term based on the slogan proclaiming his efforts at keeping America out of the war. For a few months after, he put forth most of his efforts to stopping the war but German submarines began unlimited warfare against American merchant shipping.

At the same time, Great Britain intercepted and decoded a secret message from Germany to Mexico urging Mexico to go to war against the U.S. The publishing of this information along with continued German destruction of American ships resulted in the eventual entry of the U.S. into the conflict, the first time the country prepared to fight in a conflict not on American soil. Though unprepared for war, governmental efforts and activities resulted in massive defense mobilization with America's economy directed to the war effort. Though America made important contributions of war materials, its greatest contribution to the war was manpower, soldiers desperately needed by the Allies.

Some ten months before the war ended, President Wilson had proposed a program called the Fourteen Points as a method of bringing the war to an end with an equitable peace settlement. In these Points he had five points setting out general ideals; there were eight pertaining to immediately working to resolve territorial and political problems; and the fourteenth point counseled establishing an organization of nations to help keep world peace.

When Germany agreed in 1918 to an armistice, it assumed that the peace settlement would be drawn up on the basis of these Fourteen Points. However, the peace conference in Paris ignored these points and Wilson had to be content with efforts at establishing the League of Nations. Italy, France, and Great Britain, having suffered and sacrificed far more in the war than America, wanted retribution. The treaties punished severely the Central Powers, taking away arms and territories and requiring payment of reparations. Germany was punished more than the others and, according to one clause in the treaty, was forced to assume the responsibility for causing the war.

Pre-war empires lost tremendous amounts of territories as well as the wealth of natural resources in them. New, independent nations were formed and some predominately ethnic areas came under control of nations of different cultural backgrounds. Some national boundary changes overlapped and created tensions and hard feelings as well as political and economic confusion. The wishes and desires of every national or cultural group could not possibly be realized and satisfied, resulting in disappointments for both; those who were victorious and those who were defeated. Germany received harsher terms than expected from the treaty which weakened its post-war government. Along with the worldwide depression of the 1930s, the stage was set for the rise of Adolf Hitler and his Nationalist Socialist Party and World War II.

President Wilson lost in his efforts to get the U.S. Senate to approve the peace treaty. The Senate at the time was a reflection of American public opinion and its rejection of the treaty was a rejection of Wilson. The approval of the treaty would have made the U.S. a member of the League of Nations but Americans had just come off a bloody war to ensure that democracy would exist throughout the world. Americans just did not want to accept any responsibility that resulted from its new position of power and were afraid that membership in the League of Nations would embroil the U.S. in future disputes in Europe.

Major consequences of WWII included horrendous death and destruction, millions of displaced persons, the gaining of strength and spread of Communism and Cold War tensions as a result of the beginning of the nuclear age. World War II ended more lives and caused more devastation than any other war.

Besides the losses of millions of military personnel, the devastation and destruction directly affected civilians, reducing cities, houses, and factories to ruin and rubble and totally wrecking communication and transportation systems. Millions of civilian deaths, especially in China and the Soviet Union, were the results of famine.

More than 12 million people were uprooted by war's end having no place to live. Those included were prisoners of war, those that survived Nazi concentration camps and slave labor camps, orphans, and people who escaped war-torn areas and invading armies. Changing national boundary lines also caused the mass movement of displaced persons.

Germany and Japan were completely defeated; Great Britain and France were seriously weakened; and the Soviet Union and the United States became the world's leading powers. Although allied during the war, the alliance fell apart as the Soviets pushed Communism in Europe and Asia. In spite of the tremendous destruction it suffered, the Soviet Union was stronger than ever. During the war, it took control of Lithuania, Estonia, and Latvia and by mid-1945 parts of Poland, Czechoslovakia, Finland, and Romania. It helped Communist governments gain power in Bulgaria, Romania, Hungary, Czechoslovakia, Poland, and North Korea. China fell to Mao Zedong's Communist forces in 1949. Until the fall of the Berlin Wall in 1989 and the dissolution of Communist governments in Eastern Europe and the Soviet Union, the United States and the Soviet Union faced off in what was called a Cold War. The possibility of the terrifying destruction by nuclear weapons loomed over both nations.

Skill 8.5: Identify the principal causes and analyze the major consequences of postwar reform movements.

The phrase "the civil rights movement" generally refers to the nation-wide effort made by black people and those who supported them to gain equal rights to whites and to eliminate segregation. Discussion of this movement is generally understood in terms of the period of the 1950s and 1960s.

The **key people** in the civil rights movement are:

Rosa Parks -- A black seamstress from Montgomery Alabama who, in 1955, refused to give up her seat on the bus to a white man. This event is generally understood as the spark that lit the fire of the Civil Rights Movement. She has been generally regarded as the "mother of the Civil Rights Movement."

Martin Luther King, Jr.-- the most prominent member of the Civil Rights movement. King promoted nonviolent methods of opposition to segregation. The "Letter from Birmingham Jail" explained the purpose of nonviolent action as a way to make people notice injustice. He led the march on Washington in 1963, at which he delivered the "I Have a Dream" speech. He received the 1968 Nobel Prize for Peace.

James Meredith – the first African American to enroll at the University of Mississippi.

Emmett Till – a teenage boy who was murdered in Mississippi while visiting from Chicago. The crime of which he was accused was "whistling at a white woman in a store." He was beaten and murdered, and his body was dumped in a river. His two white abductors were apprehended and tried. They were acquitted by an all-white jury. After the acquittal, they admitted their guilt, but remained free because of double jeopardy laws.

Ralph Abernathy – A major figure in the Civil Rights Movement who succeeded Martin Luther King, Jr. as head of the Southern Christian Leadership Conference

Malcolm X – a political leader and part of the Civil Rights Movement. He was a prominent Black Muslim.

Stokeley Carmichael – one of the leaders of the Black Power movement that called for independent development of political and social institutions for blacks. Carmichael called for black pride and maintenance of black culture. He was head of the Student Nonviolent Coordinating Committee.

Key events of the Civil Rights Movement include:

Brown vs. Board of Education, 1954

The murder of Emmett Till, 1955

Rosa Parks and the Montgomery Bus Boycott, 1955-56 – After refusing to give up her seat on a bus in Montgomery, Alabama, Parks was arrested, tried, and convicted of disorderly conduct and violating a local ordinance. When word reached the black community a bus boycott was organized to protest the segregation of blacks and whites on public buses. The boycott lasted 381 days, until the ordinance was lifted.

Strategy shift to "direct action" – nonviolent resistance and civil disobedience, 1955 – 1965. This action consisted mostly of bus boycotts, sit-ins, freedom rides, etc.

Formation of the Southern Christian Leadership Conference, 1957. This group, formed by Martin Luther King, Jr., John Duffy, Rev. C. D. Steele, Rev. T. J. Jemison, Rev. Fred Shuttlesworth, Ella Baker, A. Philip Randolph, Bayard Rustin and Stanley Levison. The group provided training and assistance to local efforts to fight segregation. Non-violence was its central doctrine and its major method of fighting segregation and racism.

The Desegregation of Little Rock, 1957. Following up on the decision of the Supreme Court in Brown vs. Board of Education, the Arkansas school board voted to integrate the school system. The NAACP chose Arkansas as the place to push integration because it was considered a relatively progressive Southern state. However, the governor called up the National Guard to prevent 9 black students from attending Little Rock's Central High School.

Sit-ins – In 1960, students began to stage "sit-ins" at local lunch counters and stores as a means of protesting the refusal of those businesses to desegregate. The first was in Greensboro, NC. This led to a rash of similar campaigns throughout the South. Demonstrators began to protest parks, beaches, theaters, museums, and libraries. When arrested, the protesters made "jail-no-bail" pledges. This called attention to their cause and put the financial burden of providing jail space and food on the cities.

Freedom Rides – Activists traveled by bus throughout the deep South to desegregate bus terminals (required by federal law). These protesters undertook extremely dangerous protests. Many buses were firebombed, attacked by the KKK, and beaten. They were crammed into small, airless jail cells and mistreated in many ways. Key figures in this effort included John Lewis, James Lawson, Diane Nash, Bob Moses, James Bevel, Charles McDew, Bernard Lafayette, Charles Jones, Lonnie King, Julian Bond, Hosea Williams, and Stokeley Carmichael.

The Birmingham Campaign, *1963-64.* A campaign was planned to use sit-in, kneel-ins in churches, and a march to the county building to launch a voter registration campaign. The City obtained an injunction forbidding all such protests. The protesters, including Martin Luther King, Jr., believed the injunction was unconstitutional, and defied it. They were arrested. While in jail, King wrote his famous Letter from Birmingham Jail. When the campaign began to falter, the "Children's Crusade" called students to leave school and join the protests. The events became news when more than 600 students were jailed. The next day more students joined the protest. The media was present, and broadcast to the nation, vivid pictures of fire hoses being used to knock down children and dogs attacking some of them. The resulting public outrage led the Kennedy administration to intervene. About a month later, a committee was formed to end hiring discrimination, arrange for the release of jailed protesters, and establish normative communication between blacks and whites. Four months later, the KKK bombed the Sixteenth Street Baptist Church, killing 4 girls.

The March on Washington, 1963. This was a march on Washington for jobs and freedom. It was a combined effort of all major civil rights organizations. The goals of the march were: meaningful civil rights laws, a massive federal works program, full and fair employment, decent housing, the right to vote, and adequate integrated education. It was at this march that Martin Luther King, Jr. made the famous "I Have a Dream" speech.

Mississippi Freedom Summer, 1964. Students were brought from other states to Mississippi to assist local activists in registering voters, teaching in "Freedom schools" and in forming the Mississippi Freedom Democratic Party. Three of the workers disappeared – murdered by the KKK. It took six weeks to find their bodies. The national uproar forced President Johnson to send in the FBI. Johnson was able to use public sentiment to effect passage in Congress of the Civil Rights Act of 1964.

Selma to Montgomery marches, 1965. Attempts to obtain voter registration in Selma, Alabama had been largely unsuccessful due to opposition from the city's sheriff. M.L. King came to the city to lead a series of marches. He and over 200 demonstrators were arrested and jailed. Each successive march was met with violent resistance by police. In March, a group of over 600 intended to walk from Selma to Montgomery (54 miles). News media were on hand when, 6 blocks into the march, state and local law enforcement officials attacked the marchers with billy clubs, tear gas, rubber tubes wrapped in barbed wire and bull ships. They were driven back to Selma. National broadcast of the footage provoked a nation-wide response. President Johnson again used public sentiment to achieve passage of the Voting Rights Act of 1965. This law changed the political landscape of the South irrevocably.

Key policies, legislation and court cases included the following:

Brown v. Board of Education, 1954 – the Supreme Court declared that Plessy v. Ferguson was unconstitutional. This was the ruling that had established "Separate but Equal" as the basis for segregation. With this decision, the Court ordered immediate desegregation.

Civil Rights Act of 1964 – bars discrimination in public accommodations, employment and education

Voting Rights Act of 1965 – suspended poll taxes, literacy tests and other voter tests for voter registration.

Since 1941 a number of anti-discrimination laws have been passed by the Congress. These acts have protected the civil rights of several groups of Americans. These laws include:

- Fair Employment Act of 1941
- Civil Rights Act of 1964
- Immigration and Nationality Services Act of 1965
- Voting Rights Act of 1965
- Civil Rights Act of 1968
- Age Discrimination in Employment Act of 1967
- Age Discrimination Act of 1975
- Pregnancy Discrimination Act of 1978
- Americans with Disabilities Act of 1990
- Civil Rights Act of 1991
- Employment Non-Discrimination Act

Numerous groups have used various forms of protest, attempts to sway public opinion, legal action, and congressional lobbying to obtain full protection of their civil rights under the Constitution.

"Minority rights" encompasses two ideas: the first is the normal individual rights of members of ethnic, racial, class, religious or sexual minorities; the second is collective rights of minority groups. Various civil rights movements have sought to guarantee that the individual rights of persons are not denied on the basis of being part of a minority group. The effects of these movements may be seen in guarantees of minority representation, affirmative action quotas, etc.

The disability rights movement was a successful effort to guarantee access to public buildings and transportation, equal access to education and employment, and equal protection under the law in terms of access to insurance, and other basic rights of American citizens. As a result of these efforts, public buildings and public transportation must be accessible to persons with disabilities, discrimination in hiring or housing on the basis of disability is also illegal.

A "prisoners' rights" movement has been working for many years to ensure the basic human rights of persons incarcerated for crimes.

Immigrant rights movements have provided for employment and housing rights, as well as preventing abuse of immigrants through hate crimes. In some states, immigrant rights movements have led to bi-lingual education and public information access.

Another group movement to obtain equal rights is the lesbian, gay, bisexual and transgender social movement. This movement seeks equal housing, freedom from social and employment discrimination, and equal recognition of relationships under the law.

Basic civil liberties must, from time to time, be protected through social movements. These rights are the "inalienable" rights guaranteed by the U.S. Constitution and Bill of Rights. These rights include the right to assembly, the right to privacy, freedom of religion and freedom of speech.

The women's rights movement is concerned with the freedoms of women as differentiated from broader ideas of human rights. These issues are generally different from those that affect men and boys because of biological conditions or social constructs. The rights the movement has sought to protect throughout history include:

- The right to vote
- The right to work
- The right to fair wages
- The right to bodily integrity and autonomy
- The right to own property
- The right to an education
- The right to hold public office
- Marital rights

- Parental rights
- Religious rights
- The right to serve in the military
- The right to enter into legal contracts

The movement for women's rights has resulted in many social and political changes. Many of the ideas that seemed very radical merely 100 years ago are now normative.

Some of the most famous leaders in the women's movement throughout American history are:

- Abigail Adams
- Susan B. Anthony
- Gloria E. Anzaldua
- Betty Friedan
- Olympe de Gouges
- Gloria Steinem
- Harriet Tubman
- Mary Wollstonecraft
- Virginia Woolf
- Germaine Greer

Many within the women's movement are primarily committed to justice and the natural rights of all people. This has led many members of the women's movement to be involved in the Black Civil Rights Movement, the gay rights movement, and the recent social movement to protect the rights of fathers.

After WWII, women were expected to return to the life of homebound docility of the pre-war years. But during the war they were actively recruited into the workplace, indeed into traditionally male jobs in heavy industry. The freedoms they enjoyed and the opportunity to explore their full potential were not things they were willing to give up so easily. The post-war years were a time of hope and great prosperity. Women, like minorities, began to demand their legal rights and freedoms. The women's movement, like the Civil Rights Movement and other efforts to accomplish social reform and human rights, grew from the opportunities that arose from the same periods of struggle and hardship that led others to demand their rights and freedoms.

Skill 8.6: Compare the effects of military and ideological conflicts on U.S. domestic policies and foreign relations.

Korean War ■ 1950 to 1953

Causes: Korea was under control of Japan from 1895 to the end of the Second World War in 1945. At war's end, the Soviet and U.S. military troops moved into Korea with the U.S. troops in the southern half and the Soviet troops in the northern half with the 38 degree North Latitude line as the boundary.

The General Assembly of the UN in 1947 ordered elections throughout all of Korea to select one government for the entire country. The Soviet Union would not allow the North Koreans to vote, so they set up a Communist government there. The South Koreans set up a democratic government but both claimed the entire country. At times, there were clashes between the troops from 1948 to 1950. After the U.S. removed its remaining troops in 1949 and announced in early 1950 that Korea was not part of its defense line in Asia, the Communists decided to act and invaded the south.

Participants were: North and South Korea, United States of America, Australia, New Zealand, China, Canada. France, Great Britain, Turkey, Belgium, Ethiopia, Colombia, Greece, South Africa, Luxembourg, Thailand, the Netherlands, and the Philippines. It was the first war in which a world organization played a major military role and it presented quite a challenge to the UN, which had only been in existence five years.

The war began June 25, 1950 and ended July 27, 1953. A truce was drawn up and an armistice agreement was signed ending the fighting. A permanent treaty of peace has never been signed and the country remains divided between the Communist North and the Democratic South. It was a very costly and bloody war destroying villages and homes, displacing and killing millions of people.

The Vietnam War

U.S. Involvement ■ 1957 to 1973

Causes: U.S. involvement was the second phase of three in Vietnam's history. The first phase began in 1946 when the Vietnamese fought French troops for control of the country. Vietnam prior to 1946 had been part of the French colony of Indochina (since 1861 along with Laos and Kampuchea or Cambodia). In 1954, the defeated French left and the country became divided into Communist North and Democratic South. United States' aid and influence continued as part of the U.S. "Cold War" foreign policy to help any nation threatened by Communism.

The second phase involved the U.S. commitment. The Communist Vietnamese considered the war one of national liberation, a struggle to avoid continual dominance and influence of a foreign power. A cease-fire was arranged in January 1973 and a few months later U.S. troops left for good. The third and final phase consisted of fighting between the Vietnamese but ended April 30, 1975, with the surrender of South Vietnam, the entire country being united under Communist ruler.

Participants were the United States of America, Australia, New Zealand, South and North Vietnam, South Korea, Thailand, and the Philippines. With active U.S. involvement from 1957 to 1973, it was the longest war participated in by the U.S.; was tremendously destructive and completely divided the American public in their opinions and feelings about the war. Many were frustrated and angered by the fact that it was the first war fought on foreign soil in which U.S. combat forces were totally unable to achieve their goals and objectives.

Returning veterans faced not only readjustment to normal civilian life but also faced bitterness, anger, rejection, and no heroes' welcomes. Many suffered severe physical and deep psychological problems. The war set a precedent with Congress and the American people actively challenging U.S. military and foreign policy. The conflict, though tempered markedly by time, still exists and still has a definite effect on people.

The struggle between the Communist world under Soviet Union leadership and the non-Communist world under Anglo-American leadership resulted in what became known as the Cold War. Communism crept into the Western Hemisphere with Cuban leader Fidel Castro and his regime. Most colonies in Africa, Asia, and the Middle East gained independence from European and Western influence and control. In South Africa in the early 1990s, the system of racial segregation, called "apartheid," was abolished.

The Soviet Union was the first industrialized nation to successfully begin a program of space flight and exploration, launching Sputnik and putting the first man in space. The United States also experienced success in its space program successfully landing space crews on the moon. In the late 1980s and early 1990s, the Berlin Wall was torn down and Communism fell in the Soviet Union and Eastern Europe. The 15 republics of the former USSR became independent nations with varying degrees of freedom and democracy in government and together formed the Commonwealth of Independent States (CIS). The former Communist nations of Eastern Europe also emphasized their independence with democratic forms of government.

Tremendous progress in communication and transportation has tied all parts of the earth and drawn them closer. There are still vast areas of the former Soviet Union that have unproductive land, extreme poverty, food shortages, rampant diseases, violent friction between cultures, the ever-present nuclear threat, environmental pollution, rapid reduction of natural resources, urban over-crowding, acceleration in global terrorism and violent crimes, and a diminishing middle class.

Women were very active in the reform movements of the era. Their leadership in these activities underscored the inequality of women in American society. A group of women emerged in the 1840s that was the beginning of the first women's rights movement in the nation's history. Among the early leaders of the movement were Elizabeth Cady Stanton, Lucretia Mott, and Ernestine Rose. At this time very few states recognized women's rights to vote, own property, sue for divorce, or execute contracts. In 1869, Susan B. Anthony, Ernestine Rose and Elizabeth Cady Stanton founded the National Woman Suffrage Association.

COMPETENCY 9: Understand major political, social, and economic events and developments in New Mexico history; and analyze the diverse perspectives of those who participated in these events and developments.

Skill 9.1: Examine the role played by Native American peoples in the development of New Mexico and the Southwest.

During the prehistoric period the Folsom Paleo-Indians wandered the area that is now New Mexico hunting animals. Native Americans began to settle in several areas of the state around the beginning of the Common Era. These early peoples lived in pit houses, cliff-side caves, or stone structures. The Ancestral Peublo people lived in the northwest region of the state and the Mogollon in the southwest region. Both of these groups established peaceful agricultural societies by about 1000 C.E. The reason for the disappearance of the Mogollon culture is unknown. Archaeologists believe the Pueblo left their stone settlements during the drought and later built the multi-storied adobe pueblos along the Rio Grande. These native peoples raised corn, beans and squash.

The Athapascan tribes are believed to have entered the Southwest shortly before the arrival of Spanish explorers and settlers. The Athapascans were divided into two primary groups: the Apache and the Navajo. They were a more nomadic society that did not establish permanent settlements until much later.

With the arrival of Spanish settlers in the 16th century came the Franciscan missionaries. They were quite zealous in their efforts to convert the native peoples to Christianity. The Pueblo peoples passionately resented their efforts to deprive them of their religious beliefs. In 1680 they united in a surprise revolt (the Pueblo Revolt) against the Spanish. Many of the Spanish settlers were killed and many others fled to the south. Around 12-15 years later, Diego de Vargas led the Spanish in re-conquering the area. Neglected by both Spain and Mexico, the settlers survived through the help of the Pueblo people. There was much cultural sharing between the two groups, resulting in a unique blended culture continues to typify New Mexico's people today.

By the terms of the **Treaty of Paris** which ended the Revolutionary War, a large amount of land occupied and claimed by American Indians was ceded to the United States. The British, however, did not inform the Native People of the change. The government of the new nation first tried to treat the tribes who had fought with the British as conquered people and claimed their land. This policy was later abandoned because it could not be enforced.

The next phase of the government's policy toward the American Indians was to purchase their land in treaties in order to continue national expansion. This created tension with the states and with settlers.

During the nineteenth century the nation expanded westward. This expansion and settlement of new territory forced the Native Americans to continue to move farther west. The Native Americans were gradually giving up their homelands, their sacred sites, and the burial grounds of their ancestors. Some of the American Indians chose to move west. Many, however, were relocated by force.

The Indian Removal Act of 1830 authorized the government to negotiate treaties with Native Americans to provide land west of the Mississippi River in exchange for lands east of the river. This policy resulted in the relocation of more than 100,000 Native Americans. Theoretically, the treaties were expected to result in voluntary relocation of the native people. In fact, however, many of the native chiefs were forced to sign the treaties.

One of the worst examples of "Removal" was the Treaty of New Echota. This treaty was signed by a faction of the Cherokees rather than the actual leaders of the tribe. When the leaders attempted to remain on their ancestral lands, the treaty was enforced by President Martin Van Buren. The removal of the Cherokees came to be known as "The Trail of Tears" and resulted in the deaths of more than 4000 Cherokees, mostly due to disease.

After 1821, when Mexico won independence from Spain, the new government opened the borders to trade with the U.S. The Santa Fe Trail was an outgrowth of this policy of open trade. But Mexico was not able to defend the northern regions, which permitted the immigration of Americans.

The influx of settlers and their claims to lands that had been the hunting grounds of the Native Americans led to numerous "Indian raids" and wars in the region. During and after the Civil War, the Chiricahua Apaches refused U.S. efforts to relocate them to forced "Indian settlements." It was only when Geronimo tired of the wars and saw surrender as the only way to ensure a peaceful future for his people, that peace was achieved.

The conclusion of the Civil War opened the floodgates for migration westward and settlement of new land. The availability of cheap land and the expectation of great opportunity prompted thousands, including immigrants, to travel across the Mississippi River and settle the Great Plains and California. The primary basis of the new western economy was farming, mining, and ranching. Both migration and the economy were facilitated by the expansion of the railroad and the completion of the transcontinental railroad in 1869.

Migration and settlement were not easy. As the settlers moved west they encountered Native American tribes who believed they had a natural right to the lands upon which their ancestors had lived for generations. Resentment of the encroachment of new settlers was particularly strong among the tribes that had been ordered to relocate to "Indian Country" prior to 1860. Conflict was intense and frequent until 1867 when the government established two large tracts of land called "reservations" in Oklahoma and the Dakotas to which all tribes would be confined. With the war over, troops were sent west to enforce the relocation and reservation containment policies. There were frequent wars, particularly as white settlers attempted to move onto Indian lands and as the tribes resisted this confinement.

Continuing conflict led to passage of the Dawes Act of 1887. This was a recognition that confinement to reservations was not working. The law was intended to break up the Indian communities and bring about assimilation into white culture by deeding portions of the reservation lands to individual Indians who were expected to farm their land. The policy continued until 1934.

Armed resistance essentially came to an end by 1890. The surrender of Geronimo and the massacre at Wounded Knee, led to a change of strategy by the Indians. Thereafter, the resistance strategy was to preserve their culture and traditions.

The Navajo people were particularly instrumental in the Allied victory in World War II. The language was unique and impossible for most to understand. The U.S. military decided to use the Navajo Code Talkers to send messages that could not be decoded by the Japanese.

Skill 9.2: Identify leading figures and analyze major events that shaped New Mexico's political, economic, and social development.

Francisco Vazquez de Coronado was the first European to systematically explore New Mexico in 1540 in search of fabled gold. His mission was to conquer the native people and claim the wealth of the land. He did not, however, find gold, and returned to New Spain with nothing.

Don Juan de Onate established the first European colony in New Mexico in 1598. Although the settlement was a financial failure, it established cultural roots that are influential today.

Don Pedro de Peralta was later appointed the third governor of the territory and established Santa Fe as its capital. His term of service initiated a 70-year period of Spanish settlement, exploration and missionary work.

The first church built in North America was at San Juan Pueblo. Unlike the missions established in California and Texas, these churches were typical of Spanish Colonial architecture. By the early part o f the 17th century, 50 churches had been built in New Mexico.

Some of the native peoples accepted Christianity, but others found it oppressive and resented the demands that they abandon their own native religious beliefs. This was particularly true among some of the Pueblo peoples. In 1680, after laying careful plans, the tribes ruse up under the leadership of Pope, and drive the Spanish from Santa Fe in the **Pueblo Revolt**. Within about 12 years, the Spanish returned and reclaimed the territory they had lost. Relationships between the native peoples and the Spanish were significantly better in the ensuing years, resulting in a rich blended culture.

The **Mexican Period** began in 1821, when Mexico won independence from Spain. Trade was opened with the U.S. and the **Santa Fe Trail**, which began in Missouri, brought new settlers, new money, and new lifestyles to the region.

When the U.S. declared war on Mexico in 1846, U.S. General Stephen Watts Kearny led his troops down the Santa Fe Trail and proclaimed New Mexico and American territory. In the American Civil War, New Mexico fought with Union soldiers to remain a slave-free territory.

The growth of the railroads brought access to new markets and greatly improved commerce. The southeastern plains of New Mexico rapidly became cattle kingdoms. The rival cattle barons and merchants found themselves engaged in the **Lincoln County War**, from which Billy the Kid emerged as an outlaw hero. The beef industry flourished, and made men like John Chisum famous for bringing longhorn cattle from Texas.

During and after the Civil War there was much "Indian trouble." Refusing to be consigned to poor land and confined to "reservations," the Chiricahua tribes fought for their freedom and their ancestral lands and lifestyles. These struggles finally ended when Geronimo surrendered to the U.S. Army to give his people a chance to enjoy a peaceful life.

Many of the enlistees in the Army in the regions of New Mexico were African Americans who joined after the Civil War. The Native peoples found their curly hair comparable to the buffalo tuft, and called them Buffalo Soldiers.

For more than 60 years after becoming an American territory, political and cultural factors prevented New Mexico from achieving statehood. New Mexico finally became a state in 1912, the 47th state in the union.

The rise of **Pancho Villa** in the midst of political unrest in Mexico was not supported by the U.S. Villa and his followers raided Columbus, New Mexico in 1916. The armed conflict resulted in many deaths on both sides and Villa's return to Mexico.

In addition to the contributions of the Navajo Code Talkers during World War II, two regiments from New Mexico were forced to endure the Bataan Death March in the Philippines during World War II. The top-secret Manhattan Project, directed by J. Robert Oppenheimer, exploded the first atomic bomb at Los Alamos in July 1945. Two weeks later, the U.S. dropped two atomic bombs on Japan, ending World War II.

In the decades between 1940 and 1980, the population of New Mexico tripled. Route 66 brought travel and tourism; the motion picture industry discovered spectacular sites for filming; and there were reports of a crashed UFO near Corona.

Since the beginning of the Common Era, agriculture and ranching have supported the economy of the state. During the last century, the nuclear science facility and the rapidly growing electronics industry have found ways to subsist alongside the traditional agricultural lifestyle.

Skill 9.3: Recognize historical and cultural aspects of New Mexico's uniqueness.

Historically and culturally New Mexico is a unique blend of Native American, Spanish/Mexican and Anglo/European/American influences. The Native American population has both interacted and been partially absorbed into the composite culture and maintained its uniqueness and traditions in separate territories. The agricultural and mining economy has been open to people of every heritage, allowing cultural influences to interpenetrate and to create a distinctive local culture. The Pueblo live in settled agricultural communities scattered throughout the state. The Apache, some Pueblo, some Ute and some Navajo live in federal reservations within the state. The Navajo Nation is the largest such reservation in the country.

New Mexico has the highest percentage of people of Hispanic ancestry of an US state. It also has a large Amerindian population. Predominant cultural influences include American, Colonial Spanish, Mexican, Native American and Amerindian.

Over one-third of New Mexico residents are of Hispanic origin. A majority of the Hispanic residents are descendants of the original Spanish colonists and live in the northern part of the state. A significantly smaller number of Mexican immigrants live in the southern part of the state.

The state's early isolation from external influences has produced a unique culture that is apparent in the particular unique dialect of Spanish spoken by many New Mexicans. It includes specifically New Mexican vocabulary that is often unknown to other Spanish speakers. It also preserves some late medieval Castillian vocabulary and incorporates many Native American words, as well as an Anglicized set of concepts and modern American inventions.

Skill 9.4 Analyze the influence of geographic factors on New Mexico's development.

New Mexico has only about 23 cloudy or rainy days each year. There are no extremes of heat or cold, but due to the absorption and radiation of the sun's heat by the great sandy areas, there is a wide daily range in temperature. The annual rainfall ranges from 6 inches in the southwestern valleys to 30 inches in the northern mountains. The snow accumulates to great depths on the mountain peaks and forms a steady source of water supply for many of the rivers.

The agriculture of the state is largely confined to the river valleys and irrigated sections. The cactus and yucca are abundant in the arid southern valleys. The roots of the yucca are used as a substitute for soap, and the plant is cut and shipped from some parts of the state for use in paper manufacture. The great extent of semi-arid plains covered with grama grass and salt grass affords abundant food for herds and flocks, and stock-raising has been an important branch of agriculture since the arrival of the first Spanish settlers.

The Rio Grande River, which essentially bisects the state, has supported agriculture and agrarian communities throughout New Mexico's history. The Elephant Butte Dam on the Rio Grande provides irrigation for farming. Other areas that support agriculture are the Colorado River basin and the Pecos and San Juan River regions.

The federal government protects millions of acres of national forest. The mountainous regions, in particular, have supported mining industries, notably turquoise and silver, as well as several minerals.

The landscape includes rose-colored deserts, snow-capped mountain peaks, and huge mesas. The plains have supported ranching, both cattle and sheep. These plains are covered with cactus, yucca, creosote bush, sagebrush and several desert grasses.

The geography and topography have supported a significant economy. Cattle, dairy products, sheep and other livestock are supported by the plains regions. Dryland farming produces nursery stock, hay, pecans and chili peppers, as well as onions and potatoes. The forests support an active lumber business. Mining produces uranium ore, manganese, potash, salt, perlite, copper ore, beryllium and tin, as well as natural gas, petroleum and coal. The natural beauty of the state and the presence of numerous historic and Native American communities supports a thriving tourism industry.

SUBAREA II—GEOGRAPHY AND CULTURE

COMPETENCY 10: Understand important geographic concepts and terms, and use geographic tools and resources to generate and interpret information.

Skill 10.1: Define and apply important geographic terms and concepts.

Human communities subsisted initially as gatherers – gathering berries, leaves, etc. With the invention of tools it became possible to dig for roots, hunt small animals, and catch fish from rivers and oceans. Humans observed their environments and soon learned to plant seeds and harvest crops. As people migrated to areas in which game and fertile soil were abundant, communities began to develop. When people had the knowledge to grow crops and the skills to hunt game, they began to understand division of labor. Some of the people in the community tended to agricultural needs while others hunted game.

As habitats attracted larger numbers of people, environments became crowded and there was competition. The concept of division of labor and sharing of food soon came, in more heavily populated areas, to be managed. Groups of people focused on growing crops while others concentrated on hunting. Experience led to the development of skills and of knowledge that make the work easier. Farmers began to develop new plant species and hunters began to protect animal species from other predators for their own use. This ability to manage the environment led people to settle down, to guard their resources, and to manage them.

Camps soon became villages. Villages became year-round settlements. Animals were domesticated and gathered into herds that met the needs of the village. With the settled life it was no longer necessary to "travel light." Pottery was developed for storing and cooking food.

By 8000 BCE, culture was beginning to evolve in these villages. Agriculture was developed for the production of grain crops, which led to a decreased reliance on wild plants. Domesticating animals for various purposes decreased the need to hunt wild game. Life became more settled. It was then possible to turn attention to such matters as managing water supplies, producing tools, making cloth, etc. There was both the social interaction and the opportunity to reflect upon existence. Mythologies arose and various kinds of belief systems. Rituals arose that re-enacted the mythologies that gave meaning to life. As farming and animal husbandry skills increased, the dependence upon wild game and food gathering declined. With this change came the realization that a larger number of people could be supported on the produce of farming and animal husbandry.

Two things seem to have come together to produce cultures and civilizations: a society and culture based on agriculture and the development of centers of the community with literate social and religious structures. The members of these hierarchies then managed water supply and irrigation, ritual and religious life, and exerted their own right to use a portion of the goods produced by the community for their own subsistence in return for their management.

Sharpened skills, development of more sophisticated tools, commerce with other communities, and increasing knowledge of their environment, the resources available to them, and responses to the needs to share good, order community life, and protect their possessions from outsiders led to further division of labor and community development.

As trade routes developed and travel between cities became easier, trade led to specialization. Trade enables a people to obtain the goods they desire in exchange for the goods they are able to produce. This, in turn, leads to increased attention to refinements of technique and the sharing of ideas. The knowledge of a new discovery or invention provides knowledge and technology that increases the ability to produce goods for trade.

As each community learns the value of the goods it produces and improves its ability to produce the goods in greater quantity, industry is born.

Refer to following skills in Competency 10.0 for additional geographical terms.

Skill 10.2: Recognize and apply important geographic themes.

GEOGRAPHY involves studying location and how living things and earth's features are distributed throughout the earth. It includes where animals, people, and plants live and the effects of their relationship with earth's physical features. Geographers also explore the locations of earth's features, how they got there, and why it is so important.

What geographers study can be broken down into four areas:

Location: Being able to find the exact site of anything on the earth;
Spatial relations: The relationships of earth's features, places, and groups of people with one another due to their location;
Regional characteristics: Characteristics of a place such as landform and climate, types of plants and animals, kinds of people who live there, and how they use the land; and
Forces that change the earth: Such as human activities and natural forces.

Geographical studies are divided into:

Regional: Elements and characteristics of a place or region
Topical: One earth feature or one human activity occurring throughout the entire world
Physical: Earth's physical features, what creates and changes them, their relationships to each other as well as human activities
Human: Human activity patterns and how they relate to the environment including political, cultural, historical, urban, and social geographical fields of study.

Special research methods used by geographers include mapping, interviewing, field studies, mathematics, statistics, and scientific instruments.

GEOGRAPHY

Eratosthenes was an ancient Greek mathematician who calculated the circumference of the earth.

Strabo wrote a geography of the known ancient world in 17 volumes.

Ptolemy contributed his skills in mapping and theories from studies in astronomy to geographic knowledge.

Christopher Columbus known for his famous first voyage sailing west to find the riches of the east and finding the Western Hemisphere instead.

Marco Polo, Vasco da Gama, and Magellan are three of many explorers and colonizers who contributed to geographic knowledge.

National Geographic Society is publisher of the National Geographic magazine and the funding of expeditions and other activities furthering geographic education.

Geography is the study of the earth, its people, and how people adapt to life on earth and how they use its resources. It is undeniably connected to history, economics, political science, sociology, anthropology, and even a bit of archaeology. Geography not only deals with people and the earth today but also with:
How did it all begin?
What is the background of the people of an area?
What kind of government or political system do they have?
How does that affect their ways of producing goods and the distribution of them?
What kind of relationships do these people have with other groups?
How is the way they live their lives affected by their physical environment?
In what ways do they effect change in their way of living?

All of this is tied in with their physical environment, the earth and its people

Skill 10.3: Recognize similarities and differences between maps and globes.

We use **illustrations** of various sorts because it is often easier to demonstrate a given idea visually instead of orally. Sometimes it is even easier to do so with an illustration than a description. This is especially true in the areas of education and research because humans are visually stimulated. It is a fact that any idea presented visually in some manner is always easier to understand and to comprehend than simply getting an idea across verbally, by hearing it or reading it. Among the more common illustrations used in political and social sciences are various types of **maps, graphs and charts**.

Photographs and **globes** are useful as well, but as they are limited in what kind of information that they can show, they are rarely used. Unless, as in the case of a photograph, it is of a particular political figure or a time that one wishes to visualize.

Although maps have advantages over globes and photographs, they do have a major disadvantage. This problem must be considered as well. The major problem of all maps comes about because most maps are flat and the Earth is a sphere. It is impossible to reproduce exactly on a flat surface an object shaped like a sphere. In order to put the earth's features onto a map they must be stretched in some way. This stretching is called **distortion.**

Distortion does not mean that maps are wrong it simply means that they are not perfect representations of the Earth or its parts. **Cartographers,** or mapmakers, understand the problems of distortion. They try to design them so that there is as little distortion as possible in the maps.

The process of putting the features of the Earth onto a flat surface is called **projection**. All maps are really map projections. There are many different types. Each one deals in a different way with the problem of distortion. Map projections are made in a number of ways. Some are done using complicated mathematics. However, the basic ideas behind map projections can be understood by looking at the three most common types:

(1) **Cylindrical Projections** - These are done by taking a cylinder of paper and wrapping it around a globe. A light is used to project the globe's features onto the paper. Distortion is least where the paper touches the globe. For example, suppose that the paper was wrapped so that it touched the globe at the equator, the map from this projection would have just a little distortion near the equator. However, in moving north or south of the equator, the distortion would increase as you moved further away from the equator.

The best known and most widely used cylindrical projection is the **Mercator Projection.** Gerardus Mercator, a Flemish mapmaker, first developed it in 1569.

(2). **Conical Projections** - The name for these maps come from the fact that the projection is made onto a cone of paper. The cone is made so that it touches a globe at the base of the cone only. It can also be made so that it cuts through part of the globe in two different places. Again, there is the least distortion where the paper touches the globe. If the cone touches at two different points, there is some distortion at both of them. Conical projections are most often used to map areas in the **middle latitudes**. Maps of the United States are most often conical projections. This is because most of the country lies within these latitudes.

(3). **Flat-Plane Projections** - These are made with a flat piece of paper. It touches the globe at one point only. Areas near this point show little distortion. Flat-plane projections are often used to show the areas of the north and south poles. One such flat projection is called a **Gnomonic Projection**. On this kind of map all meridians appear as straight lines, Gnomonic projections are useful because any straight line drawn between points on it forms a **Great-Circle Route**.

Great-Circle Routes can best be described by thinking of a globe and when using the globe the shortest route between two points on it can be found by simply stretching a string from one point to the other. However, if the string was extended in reality, so that it took into effect the globe's curvature, it would then make a great-circle. A great-circle is any circle that cuts a sphere, such as the globe, into two equal parts. Because of distortion, most maps do not show great-circle routes as straight lines, Gnomonic projections, however, do show the shortest distance between the two places as a straight line, because of this they are valuable for navigation. They are called Great-Circle Sailing Maps.

Maps have four main properties. They are (1) the size of the areas shown on the map. (2) The shapes of the areas, (3) Consistent scales, and (4) Straight line directions. A map can be drawn so that it is correct in one or more of these properties. No map can be correct in all of them.

Equal areas - One property which maps can have is that of equal areas, In an equal area map, the meridians and parallels are drawn so that the areas shown have the same proportions as they do on the Earth. For example, Greenland is about 118th the size of South America, thus it will be show as 118th the size on an equal area map. The **Mercator projection** is an example of a map that does not have equal areas. In it, Greenland appears to be about the same size of South America. This is because the distortion is very bad at the poles and Greenland lies near the North Pole.

Conformality - A second map property is conformality, or correct shapes. There are no maps that can show very large areas of the earth in their exact shapes.

Only globes can really do that, however Conformal Maps are as close as possible to true shapes. The United States is often shown by a Lambert Conformal Conic Projection Map.

Consistent Scales - Many maps attempt to use the same scale on all parts of the map. Generally, this is easier when maps show a relatively small part of the earth's surface. For example, a map of Florida might be a Consistent Scale Map. Generally maps showing large areas are not consistent-scale maps. This is so because of distortion. Often such maps will have two scales noted in the key. One scale, for example, might be accurate to measure distances between points along the Equator. Another might be then used to measure distances between the North Pole and the South Pole.

Maps showing physical features often try to show information about the elevation or **relief** of the land. **Elevation** is the distance above or below the sea level. The elevation is usually shown with colors, for instance, all areas on a map which are at a certain level will be shown in the same color.

Relief Maps - Show the shape of the land surface, flat, rugged, or steep. Relief maps usually give more detail than simply showing the overall elevation of the land's surface. Relief is also sometimes shown with colors, but another way to show relief is by using **contour lines**. These lines connect all points of a land surface which are the same height surrounding the particular area of land.

Thematic Maps - These are used to show more specific information, often on a single **theme**, or topic. Thematic maps show the distribution or amount of something over a certain given area for example, things such as population density, climate, economic information, cultural, political information, etc.

Skill 10.4: Use maps of locales and world regions to show relative location, direction, latitude and longitude, topography, climate, size, and shape.

Two of the most important terms in the study of geography are *absolute* and *relative* location. Both technically describe the same thing, but both are also, in many respects, as different as day and night.

First, what is **location**? We want to know this in order to determine where something is and where we can find it. We want to point to a spot on a map and say, "That is where we are" or "That is where we want to be." In another way, we want to know where something is as compared to other things. It is very difficult for many people to describe something without referring to something else. Associative reasoning is a powerful way to think.

Absolute location is the exact whereabouts of a person, place, or thing, according to any kind of geographical indicators you want to name. You could be talking about latitude and longitude or GPS or any kind of indicators at all. For example, Paris is at 48 degrees north longitude and 2 degrees east latitude. You can't get much more exact than that. If you had a map that showed every degree of latitude and longitude, you could pinpoint exactly where Paris was and have absolutely no doubt that your geographical depiction was accurate.

Many geographers prefer to use absolute location because of its precision. If you have access to maps and compasses and GPS indicators, why not describe the absolute location of something? It's much more accurate than other means of describing where something is. An absolute location can also be much simpler. Someone might ask you where the nearest post office is and you might say, "It's at the southeast corner of First Avenue and Main Street." That's about as absolute as you can get.

Relative location, on the other hand, is *always* a description that involves more than one thing. When you describe a relative location, you tell where something is by describing what is around it. The same description of where the nearest post office is in terms of absolute location might be this: "It's down the street from the supermarket, on the right side of the street, next to the dentist's office."

We use relative location to be not necessarily less precise but to be more in tune with the real world. Very few people carry exact maps or GPS locators around with them. Nearly everyone, though, can find a location if they have it described to them in terms of what is nearby.

Absolute location can be a bit more map-like and direction-oriented as well. You might say that Chicago is east of Seattle or that St. Louis is north of New Orleans. This is not nearly as involved as the post office location description. In the same way, you might say that Chicago is on Lake Michigan.

Another way to describe where people live is by the **geography** and **topography** around them. The vast majority of people on the planet live in areas that are very hospitable. Yes, people live in the Himalayas and in the Sahara, but the populations in those areas are small indeed when compared to the plains of China, India, Europe, and the United States. People naturally want to live where they won't have to work really hard just to survive, and world population patterns reflect this.

We can examine the spatial organization of the places where people live. For example, in a city, where are the factories and heavy industry buildings? Are they near airports or train stations? Are they on the edge of town, near major roads? What about housing developments? Are they near these industries, or are they far away? Where are the other industry buildings? Where are the schools and hospitals and parks? What about the police and fire stations? How close are homes to each of these things? Towns and especially cities are routinely organized into neighborhoods, so that each house or home is near to most things that its residents might need on a regular basis. This means that large cities have multiple schools, hospitals, grocery stores, fire stations, etc.

Most places in the world are in some manner close to agricultural land as well. Food makes the world go round and some cities are more agriculturally inclined than others. Rare is the city, however, that grows absolutely no crops. The kind of food grown is almost entirely dependent on the kind of land available and the climate surrounding that land. Rice doesn't grow well in the desert, for instance, nor do bananas grow well in snowy lands. Certain crops are easier to transport than others and the ones that aren't are usually grown near ports or other areas of export.

Distance is the measurement between two points of location on a map. Measurement can be in terms of feet, yards, miles, meters, or kilometers. Distance is often correct on equidistant maps only in the direction of latitude.

On a map that has a large scale, 1:125,000 or larger, distance distortion is usually insignificant. An example of a large-scale map is a standard topographic map. On these maps measuring straight line distance is simple. Distance is first measured on the map using a ruler. This measurement is then converted into a real world distance using the map's scale. For example, if we measured a distance of 10 centimeters on a map that had a scale of 1:10,000, we would multiply 10 (distance) by 10,000 (scale). Thus, the actual distance in the real world would be 100,000 centimeters.

Measuring distance along map features that are not straight is a little more difficult. One technique that can be employed for this task is to use a number of straight-line segments. The accuracy of this method is dependent on the number of straight-line segments used. Another method for measuring curvilinear map distances is to use a mechanical device called an **opisometer**. This device uses a small rotating wheel that records the distance traveled. The recorded distance is measured by this device either in centimeters or inches.

Direction is usually measured relative to the location of North or South Pole. Directions determined from these locations are said to be relative to True North or True South. The magnetic poles can also be used to measure direction. However, these points on the Earth are located in spatially different spots from the geographic North and South Pole. The North Magnetic Pole is located at 78.3° North, 104.0° West. In the Southern Hemisphere, the South Magnetic Pole is located in Commonwealth Day, Antarctica and has a geographical location of 65° South, 139° East. The magnetic poles are also not fixed overtime and shift their spatial position overtime.

There are many different climates throughout the earth. It is most unusual if a country contains just one kind of climate. Regions of climates are divided according to **latitudes**:

0 - 23 1 /2 degrees are the "low latitudes"
23 1/2 - 66 1/2 degrees are the "middle latitudes"
66 1/2 degrees to the Poles are the "high latitudes"

The **low latitudes** are comprised of the rainforest, savanna, and desert climates. The tropical rainforest climate is found in equatorial lowlands and is hot and wet. There is sun, extreme heat and rain every day. Although daily temperatures rarely rise above 90 degrees F, the daily humidity is always high, leaving everything sticky and damp. North and south of the tropical rainforests are the tropical grasslands called "savannas," the "lands of two seasons"--a winter dry season and a summer wet season. Further north and south of the tropical grasslands or savannas are the deserts. These areas are the hottest and driest parts of the earth receiving less than 10 inches of rain a year. These areas have extreme temperatures between night and day. After the sun sets, the land cools quickly dropping the temperature as much as 50 degrees F.

The **middle latitudes** contain the Mediterranean, humid-subtropical, humid-continental, marine, steppe, and desert climates. Lands containing the Mediterranean climate are considered "sunny" lands found in six areas of the world: lands bordering the Mediterranean Sea, a small portion of southwestern Africa, areas in southern and southwestern Australia, a small part of the Ukraine near the Black Sea, central Chile, and Southern California. Summers are hot and dry with mild winters. The growing season usually lasts all year and what little rain falls are during the winter months. What is rather unusual is that the Mediterranean climate is located between 30 and 40 degrees north and south latitude on the western coasts of countries.

Longitude measures the north-south position of locations on the Earth's surface relative to a point found at the center of the Earth. This central point is also located on the Earth's rotational or **polar axis**. The equator is the starting point for the measurement of latitude. The equator has a value of zero degrees. A line of latitude or **parallel** of 30° North has an angle that is 30° north of the plane represented by the equator. The maximum value that latitude can attain is either 90° North or South. These lines of latitude run parallel to the rotational axis of the Earth. There are 180° of longitude on either side of a starting meridian which is known the **Prime Meridian**. The Prime Meridian has a designated value of 0°. Measurements of longitude are also defined as being either west or east of the Prime Meridian.

Skill 10.5: Use geographic tools and resources such as aerial photographs, satellite images, geographic information systems, map projections, atlases, gazetteers, and other forms of cartography to generate, synthesize, and interpret information

Computer technology has greatly improved the collection and interpretation of scientific data. Molecular findings have been enhanced through the use of computer images. Technology has revolutionized the access to data via the internet and shared databases. The manipulation of the data has much more sophisticated software capabilities. The computer engineering advances have produced such products as MRIs and CT scans in medicine and laser technology with numerous applications refining precision.

Satellites have improved our ability to communicate and transmit radio and television signals. Navigational abilities have been greatly improved through the use of satellite signals. Sonar uses sound waves to locate objects, especially underwater. The sound waves bounce off the object and are picked up to assist in location. Seismographs record vibrations in the earth and allow us to measure earthquake activity.

Also refer to Skill 10.3.

COMPETENCY 11: Understand major physical features of the world and the natural processes that shape the earth.

Skill 11.1: Recognize the location and characteristics of major land masses, their significant landforms, and the relationship of these landforms to oceans and other bodies of water.

The earth's surface is made up of 70% water and 30% land. Physical features of the land surface include mountains, hills, plateaus, valleys, and plains. Other minor landforms include deserts, deltas, canyons, mesas, basins, foothills, marshes and swamps. Earth's water features include oceans, seas, lakes, rivers, and canals.

Mountains are landforms with rather steep slopes at least 2,000 feet or more above sea level. Mountains are found in groups called mountain chains or mountain ranges. At least one range can be found on six of the earth's seven continents. North America has the Appalachian and Rocky Mountains; South America the Andes; Asia the Himalayas; Australia the Great Dividing Range; Europe the Alps; and Africa the Atlas, Ahaggar, and Drakensburg Mountains.

Hills are elevated landforms rising to an elevation of about 500 to 2000 feet. They are found everywhere on earth including Antarctica where they are covered by ice.

Plateaus are elevated landforms usually level on top. Depending on location, they range from being an area that is very cold to one that is cool and healthful. Some plateaus are dry because they are surrounded by mountains that keep out any moisture. Some examples include the Kenya Plateau in East Africa, which is very cool. The plateau extending north from the Himalayas is extremely dry while those in Antarctica and Greenland are covered with ice and snow.

Plains are described as areas of flat or slightly rolling land, usually lower than the landforms next to them. Sometimes called lowlands (and sometimes located along **seacoasts)** they support the majority of the world's people. Some are found inland and many have been formed by large rivers. This resulted in extremely fertile soil for successful cultivation of crops and numerous large settlements of people. In North America, the vast plains areas extend from the Gulf of Mexico north to the Arctic Ocean and between the Appalachian and Rocky Mountains. In Europe, rich plains extend east from Great Britain into central Europe on into the Siberian region of Russia. Plains in river valleys are found in China (the Yangtze River valley), India (the Ganges River valley), and Southeast Asia (the Mekong River valley).

Valleys are land areas found between hills and mountains. Some have gentle slopes containing trees and plants; others have steep walls and are referred to as canyons. One example is Arizona's Grand Canyon of the Colorado River.

Deserts are large dry areas of land receiving ten inches or less of rainfall each year. Among the better known deserts are Africa's large Sahara Desert, the Arabian Desert on the Arabian Peninsula, and the desert Outback covering roughly one third of Australia.

Deltas are areas of lowlands formed by soil and sediment deposited at the mouths of rivers. The soil is generally very fertile and most fertile river deltas are important crop-growing areas. One well-known example is the delta of Egypt's Nile River, known for its production of cotton.

Mesas are the flat tops of hills or mountains usually with steep sides. Sometimes plateaus are also called mesas. Basins are considered to be low areas drained by rivers or low spots in mountains. Foothills are generally considered a low series of hills found between a plain and a mountain range. Marshes and swamps are wet lowlands providing growth of such plants as rushes and reeds.

Oceans are the largest bodies of water on the planet. The four oceans of the earth are the **Atlantic Ocean**, one-half the size of the Pacific and separating North and South America from Africa and Europe; the **Pacific Ocean**, covering almost one-third of the entire surface of the earth and separating North and South America from Asia and Australia; the **Indian Ocean**, touching Africa, Asia, and Australia; and the ice-filled **Arctic Ocean,** extending from North America and Europe to the North Pole. The waters of the Atlantic, Pacific, and Indian Oceans also touch the shores of Antarctica.

Seas are smaller than oceans and are surrounded by land. Some examples include the Mediterranean Sea found between Europe, Asia, and Africa; and the Caribbean Sea, touching the West Indies, South and Central America. A lake is a body of water surrounded by land. The Great Lakes in North America are a good example.

Rivers, considered a nation's lifeblood, usually begin as very small streams, formed by melting snow and rainfall, flowing from higher to lower land, emptying into a larger body of water, usually a sea or an ocean. Examples of important rivers for the people and countries affected by and/or dependent on them include the Nile, Niger, and Zaire Rivers of Africa; the Rhine, Danube, and Thames Rivers of Europe; the Yangtze, Ganges, Mekong, Hwang He, and Irrawaddy Rivers of Asia; the Murray-Darling in Australia; and the Orinoco in South America. River systems are made up of large rivers and numerous smaller rivers or tributaries flowing into them. Examples include the vast Amazon Rivers system in South America and the Mississippi River system in the United States.

Canals are man-made water passages constructed to connect two larger bodies of water. Famous examples include the **Panama Canal** across Panama's isthmus connecting the Atlantic and Pacific Oceans and the **Suez Canal** in the Middle East between Africa and the Arabian peninsula connecting the Red and Mediterranean Seas.

Skill 11.2: Analyze ways in which geological and hydrological processes have caused changes in the earth's physical features over time.

The processes that change the surface of the earth are of two kinds: those that wear down the surface (erosion), and those that build it up (deposition), and the chief agencies are the atmosphere, water, organic life, and internal changes in the earth's crust.

Atmospheric Effects. The processes by which rocks are broken up and formed into soil are collectively called **weathering**. The expansion of rocks by heating in the daytime and the contraction because of cooling at night, the opening of small cracks in the rocks through the freezing within them of water in cold weather, and the wear of rocks by waves, streams, and winds, cause them to break down gradually into ever finer particles. The mechanical reduction of solid rock to an aggregation of loose material is called disintegration, and the fragmental material produced by it is called *rock waste*. The chemical process by which rock is broken down is called *decomposition.*

The atmosphere contains, among other gases, oxygen, carbon dioxide, water vapor, and often a little sulfur dioxide. All of these are brought down to the surface by rain, and enter into combination with minerals in the rocks. Some minerals are rather easily dissolved, and thus the particles of other minerals are separated and loosened. The physical and chemical changes thus go hand in hand in causing the rocks to crumble, and the loose material resulting is easily carried away by rain and streams, as well as by the wind. This transportation of rock waste from one place to another, results in the lowering of the surface where the material is removed, and in the raising of the surface where the material is deposited. The processes of erosion, transportation, and deposition, known collectively as *gradation*, thus bring about marked changes in the form of the surface. Wind and rain play an important part in these processes

The atmosphere is constantly in motion and the air currents carry along more or less solid matter. An ordinary wind will move fine sand, and a strong wind will move gravel; hence winds are constantly changing some portions of the earth's surface. Such changes are most striking in sandy regions, especially on beaches and in desert lands, where the surface is very dry.

The air also helps to modify the surface of the earth through the agency of rainfall. Rills formed by the running together of numerous raindrops carve gullies and ravines in places where the land is soft. Soil is also moved down slopes by rain wash. Rain is also the source of the water of springs and streams, whose erosive effects are part of the work of the hydrosphere.

The *hydrosphere* includes both the running and the standing water on the earth's surface, whether in the oceans and seas, or in springs, rivers, lakes, and swamps. All of these are important geologic agencies. Ocean waves wear away the shore and spread the detritus over the sea floor, or cast it up to form beaches. In many places, they hollow out caves in the rocks or cut the rocks into curious forms. Ocean currents move so gently that they do not affect the form of the coast except along stretches of sandy shore, but they exert a great influence on climate, including rainfall, and so indirectly cause changes on the land. Similar processes are going on along the shores of lakes, though not as a rule so vigorously as on the seacoast.

Streams carry on much the same activity as the rills formed by raindrops. The cutting action of a stream may form a wide valley with gentle slopes, or a deep canyon with precipitous sides. The constructive work of streams, in the formation of flood plains and deltas, which are built from the sediment transported by the water, is as striking.

The part of the rain that sinks into the earth is called *ground water.* The quantity of ground water in a locality is dependent on the rainfall, the topography, and the underground conditions. It percolates downward into the rocks and fills the crevices and pore spaces in them up to a variable level, called the *water table*, which falls in a dry season and rises in a wet season. Wells, springs, geysers, and subterranean streams derive their supply from ground water. In percolating through the rocks, ground water dissolves some fo the minerals and thus enlarges the crevices. In soluble rocks, such as limestone, great caverns are sometimes formed. The dissolved mineral matter in the water of wells and springs is derived in this way. Most of it is eventually carried to the oceans by rivers, and thus the salinity of the ocean is slowly increased.

In the colder parts of the world, much of the breaking down of the solid rocks is due to the expansion resulting from the freezing of water in the crevices of rocks. Again, the alternate freezing and thawing of water in the soil loosens boulders and causes landslides and other movements of rock masses.

Ice contracts at temperatures below the freezing point, and the alternate expansion and contraction of a large mass of ice, such as that which forms over the surface of a lake, produces marked effects. When it first freezes, the ice exactly covers the lake surface, but a fall of temperature causes cracks to form because the contracting ice breaks apart. Water from beneath fills these crevices and freezes, and again there is an unbroken surface. When the temperature rises, the ice expands, and in overriding the shore it may shove up ridges of earth and stones. The rock walls on the shores of many lakes are the results of such a process. Also, the anchor-ice that forms along the banks of streams holds in its grip large masses of earth and rock that carried away when the ice breaks up in the spring, may be deposited farther downstream.

Plants and Animals. Since life first developed, plants and animals have been contributing to the processes of geologic change. They, too, use both mechanical and chemical methods. During life, plants decompose the carbon dioxide of the air; after they die, the carbon that they have stored in their tissues is added to the soil as they decay, being eventually changed again, by oxidation, into carbon dioxide. This and other compounds of organic origin help to decompose rocks and to form soil. Living plants split rocks mechanically by the growth of their roots and stems that have penetrated crevices in the rocks. Swamps, marshes, and peat bogs are examples of the effects of plant life under particular conditions. They are formed in shallow-water areas by plants that grow so profusely that natural drainage is checked. Peat represents the partial decay of vegetation in a marshy area.

Animals that live in the ground assist the process of erosion by burrowing into the soil. Humans change topography on a large scale by digging canals, leveling hills, tunneling through mountains, cultivating soil, draining swamps, constructing reservoirs, etc. Another outstanding example of the work of animal organisms is the building of coral reefs and islands. These are composed of the limy shells of small marine animals.

There are some earth movements that occur suddenly had have effects easily recorded. Earthquakes are frequent enough over the world to be commonplace, though violent quakes in thickly settled areas appal us because of the destruction wrought by them. Earthquakes are tremors in the earth's crust, caused by faulting or readjustments of rock masses.

A volcano is another geological agent whose effects are easily seen. In times past, eruptions giving rise to great lava flows have built up plateaus. Lines of volcanic cones have been formed by the partial closing of fissures through which lava has escaped.

The theory of **continental drift** was first introduced by Alfred Wegener in 1912 to explain the movement of the continents in relation to each other. It has long been noted that the shapes of the continents on either side of the Atlantic Ocean appeared to fit together. A number of geologists had speculated that all the continents had once been joined together in a single "supercontinent." Wegener first formally published the theory that the continents had "drifted apart." He was not able to substantiate a convincing explanation of how this drift occurred or of what caused it. The theory did not achieve broad acceptance until the 1960s. It later became part of the larger theory of plate tectonics.

Plate tectonics is a geological theory that attempts to explain large-scale motions within the Earth's crust. It is based on an understanding of "sea floor spreading" that was developed in the 1960s. According to this theory, the outer part of the Earth's interior is composed of two layers: crust and the rigid part of the mantle. Below this is the *asthenosphere* which essentially allows the *lithosphere* (crust and mantle) to "float". The lithosphere is believed to have broken up into plates (10 major and 10 minor). The plates move in relation to each other at the plate boundaries. The plate boundaries are where earthquakes, volcanoes, mountain-building, and ocean trench development occur.

Skill 11.3: Identify characteristics of major climate regions and examine the effect of climate on human settlement and activity

Weather is the condition of the air which surrounds the day-to-day atmospheric conditions including temperature, air pressure, wind and moisture or precipitation which includes rain, snow, hail, or sleet.

Climate is average weather or daily weather conditions for a specific region or location over a long or extended period of time. Studying the climate of an area includes information gathered on the area's monthly and yearly temperatures and its monthly and yearly amounts of precipitation. In addition, a characteristic of an area's climate is the length of its growing season. Four reasons for the different climate regions on the earth are differences in:

(1) Latitude,
(2) The amount of moisture,
(3) Temperatures in land and water, and
(4) The earth's land surface.

There are many different climates throughout the earth. It is most unusual if a country contains just one kind of climate. Regions of climates are divided according to latitudes:

0 - 23 1 /2 degrees are the "low latitudes"
23 1/2 - 66 1/2 degrees are the "middle latitudes"
66 1/2 degrees to the Poles are the "high latitudes"

The **low latitudes** are comprised of the rainforest, savanna, and desert climates. The tropical rainforest climate is found in equatorial lowlands and is hot and wet. There is sun, extreme heat and rain--everyday. Although daily temperatures rarely rise above 90 degrees F, the daily humidity is always high, leaving everything sticky and damp. North and south of the tropical rainforests are the tropical grasslands called "savannas," the "lands of two seasons"--a winter dry season and a summer wet season. Further north and south of the tropical grasslands or savannas are the deserts. These areas are the hottest and driest parts of the earth receiving less than 10 inches of rain a year.

These areas have extreme temperatures between night and day. After the sun sets, the land cools quickly dropping the temperature as much as 50 degrees F.

The **middle latitudes** contain the Mediterranean, humid-subtropical, humid-continental, marine, steppe, and desert climates. Lands containing the Mediterranean climate are considered "sunny" lands found in six areas of the world: lands bordering the Mediterranean Sea, a small portion of southwestern Africa, areas in southern and southwestern Australia, a small part of the Ukraine near the Black Sea, central Chile, and Southern California. Summers are hot and dry with mild winters. The growing season usually lasts all year and what little rain falls are during the winter months. What is rather unusual is that the Mediterranean climate is located between 30 and 40 degrees north and south latitude on the western coasts of countries.

The humid **subtropical climate** is found north and south of the tropics and is moist indeed. The areas having this type of climate are found on the eastern side of their continents and include Japan, mainland China, Australia, Africa, South America, and the United States--the southeastern coasts of these areas. An interesting feature of their locations is that warm ocean currents are found there. The winds that blow across these currents bring in warm moist air all year round. Long, warm summers; short, mild winters; a long growing season allow for different crops to be grown several times a year. All contribute to the productivity of this climate type which supports more people than any of the other climates.

The **marine climate** is found in Western Europe, the British Isles, the U.S. Pacific Northwest, the western coast of Canada and southern Chile, along with southern New Zealand and southeastern Australia. A common characteristic of these lands is that they are either near water or surrounded by it. The ocean winds are wet and warm bringing a mild, rainy climate to these areas. In the summer, the daily temperatures average at or below 70 degrees F. During the winter, because of the warming effect of the ocean waters, the temperatures rarely fall below freezing.

In northern and central United States, northern China, south central and southeastern Canada, and the western and southeastern parts of the former Soviet Union is found the **"climate of four seasons,"** the **humid continental climate--spring,** summer, fall, and winter. Cold winters, hot summers, and enough rainfall to grow a variety of crops are the major characteristics of this climate. In areas where the humid continental climate is found are some of the world's best farmlands as well as important activities such as trading and mining. Differences in temperatures throughout the year are determined by the distance a place is inland, away from the coasts.

The **steppe or prairie climate** is located in the interiors of large continents like Asia and North America. These dry flatlands are far from ocean breezes and are called prairies or the Great Plains in Canada and the United States and steppes in Asia. Although the summers are hot and the winters are cold as in the humid continental climate, the big difference is rainfall. In the steppe climate, rainfall is light and uncertain, 10 to 20 inches a year mainly in spring and summer and is considered normal. Where rain is more plentiful, grass grows; in areas of less, the steppes or prairies gradually become deserts.

These are found in the Gobi Desert of Asia, central and western Australia, southwestern United States, and in the smaller deserts found in Pakistan, Argentina, and Africa south of the Equator.

The two major climates found in the high latitudes are **"tundra" and "taiga."** The word "tundra" meaning "marshy plain" is a Russian word and aptly describes the climatic conditions in the northern areas of Russia, Europe, and Canada. Winters are extremely cold and very long. Most of the year the ground is frozen but becomes rather mushy during the very short summer months. Surprisingly less snow falls in the area of the tundra than in the eastern part of the United States. However, due to the harshness of the extreme cold, very few people live there and no crops can be raised. Despite having a small human population, many plants and animals are found there.

The **"taiga"** is the northern forest region and is located south of the tundra. In fact, the Russian word "taiga" means 'forest." The world's largest forestlands are found here along with vast mineral wealth and forbearing animals. The climate is extreme that very few people live here, not being able to raise crops due to the extremely short growing season. The winter temperatures are colder and the summer temperatures are hotter than those in the tundra are because the taiga climate region is farther from the waters of the Arctic Ocean. The taiga is found in the northern parts of Russia, Sweden, Norway, Finland, Canada, and Alaska with most of their lands covered with marshes and swamps.

In certain areas of the earth there exists a type of climate unique to areas with high mountains, usually different from their surroundings. This type of climate is called a **"vertical climate"** because the temperatures, crops, vegetation, and human activities change and become different as one ascends the different levels of elevation. At the foot of the mountain, a hot and rainy climate is found with the cultivation of many lowland crops. As one climbs higher, the air becomes **cooler,** the climate changes sharply and different economic activities change, such as grazing sheep and growing corn. At the top of many mountains, snow is found year round.

Skill 11.4: Analyze relationships among various regional and global patterns of geographic phenomena.

See Skills 11.1 and 11.4

COMPETENCY 12: Understand major physical and cultural regions of the world, analyze geographic relationships within and between regions, and recognize the diverse perspectives of different human groups and cultures.

Skill 12.1: Recognize major cultural groups associated with particular regions.

Social scientists use the term **culture** to describe the way of life of a group of people. This would include not only art, music, and literature but also beliefs, customs, languages, traditions, inventions--in short, any way of life whether complex or simple. The term **geography** is defined as the study of earth's features and living things as to their location, relationship with each other, how they came to be there, and why it is so important.

Physical geography is concerned with the locations of such earth features as climate, water, and land; how these relate to and affect each other and human activities; and what forces shaped and changed them. All three of these earth features affect the lives of all humans having a direct influence on what is made and produced, where it occurs, how it occurs, and what makes it possible. The combination of the different climate conditions and types of landforms and other surface features work together all around the earth to give the many varied cultures their unique characteristics and distinctions.

Cultural geography studies the location, characteristics, and influence of the physical environment on different cultures around the earth. Also included in these studies are comparisons and influences of the many varied cultures. Ease of travel and up-to-the-minute, state-of-the-art communication techniques ease the difficulties of understanding cultural differences making it easier to come in contact with them.

Skill 12.2: Examine how the interaction of ethnic, regional, and national cultures influences specific situations or events.

The Dutch settlers of the early colonial period introduced many goods to North America that profoundly affected the nature of the development of both the state and the nation. The trade of the Dutch West India Company provided the foundation for an economy based on trade and commerce.

As African Americans left the rural South and migrated to the North in search of opportunity, many settled in Harlem in New York City. By the 1920s Harlem had become a center of life and activity for persons of color. The music, art, and literature of this community gave birth to a cultural movement known as **the Harlem Renaissance**. The artistic expressions that emerged from this community in the 1920s and 1930s celebrated the black experience, black traditions, and the voices of black America.

Major writers and works of this movement include:

- Langston Hughes – *The Weary Blues*
- Nella Larsen – *Passing*
- Zora Neale Hurston – *Their Eyes Were Watching God*
- Claude McKay
- Countee Cullen
- Jean Toomer

Although Puerto Rico became a territory of the U.S. at the end of the Spanish American War, there was little immigration during the first half of the century. The transition from Spanish colony to U.S. possession was not easy for the people of Puerto Rico. Residents have been U.S. citizens since 1917, but they have no representation in the Congress. Technically, moving from the island to the U.S. mainland is considered internal migration rather than immigration. This does not, however, recognize that leaving an island with a distinct culture and identity involves the same cultural conflicts and intellectual, language and other adjustments as those faced by most immigrants. A severe economic depression created widespread poverty in the early part of the 20th century. Few Puerto Ricans were able to afford the fare to travel by boat to the mainland. In 1910, there were only about 2,000 Puerto Ricans living on the mainland; most created small enclaves in New York City. By 1945, there were 13,000 Puerto Ricans in New York City. But by 1946, there were more than 50,000. And for each of the next ten years, over 25,000 more would immigrate each year. By the mid-1960s, there were more than a million Puerto Ricans on the mainland.

The primary factors that account for the sudden migration are:

- Continuing economic depression in Puerto Rico,
- Recruitment for workers from Puerto Rico by U.S. factory owners and employment agencies,
- The return of thousands of war veterans to Puerto Rico who wanted more than the island could offer,
- Most important, however, was the sudden availability of air travel at an affordable cost.

Many of the immigrant Puerto Ricans established communities in major east coast cities and mid-Atlantic farming regions, and also in the mill towns of New England. A very large number of these immigrants settled in the northeastern part of Manhattan that came to be known as **Spanish Harlem**. They quickly became an important factor in the city's political and cultural life. Although the first generation of migrants faced prejudice, unemployment, discrimination, and poverty, most remained and learned to thrive.

Today, Puerto Rican immigrants and their descendants have developed several means of preserving and teaching their heritage. Their communities are strong and integrated into the mainstream of the society. They have contributed to the growth of the nation and the inclusion within every area of American life from politics to education to sports and the arts.

See Competency 9 for New Mexico specific information.

Skill 12.3: Demonstrate knowledge of the development and interrelationship of belief systems in different regions of the world

Belief systems, like other cultural elements or institutions, spread through human interaction. It is thus natural that religions and belief systems may have regional or cultural markers that are transmitted across regions. Religions and belief systems general originate in a particular region, with elements that are culturally or regionally defined or influenced. As belief systems are introduced to new groups or societies, some of those regional and cultural markers will also penetrate the new society. By the same token, as interaction between the originating society and the new society continues and the belief system finds new expression, some regional or cultural elements introduced by the new society will be carried back to the originating culture.

Belief systems are introduced to new societies in a variety of ways. One method is military and political conquest. As the originating society conquers a new territory and incorporates it into the political entity, belief systems are frequently either peaceably spread to the conquered people or forced upon them in the name of cultural unity. This has occurred frequently in human history. The rise and spread of the Islamic Empire both converted and forced the conversion of conquered peoples to Islam. Another example may be seen in the conversion of the Emperor Constantine to Christianity and his imposition of Christianity upon Rome as the national religion.

Belief systems are also introduced through other types of human interaction. This occurs through commercial interaction, the identification of common or similar primitive mythologies (for example, similar creation and great flood myths). Educational interaction and cultural sharing between cultures also frequently carries religious belief systems, as well.

Skill 12.4: Identify economic, environmental, and cultural factors contributing to demographic change and analyze geographic relationships such as population density and spatial distribution patterns

Physical locations of the earth's surface features include the four major hemispheres and the parts of the earth's continents in them. Political locations are the political divisions, if any, within each continent. Both physical and political locations are precisely determined in two ways: (1) Surveying is done to determine boundary lines and distance from other features. (2) Exact locations are precisely determined by imaginary lines of latitude (parallels) and longitude (meridians). The intersection of these lines at right angles forms a grid, making it impossible to pinpoint an exact location of any place using any two grip coordinates.

The **Eastern Hemisphere**, located between the North and South Poles and between the Prime Meridian (0 degrees longitude) east to the International Date Line at 180 degrees longitude, consists of most of Europe, all of Australia, most of Africa, and all of Asia, except for a tiny piece of the easternmost part of Russia that extends east of 180 degrees longitude.

The Western Hemisphere, located between the North and South Poles and between the Prime Meridian (0 degrees longitude) west to the International Date Line at 180 degrees longitude, consists of all of North and South America, a tiny part of the easternmost part of Russia that extends east of 180 degrees longitude, and a part of Europe that extends west of the Prime Meridian (0 degrees longitude).

The **Northern Hemisphere**, located between the North Pole and the Equator, contains all of the continents of Europe and North America and parts of South America, Africa, and most of Asia.

The **Southern Hemisphere**, located between the South Pole and the Equator, contains all of Australia, a small part of Asia, about one-third of Africa, most of South America, and all of Antarctica.

Of the seven continents, only one contains just one entire country and is the only island continent, Australia. Its political divisions consist of six states and one territory: Western Australia, South Australia, Tasmania, Victoria, New South Wales, Queensland, and Northern Territory.

Africa is made up of 54 separate countries, the major ones being Egypt, Nigeria, South Africa, Zaire, Kenya, Algeria, Morocco, and the large island of Madagascar.

Asia consists of 49 separate countries, some of which include China, Japan, India, Turkey, Israel, Iraq, Iran, Indonesia, Jordan, Vietnam, Thailand, and the Philippines.

Europe's 43 separate nations include France, Russia, Malta, Denmark, Hungary, Greece, Bosnia and Herzegovina.

North America consists of Canada and the United States of America and the island nations of the West Indies and the "land bridge" of Middle America, including Cuba, Jamaica, Mexico, Panama, and others.

Thirteen separate nations together occupy the continent of South America, among them such nations as Brazil, Paraguay, Ecuador, and Suriname.

The continent of Antarctica has no political boundaries or divisions but is the location of a number of science and research stations managed by nations such as Russia, Japan, France, Australia, and India.

Social scientists use the term culture to describe the way of life of a group of people. This would include not only art, music, and literature but also beliefs, customs, languages, traditions, inventions--in short, any way of life whether complex or simple. The term geography is defined as the study of earth's features and living things as to their location, relationship with each other, how they came to be there, and why so important.

Physical geography is concerned with the locations of such earth features as climate, water, and land; how these relate to and affect each other and human activities; and what forces shaped and changed them. All three of these earth features affect the lives of all humans having a direct influence on what is made and produced, where it occurs, how it occurs, and what makes it possible. The combination of the different climate conditions and types of landforms and other surface features work together all around the earth to give the many varied cultures their unique characteristics and distinctions.

Cultural geography studies the location, characteristics, and influence of the physical environment on different cultures around the earth. Also included in these studies are comparisons and influences of the many varied cultures. Ease of travel and up-to-the-minute, state-of-the-art communication techniques ease the difficulties of understanding cultural differences making it easier to come in contact with them

Skill 12.5: Analyze the effect of physical and cultural factors on settlement patterns, land use decisions, ecosystem changes, and the transmission of customs and ideas.

Land use is the function of the land – what use is made of it. Land use and development models are theories that attempt to explain the layout of urban areas, primarily in "more economically developed countries" or in "less economically developed countries".

Two primary land use models are generally applied to urban regions. These are: (1) The Burgess model (also called the concentric model), in which cities are seen to develop in a series of concentric circles with the central business district at the center, ringed by the factories and industrial usage area, ringed by the low class residential area, then the middle class residential area, and finally the high class residential area (often suburbs); and (2) The Hoyt model (also called the Sector Model), in which the central business district occupies a central area of a circle, with factories and industry occupying an elongated area that abuts the city center, and with the low class residential area surrounding the industrial area, and the middle class residential area forming a semi-circle toward the other side of the city center, and a small upper class residential sector extending from the city center out through the middle of the middle-class residential area.

In rural areas, land use will probably include agriculture, forestry, and possibly fishing. The Von Thunen Model observes a city as the center of a state or region, from which a series of concentric circles emanates, each devoted to particular rural land usage patterns: the first ring from the city would be devoted to dairy farming and intensive farming, which allows produce to reach the market quickly. The second zone would focus on timber and firewood for fuel and building materials, which, because of its weight, needs to be relatively close to the city. The third zone would be dedicated to extensive field crops such as grains. The fourth zone would be dedicated to ranching and/or animal husbandry. Beyond this unoccupied wilderness would remain.

The purpose and aim of social policy is to improve human welfare and to meet basic human needs within the society. Social policy addresses basic human needs for the sustainability of the individual and the society. The concerns of social policy, then, include food, clean water, shelter, clothing, education, health, and social security. Social policy is part of public policy, determined by the city, the state, the nation, or the multi-national organization responsible for human welfare in a particular region.

Environmental policy is concerned with the sustainability of the earth, the region under the administration of the governing group or individual or a local habitat. The concern of environmental policy is the preservation of the region, habitat or ecosystem.

Because humans, both individually and in community, rely upon the environment to sustain human life, social and environmental policy must be mutually supportable. Because humans, both individually and in community, live upon the earth, draw upon the natural resources of the earth, and affect the environment in many ways, environmental and social policy must be mutually supportive.

If modern societies have no understanding of the limitations upon natural resources or how their actions affect the environment, and they act without regard for the sustainability of the earth, it will become impossible for the earth to sustain human existence. At the same time, the resources of the earth are necessary to support the human welfare. Environmental policies must recognize that the planet is the home of humans and other species.

For centuries, social policies, economic policies, and political policies have ignored the impact of human existence and human civilization upon the environment. Human civilization has disrupted the ecological balance, contributed to the extinction of animal and plant species, and destroyed ecosystems through uncontrolled harvesting.

In an age of global warming, unprecedented demand upon natural resources, and a shrinking planet, social and environmental policies must become increasingly interdependent if the planet is to continue to support life and human civilization.

COMPETENCY 13: Understand major physical and cultural regions of New Mexico and the United States and analyze geographic relationships within and between regions.

Skill 13.1: Recognize basic physical characteristics of the United States and New Mexico

The United States of America stretches from the Atlantic to the Pacific Oceans and from the contiguous border of Canada to the Rio Grande River dividing the US and Mexico.

Mountains are landforms with rather steep slopes at least 2,000 feet or more above sea level. Mountains are found in groups called mountain chains or mountain ranges. The United States has the Appalachian and Rocky Mountains.

Plains are described as areas of flat or slightly rolling land, usually lower than the landforms next to them. Sometimes called lowlands (and sometimes located along **seacoasts)** they support the majority of the world's people. Some are found inland and many have been formed by large rivers. This resulted in extremely fertile soil for successful cultivation of crops and numerous large settlements of people. In North America, the vast plains areas extend from the Gulf of Mexico north to the Arctic Ocean and between the Appalachian and Rocky Mountains.

Valleys are land areas found between hills and mountains. Some have gentle slopes containing trees and plants; others have steep walls and are referred to as canyons. One example is Arizona's Grand Canyon of the Colorado River.

Oceans are the largest bodies of water on the planet. The four oceans of the earth are the **Atlantic Ocean**, one-half the size of the Pacific and separating North and South America from Africa and Europe; the **Pacific Ocean**, covering almost one-third of the entire surface of the earth and separating North and South America from Asia and Australia; the **Indian Ocean**, touching Africa, Asia, and Australia; and the ice-filled **Arctic Ocean,** extending from North America and Europe to the North Pole. The waters of the Atlantic, Pacific, and Indian Oceans also touch the shores of Antarctica.

Rivers, considered a nation's lifeblood, usually begin as very small streams, formed by melting snow and rainfall, flowing from higher to lower land, emptying into a larger body of water, usually a sea or an ocean. River systems are made up of large rivers and numerous smaller rivers or tributaries flowing into them. The Mississippi River system in the United States is an example.

Deltas are areas of lowlands formed by soil and sediment deposited at the mouths of rivers. The soil is generally very fertile and most fertile river deltas are important crop-growing areas. One example is the delta of the Mississippi River in the Gulf of Mexico.

The United States has abundant natural resources. Even with a population that now tops 300 million the possibility for coaxing more natural resources from the land and the waters is good. It is not inexhaustible, however.

Some regions of the U.S. are known for certain things. Oil can be found in great numbers in Texas, Oklahoma, Alaska, and a handful of other states. Most of these states make oil drilling and production a big business, with output reaching staggering numbers in some cases. The oil is used to power machinery and transportation devices the world over. The ideal is to achieve a balance between wringing as much oil out of the land as possible while also preserving the land the oil is found under. This balance is not always achieved; in some cases, it is never achieved or even attempted.

Another natural resource in abundance in the U.S. is natural gas. This resource is found in Texas, Oklahoma, Wyoming, Utah, Colorado, Louisiana, Arkansas, Michigan, North Carolina, Pennsylvania, and New York. Concentrations of natural gas can be found in other states as well. This resource is transported through pipes into homes and other buildings in order to provide energy for people and businesses. Like oil, natural gas comes from deep within the ground. It is both easy and difficult to get it out of the ground. Some deposits are easier to get at than others, and some methods of extraction are simpler and more cost-effective than others. Natural gas is more "natural" in nature than oil and can be used for things that oil can and cannot: For example, natural gas now powers buses, trains, some cars, and other transportation devices. You wouldn't necessarily find powering a family's kitchen stove, however.

Coal is another natural resource found in great amounts in the U.S., whose people use it for energy. Coal can be found in 38 of the 50 U.S. states. Among the top coal-producing states are Montana, Illinois, Wyoming, West Virginia, Kentucky, Pennsylvania, Ohio, Colorado, Texas, and Indiana. A full 24 percent of the world's recoverable reserves of coal can be found within the borders of the United States. Coal can be found on the surface or underground. Both methods have their associated costs and risks, including harmful effects on the land left behind and air around the requisite coal mines.

A host of other minerals are to be found and mined in the U.S. Among them are chromium, copper, gypsum, iron oxide, phosphate, salt, selenium, silica, silicon, silver, sulfur, tin, tungsten, and zinc. In every case, these minerals are found to varying degrees in certain parts of the country. The way they are extracted from the earth varies according to the type of mineral being extracted; some are easier to extract than others, and the mining of some leaves behind horrible scars, from which the land does not easily recover.

In nearly every case, the supply of such natural resources was discovered and taken advantage of, to the tune of human settlement nearby. Oil wells and oil fields have oil workers living nearby. Coal mines have coal miners living nearby. This is in addition to the processing facilities needed to extract those resources. Such development and land use are likely here to stay, since the populations will likely not move away once the resource supply is exhausted. In this way, the processing of natural resources has changed the land forever.

The **Rio Grande River**, which essentially bisects the state, has supported agriculture and agrarian communities throughout New Mexico's history. The Elephant Butte Dam on the Rio Grande provides irrigation for farming. Other areas that support agriculture are the Colorado River basin and the Pecos and San Juan River regions.

The federal government protects millions of acres of national forest. The mountainous regions, in particular, have supported mining industries, notably turquoise and silver, as well as several minerals.

The landscape includes rose-colored deserts, snow-capped mountain peaks, and huge mesas. The plains have supported ranching, both cattle and sheep. These plains are covered with cactus, yucca, creosote bush, sagebrush and several desert grasses.

The geography and topography have supported a significant economy. Cattle, dairy products, sheep and other livestock are supported by the plains regions. Dryland farming produces nursery stock, hay, pecans and chili peppers, as well as onions and potatoes. The forests support an active lumber business. Mining produces uranium ore, manganese, potash, salt, perlite, copper ore, beryllium and tin, as well as natural gas, petroleum and coal. The natural beauty of the state and the presence of numerous historic and Native American communities support a thriving tourism industry.

Skill 13.2: Identify basic features of state and national resource bases and analyze geological, climatic, and biological factors that have determined the location of major state and national resources.

Refer to Skill 13.1.

Skill 13.3: Examine basic types of land use and development in New Mexico and the United States

Far and way the largest factor influencing land use is population and the growth thereof. A burgeoning population demands a lot from the land it surrounds and eventually incorporates, for food, living, and industrial use. The more people who want to live in a certain area, the more the land in that area will have to be transformed to meet that population need. In some cases, the land is simply appropriated. Naturally aerated land is perfect for farms and ranches, with an abundance of water and natural food for the crops and animals; in other cases however, the land is transformed—agricultural land becoming industrial land, for example, or farmland being plowed over in favor of living space. In all cases, the land is being used to support the population, which is growing and expanding its needs and demands, at the expense of the land.

Geography is another influence on land use, sometimes as a limiter and sometimes as an invitation. Highly inhospitable lands are usually not all that populated because of the inherently harsh living conditions. We just don't see cities of thousands of people built into the sides of the world's tallest mountains. (The population situation is not that desperate yet; perhaps, in the future, such cities will exist out of necessity.) In the same way a settlement in the middle of a desert will most likely becoming a growing concern (unless, of course, it is Las Vegas, which is a main exception to this rule). Geography doesn't always have to be a limiter, however. Fertile land that is excellent for farming will, in most cases, be being put to good agricultural use. Land that lends itself to good fortification will, naturally, be inhabited by people looking to defend themselves from invasion and other forms of outside influence. In even more simple terms, the very presence of a large body of water will routinely result in the human use of that water in some way, as a source of drinking water for people and animals or as a source of nourishment for crops. Rare indeed is the body of water that has not been appropriated in some form or fashion by human hands.

Geography can also form natural boundaries for settlements and civilizations. Mountain ranges and large bodies of water make effective borders between states and countries. If a civilization that has a mountain range or a river or ocean as a boundary wants to grow, it might be forced to grow upward rather than outward, at least in those locations bordered by these landforms or bodies of water.

Prime examples of this are New York City and San Francisco, both of which have limited land on which to build but which use that land to the fullest by building tall skyscrapers that house myriad people and businesses.

In all of these things, necessity is the most basic thing driving land use. Growing populations *need* more land, and geographically challenged civilizations *need* to get creative in using their land.

Land-use patterns vary substantially by region. Factors that influence the use of land include difference in climate, soil make-up, topography and population dispersal. There are several different types of land use:

Cropland – Makes up 20% of US land use. This category includes land that is actively being used to grow crops as well as idle cropland. Cropland is roughly concentrated in the central regions of the contiguous United States. Cropland is the majority of land-use in the Northern Plain and the Corn Belt and the Southern Plains, Lake States, and Delta States also having cropland shares above the national average.

Grassland Pasture and Range – Makes up 26% of US land use. This category includes land used for grazing livestock, ranching and animal husbandry. Lower levels of precipitation make land in the West more suitable for grazing. The Mountain region and Southern Plains also have a majority of land in this land-use type. The Northern Plains and the Pacific region also have relative large amounts of grazing land.

Forestland – Makes up 29% of US land use. Land used to grow timber for building and fuel. This type of land-use is most prevalent in the Eastern regions such as the Northeast, Appalachian, Southeast, and Delta States. The Lake States and the Pacific region also have a large share of forest-use land because the topography and climate of these regions are conductive to growing trees.

Urban uses – 3% of land use. The Northeast and Southeast have the highest percentage of urban-use land.

Special Uses – 13% of US land use. Special uses encompasses land used for national and state parks, roads and recreational areas.

Miscellaneous Uses – 10% of US land use. This is most of other types of land including swamps, tundras, bare rock areas, marshes, etc.

Land use and development models are theories that attempt to explain the layout of urban areas, primarily in “more economically developed countries” or in “less economically developed countries”.

Two primary land use models are generally applied to urban regions. These are: (1) The Burgess model (also called the concentric model), in which cities are seen to develop in a series of concentric circles with the central business district at the center, ringed by the factories and industrial usage area, ringed by the low class residential area, then the middle class residential area, and finally the high class residential area (often suburbs); and (2) The Hoyt model (also called the Sector Model), in which the central business district occupies a central area of a circle, with factories and industry occupying an elongated area that abuts the city center, and with the low class residential area surrounding the industrial area, and the middle class residential area forming a semi-circle toward the other side of the city center, and a small upper class residential sector extending from the city center out through the middle of the middle-class residential area.

In rural areas, land use will probably include agriculture, forestry, and possibly fishing. The Von Thunen Model observes a city as the center of a state or region, from which a series of concentric circles emanates, each devoted to particular rural land usage patterns: the first ring from the city would be devoted to dairy farming and intensive farming, which allows produce to reach the market quickly. The second zone would focus on forestland, which, because of its weight, needs to be relatively close to the city. The third zone would be dedicated to extensive field cropland.
The fourth zone would be dedicated to grassland. Beyond this miscellaneous land would exist.

Skill 13.4: Recognize patterns of urban/rural settlement in New Mexico and the United States and examine the effect of different patterns of urban/rural settlement on the environment

The United States has always been a destination for people from other countries looking to improve their lot. Through most of its history, the majority of newcomers to the US were whites from Europe, particularly in the period between 1890 and 1930, when there was a comparatively liberal immigration policy. Before the Civil War, African slaves who had been brought to the US were primarily in the southern states. Following emancipation, many blacks moved to urban areas where employment was more easily found.

Beginning around 1980, a shift in the nationality of new immigrants began, with an increase in the number of immigrants from Asian and Latin American countries. Political unrest and economic downturns led to surges in immigrants from troubled countries such as the Dominican Republic and Cambodia. The disparity between the US and Mexican economies created a situation where laborers from Mexico could find ample work in America.

Initially, the increase in Latin American and Asian immigration affected the few traditional "gateway" states such as New York, Florida, Texas and California. In the decades since, immigration has moved increasingly into interior areas of the US such as the midwestern states of Iowa and Nebraska, where agricultural and meatpacking industries provide a source of employment for immigrant labor. This movement of immigrants from the border states has had the effect of spreading ethnic and cultural diversity into small, previously homogenous towns, making a permanent impact on American culture.

See Competency 9 and related topics on New Mexico.

Skill 13.5: Analyze cross-cultural exchanges and the efforts of various groups to maintain their cultural identities

Cultural identity is the identification of individuals or groups as they are influenced by their belonging to a particular group or culture. This refers to the sense of whom one is, what values are important, and what racial or ethnic characteristics are important in one's self-understanding and manner of interacting with the world and with others. In a nation with a well-deserved reputation as a "melting pot" the attachment to cultural identities can become a divisive factor in communities and societies. Cosmopolitanism, its alternative, tends to blur those cultural differences in the creation of a shared new culture.

Throughout the history of the nation, groups have defined themselves and/or assimilated into the larger population to varying degrees. In order for a society to function as a cohesive and unifying force, there must be some degree of enculturation of all groups. The alternative is a competing, and often conflicting, collection of sub-groups that are not able to cohere into a society. This failure to assimilate will often result in culture wars as values and lifestyles come into conflict.

Cross-cultural exchanges, however, can enrich every involved group of persons with the discovery of shared values and needs, as well as an appreciation for unique cultural characteristics of each. For the most part, the history of the nation has been the story of successful enculturation and cultural enrichment. The notable failures, often resulting from one sort of prejudice and intolerance or another, are well known. For example, cultural biases have led to the oppression of the Irish or the Chinese immigrants in various parts of the country. Racial biases have led to various kinds of disenfranchisement and oppression of other groups of immigrants. Perhaps most notably, the bias of the European settlers against the civilization and culture of the Native peoples of North America has caused mass extermination, relocation, and isolation.

COMPETENCY 14: Understand the relationship between geography and history and analyze the effects of human activity on the environment.

Skill 14.1: Examine ways in which historical developments and events have been influenced by geographic factors.

The earliest known civilizations developed in the Tigris-Euphrates valley of Mesopotamia (modern Iraq) and the Nile valley of Egypt between 4000 BCE and 3000 BCE. Because these civilizations arose in river valleys, they are known as *fluvial civilizations*. Geography and the physical environment played a critical role in the rise and the survival of both of these civilizations.

The Fertile Crescent was bounded on the West by the Mediterranean, on the South by the Arabian Desert, on the north by the Taurus Mountains, and on the east by the Zagros Mountains.

First, the rivers provided a source of water that would sustain life, including animal life. The hunters of the society had ample access to a variety of animals, initially for hunting to provide food, as well as hides, bones, antlers, etc. from which clothing, tools and art could be made. Second the proximity to water provided a natural attraction to animals which could be herded and husbanded to provide a stable supply of food and animal products. Third, the rivers of these regions overflowed their banks each year, leaving behind a deposit of very rich soil. As these early people began to experiment with growing crops rather than gathering food, the soil was fertile and water was readily available to produce sizeable harvests. In time, the people developed systems of irrigation that channeled water to the crops without significant human effort on a continuing basis.

The designation "Fertile Crescent" was applied by the famous historian and Egyptologist James Breasted to the part of the Near East that extended from the Persian Gulf to the Sinai Peninsula. It included Mesopotamia, Syria and Palestine. This region was marked by almost constant invasions and migrations. These invaders and migrants seemed to have destroyed the culture and civilization that existed. Upon taking a longer view, however, it becomes apparent that they actually absorbed and supplemented the civilization that existed before their arrival. This is one of the reasons the civilization developed so quickly and created so such an advanced culture.

Skill 14.2: Analyze interactions between human beings and the physical environment.

Ecology is the study of how living organisms interact with the physical aspects of their surroundings (their environment), including soil, water, air, and other living things. **Biogeography** is the study of how the surface features of the earth – form, movement, and climate – affect living things.

Three levels of environmental understanding are critical:

1. An **ecosystem** is a community (of any size) consisting of a physical environment and the organisms that live within it.

2. A **biome** is a large area of land with characteristic climate, soil, and mixture of plants and animals. Biomes are made up of groups of ecosystems. Major biomes are: desert, chaparral, savanna, tropical rain forest, temperate grassland, temperate deciduous forest, taiga, and tundra.

3. A **habitat** is the set of surroundings within which members of a species normally live. Elements of the habitat include soil, water, predators, and competitors.

Within habitats interactions between members of the species occur. These interactions occur between members of the same species and between members of different species. Interaction tends to be of three types:

1. **Competition**. Competition occurs between members of the same species or between members of different species for resources required to continue life, to grow, or to reproduce. For example, competition for acorns can occur between squirrels or it can occur between squirrels and woodpeckers. One species can either push out or cause the demise of another species if it is better adapted to obtain the resource. When a new species is introduced into a habitat, the result can be a loss of the native species and/or significant change to the habitat. For example, the introduction of the Asian plant Kudzu into the American South, has resulted in the destruction of several species because Kudzu grows and spreads very quickly and smothers everything in its path.

2. **Predation**. Predators are organisms that live by hunting and eating other organisms. The species best suited for hunting other species in the habitat will be the species that survives. Larger species that have better hunting skills reduce the amount of prey available for smaller and/or weaker species. This affects both the amount of available prey and the diversity of species that are able to survive in the habitat.

3. **Symbiosis** is a condition in which two organisms of different species are able to live in the same environment over an extended period of time without harming one another. In some cases one species may benefit without harming the other. In other cases both species benefit.

Different organisms are by nature best suited for existence in particular environments. When an organism is displaced to a different environment or when the environment changes for some reason, its ability to survive is determined by its ability to *adapt* to the new environment. Adaptation can take the form of structural change, physiological change, or behavioral modification.

Biodiversity refers to the variety of species and organisms, as well as the variety of habitats available on the earth. Biodiversity provides the life-support system for the various habitats and species. The greater the degree of biodiversity, the more species and habitats will continue to survive.

When human and other population and migration changes, climate changes, or natural disasters disrupt the delicate balance of a habitat or an ecosystem, species either adapt or become extinct.

Natural changes can occur that alter habitats – floods, volcanoes, storms, earthquakes. These changes can affect the species that exist within the habitat, either by causing extinction or by changing the environment in a way that will no longer support the life systems. Climate changes can have similar effects. Inhabiting species, however, can also alter habitats, particularly through migration. Human civilization, population growth, and efforts to control the environment can have many negative effects on various habitats. Humans change their environments to suit their particular needs and interests. This can result in changes that result in the extinction of species or changes to the habitat itself. For example, deforestation damages the stability of mountain surfaces. One particularly devastating example is in the removal of the grasses of the Great Plains for agriculture. Tilling the ground and planting crops left the soil unprotected. Sustained drought dried out the soil into dust. When windstorms occurred, the topsoil was stripped away and blown all the way to the Atlantic Ocean.

Skill 14.3: Examine the impact of technological innovations on the physical environment and on human concepts of geography.

Natural resources are features of the earth's surface or substances that occur naturally and are considered to have value in their original form. Natural resources that are extracted, or purified become commodities. Thus, mining, oil extraction, fishing and forestry are generally considered natural resource industries.

Natural resources are classified into renewable and non-renewable resources. Renewable resources are living resources that can renew themselves if they are not over-harvested. These include fish, coffee, forests, etc. Non-living renewable natural resources include water, wind, soil, tides and solar radiation.

The natural resources of a nation often determine its economy and its wealth. This, in turn, contributes to the nation's political influence. A nation with significant resources in raw metallic ores, petroleum deposits, coal, etc. will develop an economy and a culture based, at least to some degree, on the extraction and refinement of those raw materials. Such natural resources as rain forests provide the raw materials for the development of medicines and other products.

Civilizations require supplies of water and food products. Agricultural communities will develop in regions with arable land that can produce crops for its own needs and for other regions. The ability to move water to high-demand areas and to harness the power of water and wind to provide energy is another use of natural resources.

Societies that support their economy by managing, harvesting, extracting, and utilizing natural resources develop cultural identities that reflect the means of subsistence. These societies and cultures will develop the means of sustaining and protecting both the resources and the ecosystems.

Since the dawn of agriculture, humans have modified their environment to suit their needs and to provide food and shelter. These changes always impact the environment, sometimes adversely from a human perspective.

Agriculture, for instance, often involves loosening topsoil by plowing before planting. This in turn affects how water and wind act on the soil, and can lead to erosion. In extreme cases, erosion can leave a plot of agricultural land unsuitable for use. Technological advances have led to a modern method of farming that relies less on plowing the soil before planting, but more on chemical fertilizers, pesticides and herbicides. These chemicals can find their way into groundwater, affecting the environment.

Cities are large examples of how technological change has allowed humans to modify their environment to suit their needs. At the end of the 18th Century, advances made in England in the construction of canals were brought to New York and an ambitious project to connect Lake Erie with the Hudson River by canal was planned. The Erie Canal was built through miles of virgin wilderness, opening natural areas to settlement and commerce. Towns along the canal grew and thrived, including Buffalo, Rochester and Albany. The canal also opened westward expansion beyond the borders of New York by opening a route between the Midwest and the East Coast.

Further advances in transportation and building methods allow for larger and denser communities, which themselves impact the environment in many ways. Concentrated consumption of fuels by automobiles and home heating systems affect the quality of the air in and around cities. The lack of exposed ground means that rainwater runs off of roads and rooftops into sewer systems instead of seeping into the ground, and often makes its way into nearby streams or rivers, carrying urban debris with it.

Skill 14.4: Evaluate the social and economic effects of environmental change and ecological crises.

The populations of both the United States and the world as a whole are growing. With growth in population comes an increase in demand for land use, of one form or another. Common land use needs include farming, living space, and industrial development.

Agriculture is a prime means of land use. Certain kinds of land are more amenable to certain kinds of crops. Nearby water is a primary concern as well. The larger a population, the more its people need to consume in terms of food and drink. With very few exceptions, a larger population has a greater demand for nourishment. Even with today's technological advancements, the amount of land that has to be devoted to agriculture in order to feed that country's and world's population is high and growing all the time. Meeting those needs is a monumental challenge for land use planners.

Living space is another prime means of land use. People have to live *somewhere*. The vast majority of people live in settlements of varying sizes, from collectives on up to megalopolises. The larger a population, the greater its housing needs. Especially in America, the desire to expand the amount of land needed for housing has created a much "wider" realm of living space land than has existed before. The coming of the automobile has enabled people to live far away from any sort of civilization, yet enjoy the fruits of that civilization by driving to town for food, water, and other necessities and/or provide their own necessities through various means.

Another common kind of land use is industrial development. The coming of the Industrial Revolution made it much easier to build and maintain factories to make things of all shapes and sizes at an accelerated rate. Factories produce household goods in addition to employing people. Other industries produce or process the food and water generated by agricultural land.

As a civilization expands, the amount of land it requires for its own use grows. A former desert area can suddenly become a very large city. Las Vegas is a perfect example of this. The city, one of the fastest-growing in the U.S., was created wholesale in one of the most inhospitable of places in the country. Yet it works because its infrastructure was created solidly from the beginning and, perhaps more importantly, because it has room to expand in size. Agricultural land or living space land that is transformed from "wild" land can be a source of food for a population; it can also be a source of concern for its population-watchers. Land that is transformed for human use at the expense of Nature can lead to problems down the line. A prime example of this is the building up of a human presence on a flood plain: People know the flood risks for waterways, yet they continue to build closer and closer to those waterways, especially agriculturally because the land is so fertile from the water but also for living space because it's flat land that doesn't have to be leveled in order to build on it. Another example of this is overgrazing that leads to desertification: More and more animals in one place create a demand for natural food that is higher than the natural supply, resulting in an elimination of that food supply and an increase in the aridity of the land, in some cases creating desert where none existed previously.

Needs also compete with one another for land. Agriculture land is being sold to housing developers all the time, with the result being that the people who move in to the homes built on that land have to go elsewhere for their food. Desertification can result from this as well, as people build homes on top of previously well-watered land and use all of that water for their living needs.

COMPETENCY 15: Understand the diverse and dynamic nature of culture.

Skill 15.1: Demonstrate knowledge of basic anthropological concepts.

ANTHROPOLOGY is the scientific study of human culture and humanity, the relationship between man and his culture. Anthropologists study different groups, how they relate to other cultures, and patterns of behavior, similarities and differences. Their research is two fold: cross-cultural and comparative. The major method of study is referred to as "participant observation." The anthropologist studies and learns about the people being studied by living among them and participating with them in their daily lives. Other methods may be used but this is the most characteristic method used.

Innovation is the introduction of new ways of performing work or organizing societies, and can spur drastic changes in a culture. Prior to the innovation of agriculture, for instance, human cultures were largely nomadic and survived by hunting and gathering their food. Agriculture led directly to the development of permanent settlements and a radical change in social organization. Likewise, technological innovations in the Industrial Revolution of the 19th Century changed the way work was performed and transformed the economic institutions of western cultures. Recent innovations in communications are changing the way cultures interact today.

Cultural diffusion is the movement of cultural ideas or materials between populations independent of the movement of those populations. Cultural diffusion can take place when two populations are close to one another, through direct interaction, or across great distances, through mass media and other routes. American movies are popular all over the world, for instance. Within the US, hockey, traditionally a Canadian pastime, has become a popular sport. These are both examples of cultural diffusion.

Adaptation is the process that individuals and societies go through in changing their behavior and organization to cope with social, economic and environmental pressures.

Acculturation is an exchange or adoption of cultural features when two cultures come into regular direct contact. An example of acculturation is the adoption of Christianity and western dress by many Native Americans in the United States.

Assimilation is the process of a minority ethnic group largely adopting the culture of the larger group it exists within. These groups are typically immigrants moving to a new country, as with the European immigrants who traveled to the United States at the beginning of the 20th Century who assimilated to American culture.

Extinction is the complete disappearance of a culture. Extinction can occur suddenly, from disease, famine or war when the people are completely destroyed, or slowly over time as a culture adapts, acculturates or assimilates to the point where its original features are lost.

ARCHAEOLOGY is the scientific study of past human cultures by studying the remains they left behind--objects such as pottery, bones, buildings, tools, and artwork. Archaeologists locate and examine any evidence to help explain the way people lived in past times. They use special equipment and techniques to gather the evidence and make special effort to keep detailed records of their findings because a lot of their research results in destruction of the remains being studied. The first step is to locate an archaeological site using various methods. Next, surveying the site takes place starting with a detailed description of the site with notes, maps, photographs, and collecting artifacts from the surface. Excavating follows either by digging for buried objects or by diving and working in submersible decompression chambers, when underwater. They record and preserve the evidence for eventual classification, dating, and evaluating their find.

PSYCHOLOGY involves scientifically studying behavior and mental processes. The ways people and animals relate to each other are observed and recorded. Psychologists scrutinize specific patterns, which will enable them to discern and predict certain behaviors, using scientific methods to verify their ideas. In this way they have been able to learn how to help people fulfill their individual human potential and strengthen understanding between individuals as well as groups and in nations and cultures. The results of the research of psychologists have deepened our understanding of the reasons for people's behavior.

Psychology is not only closely connected to the natural science of biology and the medical field of psychiatry but it is also connected to the social science areas of anthropology and sociology which have to do with people in society. Along with the sociologists and anthropologists, psychologists also study humans in their social settings, analyzing their attitudes and relationships. The disciplines of anthropology psychology, and sociology often research the same kinds of problems but from different points of view, with the emphasis in psychology on individual behavior, how an individual's actions are influenced by feelings and beliefs.

In their research, psychologists develop hypotheses, and then test them using the scientific method. These methods used in psychological research include:

naturalistic observation which includes observing the behavior of animals and humans in their natural surroundings or environment
systematic assessment, which describes assorted ways to measure the feelings, thoughts, and personality traits of people using case histories, public opinion polls or surveys, and standardized tests. These three types of assessments enable psychologists to acquire information not available through naturalistic observations
experimentation enables psychologists to find and corroborate the cause-and-effect relationships in behavior, usually by randomly dividing the subjects into two groups: experimental group and control group

SOCIOLOGY is the study of human society: the individuals, groups, and institutions making up human society. It includes every feature of human social conditions. It deals with the predominant behaviors, attitudes, and types of relationships within a society, which is defined as a group of people with a similar cultural background living in a specific geographical area. Sociology is divided into five major areas of study:

Population studies: General social patterns of groups of people living in a certain geographical area,
Social behaviors: Changes in attitudes, morale, leadership, conformity, and others,
Social institutions: Organized groups of people performing specific functions within a society such as churches, schools, hospitals, business organizations, and governments
Cultural influences: Including customs, knowledge, arts, religious beliefs, and language, and
Social change: Such as wars, revolutions, inventions, fashions, and other events or activities.

Sociologists use three major methods to test and verify theories:

(1) Surveys;
(2) Controlled experiments; and
(3) Field observation.

Skill 15.2: Recognize how language, literature, the arts, media, architecture, artifacts, traditions, beliefs, values, and behaviors interact and contribute to the preservation, development, and transmission of culture.

Literature has been an attempt to come to terms with the nature and the cost of war, of the meaning of the human struggle for freedom and the ability to enjoy basic human and civil rights. Literature has cried out against change and it has embraced change. By the beginning of the 20th century, literature was reflecting the struggle of the modern individual to find a place and a meaning in a new world that seemed like a jungle. But literature has reflected the observation that not only does the modern human not know how to find meaning, he/she does not actually know what he/she is seeking. It is this crisis of identity that has been the subject of most modern literature. This can be seen is the writings of Joseph Conrad, Sigmund Freud, James Joyce, Eugene O'Neill, Luigi Pirandello, Samuel Beckett, George Bernard Shaw, T.S. Eliot, Kafka, Camus, Pasternak, Graham Greene, Tennessee Williams, and a host of others.

In art and architecture, there has been a search for new forms and for basic symbols that would speak a universal language. This fragmentation and anxiety has found expression in cubism and surrealism. In painting, one need only consider the works of Cezanne and Picasso and Dali. In Sculpture, artists took one of two directions: either looking back and preserving the conventional ideals of beauty, or experimenting with distortion and the abstract concepts of time and force. Architecture tended to move toward more functional lines and expressions.

In religion and philosophy there have been great changes as well. For much of the period, religious interpretation tended to swing like a pendulum between the liberal and the conservative. By the end of the 21st century, however, the struggle for meaning and identity had resulted in a generalized conservative trend. This tendency can be seen in most religions yet today. Religion and philosophy are, to be sure, the means of self-definition and the understanding of one's place in the universe. Recent conservative trends, however, have had a polarizing effect. Issues of the relationship of Church and State have arisen and been resolved in most countries during this period. Yet, at the same time there has been an increasing effort to understand the religious beliefs of others, either to create new ways to define one's religion over and against other religions, or as the basis of new attacks on the values and teachings of other religions. This same struggle resulted in the rise of the philosophical movement known as existentialism, as seen in the writings of Soren Kierkegaard, Karl Jaspers, and Jean-Paul Sartre.

Skill 15.3: Examine examples of cultural unity and diversity within and across groups.

Ethnocentrism and **cultural relativity** are terms used by sociologists to describe two ways of thinking about other cultures in relation to one's own culture. These terms have been expanded to describe two general ways that cultures view themselves and other cultures.

Ethnocentrism, as the word suggests, considers one's own culture to be the central and usually superior culture, and views all other cultures in terms of how they are different. An ethnocentric view usually considers these different practices in other cultures as inferior, or even "savage."

Psychologists have suggested that ethnocentrism is a naturally occurring attitude. For the large part, people are most comfortable among other people who share their same upbringing, language and cultural background, and are likely to judge other cultural behaviors as alien or foreign.

In the objective study of other cultures, however, ethnocentrism can skew the way the behaviors of other cultures are interpreted. Current thinking is that the study of another culture should not be made in terms of the observer's own culture, but only in relation to that culture's other attributes. This is called cultural relativity. Cultural relativity aims to remove the biases and prejudices inherent in ethnocentrism to produce a clearer and more complete picture of other cultures.

Critics of ethnocentrism point to the negative results that cultural prejudice can have not only in academic research but also in everyday life. Critics of cultural relativity claim that it removes moral judgment from the observation and acceptance of other cultures. For instance, a cultural relativist might not offer a judgment on a culture that traditionally kills a wife when her husband dies. A critic of this approach might hold that killing a person under these circumstances is wrong, independent of that culture's beliefs or traditions.

Skill 15.4: Analyze ways in which groups, societies, and cultures meet human needs

Review Competency 14.0.

Skill 15.5: Recognize social and cultural differences between preindustrial and postindustrial societies.

Social Stratification is the division of a society into different levels based on factors such as race, religion, economic standing or family heritage. Various types of social stratification may be closely related. For instance stratification by race may result in people of one race being relegated to a certain economic class as well.

The pioneering sociologist Max Weber theorized that there are three components of social stratification: class, status and political.

Social class, as Weber defined it, is based on economics and a person's relationship to the economic market e.g. a factory worker is of a different social class than a factory owner. Social status is based on non-economic factors like honor or religion. Political status is based on the relationships and influence one has in the political domain.

The economic revolutionary Karl Marx identified social stratification as the source of exploitation of one level of society by another, and based his theory of revolution and economic reform on this belief.

Mobility between social strata may differ between societies. In some societies, a person may move up or down in social class owing to changes in one's personal economic fortunes, for instance. Political status can change when prevailing political thought shifts. Some systems of stratification are quite formal, however, as in the former caste system in India. In these systems, lines between strata are more rigid, with employment, marriage and other social activities tightly defined by one's position.

Sociologists have identified five different types of institutions around which societies are structured: family, education, government, religion and economy. These institutions provide a framework for members of a society to learn about and participate in a society, and allow for a society to perpetuate its beliefs and values to succeeding generations.

The **family** is the primary social unit in most societies. It is through the family that children learn the most essential skills for functioning in their society such as language and appropriate forms of interaction. The size of the family unit varies among cultures, with some including grandparents, aunts, uncles and cousins as part of the basic family, who may all live together. The family is also related to a society's economic institutions, as families often purchase and consume goods as a unit. A family that works to produce its own food and clothing, as was the case historically in many societies, is also a unit of economic production.

Education is an important institution in a society, as it allows for the formal passing on of a culture's collected knowledge. The institution of education is connected to the family, as that is where a child's earliest education takes place. Educational traditions within a society are also closely associated with economic institutions, as some levels of employment require specific academic achievement.

A society's **governmental** institutions often embody its beliefs and values. Laws, for instance, reflect a society's values by enforcing its ideas of right and wrong. The structure of a society's government can reflect a society's ideals about the role of an individual in his society. A democracy may emphasize that an individual's rights are more important than the needs of the larger society, while a socialist governmental institution may place the needs of the whole group first in importance.

Religion is frequently the institution from which spring a society's primary beliefs and values, and can be closely related to other social institutions. Many religions have definite teachings on the structure and importance of the family, for instance. In some societies, the head of the government is also the head of the predominant religion, or the government may be operated on religious principles. Historically, formal educational institutions in many societies were primarily religious, and all religions include an educational aspect to teach their beliefs.

A society's **economic** institutions define how an individual can contribute and receive economic reward from his society. Economic institutions are usually closely tied to governmental institutions, each informing and regulating the other. They are linked to family institutions, as workers are often supporting more than one person with their wages. A society's economic institutions might affect its educational goals by creating a demand for certain skills and knowledge.

Refer to Skills 5.1 and 7.5.

Skill 15.6 Analyze the relationship between language and culture.

Language is inextricably joined with culture. Each complements the other in various important ways, through a number of varied means. First and foremost, language is a means for members of a society or civilization to communicate with one another. Language, be it words or syllables or pictures, is the transmittal of concepts from one person to another or to many. The back-and-forth of conversation is a way for people to share their concerns, fears, and accomplishments—not to mention the trivialities of everyday life. People use words all the time, to communicate complex and simple concepts, to have serious discussions or throwaway conversations.

Language is also a means to communicate culture to "outsiders." People from one civilization describe their culture, customs, and other particulars to "outsiders" by using language. The way they say certain things and the various elements, words, and even syllables that they emphasize say a lot about their language, their values, and their culture.

Language doesn't always mean words. One very powerful means of communicating is "body language," the nonverbal communication that augments or takes the place of words. People who speak different languages can successfully communicate with each other through body language even though neither shares the other's tongue. Body language is both facial expressions and other body movements. Sometimes, both are used in conjunction with each other to present an overall picture.

Another way that language and culture are intertwined is in the learning of a language by someone who doesn't speak it natively. For example, a native English speaker might be studying German. By learning not only the various German words but also the way in which German sentences are structured and the way in which German speakers think, students of the German language can gain valuable insights into the culture of Germany. The German language is put together quite logically, which is, by and large, an apt description of the German people and culture: The trains run on time, the people like to be prepared, and the sentence structure "just makes sense."

German, in addition to Spanish and French, has formal and informal versions of many words as well. The proper one is used depending on how well you know someone or on how far up or down on the social ladder you are from the person to whom you are talking. English doesn't really have a corresponding construction. What that says about the civilizations that house the native speakers can be debated by experts. Language, then, for the most part, is a mirror, a prism of a culture. Words, signals, and symbols can communicate the particulars of a culture to anyone willing to look, listen, or otherwise pay attention.

COMPETENCY 16: Understand how culture, physical environment, individuals, groups, and institutions shape group and personal identities.

Skill 16.1: Define the concepts of role, status, culture, and social class, and use them to analyze connections and interactions among individuals, groups, and institutions in society.

Socialization is the process by which humans learn the expectations their society has for their behavior, in order that they might successfully function within that society.

Socialization takes place primarily in children as they learn and are taught the rules and norms of their culture. Children grow up eating the common foods of a culture, and develop a "taste" for these foods, for example. By observing adults and older children, they learn about gender roles, and appropriate ways to interact.

Socialization also takes place among adults who change their environment and are expected to adopt new behaviors. Joining the military, for example, requires a different type of dress and behavior than civilian culture. Taking a new job or going to a new school are other examples of situations where adults must re-socialize.

Two primary ways that socialization takes place are through positive and negative sanctions. Positive sanctions are rewards for appropriate or desirable behavior, and negative sanctions are punishments for inappropriate behavior. Recognition from peers and praise from a parent are examples of positive sanctions that reinforce expected social behaviors. Negative sanctions might include teasing by peers for unusual behavior, or punishment by a parent.

Sanctions can be either formal or informal. Public awards and prizes are ways a society formally reinforces positive behaviors. Laws that provide for punishment of specific infractions are formal negative sanctions.

Skill 16.2: Recognize how perceptions, attitudes, values, beliefs, and media and technology affect the development of personal identity and decision making.

Personal identity is defined by Encarta Dictionary as what identifies somebody or something; somebody's essential self, the characteristics that somebody recognizes as belonging uniquely to himself or herself and constituting his or her individual personality for life.

It is important to understand adolescent identity as it defines who a child/student is. For example, consider the high achieving student who is encouraged and praised for stellar academic achievement and success in athletics, versus those students who perceive themselves to be different because of their sexual orientation or race or customs. The latter are challenged by low expectations may be unable to challenge themselves because they have been expected to isolate themselves or to under-perform. These students perceive themselves to be different. With proper encouragement, it may be possible to help students who initially resisted success because of fear or prejudice to turn themselves around and forge new identities. The print media barrages young females with displays of females in the image of the "waif" model. There have been suggestions that there is a correlation in the increasing number of cases of anorexia in young girls. So here self-identity is the girl who sees herself as not measuring up to society's norms.

The media plays an extensive role in the lives of children. The "MTV-generation" has been exposed to a wide range of images and promoted overt sexuality in the guise of "Spring Break" type shows, typically underwritten by makers/distributors of alcoholic beverages. These images are displayed and replayed repeatedly over the airwaves and on the Internet. Marketers have targeted the 8-18 age groups because these children hold the keys to parent's buying decisions. Advertisements are aimed at children; children's programming is rift with subtle sales pitches for dolls, games, toys, costumes, holiday themed items. Children shape their identity by the amount of toys ("collect them all") cost of toys, (American Girl Dolls at $100 each) or by attaining the hard-to-find toy (X-Box in 2005 at $300 each) because that is what the American society values.

Ancient Greece is often called the "Cradle of Western Civilization" because of the enormous influence it had not only on the time in which it flourished, but on western culture ever since.

Early Greek institutions have survived for thousands of years, and have influenced the entire world. The **Athenian form of democracy**, with each citizen having an equal vote in his own government, is a philosophy upon which all modern democracies are based. In the United States, the Greek tradition of democracy was honored in the choice of **Greek architectural** styles for the nation's government buildings. The modern **Olympic Games** are a revival of an ancient Greek tradition and many of the events are recreations of original contests.

The works of the Greek **epic poet** Homer are considered the earliest in western literature, and are still read and taught today. The tradition of the theater was born in Greece, with the plays of Aristophanes and others. In philosophy, Aristotle developed an approach to learning that emphasized observation and thought, and Socrates and Plato contemplated the nature of being and the origins and ideals of government and political relations. Greek mythology has been the source of inspiration for literature into the present day.

In the field of mathematics, Pythagoras and Euclid laid the foundation of geometry and Archimedes calculated the value of pi. Herodotus and Thucydides were the first to apply research and interpretation to written history.

In the arts, Greek sensibilities were held as perfect forms to which others might strive. In sculpture, the Greeks achieved an idealistic aesthetic that had not been perfected before that time.

The Greek civilization served as an inspiration to the Roman Republic, which followed in its tradition of democracy, and was directly influenced by its achievements in art and science. Later, during the Renaissance, European scholars and artists would rediscover ancient Greece's love for dedicated inquiry and artistic expression, leading to a surge in scientific discoveries and advancements in the arts.

The ancient civilization of Rome owed much to the Greeks. Romans admired Greek architecture and arts, and built upon these traditions to create a distinct tradition of their own that would influence the western world for centuries.

In government, the Romans took the Athenian concept of democracy and built it into a complex system of representative government that included executive, legislative and judicial functions. In the arts, Romans created a realistic approach to portraiture, in contrast to the more idealized form of the Greeks. In architecture, Rome borrowed directly from the Greek tradition, but also developed the dome and the arch, allowing for larger and more dramatic forms. The Romans continued the Greek tradition of learning, often employing Greeks to educate their children.

The Roman Republic flourished in the centuries leading up to the advent of the Christian era. An organized bureaucracy and active political population provided elite Roman citizens with the means to ascend to positions of considerable authority.

The Roman Empire extended through much of Europe and Roman culture extended with it. Everywhere the Romans went, they built roads, established cities, and left their mark on the local population. The Roman language, Latin, spread as well and was transformed into the Romance languages of French and Spanish. The Roman alphabet, which was based on the Greek transformation of Phoenician letters, was adopted throughout the empire and is still used today.

The empire itself has served as a model for modern government, especially in federal systems such as that found in the United States. The eventual decline and fall of the empire has been a subject that has occupied historians for centuries.

Skill 16.3: Examine the role of institutions in promoting continuity and change, and analyze institutional influences on people, events, and cultures in historical and contemporary contexts.

Ancient Greece is often called the "Cradle of Western Civilization" because of the enormous influence it had not only on the time in which it flourished, but on western culture ever since.

Early Greek institutions have survived for thousands of years, and have influenced the entire world. The **Athenian form of democracy**, with each citizen having an equal vote in his own government, is a philosophy upon which all modern democracies are based. In the United States, the Greek tradition of democracy was honored in the choice of **Greek architectural** styles for the nation's government buildings. The modern **Olympic Games** are a revival of an ancient Greek tradition and many of the events are recreations of original contests.

The works of the Greek epic poet Homer are considered the earliest in western literature, and are still read and taught today. The tradition of the theater was born in Greece, with the plays of Aristophanes and others. In philosophy, Aristotle developed an approach to learning that emphasized observation and thought, and Socrates and Plato contemplated the nature of being and the origins and ideals of government and political relations. Greek mythology has been the source of inspiration for literature into the present day.

In the field of mathematics, Pythagoras and Euclid laid the foundation of geometry and Archimedes calculated the value of pi. Herodotus and Thucydides were the first to apply research and interpretation to written history.

In the arts, Greek sensibilities were held as perfect forms to which others might strive. In sculpture, the Greeks achieved an idealistic aesthetic that had not been perfected before that time.

The Greek civilization served as an inspiration to the Roman Republic, which followed in its tradition of democracy, and was directly influenced by its achievements in art and science. Later, during the Renaissance, European scholars and artists would rediscover ancient Greece's love for dedicated inquiry and artistic expression, leading to a surge in scientific discoveries and advancements in the arts.

The ancient civilization of Rome owed much to the Greeks. Romans admired Greek architecture and arts, and built upon these traditions to create a distinct tradition of their own that would influence the western world for centuries.

In government, the Romans took the Athenian concept of democracy and built it into a complex system of representative government that included executive, legislative and judicial functions. In the arts, Romans created a realistic approach to portraiture, in contrast to the more idealized form of the Greeks. In architecture, Rome borrowed directly from the Greek tradition, but also developed the dome and the arch, allowing for larger and more dramatic forms. The Romans continued the Greek tradition of learning, often employing Greeks to educate their children.

The Roman Republic flourished in the centuries leading up to the advent of the Christian era. An organized bureaucracy and active political population provided elite Roman citizens with the means to ascend to positions of considerable authority. The Roman Empire extended through much of Europe and Roman culture extended with it. Everywhere the Romans went, they built roads, established cities, and left their mark on the local population. The Roman language, Latin, spread as well and was transformed into the Romance languages of French and Spanish. The Roman alphabet, which was based on the Greek transformation of Phoenician letters, was adopted throughout the empire and is still used today. The empire itself has served as a model for modern government, especially in federal systems such as that found in the United States. The eventual decline and fall of the empire has been a subject that has occupied historians for centuries.

The rise of Christianity in early modern Europe was due as much to the iron hand of feudalism as it was to the Church itself. Feudalism, more than any other element, helped the Church get its grip on Europe. That grip, some would argue, has yet to be relinquished. Like the caste system in India, feudalism kept people in strict control according to their social class. If you were a peasant, you had been born that way and you had an excellent chance of staying that way for your entire life. The rich and powerful were also the highest class in society, and the friends of the rich and powerful were the clergy.

In a way that governments never could, Christianity unified Europe. Especially with the pope at the head of the religion, the peoples of Europe could correctly be called Christendom because they all had the same beliefs, the same worries, and the same tasks to perform in order to achieve the salvation that they so desperately sought. The Church was only too happy to capitalize on this power, which increased throughout the Middle Ages until it met a stalwart from Germany named Martin Luther.

Skill 16.4: Analyze ways in which conflict can occur between individual and/or community belief systems, government policies, and laws in historical and contemporary contexts.

The First Amendment to the Constitution prohibits a state-sponsored religion while also prohibiting the government from interfering with its people's exercise of their religions. These have been two of the most fundamental tenets and faithfully upheld provisions of the Constitution since their inception.

One common term still bandied about is the "wall of separation between church and state" that the First Amendment builds. We have this phrase thanks to Thomas Jefferson, himself a committed Deist who wanted no part of an entangling of government and religion. In the 200 years since Jefferson first wrote this phrase, such entanglement has been discouraged numerous times.

From the earliest days of the nineteenth century, this tendency to keep the two entities separate has been challenged, intentionally or not, by parochial school. These schools are run by religious organizations, like churches, and provide their students with not only a secular education but also religious instruction. It would seem to be a straightforward conclusion that the funding of one of these schools by the state or federal government would violate the doctrine of separation between church and state, but churches have tried nonetheless. The Court has consistently ruled against public funding for parochial schools. And since these things are rarely as straightforward as they assume, it is true as well that the Supreme Court has upheld a series of laws that provided state-sponsored spending for religious schools.

In particular, in *Cochran* v. *Louisiana State Board of Educators* (1930), the Court ruled that a law that provided textbook funds for students of secular and parochial schools did not violate the First Amendment because the funds were intended to benefit the students, not the religious entities that sponsored the schools. The effectiveness of that decision has weakened in the 70 years since it was issued, as subsequent Justices found fault with it to one degree or another.

One thing that all Justices seem to agree on, however, is the inadmissibility of prayer in school. The famous *Engle* v. *Vitale* is an excellent example, in which the Court invalidated a school policy of beginning each class day with a school wide prayer. This principle was reaffirmed in *Wallace* v. *Jaffree* (1985), in which the Court invalidated a day-opening moment of silence because the law that mandated it made clear that it was intended as a time for prayer. Students can certainly pray silently any time they wish; the problem was with the state's and the school's mandating a specified prayer time.

Universities have been permitted to allow religious groups' meetings on university property, provided that secular groups have the same meeting opportunity.

Another element of the First Amendment religion phrasing that has come to be contentious is the "Free Exercise Clause," the ability to practice your religion as you see fit. In the twentieth century, many businesses in America closed on Sunday, the traditional day of worship for Christians. This practice was enforced by laws in many states, called "Blue Laws," which in many cases required businesses to close on Sunday. Since Jewish people honored their Sabbath on Saturday, not Sunday, they felt disenfranchised by such laws. The case was *Braunfeld* v. *Brown* (1961), and the Court ruled for the Blue Laws, saying that the loss of business that Jewish owners suffered by closing Sunday in addition to Saturday (which they did because of *their* religious beliefs) was not a state-mandated restriction of their religious beliefs but, rather, a secular policy. Other famous religious beliefs-government mandated cases have involved the Amish religion's prohibition of education beyond eighth grade (*Wisconsin* v. *Yoder*, 1972 and *United States* v. *Lee*, 1982).

A particularly contentious issue has arisen in the last 20 years, involving the Native American use of peyote, a narcotic in religious ceremonies. Technically, according to American law, the use of such a drug is illegal; Native Americans, however, claim that they use it as part of sacred practices that supersede the laws of the land. The result has been a federal law protecting such practices, extending to the growth and cultivation of said substance but only for religious means.

Perhaps the most contentious church-state conflict has been public displays of religious images on state-owned property. In the news recently have been the Ten Commandments, the Christian and Jewish religions' ancient set of laws that happen to include religious elements. Various groups have tried to prevent such displays of these laws and statues from appearing on courthouse walls and lawns, but the Court has consistently treated the Commandments as a part of legal history. Other battles have involved depictions of scenes from the Jesus story on state-owned property, especially at Christmastime. In most cases, the Court has ruled that such displays are permissible as long as the holiday display also included images of Santa Claus and other recognizably secular parts of the Christmas holiday (*Lynch* v. *Donnelly*, 1984).

Skill 16.5: Apply ideas, theories, and modes of inquiry drawn from anthropology, psychology, and sociology to examine general social phenomena and issues related to gender, ethnicity, and intercultural understanding

Sociology is the study of human society: the individuals, groups, and institutions making up human society. It includes every feature of human social conditions. It deals with the predominant behaviors, attitudes, and types of relationships within a society, which is defined as a group of people with a similar cultural background living in a specific geographical area. Sociology is divided into five major areas of study:

Sociology studies human society with its attitudes, behaviors, conditions, and relationships with others. It is closely related to anthropology, especially applied to groups outside of one's region, nation, or hemisphere. History puts it in perspective with an historical background. Political Science is tied to sociology with the impact of political and governmental regulation of activities. Awareness of, influence of, and use of the physical environment as studied in geography also contributes to understanding. Economic activities are a part of human society. The field of psychology is also related

Population studies: General social patterns of groups of people living in a certain geographical area,
Social behaviors: Changes in attitudes, morale, leadership, conformity, and others,
Social institutions: Organized groups of people performing specific functions within a society such as churches, schools, hospitals, business organizations, and governments
Cultural influences: Including customs, knowledge, arts, religious beliefs, and language, and
Social change: Such as wars, revolutions, inventions, fashions, and other events or activities.

Sociologists use three major methods to test and verify theories:

(1) Surveys;
(2) Controlled experiments; and
(3) Field observation....

Some important figures in the field of sociology include the following:

Auguste Comte the French philosopher who coined the term "sociology" and developed the theory called "positivism," which stated that social behavior and events could be measured scientifically.

Karl Marx and Friedrich Engels supported the theory of "economic determinism" which stated that all social patterns and institutions were controlled by economic factors, which formed much of the basis of Communism.

Herbert Spencer stated that human society's development was a process occurring gradually, evolving from lower to higher forms, very much like biological evolution.

Emile Durkheim was the French sociologist who was one of the first to use scientific research methods.

Max Weber stated that sociological theories are probably generalizations.

For more information on sociology, check out:
http://www.sociosite.net/databases.php#USA
http://www.socioweb.com/

ANTHROPOLOGY is the scientific study of human culture and humanity, the relationship between man and his culture. Anthropologists study different groups, how they relate to other cultures, and patterns of behavior, similarities and differences. Their research is two fold: cross-cultural and comparative. The major method of study is referred to as "participant observation." The anthropologist studies and learns about the people being studied by living among them and participating with them in their daily lives. Other methods may be used but this is the most characteristic method used....

Margaret Mead, in the 1920s lived among the Samoans, observing their ways of life, resulting in the book "Coming of Age in Samoa."... The Leakey family, Louis, his wife Mary, and son Richard, all of whom did much field work to further the study of human origins.
For more information:
http://vlib.anthrotech.com/
http://www.archeodroit.net/anthro/Contents/contents.html

Psychology is defined as scientifically studying mental processes and behavior. It is related to anthropology and sociology, two social sciences that also study people in society. All three closely consider relationships and attitudes of humans within their social settings. Anthropology considers humans within their cultures, how they live, what they make or produce, how different groups or cultures relate to each other. Sociology follows the angle of looking at behaviors, attitudes, conditions, and relationships in human society. Psychology focuses on individual behavior and how actions are influenced by feelings and beliefs...

Psychology involves scientifically studying behavior and mental processes. The ways people and animals relate to each other are observed and recorded. Psychologists scrutinize specific patterns, which will enable them to discern and predict certain behaviors, using scientific methods to verify their ideas. In this way they have been able to learn how to help people fulfill their individual human potential and strengthen understanding between individuals as well as groups and in nations and cultures. The results of the research of psychologists have deepened our understanding of the reasons for people's behavior.

Psychology is not only closely connected to the natural science of biology and the medical field of psychiatry but it is also connected to the social science areas of anthropology and sociology which have to do with people in society. Along with the sociologists and anthropologists, psychologists also study humans in their social settings, analyzing their attitudes and relationships. The disciplines of anthropology psychology and sociology often research the same kinds of problems but from different points of view, with the emphasis in psychology on individual behavior, how an individual's actions are influenced by feelings and beliefs.

In their research, psychologists develop hypotheses, and then test them using the scientific method. These methods used in psychological research include:

naturalistic observation which includes observing the behavior of animals and humans in their natural surroundings or environment

systematic assessment, which describes assorted ways to measure the feelings, thoughts, and personality traits of people using case histories, public opinion polls or surveys, and standardized tests. These three types of assessments enable psychologists to acquire information not available through naturalistic observations

experimentation enables psychologists to find and corroborate the cause-and-effect relationships in behavior, usually by randomly dividing the subjects into two groups: experimental group and control group

Aristotle is the Greek philosopher often credited with the beginnings of psychology. He was mainly interested in the human mind's accomplishments. He believed that the body was separate from the mind or soul, which the Greeks referred to as the "psyche". He believed that the highest human virtues came from the psyche, which helped people to reason.

Rene Descartes was a French philosopher who described the strong influence of the body and mind on each other because of their being separate and suggested that the pineal gland in the brain was where this interaction took place. He developed the doctrine of "nativism", the beliefs that people were born able to think and reason.

Thomas Hobbes, John Locke, David Hume, and George Berkeley were men who were called "empiricists", a name given to those who rejected Descartes' doctrine of nativism. These four men believed that at birth a person's mind is empty that one gains knowledge of the outside world through the senses, and that people get ideas from their life's experiences.

Johannes P. Muller and Hermann L.F. von Hemholtz, were two German scientists pioneered the first organized studies of perception and sensation, showing the feasibility of the scientific study of the physical processes that support mental activity.

William James started what became the first psychology laboratory in the world.

William Wundt was a German philosopher trained in physiology and medicine who published the first journal dealing with experimental psychology.

It should be noted that the work of Wundt and James put psychology in a field by itself, separate from philosophy. Their work, along with others, led to the method of research called "introspection," training their subjects to observe and as accurately as possible record their feelings, experiences, and mental processes.

John B. Watson an American psychologist who introduced the research technique of "behaviorism", the belief that the only reliable source of information was observable behavior, not inner experiences.

Ivan Pavlov and B.F. Skinner made significant contributions to this school of behaviorism, a reaction to the emphasis on introspection. The behaviorists believed that the environment was the important influence on one's behavior and looked for any correlation between environmental stimuli and observable behavior.

Max Wertheimer started the school of Gestalt psychology. The word "**Gestalt**" is German and means a shape, pattern, or form. The proponents of this form of research studied behavior, not as different incidents of response to stimuli but as an organized pattern.

Sigmund Freud was an Austrian physician who founded the school of psychoanalysis; the theory that repressed inner forces buried in the subconscious determined behavior and that these repressed feelings possibly affected personality problems, self-destructive behavior, and possibly physical symptoms. Freud developed a number of techniques to treat repression, including free association.

The practice of modern psychology includes the teachings of the earlier schools as well as the development of additional ones such as stimulus-response, cognitive, and humanistic psychology.

For more information on psychology:

http://www.psychology.org/
http://www.apa.org/

SUBAREA III—ECONOMICS

COMPETENCY 17: Understand important economic concepts, terms, and theories, and use that knowledge to analyze basic economic phenomena.

Skill 17.1 Define important economic terms and concepts and use them to analyze general economic phenomena and specific economic problems

Economics is the study of how a society allocates its scare resources to satisfy what are basically unlimited and competing wants. A fundamental fact of economics is that resources are scare and that wants are infinite. Nations have different resource endowments that determine what goods and services they can produce. The fact that scarce resources have to satisfy unlimited wants means that choices have to be made. If society uses its resources to produce good A then it doesn't have those resources to produce good B. More of good A means less of good B. This trade-off is referred to as the opportunity cost, or the value of the sacrificed alternative.

Demand is based on consumer preferences and satisfaction and refers to the quantities of a good or service that buyers are willing and able to buy at different prices during a given period of time. Supply is based on costs of production and refers to the quantities that sellers are willing and able to sell at different prices during a given period of time. The determination of market equilibrium price is where the buying decisions of buyers coincide with the selling decision of sellers. This is where the demand and supply curves intersect on a graph.

Economies of scale refer to the relationship between long run average costs and output level. A firm experiences economies of scale when it average costs decrease as output increases. This means that a firm can expand to take advantage of lower costs. Specialization refers to division of labor. Tasks are divided so no one individual performs all of the tasks in the production process.

Entrepreneurship is one of the four factors of production. The entrepreneur is the individual that has the ability to combine the land, labor and capital to produce a good or service. The entrepreneur is the one who bears the risks of failure and loss and he is the one who will gain from the profits if the product is successful.

Skill 17.2 Recognize the contributions of major economic thinkers.

Laissez-faire economics, or pure capitalism, is based on free markets without government interference in the market place. The role for government was to establish the framework for the functioning of the economy, determining things like standards of weights and measures, providing public goods, etc.

Adam Smith, author of **The Wealth of Nations**, believed that free markets should exist without government interference because any interference interfered with the rights and liberties of the market participants even though laissez-faire economics results in an unequal distribution of income. The economy, if left alone, would function as if an invisible hand guided it to an efficient allocation of resources.

Parson Malthus was an economist whose theories led to economics being called the dismal science. His theory can best be summed as saying that the population growth would exceed the growth of the food supply. This would result in the lower classes experiences increasing poverty.

Karl Marx viewed economics in a different perspective. He felt that labor was the value determining factor. Since it was labor that gave a commodity value, labor was entitled to the value of what it produced, or the surplus. The capitalist didn't do anything to earn the surplus. He appropriated it from labor and, therefore, exploited labor. This is the basis for Marxian economics. Marx goes on to apply the doctrine of historical necessity and the Hegelian triad to history and predicts a revolution based on the exploitation of labor. Marxian theories were the basis for the former Soviet and Eastern block economies.

The theories of John Maynard Keynes are the basis for modern macroeconomics. Keynesian theory is demand-side theory. Keynes felt that the level of economic activity in an economy is determined by the level of aggregate spending. If there is excess aggregate demand, or spending, then the economy can't produce enough output to satisfy that demand, and the result is increasing prices, or inflation. The way to cure the inflation is for government to implement contractionary fiscal policy; raise taxes or lower government spending. This will slow down an economy that is expanding too quickly. If there is a deficiency in aggregate demand, then there is not enough spending in the economy to cause suppliers to produce enough output to employ the labor force. The Keynesian solution is to stimulate the economy with expansionary fiscal policy, to lower taxes and/or increase spending. In the Keynesian framework, government policy action is required to rid the economy of inflation and unemployment. The economy will not self-correct.

Milton Friedman disagrees with Keynes on the role of fiscal policy. Friedman and the Monetarists believe that money supply is the most important variable affecting the level of economic activity. The equation describing the economy is MV=PQ, where M = money supply, V = velocity, P = price level and Q equals the number of transactions in the economy. Increasing the money supply directly leads to a higher level of economic activity; decreasing the money supply directly causes a lower level of economic activity. Monetarists do not advocate the use of fiscal or monetary policy. Fiscal policy can be negated by the crowding out effect, a situation where an increase in government spending to stimulate the economy is offset by a decrease in private sector spending. Monetary policy can result in an overcorrection because of time lags. The expansionary monetary policy the government implements in the current time period to counter unemployment results in inflation in a later time period. Monetarists and Keynesians differ in their beliefs on the effectiveness of monetary and fiscal policy.

Skill 17.3 Compare and apply the different perspectives of macro- and microeconomics.

Economics is divided into two broad categories: macroeconomics and microeconomics. Macroeconomics is a study of the aggregates that comprise the economy on the national level: output, consumption, investment, government spending and net exports. Macroeconomics is concerned with a study of the economy's overall economic performance, or what is called the Gross Domestic Product or GDP. It is concerned with inflation and unemployment and what to do to solve these problems. There are different macro theories about the functioning of the macro economy. These are Keynesian, Monetarists, and Supply Side theories. Macroeconomics is also concerned with growth theory and how does an economy develop and grow over time.

Microeconomics is a study of the economy at the industry or firm level. Microeconomics is concerned with things like consumer behavior, output and input markets and the distribution of income. Consumer behavior is concerned with how consumers make their consumption decisions. The study of the output markets is a study of market structure. There are four kinds of market structures in the output market; perfect competition, monopoly, monopolistic competition and oligopoly. For the most part, perfect competition is a theoretical extreme, most closely approximated by agriculture. The numerous firms sell a product identical to that sold by all other firms in the industry and have no control over the price. Buyers and sellers have full market information and there are no barriers to entry. A barrier to entry is anything that makes it difficult for firms to enter or leave the industry. The opposite of a perfectly competitive firm is a monopolist. Monopoly is a market structure in which there is only one seller who can control his price. The firm is equal to the industry.

A monopolist becomes a monopolist and remains a monopolist because of barriers to entry, which are very high. These barriers to entry, like a very high fixed cost structure, function to keep new firms from entering the industry. Monopoly is illegal in the U.S. economy. In between the two extremes are the two market structures that all U.S. firms fall into. Oligopoly is a market structure in which there are a few sellers of products that may be either homogeneous, like steel, or heterogeneous, like automobiles. There are high barriers to entry, which is why there are only a few firms in each industry. Monopolistic competition is the situation you see in shopping centers. There are numerous firms, each selling products that are similar, but not identical, like brand name shoes or clothing. Barriers to entry are not as high as in oligopoly which is why there are more firms. Input markets are the markets in which factors of production are hired and factor incomes are earned. Factors earn an amount of income that is determined by their scarcity and contribution.

Skill 17.4 Analyze economic phenomena from the perspective of different economic theories.

Demand-side economics is the traditional macroeconomic approach to the economy and is based on Keynesian economics. This school of thought explains the levels of output, income and employment in terms of the level of aggregate spending in the economy. A recession occurs when there is a deficiency in aggregate spending. There is not sufficient demand in the economy to cause the labor force to be employed. The government needs to stimulate the economy by monetary and/or fiscal policy to stimulate a higher level of spending. This will cause a rightward shift of the aggregate demand curve. The increase in demand will cause suppliers to hire more workers to produce the additional output they are producing. Keynes believed that only fiscal policy was effective. Inflation was caused by the opposite situation. There is excess aggregate demand in the economy. Since producers can't produce any more output (assumption of full employment) the only effect is inflation. Here the role for government is to slow down and economy that is expanding too quickly. The way to do this is to use contractionary monetary and/or fiscal policy. In the Keynesian model, unemployment and inflation are mutually exclusive; they can't both occur at the same time.

Supply side economics came into being in the 1980s to address the issue of stagflation. This was a situation where the economy experienced rising inflation and unemployment, something that the demand side model couldn't explain or solve. The economy's problems were caused by a shifting aggregate supply curve, not the aggregate demand curve. Therefore the solution was to implement policies aimed at causing an increase in aggregate supply. These policies became knows as supply side economics. They included tax incentives to induce people to work, programs aimed at improving the quality of the labor force, deregulation and improvement of the infrastructure. These were the policies of the Regan administration.

COMPETENCY 18: Understand various types of economic systems and analyze the structure, principles, and operation of different models of economic organization.

Skill 18.1 Recognize basic characteristics of traditional, command, market, and mixed economies.

The traditional economy is one based on custom. This usually describes the situation that exists in many less developed countries. The people do things the way their ancestors did so they are not too technologically advanced. Since their whole mindset is directed toward tradition, they are not very interested in technology, equipment and new ways of doing things. Technology and equipment are viewed as a threat to the old way of doing things and to their tradition. There is very little upward mobility for the same reason.

The model of capitalism is based on private ownership of the means of production and operates on the basis of free markets, on both the input and output side. The free markets function to coordinate market activity and to achieve an efficient allocation of resources. Laissez-faire capitalism is based on the premise of no government intervention in the economy. The market will eliminate any unemployment or inflation that occurs. Government needs only to provide the framework for the functioning of the economy and to protect private property. The role of financial incentives is crucial for it results in risk-taking and research and development.

A command economy is almost the exact opposite of a market economy. A command economy is based on government ownership of the means of production and the use of planning to take the place of the market. Instead of the market determining the output mix and the allocation of resources, the bureaucracy fulfills this role by determining the output mix and establishing production target for the enterprises, which are publicly owned. The result is inefficiency. There is little interest in innovation and research because there is not financial reward for the innovator.

A mixed economy uses a combination of markets and planning, with the degree of each varying according to country. The real world can be described as mixed economies, each with varying degrees of planning. The use of markets results in the greatest efficiency since markets direct resources in and out of industries according to changing profit conditions. However, government is needed to perform various functions. The degree of government involvement in the economy can vary in mixed economies. Government is needed to keep the economy stable during periods of inflation and unemployment.

All of the major economies of the world are **mixed economies**. They use markets but have different degrees of government involvement in the functioning of the markets and in the provision of public goods. For example, in some countries health care and education are provided by government and are not a part of the private sector. In the United States, most health care and higher education is private and at the expense of the consumer.

Skill 18.2 Analyze how different types of economic systems address fundamental questions concerning resource allocation, production, and distribution.

Economic systems refer to the arrangements a society has devised to answer what are known as the Three Questions: What goods to produce, How to produce the goods, and For Whom are the goods being produced, or how is the allocation of the output determined. Different economic systems answer these questions in different ways. These are the different "isms" that exist that define the method of resource and output allocation.

A market economy answers these questions in terms of demand and supply and the use of markets. Consumers vote for the products they want with their dollar spending. Goods acquiring enough dollar votes are profitable, signaling to the producers that society wants their scarce resources used in this way. This is how the "What" question is answered. The producer then hires inputs in accordance with the goods consumers want, looking for the most efficient or lowest cost method of production. The lower the firm's costs for any given level of revenue, the higher the firm's profits. This is the way in which the "How" question is answered in a market economy. The "For Whom" question is answered in the marketplace by the determination of the equilibrium price. Price serves to ration the good to those who can and will transact at the market price of better. Those who can't or won't are excluded from the market. The United States has a market economy.

The opposite of the market economy is called the centrally planned economy. This used to be called Communism, even though the term in not correct in a strict Marxian sense. In a planned economy, the means of production are publicly owned, with little, if any public ownership. Instead of the Three Questions being solved by markets, they have a planning authority that makes the decisions in place of markets. The planning authority decides what will be produced and how. Since most planned economies directed resources into the production of capital and military goods, there was little remaining for consumer goods and the result was chronic shortages. Price functioned as an accounting measure and did not reflect scarcity. The former Soviet Union and most of the Eastern Bloc countries were planned economies of this sort.

In between the two extremes is market socialism. This is a mixed economic system that uses both markets and planning. Planning is usually used to direct resources at the upper levels of the economy, with markets being used to determine prices of consumer goods and wages. This kind of economic system answers the three questions with planning and markets. The former Yugoslavia was a market socialist economy.

You can put each nation of the world on a continuum in terms of these characteristics and rank them from most capitalistic to most the planned. The United States would probably rank as the most capitalistic and North Korea would probably rank as the most planned, but this doesn't mean that the United States doesn't engage in planning or that economies like mainland China don't use markets.

Skill 18.3 Analyze and compare the structure, operation, and role of government in different economic systems.

A market economy functions on the basis of the financial incentive and personal freedom. Private property and private ownership of the means of production are the major characteristics. Firms use society's scarce resources to produce the goods that consumers want. Firms know they have a good that society wants when they earn profit. Firms have a good that consumers don't want when they consistently incur losses. Firms with consistent losses eventually go out of business and those resources shift into other industries, producing goods that consumers do want. Consumers are, in effect, voting for the goods and services they want and don't want, with their dollars. Technological progress is advanced because of the financial incentives, whether they are personal or corporate. Firms invest in research and development activities to find newer and more efficient technologies that result in greater output at lower prices. Individuals risk their own time and money on inventions because of the potential financial rewards. They live in the structure of a market economy that allows them the liberty of choosing what to do with their own resources within the confines of the law. Students study whatever it is that they want to major in. The role for government is to provide the environment for the functioning of the economy not to interfere is the functioning of individuals and firms.

In a planned economy, particularly one based on public ownership of the means of production, a planning entity substitutes for the market, to varying degrees from partial to total. Instead of consumers voting with their dollars, they have a bureaucratic entity trying to substitute for the functions of supply and demand in making production decisions. This is why planned economies are often plagued by a misallocation of resources that result in shortages and surpluses.

In most cases, the incentive for technological progress and innovation is absent because of the lack of financial rewards. There is no financial incentive for the inventor. There is no financial incentive for the firm to engage in R & D activities, even if they have the authorization to do so. What's in it for them? Many planned economies have less personal and political freedom than do market economies. The economy needs resources for a particular area. The labor force is directed into that area by assignment, for the most part, not by financial incentives. They attract more engineers not by offering a higher salary and more perks for engineers, but by assigning people to be engineers. Their schooling isn't financed if they don't study the required disciplines. Most planned economies are usually headed by dictators whereas market economies have elected officials. A populace does not vote for and elect those officials who suppress them.

Government plays a much bigger role in the day to day lives of the population and businesses in an economy where the means of production are publicly owned than when they are privately owned.

Skill 18.4 Analyze ways in which various economic systems and institutions influence individuals, families, businesses, communities, and government.

Economic systems affect individuals, families, businesses, communities and government. Market economies and command economy's have different effects. A market economy is based on supply and demand. Supply and demand are what make markets function efficiently. Supply is defined as the quantity of a good or service that a producer is willing to make available at different prices during a specified period of time. The producers' decisions are based on costs of production. Demand is defined as the quantity of goods and services that a buyer is willing and able to buy at different prices during a specified period of time. The consumers' decisions are based on both income and preferences. A market equilibrium occurs where the selling decisions of producers are equal to the buying decision of consumers, or where the supply and demand curves intersect. This gives us the market equilibrium price and quantity and results in an efficient allocation of resources in accordance with consumer preferences. In other words, producers are using society's resources to produce the goods and services that society wants. Producers know this because they have a profitable business.

Incentives and substitutes affect the market situation. Incentives for consumers are things like sales, coupons, rebates, etc. The incentives results in increased sales for the firm, even though there is a cost to the incentives. There is a change in the market equilibrium situation and possibly market shares. The increased demand coupled with brand loyalty means the firm will be able to raise prices at some point and not loose their customers. On the production side, incentives to innovate result in increased output at lower costs, or more profit and greater market share for the innovating firm. The individual inventor also experiences financial rewards. Many firms reward employees who propose good time or money saving suggestions.

Many of these effects are absent without the use of markets, as in a command economy. Supply and demand serve the function on registering the wishes and decisions of producers and consumers with the market tabulating these results. This leads to efficiency. Using a bureaucrat to substitute for the role of supply and demand, leads to inefficiency in both production and consumption. Consumers are no longer directing the allocation of resources with their dollar voting. They may not be getting the goods and services that they want their society's resources used for because, more often then not, the production of consumption goods is being suppressed as resources are directed into the production of military, industrial and public goods. Prices are not efficient because they don't have their allocation function. Incentives don't function in the same way. Consumers don't buy what they don't want even if it's on sale. The result in trying to substitute in some way for the supply and demand functions of the market is inefficiency in both production and consumption. When government is the enterprise owner as in a command-economy, society's resources are not being used efficiently and they are not being used to produce what society wants produced. This means higher production costs and more waste.

COMPETENCY 19: Understand the components, structure, organization, and operation of the U.S. economy.

Skill 19.1 Recognize basic values and principles of the U.S. economic system.

Financial incentives are the key to the functioning of a market economy. All market participants are willing to take a risk for the opportunity of being a financial success. Entrepreneurs are willing to undertake the risk of new business ventures for the purpose of monetary gain. Resources move into higher than normal rate of return industries because they are attracted by the profit potential. Inventors are willing to take the risk of spending time and money trying to come up with new products in the hope of monetary gain. All of these represent the ways financial incentives operate in a market economy.

Consumers vote for the products they want with their dollar spending. Goods acquiring enough dollar votes are profitable, signaling to the producers that society wants their scarce resources used in this way. This is the process of consumer sovereignty. The producer then hires inputs in accordance with the goods consumers want, looking for the most efficient or lowest cost method of production. The lower the firm's costs for any given level of revenue, the higher the firm's profits. If a good does not acquire enough dollar votes, then the firm isn't profitable. Consumers are letting producers know that they don't want society's scarce resources used for the production of the good.

The existence of economic profits in an industry functions as a market signal to firms to enter the industry. Economic profits means there is an above normal rate of return in this industry. As the number of firms increases, the market supply curve shifts to the right. Assuming cost curves stay the same, the expansion continues until the economic profits are eliminated and the industry is earning a normal rate of return. Depending on the level of capital intensity, this process might take a few years or it might take many years. The easier it is to shift resources from one industry to another, the faster the process will be. But the expansion will continue as long as there are economic profits to attract firms. Resources will go where they earn the highest rate of return especially if they were in a situation earning a lower than normal rate of return. Firms are free to use their resources in any way they want within the confines of the prevailing legal system.

Without a profit incentive there would be no reason for firms to spend millions and billions on research and development and technological progress would be almost nonexistent. The entrepreneur is willing to take the risks. He knows there is a good probability that his business will fail, but there is also a chance that it will succeed and there is a remote chance that it will be another Microsoft. Given this chance, entrepreneurs are willing to take the chance and risk their own money and investors are also willing to risk money on the chance that the business venture will be successful or very successful. If the venture isn't successful, meaning it isn't receiving those dollar votes that make it profitable, the consumers are telling that business that they don't want their scarce resources used in that way. Profits are the market signal that entrepreneurs and firms look for.

Skill 19.2 Analyze interactions among the various institutions that comprise the U.S. economic system as they relate to wealth, capital formation, and income distribution.

Households, businesses and government are related through the circular flow diagram. They are all integral parts of the macro economy. There are two markets. The input market is where factor owners sell their factors and employers hire their inputs. Sometimes labor is organized into labor unions in the input market. The purpose of the labor union is to negotiate the work contract with the employer and to establish a procedure for grievances. They hope to acquire a larger share of income for their members. The output market is where firms sell the output they produce with their inputs. It's where factors owners spend their incomes on goods and services. There are two sectors, households and businesses. Households sell their factors in the input market and use their income to purchase goods and services in the output market. So wages, interest, rent and profit flow from the business sector to the household sector. Since factor incomes are based on scarcity of the factor and contribution of the factor, the result in an unequal distribution of income. Not all factors are equal. Households that earn their factor incomes in the factor market spend their incomes on goods and services produced by businesses and sold in the output market. Receipts for goods and services flow from households to businesses. Government receives tax payments from households and businesses and provides services to businesses and households. Each of the three is a component of the aggregate sectors of the economy and as such makes a contribution to the GDP.

Adding **financial institutions** to the picture shows how monetary policy is implemented by the Federal Reserve. There are three components of monetary policy: the reserve ratio, the discount rate and open market operations. Changes in any of these three components affect the amount of money in the banking system and thus, the level of spending in the economy. The reserve ratio refers to the portion of deposits that banks are required to hold as vault cash or on deposit with the Fed. The purpose of this reserve ratio is to give the Fed a way to control the money supply. These funds can't be used for any other purpose. When the Fed changes the reserve ratio, it changes the money creation and lending ability of the banking system. When the Fed wants to expand the money supply it lowers the reserve ratio, leaving banks with more money to loan. This is one aspect of expansionary monetary policy. When the reserve ratio is increased, this results in banks having less money to make loans with, which is a form of contractionary monetary policy, which leads to a lower level of spending in the economy. Another way in which monetary policy is implemented is by changing the discount rate. When banks have temporary cash shortages, they can borrow from the Fed. The interest rate on the funds they borrow is called the discount rate. Raising and lowering the discount rate is a way of controlling the money supply. Lowering the discount rate encourages banks to borrow from the Fed, instead of restricting their lending to deal with the temporary cash shortage. By encouraging banks to borrow, their lending ability is increased and this results in a higher level of spending in the economy. Lowering the discount rate is a form of expansionary monetary policy. Discouraging bank lending by raising the discount rate, then is a form of contractionary monetary policy. A well developed banking system is necessary for capital formation, or investment purposes.

Skill 19.3 Recognize factors affecting the formulation of U.S. economic policy and apply this knowledge to the analysis of economic issues and problems.

Gross Domestic Product, or GDP, is computed by either the expenditures approach or the incomes approach is a measure of the overall performance of the national economy. From GDP, government policy makers can determine what is happening in the economy and where the problem areas are. The GDP is a way of measuring economic growth. Then they can devise policies to help those problem areas. The overall macroeconomic instability problems of inflation and unemployment are, for the most part, caused by the inequality of aggregate demand and aggregate supply. An economy that is growing too rapidly and has too high a level of spending has inflation, a period of rises in the price level. Inflation results in a dollar with less purchasing power and represents a situation where the appropriate governmental action is to slow down the economy. The government will implement policies that results in less spending in the economy to end the inflation.

When there isn't enough spending in the economy, producers who have surplus merchandise, lower production levels and layoff workers, or there is unemployment. The appropriate action for government is to stimulate the economy, to take actions that result in higher levels of spending. The increase in demand leads to higher levels of employment.

Government can implement contractionary policies for inflation or expansionary policies for unemployment in two ways. Fiscal policy refers to changes in the level of government spending and/or taxes. Expansionary fiscal policy consists on raising government spending and/or lower taxes to increase spending in the economy thus eliminating unemployment. Contractionary policies, to stop inflation, consist of a decrease in government spending and/or an increase in taxes, both of which lower the levels of spending in the economy. Fiscal policy requires legislative action. Laws have to be enacted.

The other policy tool open to the government is monetary policy. Monetary policy is implemented by the Fed through changing the level of money in the banking system. Simply put, banks earn income by making loans. People and business borrow from banks and spend the borrowed funds. If the Fed changes the amount of funds that banks have available to loan out, they change the level of spending in the economy. There are three ways that the Fed can do this. First of all, banks cannot loan out all of their deposits. They are required to hold a certain percentage as **reserves**. The percentage is called the reserve ratio. Raising the reserve ratio leaves banks with fewer reserves to loan out and is therefore an aspect of contractionary monetary policy (used during recessions). Lowering the reserve ratio, then increases lending ability and spending and is an aspect of expansionary monetary policy. A second mechanism for implementing monetary policy is called the Discount Rate, which is the rate of interest charged by the Fed to banks that borrow from it. Lowering the Discount Rate encourages banks to borrow and make loans, thus leading to higher levels of spending, or is a form of expansionary monetary policy. Contractionary monetary policy would be indicated by an increase in the Discount Rate. The third means of influencing the money supply is through Open Market Operations. This is when the Fed buys or sells bonds in the open market. When the Fed buys bonds from the public or banks, the Fed pays with dollars that are put into circulation. Thus, the Fed buying bonds represents a form of expansionary monetary policy – there are more dollars in the system for loans and spending. The Fed selling bonds is a form of contractionary monetary policy.

Since today's financial markets are international, banks can borrow and lend in foreign markets. They aren't constrained by the domestic market. Financial capital goes where it earns the highest rate of return, regardless of national boundaries. This means that if the Fed is trying to implement contractionary monetary policy, banks and businesses can just borrow in international markets, and get around the Fed's contractionary policies, at least in the short-run.

Skill 19.4 Analyze the influence of economic institutions and educational choices on career selection and opportunity in the United States.

Financial incentives are the key to the functioning of a market economy but also to the majority of career selection. . All market participants, including students, are willing to take a risk for the opportunity of being a financial success. Entrepreneurs are willing to undertake the risk of new business ventures for the purpose of monetary gain. Resources move into higher than normal rate of return industries because they are attracted by the profit potential. Inventors are willing to take the risk of spending time and money trying to come up with new products in the hope of monetary gain. All of these represent the ways financial incentives operate in a market economy.

Resources will go where they earn the highest rate of return especially if they were in a situation earning a lower than normal rate of return. Labor is one of the resources that will go where it receives the highest incentive. When workers are needed in a particular occupation, there will be more scholarship money available to entice students into the field. Starting salaries will be higher for the same reasons.

A market economy allows individuals the rights to take chances. The entrepreneur is willing to take the risks. He knows there is a good probability that his business will fail, but there is also a chance that it will succeed and there is a remote chance that it will be another Microsoft. Given this chance, entrepreneurs are willing to take the chance and risk their own money and investors are also willing to risk money on the chance that the business venture will be successful or very successful. If the venture isn't successful meaning it isn't receiving those dollar votes that make it profitable, the consumers are telling that business that they don't want their scarce resources used in that way. Profits are the market signal that indicates the proper allocation of resources in accordance with consumer preferences. Excess profits, or an above normal rate of return, signal an expansion as resources are attracted into the industry.

COMPETENCY 20.0 Understand the international economic structure and the role of interdependence in the contemporary global economy.

Skill 20.1 Define and apply basic concepts of international economics.

The theory of **comparative advantage** says that trade should be based on the comparative opportunity costs between two nations. The nation that can produce a good more cheaply should specialize in the production of that good and trade for the good in which it has the comparative disadvantage. In this way both nations will experience gains from trade. A basis for trade exists if there are differing comparative costs in each country. Suppose country A can produce ten units of good X or ten units of good Y with its resources. Country B can produce thirty units of X or ten units of Y with its resources. What are the relative costs in each country? In country A one X costs one unit of Y and in country B one X costs three units of Y. Good Y is cheaper in country B than it is in country A, 1/3X = 1 Y in country B versus 1Y = 1X in country A. Country B has the comparative advantage in the production of Y and country A has the comparative advantage in the production of good X. According to trade theory each country should specialize in the production of the good in which it has the comparative advantage. Country B will devote all of its resources to the production of good Y and country A will devote of its resources to the production of good X. Each country will trade for the good in which it has the comparative disadvantage.

To determine the gains from trade, we must first consider the pre-trade production and consumption positions of both countries. In A, the pre-trade position was where they could have either 10 units of X or 10 units of Y or any combination in between. Let's assume country A chose a combination of 7Y and 3X. In country B, their resources allowed either 30 units of Y or 10 units of X or any combination in between. Let's assume country B chose the combination of 18Y and 4 X. Now let's consider the production and consumption situation before and after trade. Before trade, the total production of good Y was 18 from country B and 7 from country A for a total of 25Y. After trade, total world production is 30Y, with country B specializing in the production of Y. For good X, the pre-trade situation was 3 units of X from country A and 4 units of X from country B, for a total of 7 units of X. After trade, with country A specializing in the production of X, total world production of X is 10 units. Specialization and trade according to comparative advantage results in the world having 30Y rather than 25Y and 10X instead of 7X. This increase is referred to as the gains from trade. Both countries have higher consumption levels of both good due to specialization. This example refers to free unrestricted trade. Trade barriers introduce distortions.

When nations trade the traded goods and services must be paid for. This involves the use of foreign exchange. The exchange rates of most currencies today are determined in a floating exchange rate regime. In a clean float, supply and demand factors for each currency in terms of another are what determine the equilibrium price or the **exchange rate**. A clean float is a market functioning without any government interference, purely on the basis of demand and supply. Sometimes nations will intervene in the market to affect the value of their currency vis-à-vis the other currency. This situation is referred to as a managed or **dirty float.** A government is not required to intervene to maintain a currency value, as they were under a regime of fixed exchange rates. A government that intervenes in the currency market now does so because it wants to, not because it is required to intervene to maintain a certain exchange rate value. For example, if the U.S. government thinks the dollar is depreciating too much against the Canadian dollar, the U.S. government will buy U.S. dollars in the open market and pay for them with Canadian dollars. This increases the demand for U.S. dollars and increases the supply of Canadian dollars. The U.S. dollar appreciates, or increases in value, and the Canadian dollar depreciates, or decreases in value, in response to the government intervention. A stronger U.S. dollar means Canadian goods are cheaper for Americans, and American goods are more expensive for Canadians.

All nations have records of their international transactions. A nation's international transactions are recorded in the Balance of Payments. The Balance of Payment consists of two major accounts: the Current Account, which gives the figures for the exchange of goods, services and unilateral transfers; and the Capital Accounts which provides the figures for capital flows resulting from the exchange of real and financial assets. The Current Account contains the Balance of Trade, which are a nation's merchandise imports minus its merchandise exports. If the nation's exports are greater than its imports, it has a trade surplus. If its imports are greater than its exports, it has a trade deficit. Adding in the category of exports and imports of services gives the Balance on Goods and Services. Adding unilateral transfers, military expenditures and other miscellaneous items yields the Balance on Current Account. The Capital Accounts consists of strictly financial items in various categories. The last category is Statistical Discrepancies which is a balancing entry so that the overall Balance of Payments always balances. This has to do with floating exchange rate regimes. It is the trade account that is watched closely today.

Skill 20.2 Recognize the functions of major institutions of international trade and finance.

The International Monetary Fund (IMF) is one of the international organizations that was founded by the Bretton Woods agreement at the end of world War II. The IMF is concerned with exchange rates and Balance of Payments and assists nations who have exchange rate or balance of payments problems. Balance of Payments is no longer an issue with floating exchange rates. Exchange rate stability is not an issue as it was in the 1960s and early 1970s when exchange markets went from crisis to crisis until exchange rates began to float. Closely related to these problems are problems within the domestic economy like inflation or unemployment. The IMF will make loans to nations who experience problems if they follow prescribed recommendations to correct their internal domestic problems.

The **GATT or General Agreements on Tariffs and Trade** was founded in 1947 and today, as the **World Trade Organization** or WTO, has 147 member nations. It was based on three principles. The first was Most Favored National status for all members. This means trade based on comparative advantage without tariffs or trade barriers. The second principle was elimination of quotas and third, reduction of trade barriers through multi-lateral trade negotiations. The WTO is the successor to the GATT and came into being in 1995. Its object is to promote free trade. As such it administers trade agreements, settles disputes, and provides a forum for trade discussions and negotiations.

Skill 20.3 Analyze interactions between domestic and global economic systems.

The **North American Free Trade Agreement (NAFTA),** the **Association of South East Asian Nations (ASEAN)** and the **European Union (EU)** are forms of regional economic integration. Economic integration is a method of trade liberalization on a regional basis. NAFTA represents the lowest form or first step in the regional trade integration process. A free trade area consists for two or more countries that abolish tariffs and other trade barriers among themselves but maintain their own trade barriers against the rest of the world. A free trade area allows for specialization and trade on the basis of comparative advantage within the area. The next stage in the integration process is a customs union, which is a free trade area that has common external tariffs against non-members. The third stage is a common market which is a customs union with free factor mobility within the area. Factors migrate where they find the best payment within the area. The fourth state is economic union where the common market members have common or coordinated economic and social policies. The final stage is monetary union where the area has a common currency. This is what Europe is working toward. They have a common market with elements of the fourth and fifth stages of integration.

The WTO does not change or blur the significance of political borders and territorial sovereignty in the same way that economic integration does, although the WTO is a way of settling trade disputes that arise from the different integration agreements. In the advanced stages of economic integration the political borders remain, but economic and social policies are common or coordinated and in monetary union, there is one common currency. Each nation is still its own independent entity but they do give up some sovereignty in the interest of having a successful union.

Skill 20.4 Analyze alternative models of economic growth and development.

There is more than one strategy of economic growth and development and the strategy that a country selects must be consistent with its situation. The strategy chosen by the United States may not be well suited for less developed countries (LDC). Most of the developing countries are producers of agricultural products. Many of these countries need agricultural growth in order to feed their own population. For many this requires investment in equipment and machinery that they can't afford. In some cases, they need land reform so people have workable plots of land. Hand in hand with the problem of agricultural growth is the problem of population growth. Many LDCs have large populations and a labor force that suffers from unemployment or underemployment. They need some method of controlling the growth of the population and giving the labor force the necessary training it requires. An increase in a resource, like labor, should be a factor contributing to economic growth, but that labor force must be productive and employed.

One method of growth is through commodity. Most LDCs are producers of primary products like minerals and ore and other natural resources. Many developed countries are dependent on the LDCs for these commodities. LDCs complain of price instability in the markets for these products. When a nation's economy is dependent on two or three primary commodities, any change in demand or supply results in big changes in the economies of the producers. This is why they have developed buffer stocks as a form of price stabilization to try to insulate the economies from market instability. The oil producing countries went a step further and formed a **cartel**. Cartelization is a form of collusion. It is when all of the producers act together and function as a monopolist. The purpose or the cartel is to raise price by restricting supply. The cartel can only work if it has production controls that all of the members adhere to. The big problem with cartels is cheating. This occurs when one of more cartel member doesn't follow the production controls. In spite of this, **OPEC (Organization of Petroleum Exporting Countries)** has been a very successful control.

Import substitution and export development are two other growth strategies. Import substitution is a strategy of protecting the domestic industry with trade barriers so the population buys the domestically produced product. Sheltering the domestic industry allows it to grow to a point where it will hopefully be competitive in world markets. It also leads to higher employment levels in the domestic country. The problem is they may be sheltering an industry that will never be competitive, especially if the industry isn't consistent with the resource base and technology of the domestic country. They will require imports of those products. Export development is closer to the principle of comparative advantage. The country exports the goods that its resources are suited for and imports those goods that its resources are not suited for. Export development as a growth strategy has been more successful than import substitution.

SUBAREA 4: POLITICAL SCIENCE AND GOVERNMENT

COMPETENCY 21: Understand important political science concepts, terms, and theories; and recognize major characteristics of various political systems.

Skill 21.1: Recognize the origins and purposes of government and analyze the impact of government on human activity at the local, state, national, and international levels.

Historically the functions of government, or people's concepts of government and its purpose and function, have varied considerably. In the theory of political science, the function of government is to secure the common welfare of the members of the given society over which it exercises control. In different historical eras, governments have attempted to achieve the common welfare by various means in accordance with the traditions and ideology of the given society. Among *primitive peoples*, systems of control were rudimentary at best. They arose directly from the ideas of right and wrong that had been established in the group and were common in that particular society. Control being exercised most often by means of group pressure, most often in the forms of taboos and superstitions and in many cases by ostracism, or banishment from the group. Thus, in most cases, because of the extreme tribal nature of society in those early times, this led to very unpleasant circumstances for the individual so treated. Without the protection of the group, a lone individual was most often in for a sad and very short, fate. (No other group would accept such an individual into their midst and survival alone was extremely difficult if not impossible).

Among more *civilized peoples*, governments began to assume more institutional forms. They rested on a well-defined legal basis. They imposed penalties on violators of the social order. They used force, which was supported and sanctioned by their people. The government was charged to establish the social order and was supposed to do so in order to be able to discharge its functions.

Eventually the ideas of government, who should govern and how, came to be considered by various thinkers and philosophers. The most influential of these and those who had the most influence on our present society were the ancient Greek philosophers such as Plato and Aristotle.

Aristotle's conception of government was based on a simple idea. The function of government was to provide for the general welfare of its people. A good government, and one that should be supported, was one that did so in the best way possible, with the least pressure on the people. Bad governments were those that subordinated the general welfare to that of the individuals who ruled. At no time should any function of any government be that of personal interest of any one individual, no matter who that individual was.

This does not mean that Aristotle had no sympathy for the individual or individual happiness (as at times Plato has been accused by those who read his "***Republic,***" which was the first important philosophical text to explore these issues). Rather Aristotle believed that a society is greater than the sum of its parts, or that "the good of the many outweighs the good of the few and also of the one".

Yet, a good government and one that is carrying out its functions well, will always weigh the relative merits of what is good for a given individual in society and what is good for the society as a whole.

This basic concept has continued to our own time and has found its fullest expression in the idea of representative democracy and political and personal freedom. In addition, a government that maintains good social order, while allowing the greatest possible exercise of autonomy for individuals to achieve

Skill 21.2: Use basic concepts of political science to analyze general political phenomena and specific political issues.

The American nation was founded very much with the idea that the people would have a large degree of autonomy and liberty. The famous maxim "no taxation without representation" was a rallying cry for the Revolution, not only because the people didn't want to suffer the increasingly oppressive series of taxes imposed on them by the British Parliament, but also because the people could not in any way influence the lawmakers in Parliament in regard to those taxes. No American colonist had a seat in Parliament, and no American colonist could vote for members of Parliament.

One of the most famous words in the Declaration of Independence is "**liberty**," the pursuit of which all people should be free to attempt. That idea, that a people should be free to pursue their own course, even to the extent of making their own mistakes, has dominated political thought in the 200-plus years of the American republic.

Another key concept in the American ideal is **equality**, the idea that every person has the same rights and responsibilities under the law. The Great Britain that the American colonists knew was one of a stratified society, with social classes firmly in place. Not everyone was equal under the law or in the coffers; and it was clear for all to see that the more money and power a person had, the easier it was for that person to avoid things like serving in the army and being charged with a crime. The goal of the Declaration of Independence and the Constitution was to provide equality for all who read those documents. The reality, though, was vastly different for large sectors of society, including women and non-white Americans.

This feeds into the idea of basic opportunity. The so-called "American Dream" is that every individual has an equal chance to make his or her fortune in a new land and that the country that is the United States will welcome and even encourage that initiative. The history of the country is filled with stories of people who ventured to

America and made their fortunes in the Land of Opportunity. Unfortunately for anyone who wasn't a white male, that basic opportunity was sometimes a difficult thing to achieve.

The political concepts of legitimacy, **power, authority and responsibility** are all inter-related. Legitimacy refers to the moral correctness of political system. If the political system is deemed to be morally correct then it will be accepted by its' citizens. The citizen will agree to obey the laws and rules of that system because the citizen accepts its legitimacy. When the citizens no lower accept the legitimacy of a regime, then the political system is overthrown. This is not the same thing as an election. An election is a part of the political system. Capitalism is a political system with legitimacy. Democracy is a political system with legitimacy. A political system's legitimacy is enhanced when it is recognized or acknowledged by another government.

Political authority refers to the people in the various offices within the political system. Their political authority lies in their ability to coerce people to comply with the wishes of the political system. Their political authority stems from the acceptance of the legitimacy of the political system or the citizens wouldn't accept their ability to coerce.

Political power refers to the ability of those with political authority to do or to influence. If a legitimate representative of the political system doesn't have his orders obeyed, there is always the military to enforce those orders.

Political responsibility is the moral obligation of citizens and government to do the morally correct thing. For example in the case of genocide and other atrocities, the political responsibility is to speak out and fight the atrocities.

There is no such thing as political authority and political power with legitimacy.

Skill 21.3: Analyze relationships between various historical developments and the evolution of political thought.

When looking at the modern major philosophies of the nature of government we will by necessity be looking at the works of men such as, ***Niccolo Machiavelli, Thomas Hobbes, John Locke, Jean-Jacques Rousseau,*** **and** ***Karl Marx***. Now this list is by no means exhaustive. However, in distinguishing political science from political philosophy, and by using the term "modern" in a broad sense, we will examine those thinkers whose works have had an actual practical effect on society, as opposed to simply trying to interpret human events. In other words, we will examine those ideas that people at different times have really tried to put into effect or have had in the end the longest lasting and widest influence.

Niccolo Machiavelli (1469-1527) One of the most important thinkers on politics and the nature of political power. His most famous work is ***The Prince*** (1532). In it, Machiavelli describes the means of gaining and holding onto political power. He looked at his work as a simple recitation of obvious facts. All political leaders want to stay in power, so very well, this is how you should do it. In reality, he was really describing the situation in his time. Nevertheless, his work has survived because it is a masterful piece that makes practical sense. A work that many a leader since has looked to as a guide for his or her own behavior. Throughout his career, Machiavelli had sought to describe a state that would be capable of resisting foreign attack and in maintaining internal order and discipline. His writings are concerned with the principles upon which such a state could be founded and with the means on which they can be implemented and maintained. In ***The Prince***, he describes the method by which a "prince" (ruler) could acquire and maintain political power. This study has often been regarded as a defense of the despotism and tyranny of such rulers as Cesare Borgia (1476? -1507 Italian ruler). However, it is in actuality based on Machiavelli's belief that a ruler is not bound by traditional ethical norms. In his view, a prince should be concerned only with power and should be bound only by rules that would lead to success in political actions. Machiavelli believed that these rules could be discovered by deduction from the political practices of the time, as well as from those of earlier times. Specifically he used examples from ancient Greece and Rome and later times, seeing what worked and what did not, spelling out his theses in simple to understand and follow ideas. For instance, many of his classic quotes are:

"It is better to be feared than loved ... but one must strive not to be hated'.

"A prince need trouble little about conspiracies when the people are well disposed, but when they are hostile and hold him in hatred, then he must fear everything and everybody."

> *"A wise prince leaves his subjects their property, for a man will sooner forgive the death of his brother than the loss of his patrimony".*
> *"A prince must show himself a lover of merit, give preferment to the able and honor those who excel in every ad'*

"A man who wishes to make a profession of goodness in everything must necessarily come to grief among so many who are not good. Therefore, it is necessary ... to learn how not to be good, and to use this knowledge and not use it, according to the necessity of the case".

"The first impression that one gets of a ruler and of his brains is from seeing the men he has about him".
"There is no other way of guarding one's self against flattery than by letting men understand that they will not offend you by speaking the truth; but when every one can tell you the truth you lose their respect'.

"I certainly think that it is better to be impetuous than cautious, for fortune is a woman, and if it is necessary.. . to conquer her by force".

Thomas Hobbes (1588-1679*)* Author of the book ***Leviathan*** *(l651)* which was actually written as a reaction to the disorders caused by the English civil wars which had culminated with the execution of King Charles I. Hobbes perceived people as rational beings, but unlike Locke and Jefferson, he had no faith in their abilities to live in harmony with one another without a government. The trouble was, as Hobbes saw it, people were selfish and the strong would take from the weak. However, the weak being rational would in turn band together against the strong. For Hobbes, the state of nature became a chaotic state in which every person becomes the enemy of every other. It became a war of all against all, with terrible consequences for all. Hobbes wrote thus:

"In such condition there is no place for industry, because the fruit thereupon is uncertain and consequently no culture of the Earth; no navigation nor use of the commodities that may be imported by sea; no commodious building; no instruments of moving or removing such things as require much force; no knowledge of the face of the Earth; no account of time; no arts; no letters; no society; and which is worst of all, continual fear and danger of violent death; and the life of man solitary, poor, nasty, brutish, and short".

The solution proposed by Hobbes was for the citizens to enter a contract of "commonwealth" with one another. The conditions of the contract were that all of the citizens would agree to surrender all of their powers to a sovereign power, the ***"Leviathan"***, on condition that every other citizen would do so also. The Leviathan would then protect the citizens of the commonwealth and provide a system of law and order. In return, the citizens owed the Leviathan their absolute obedience. Thus there was only one agreement and to break it would mean the return of society to its uncivilized, chaotic past. The only reason for disobeying the leviathan then was if it failed in its main duty of protecting the society from disorder and protecting the life and property of the citizenry.

The interesting thing to remember is that Hobbes' aims were actually liberal in nature. He wanted to produce a society in which people would be free to advance and enjoy life. His lack of faith in their ability to govern themselves forced him to conclude that an absolute ruler was then necessary in order to bring about the desired liberal society.

John Locke (1632-1704) An important thinker on the nature of democracy. He regarded the mind of man at birth as a tabula rasa, a blank slate upon which experience imprints knowledge and behavior. He did not believe in the idea of intuition or theories of innate knowledge. Locke also believed that all men are born good, independent and equal. That it is their actions that will determine their fate. Locke's views, in his most important work, ***Two Treatises of Civil Government*** (1690) attacked the theory of the divine right of kings and the nature of the state as conceived by *Thomas Hobbes.* Locke argued that sovereignty did not reside in the state, but with the people. The state is supreme, but only if it is bound by civil and what he called **"natural'** law. Many of Locke's political ideas, such as those relating to natural rights, property rights, the duty of the government to protect these rights and the rule of the majority, were embodied in the Constitution of the United States. He further held that revolution was not only a right, but also often an obligation and advocated a system of checks and balances in government. A government comprised of three branches of which the legislative is more powerful than either the executive or the judicial. He also believed in the separation of the church and state. As is apparent all of these ideas were to be incorporated in the Constitution of the United States. As such Locke is considered in many ways the true founding father of our Constitution and government system. He remains one of history's most influential political thinkers to this day.

Jean-Jacques Rousseau (1712-1778), one of the most famous and influential political theorists before the French Revolution. His most important and most studied work is **The Social Contract** (1762). He was concerned with what should be the proper form of society and government. However, unlike Hobbes, Rousseau did not view the state of nature as one of absolute chaos. The problem as Rousseau saw it was that the natural harmony of the state of nature was due to people's intuitive goodness not to their actual reason. Reason only developed once a civilized society was established.

The intuitive goodness was easily overwhelmed however by arguments for institutions of social control, which likened rulers to father figures and extolled the virtues of obedience to such figures. To a remarkable extent, strong leaders have, in Rousseau's judgment, already succeeded not only in extracting obedience from the citizens that they ruled, but also more importantly, have managed to justify such obedience as necessary.

"Man is born free, and everywhere he is in chains"

This is one of Rousseau's most famous quotes from "*The Social Contract*" he also went on to state:

"The strongest is never strong enough to be always the master, unless he transforms his might into right and obedience into duty. Hence the right of the strongest, a right which looks like an ironical pleasantry, but in fact is a well-established principle".

However, Rousseau denied that might make right. The only authority which citizens ought to obey is a legitimate one and the only legitimate authority would be one which:

"Defends and protects the person and property of each member with the whole force of the community, and where each, while joining with all the rest, still obeys no one but himself..."

The solution as Rousseau saw it was the *"Social Contract', a* contract which does bear a strong resemblance to many of Hobbes' ideas. The main principle was that each individual gives up all of their rights, not just certain rights, to the community as a whole. Nevertheless, this community is not as independent a force as in Hobbes' "Leviathan", rather it is an expression of the "general will" of the citizens themselves. By means of it, each citizen becomes the subject of every act of government. The citizens in effect will give up their "primitive", or "natural" freedoms in exchange for the "higher" freedom to follow the general will. Rousseau also had a strong psychological as well as political purpose in his ideology. The governmental power he envisioned was one, which would not and could not harm the individual members of the community because it was composed of them.

Rousseau attempted to unite the individual citizen with the government in such a way, and with such a strong psychological bond that the citizen would submit to the general will. Although the people's private interest might seem to be contrary at times to the general will. At the same time, Rousseau wanted the submission of private interests to the general will to involve no real sacrifice. The general will represented what the citizen really wanted as a citizen of a community as opposed to what the citizen might want as a selfish individual.

In fact, if the whole community forced dissenters to conform to the general will, it would not bother Rousseau because to him such coercion of the individual *means nothing more or less than that he will be forced to be free".* For Rousseau, <u>conformity to the general will was the highest form of freedom, obeying the general will was nothing more than obeying what was, in fact, actually the best for oneself.</u>

Karl Marx (1818-1883), was perhaps the most influential theorist of the 19th century and his influence has continued in various forms until this day. Contrary to popular belief, he was not the first to believe in socialist ideas, many of which had been around for some time and in various forms. Nevertheless, he was the first to call his system truly "scientific" or "**Scientific Socialism**". (Also called Marxian Socialism or as it is more widely known Marxism). It was opposed to other forms of socialism that had been called, (with some derision), "**Utopian Socialism**", (socialist ideas which though sounded good, nevertheless, would never really work in the real world). In fact, it is this very idea of Marxism being "scientific" that has been appealing to so many thinkers in modern history. (This and the underlying aspect of prophecy and redemption that is inherent, though seldom acknowledged, in Marxist ideology, has made it that much more attractive to those looking for something to believe in). Marx expounded his ideas in two major theoretical works, ***The Communist Manifesto*** (1848*)* and ***Das Capital*** ("Capital"), (vol.1 1867*).*

Skill 21.4: Recognize basic characteristics of various governmental systems and examine commonalities and differences among nations

The differences between democracy vs. totalitarianism and authoritarianism are an easier comparison to make since most understand the general differences, if not the specifics. While the differences between ***totalitarianism*** and ***authoritarianism*** is not as readily apparent, indeed most do not understand that there is a difference. That being the case, on the political spectrum democracy stands on one side and totalitarianism and authoritarianism both stand on the other. We will consider the differences between those two first. The difference between the two of them and democracy is in actuality a very great difference between totalitarianism and authoritarianism. That is why there are two different expressions, they are names for two different ideas, and that is where we will start.

Consider the two names. We see that totalitarianism is derived from the word ***total,*** while authoritarianism is derived from the word ***authority***. The essential idea is that while many may use the two expressions together and interchangeably, in regards to political movements such as Fascism, Communism, and similar types of regimes, there are really two different ideas. The difference is that a *totalitarian* system doesn't recognize the right for any aspect of society to be outside the influence of the state. Such a government sees itself as having a legitimate concern with all levels of human existence. Not only in regards to freedom of speech, or press, but even to social and religious institutions it tries to achieve a complete conformity to its ideals. Thus, those ideologies that presume to speak to all of society's ills, such as communism and fascism, look to this model for what they attempt to create in society. As Benito Mussolini said "*nothing outside of the state, nothing instead of the state".*

Those regimes that conform to the ***authoritarian*** model never presume to seek such a complete reordering of society. Thus, those dictatorships that arise without this social pretentious can best be described as authoritarian. They do usually leave some autonomous institutions, such as the Church, alone as long as they do not interfere with the state authority. This model can be seen in the history of Central and South America, where regimes, usually representing the interests of the upper classes, came to power and instituted dictatorships that seek to concentrate all political power in a few hands. While at the same time, no overall embracing ideology of control is even thought about, let alone attempted. This is seen in many of these countries. The Church soon becomes an institution of opposition to the state authority. After an initial period of acceptance, if the state was originally seen as providing order in the society and fighting communism. The only regimes where the drive for total society changing control was attempted was in those regimes in Cuba and Nicaragua that held to the Marxist-Communist world view.

Democracy is a much more familiar system to most. In the United States, it is the system under which we live. The term comes from the Greek "for the rule of the people" and that is just what it is. The two most prevalent types are ***direct*** and ***indirect*** democracy, (see ***Direct Democracy*** and ***Indirect Democracy,*** Section 1.1). Direct democracy usually involves all the people in a given area coming together to vote and decide on issues that will affect them. It is used only when the population involved is relatively small, for instance a local town meeting. An **indirect democracy** involves much larger areas and populations and involves the sending of representatives to a legislative body to vote on issues affecting the people. Such a system can be comprised of a ***Presidential*** or ***Parliamentary*** system. In the United States, we follow an indirect or representative democracy of the presidential type.

Oligarchy is a form of government where most or all political power effectively rests with a small segment of society (typically the most powerful, whether by wealth, family, military strength, or political influence). The word *oligarchy* is from the Greek words for "few" and "rule," hence, the rule of a few. Some political theorists have argued that all governments are inevitably oligarchies no matter the supposed political system.

Autocracy is a form of government in which political power rests in the hands of a single individual. The term comes from the Greek (autokrator) for "rules of one's self.

Skill 21.5: Analyze the emergence of different types of government in the world

Anarchism - Political movement believing in the elimination of all government and its replacement by a cooperative community of individuals. Sometimes it has involved political violence such as assassinations of important political or governmental figures. The historical banner of the movement is a black flag.

Communism - A belief as well as a political system, characterized by the ideology of class conflict and revolution, one party state and dictatorship, repressive police apparatus, and government ownership of the means of production and distribution of goods and services. A revolutionary ideology preaching the eventual overthrow of all other political orders and the establishment of one world Communist government. Same as Marxism. The historical banner of the movement is a red flag and variation of stars, hammer and sickles, representing the various types of workers.

Dictatorship - The rule by an individual or small group of individuals (Oligarchy) that centralizes all political control in itself and enforces its will with a terrorist police force.

Fascism - A belief as well as a political system, opposed ideologically to Communism, though similar in basic structure, with a one party state, centralized political control and a repressive police system. It however tolerates private ownership of the means of production, though it maintains tight overall control. Central to its belief is the idolization of the Leader, a "Cult of the Personality," and most often an expansionist ideology. Examples have been German Nazism and Italian Fascism.

Monarchy - The rule of a nation by a Monarch, (a non-elected usually hereditary leader), most often a king or queen. It may or may not be accompanied by some measure of democratic open institutions and elections at various levels. A modern example is Great Britain, where it is called a Constitutional Monarchy.

Parliamentary System - A system of government with a legislature, usually involving a multiplicity of political parties and often coalition politics. There is division between the head of state and head of government. Head of government is usually known as a Prime Minister who is also usually the head of the largest party. The head of government and cabinet usually both sit and vote in the parliament. Head of state is most often an elected president, (though in the case of a constitutional monarchy, like Great Britain, the sovereign may take the place of a president as head of state). A government may fall when a majority in parliament votes "no confidence" in the government.

Presidential System - A system of government with a legislature, can involve few or many political parties, no division between head of state and head of government. The President serves in both capacities. The President is elected either by direct or indirect election. A President and cabinet usually do not sit or vote in the legislature and the President may or may not be the head of the largest political party. A President can thus rule even without a majority in the legislature. He can only be removed from office before an election for major infractions of the law.

Socialism - Political belief and system in which the state takes a guiding role in the national economy and provides extensive social services to its population. It may or may not own outright means of production, but even where it does not, it exercises tight control. It usually promotes democracy, (Democratic-Socialism), though the heavy state involvement produces excessive bureaucracy and usually inefficiency. Taken to an extreme it may lead to Communism as government control increases and democratic practice decreases. Ideologically the two movements are very similar in both belief and practice, as Socialists also preach the superiority of their system to all others and that it will become the eventual natural order. It is also considered for that reason a variant of Marxism. It also has used a red flag as a symbol.

COMPETENCY 22.0: Understand principles of democratic self-government in the United States and the rights and responsibilities of citizens in a democratic society.

Skill 22.1: Recognize the ideals and issues expressed in the Declaration of Independence and analyze the fundamental ideas and purposes of the U.S. Constitution and the Constitution of the State of New Mexico.

Declaration of Independence - The Declaration of Independence was the founding document of the United States of America. The Articles of Confederation were the first attempt of the newly independent states to reach a new understanding amongst themselves. The Declaration was intended to demonstrate the reasons that the colonies were seeking separation from Great Britain. Conceived by and written for the most part by Thomas Jefferson, it is not only important for what it says, but also for how it says it. The Declaration is in many respects a poetic document. Instead of a simple recitation of the colonists' grievances, it set out clearly the reasons why the colonists were seeking their freedom from Great Britain. They had tried all means to resolve the dispute peacefully. It was the right of a people, when all other methods of addressing their grievances have been tried and failed, to separate themselves from that power that was keeping them from fully expressing their rights to "**life, liberty, and the pursuit of happiness**".

Articles of Confederation - This was the first political system under which the newly independent colonies tried to organize themselves. It was drafted after the Declaration of Independence in 1776, was passed by the Continental Congress on November 15, 1777, ratified by the thirteen states, and took effect on March 1, 1781.

The newly independent states were unwilling to give too much power to a national government. They were already fighting Great Britain. They did not want to replace one harsh ruler with another. After many debates, the form of the Articles was accepted. Each state agreed to send delegates to the Congress. Each state had one vote in the Congress. The Articles gave Congress the power to declare war, appoint military officers, and coin money. The Congress was also responsible for foreign affairs. The Articles of Confederation limited the powers of Congress by giving the states final authority. Although Congress could pass laws, at least nine of the thirteen states had to approve a law before it went into effect. Congress could not pass any laws regarding taxes. To get money, Congress had to ask each state for it, no state could be forced to pay.

Thus, the Articles created a loose alliance among the thirteen states. The national government was weak, in part, because it didn't have a strong chief executive to carry out laws passed by the legislature. This weak national government might have worked if the states were able to get along with each other. However, many different disputes arose and there was no way of settling them. Thus, the delegates went to meet again to try to fix the Articles; instead they ended up scrapping them and created a new Constitution that learned from these earlier mistakes.

They created a government that as Benjamin Franklin said, *"though it may not be the best there is";* he said that he, *"wasn't sure that it could be possible to create one better".* A fact that might be true considering that the Constitution has lasted, through civil war, foreign wars, depression, and social revolution for over 200 years.

It is truly a living document because of its ability to remain strong while allowing itself to be changed with changing times.

The Declaration of independence is an outgrowth of both ancient Greek ideas of democracy and individual rights and the ideas of the European Enlightenment and the Renaissance, especially the ideology of the political thinker ***John Locke***. Thomas Jefferson (1743-1826) the principle author of the Declaration borrowed much from Locke's theories and writings *(See **John Locke*** Section 5.3).

Essentially, Jefferson applied Locke's principles to the contemporary American situation. Jefferson argued that the currently reigning King George III had repeatedly violated the rights of the colonists as subjects of the British Crown. Disdaining the colonial petition for redress of grievances (a right guaranteed by the Declaration of Rights of 1689), the King seemed bent upon establishing an "absolute tyranny" over the colonies. Such disgraceful behavior itself violated the reasons for which government had been instituted. The American colonists were left with no choice, *"it is their right, it is their duty, to throw off such a government, and to provide new guards for their future security"* so wrote Thomas Jefferson.

Yet, though his fundamental principles were derived from Locke's, Jefferson was bolder than his intellectual mentor was. He went farther in that his view of natural rights was much broader than Locke's and less tied to the idea of property rights.

For instance, though both Jefferson and Locke believed very strongly in property rights, especially as a guard for individual liberty, the famous line in the Declaration about people being endowed with the inalienable right to "life, liberty and the pursuit of happiness", was originally Locke's idea. It was "life, liberty, and *private property".* Jefferson didn't want to tie the idea of rights to any one particular circumstance however he changed Locke's original specific reliance on property and substituted the more general idea of human happiness as being a fundamental right that is the duty of a government to protect.

Locke and Jefferson both stressed that the individual citizen's rights are prior to and more important than any obligation to the state. Government is the servant of the people. The officials of government hold their positions at the sufferance of the people. Their job is to ensure that the rights of the people are preserved and protected by that government. The citizen come first, the government comes second. The Declaration thus produced turned out to be one of the most important and historic documents that expounded the inherent rights of all peoples; a document still looked up to as an ideal and an example.

Skill 22.2: Recognize important sources of political, legal, and personal rights.

The terms "**civil liberties**" and "**civil rights**" are often used interchangeably, but there are some fine distinctions between the two terms. The term civil liberties is more often used to imply that the state has a positive role to play in assuring that all its' citizens will have equal protection and justice under the law with equal opportunities to exercise their privileges of citizenship and to participate fully in the life of the nation, regardless of race, religion, sex, color or creed. The term civil rights is used more often to refer to rights that may be described as guarantees that are specified as against the state authority implying limitations on the actions of the state to interfere with citizens' liberties. Although the term "civil rights" has thus been identified with the ideal of equality and the term "civil liberties" with the idea of freedom, the two concepts are really inseparable and interacting. Equality implies the proper ordering of liberty in a society so that one individual's freedom does not infringe on the rights of others.

The beginnings of civil liberties and the idea of civil rights in the United States go back to the ideas of the ancient Greeks. The experience of the early struggle for civil rights against the British and the very philosophies that led people to come to the New World in the first place were still fresh in people's minds. Religious freedom, political freedom, and the right to live one's life as one sees fit are basic to the American ideal. These were embodied in the ideas expressed in the Declaration of Independence and the Constitution.

All these ideas found their final expression in the United States Constitution's first ten amendments, known as the **Bill of Rights**. In 1789, the first Congress passed these first amendments and by December 1791, three-fourths of the states at that time had ratified them. The Bill of Rights protects certain liberties and basic rights. James Madison who wrote the amendments said that the Bill of Rights does not give Americans these rights. People, Madison said, already have these rights. They are natural rights that belong to all human beings. The Bill of Rights simply prevents the governments from taking away these rights.

To summarize:

The first amendment guarantees the basic rights of freedom of religion, freedom of speech, freedom of the press, and freedom of assembly.

The next three amendments came out of the colonists' struggle with Great Britain. For example, the third amendment prevents Congress from forcing citizens to keep troops in their homes. Before the Revolution, Great Britain tried to coerce the colonists to house soldiers.

Amendments five through eight protect citizens who are accused of crimes and are brought to trial. Every citizen has the right to due process of law, (due process as defined earlier, being that the government must follow the same fair rules for everyone brought to trial.) These rules include the right to a trial by an impartial jury, the right to be defended by a lawyer, and the right to a speedy trial.

The last two amendments limit the powers of the federal government to those that are expressly granted in the Constitution, any rights not expressly mentioned in the Constitution, thus, belong to the states or to the people.

In regards to specific guarantees:

Freedom of Religion: Religious freedom has not been seriously threatened in the United States historically. The policy of the government has been guided by the premise that church and state should be separate. However, when religious practices have been at cross-purposes with attitudes prevailing in the nation at particular times, there has been restrictions placed on these practices. Some of these have been restrictions against the practice of polygamy that is supported by certain religious groups. The idea of animal sacrifice that is promoted by some religious beliefs is generally prohibited. The use of mind0altering illegal substances that some use in religious rituals has been restricted. In the United States, all recognized religious institutions are tax-exempt in following the idea of separation of church and state, and therefore, there have been many quasi-religious groups that have in the past tried to take advantage of this fact. All of these issues continue, and most likely will continue to occupy both political and legal considerations for some time to come.

Freedom of Speech, Press, and Assembly: These rights historically have been given wide latitude in their practices, though there has been instances when one or the other have been limited for various reasons. The classic limitation, for instance, in regards to freedom of speech, has been the famous precept that an individual is prohibited from yelling fire! in a crowded theatre. This prohibition is an example of the state saying that freedom of speech does not extend to speech that might endanger other people. There is also a prohibition against **slander,** or the knowingly stating of a deliberate falsehood against one party by another. There are many regulations regarding freedom of the press, the most common example are the various laws against **libel**, (or the printing of a known falsehood). In times of national emergency, various restrictions have been placed on the rights of press, speech and sometimes assembly.

The legal system in recent years has also undergone a number of serious changes or challenges, with the interpretation of some constitutional guarantees.

America also has a number of organizations that present themselves as champions of the fight for civil liberties and civil rights in this country. Much criticism, however, has been raised at times against these groups as to whether or not they are really protecting rights, or following a specific ideology, perhaps attempting to create "new" rights, or in many cases, looking at the strict letter of the law, as opposed to what the law actually intends.

"Rights" come with a measure of responsibility and respect for the public order, all of which must be taken into consideration.

Overall, the American experience has been one of exemplary conduct in regards to the protection of individual rights. Where there has been a lag in its practice, notably the refusal to grant full and equal rights to blacks, the fact of their enslavement, and the second class status of women for much of American history, negates the good that the country has done in other areas. Other than the American Civil War, the country has proved itself to be more or less resilient in being able, for the most part, peacefully, to change when it has not lived up to its' stated ideals in practice. What has been called "the virtual bloodless civil rights revolution" is a case in point.

Though much effort and suffering accompanied the struggle, in the end it did succeed in changing the foundation of society in such a profound way that would have been unheard of in many other countries without the strong tradition of freedom and liberty that was, and is, the underlying feature of American society.

How best to move forward with ensuring civil liberties and civil rights for all continues to dominate the national debate. In recent times, issues seem to revolve not around individual rights but what has been called "group rights". At the forefront of the debate is whether some specific remedies like affirmative action, quotas, gerrymandering and various other forms of preferential treatment are actually fair or just as bad as the ills they are supposed to cure. At the present, no easy answers seem to be forthcoming. It is a testament to the American system that it has shown itself able to enter into these debates, to find solutions and tended to come out stronger.

The fact that the United States has the longest single constitutional history in the modern era is just one reason to be optimistic about the future of American liberty.

Skill 22.3: Examine the rights, responsibilities, and privileges of individuals in relation to family, social group, career, community, and nation.

A citizen in a democratic society is expected to do certain things in order to remain such a citizen. First and foremost, that person is expected to follow the laws of that society. The vast majority of the laws of a democratic society have been enacted to facilitate the continuance of that society. Many of these laws also have the rights of the citizens in mind. It is certainly easier to follow some of these laws than others. Throughout the history of democratic societies, however, laws have been passed that seem to violate the very spirit of the rights of those citizens. In such cases, people have worked to overturn such laws, either directly or by means of pursuing judicial solutions or indirectly by way of making sure that the lawmakers who created such laws are not re-elected. This reinforces the idea that citizens have a responsibility to themselves as well and that if government is infringing on their basic rights, they have a natural right to speak up and do something about it. Related to this is the idea that the government of a democratic society exists in part to protect the rights of its citizens. People expect such protection, in both real and virtual terms. Real terms include civil and countrywide defense, and virtual terms include laws and the people who make them. If such protection standards are not being met, then the citizens have the right and even the duty to demand such protection and work to see that it is maintained or restored.

Citizens of a democratic society are also expected to participate in the political process, either directly or indirectly. In theory, anyone who is a citizen of a democratic society can get himself or herself elected to *something*, be it at the local, state, or federal level. Other ways to participate in the political process include donating time and/or money to the political campaigns of others and speaking out on behalf of or against certain issues. The most basic level of participation in the political process is to vote.

A democratic society is built on the theory of participatory government. Citizens of such a society expect that political debates on important issues will be public and ongoing, so that they can keep themselves informed on how their representatives view such issues. Information is meant to be shared, especially in a democratic society. If major political meetings begin to take place in private, without witnesses or records, then the citizens have the right to demand that such proceedings be made current, for only then can they know whether their government is acting on their behalf.

Skill 22.4: Recognize the continuing influence of the key ideas of individual human dignity, liberty, justice, equality, and the rule of law.

The cause of human rights has been advanced significantly since the 18th Century, both in theory and in fact. Several fundamental statements of human rights have extended and established human rights throughout the world.

The U.S. Declaration of Independence declared that certain truths are self-evident: all men are created equal, that they are inherently endowed with certain unalienable rights that no government should ever violate. These rights include the right to life, liberty and the pursuit of happiness. When a government infringes upon those rights or fails to protect those rights, it is both the right and the duty of the people to overthrow that government and to establish in its place a new government that will protect those rights.

The Declaration of the Rights of Man and of the Citizen is a document created by the French National Assembly and issued in 1789. It sets forth the "natural, inalienable and sacred rights of man." It proclaims the following rights:

- Men are born and remain free and equal in rights. Social distinctions may only be founded upon the general good.
- The aim of all political association is the preservation of the natural and imprescriptible rights of man: liberty, property, security and resistance to oppression.
- All sovereignty resides essentially in the nation. No body or individual may exercise any authority which does not proceed directly from the nation.
- Liberty is the freedom to do everything which injures no one else; hence the exercise of these rights has no limits except those which assure to the other members of the society the enjoyment of the same rights. These limits can only be determined by law.
- Law can only prohibit such actions as are hurtful to society.
- Law is the expression of the general will. Every citizen has a right to participate in the formation of law. It must be the same for all. All citizens, being equal in the eyes of the law, are equally eligible to all dignities and to all public positions and occupations, according to their abilities.
- No person shall be accused, arrested or imprisoned except in the cases and according to the forms prescribed by law.
- The law shall provide for such punishments only as are strictly and obviously necessary.
- All persons are held innocent until they have been declared guilty. If it is necessary to arrest a person, all harshness not essential to the securing of the prisoner's person shall be severely repressed by law.

- No one shall be disquieted on account of his opinions, including religious views, provided their manifestation does not disturb the peace.
- The free communication of ideas and opinions is one of the most precious

of the rights of man.

- The security of the rights of man and of the citizen requires public military force. These forces are, therefore, established for the good of all and not for the personal advantage of those to whom they shall be entrusted.
- A common contribution is essential for the maintenance of the public forces and for the cost of administration. This should be equitably distributed among all the citizens in proportion to their means.
- All the citizens have a right to decide, either personally or by their representatives, as to the necessity of the public contribution.
- Society has the right to require of every public agent an account of his administration.

- A society in which the observance of the law is not assured, nor the separation of powers defined, has no constitution at all.
- Since property is an inviolable and sacred right, no one shall be deprived thereof except where public necessity, legally determined, shall clearly demand it, and then only on condition that the owner shall have been previously and equitably indemnified.

The United Nations Declaration of Universal Human Rights (1948). The declaration opens with these words: "Whereas recognition of the inherent dignity and of the equal and inalienable rights of all members of the human family is the foundation of freedom, justice and peace in the world. Whereas disregard and contempt for human rights have resulted in barbarous acts which have outraged the conscience of mankind, and the advent of a world in which human beings shall enjoy freedom of speech and belief and freedom from fear and want has been proclaimed as the highest aspiration of the common people."

1. All human beings are born free and equal in dignity and rights. They are endowed with reason and conscience and should act towards one another in a spirit of brotherhood.
2. Everyone is entitled to all the rights and freedoms set forth in this Declaration, without distinction of any kind.
3. Everyone has the right to life, liberty and security of person.
4. No one shall be held in slavery or servitude.
5. No one shall be subjected to torture or to cruel, inhuman or degrading treatment or punishment.
6. Everyone has the right to recognition everywhere as a person before the law.
7. All are equal before the law and are entitled without any discrimination to equal protection of the law.
8. Everyone has the right to an effective remedy by the competent national tribunals for acts violating the fundamental rights granted him by the constitution of by law.
9. No one shall be subjected to arbitrary arrest, detention or exile.

10. Everyone is entitled in full equality to a fair and public hearing by an independent and impartial tribunal, in the determination of his rights and obligations and of any criminal charge against him.
11. Everyone charged with a penal offence has the right to be presumed innocent until proved guilty according to law in a public trial at which he has had all the guarantees necessary for his defence. No one shall be held guilty of any penal offence on account of any act or omission which did not constitute a penal offence, under national or international law, at the time when it was committed
12. No one shall be subjected to arbitrary interference with his privacy, family, home or correspondence, nor to attacks upon his honour and reputation.
13. Everyone has the right to freedom of movement and residence within the borders of each state. Everyone has the right to leave any country, including his own, and to return to his country.
14. Everyone has the right to seek and to enjoy in other countries asylum from persecution. This right may not be invoked in the case of prosecutions genuinely arising from non-political crimes or from acts contrary to the purposes and principles of the United Nations.
15. Everyone has the right to a nationality. No one shall be arbitrarily deprived of his nationality nor denied the right to change his nationality.
16. Men and women of full age have the right to marry and to found a family. They are entitled to equal rights as to marriage, during marriage and at its dissolution. Marriage shall be entered into only with the free and full consent of the intending spouses. The family is the natural and fundamental group unit of society and is entitled to protection by society and the State.
17. Everyone has the right to own property alone or in association with others. No one shall be arbitrarily deprived of his property.
18. Everyone has the right to freedom of thought, conscience and religion, including the right to change his religion or belief, and freedom to manifest his religion or belief in teaching, practice, worship and observance.
19. Everyone has the right to freedom of opinion and expression.
20. Everyone has the fight to freedom of peaceful assembly and association. No one may be compelled to belong to an association
21. Everyone has the right to take part in the government of his country, directly or through freely chosen representatives. Everyone has the right of equal access to public service in his country. The will of the people shall be the basis of the authority of government.

22. Everyone has the right to social security and is entitled to realization of the economic, social and cultural rights indispensable for his dignity and the free development of his personality.
23. Everyone has the right to work. Everyone, without any discrimination, has the right to equal pay for equal work. Everyone who works has the right to just and favourable remuneration. Everyone has the right to form and to join trade unions for the protection of his interests.
24. Everyone has the right to rest and leisure, including reasonable limitation of working hours and periodic holidays with pay.
25. Everyone has the right to a standard of living adequate for the health and well-being of himself and his family, and the right to security in the event of unemployment, sickness, disability, widowhood, old age or other lack of livelihood in circumstances beyond his control. Motherhood and childhood are entitled to special care and assistance. All children shall enjoy the same social protection.
26. Everyone has the right to education. Education shall be directed to the full development of the human personality and to the strengthening of respect for human rights and fundamental freedoms. Parents have a prior right to choose the kind of education that shall be given to their children.
27. Everyone has the right freely to participate in the cultural life of the community. Everyone has the right to the protection of the moral and materials interests resulting from any scientific, literary or artistic production of which he is the author.
28. Everyone is entitled to a social and international order in which the rights and freedoms set forth in this Declaration can be fully realized.

The United Nations Convention on the Rights of the Child brings together the rights of children as they are enumerated in other international documents. In this document, those rights are clearly and completely stated, along with the explanation of the guiding principals that define the way society views children. The goal of the document is to clarify the environment that is necessary to enable every human being to develop to their full potential. The Convention calls for resources and contributions to be made to ensure the full development and survival of all children. The document also requires the establishment of appropriate means to protect children from neglect, exploitation and abuse. The document also recognizes that parents have the most important role in raising children.

Skill 22.5: Analyze developments that have expanded the rights of individuals and groups in U.S. public life.

The **Seneca Falls Convention** was a gathering of women and men in 1848, in the New York mill town of Seneca Falls, to address the rights of women in the United States. The growing momentum of the anti-slavery movement and discussion over the rights of black citizens had drawn attention to the rights of female citizens, who could not vote or hold important positions in American government. Some 300 people attended the convention, which culminated in the publication of a "Declaration of Sentiments," which was modeled on the Declaration of Independence and called for equal participation for women.

The Seneca Falls Convention is considered and early milestone in the feminist movement. Following is just a partial list of well-known Americans who contributed their leadership and talents in various fields and reforms:

Lucretia Mott and Elizabeth Cady Stanton for **women's rights**

Emma Hart Willard, Catharine Esther Beecher, and Mary Lyon for **education for women**

Dr. Elizabeth Blackwell, the **first woman doctor**

Antoinette Louisa Blackwell, the **first female minister**

Dorothea Lynde Dix for **reforms in prisons and insane asylums** Elihu Burritt and William Ladd for **peace movements**

Robert Owen for a **Utopian society**

Horace Mann, Henry Barmard, Calvin E. Stowe, Caleb Mills, and John Swett for **public education**

Benjamin Lundy, David Walker, William Lloyd Garrison, Isaac Hooper, Arthur and Lewis Tappan, Theodore Weld, Frederick Douglass, Harriet Tubman, James G. Birney, Henry Highland Garnet, James Forten, Robert Purvis, Harriet Beecher Stowe, Wendell Phillips, and John Brown for **abolition of slavery and the Underground Railroad**

Louisa Mae Alcott, James Fenimore Cooper, Washington Irving, Walt Whitman, Henry David Thoreau, Ralph Waldo Emerson, Herman Melville, Richard Henry Dana, Nathaniel Hawthorne, Henry Wadsworth Longfellow, John Greenleaf Whittier, Edgar Allan Poe, Oliver Wendell Holmes, **famous writers**

John C. Fremont, Zebulon Pike, Kit Carson, **explorers**

Henry Clay, Daniel Webster, Stephen Douglas, John C. Calhoun, American **statesmen** Robert Fulton, Cyrus McCormick, Eli Whitney, **inventors**

Noah Webster, American **dictionary and spellers**

See Skill 6.5 for detailed information on the Civil Rights movement.

COMPETENCY 23: Understand the structure, organization, and operation of government in the United States at the national, state, and local levels.

Skill 23.1: Analyze the concept of federalism and recognize its evolution in American political thought and practice.

Federalism in colonial America meant belief in a strong central government. The Articles of Confederation provided for a weak central government, and lawmakers and citizens alike saw the unlikelihood of such an idea. One of the debates that shaped the ratification of the Constitution was the idea that the national government would be superior in status to state and local governments. Indeed, the national government is often called the *federal* government as well. In this historical political debate, those who favored a strong federal debate were called Federalists and those opposed styled themselves anti-Federalists.

Beginning with opinions written by Chief Justice John Marshall (including *Gibbons* v. *Ogden* and *McCulloch* v. *Maryland*), a series of Supreme Court decisions affirmed the supremacy of the federal government over that of the states. After all, if a state could tax the federal government, as was argued in *McCulloch*, then the federal government could theoretically yield its authority to that state, giving it supremacy over every other state; and *that* would undermine the authority of the federal government, not only in the minds of the judges of the federal and state courts but also in the hearts and minds of the people, of both the United States and other countries. This tradition has continued to the present day, with states being unable to sue the federal government, disputes between states being settled by federal courts, and foreign threats being answered by a national defense force. In today's political discussions, the idea of states' superseding the federal government seems foreign indeed.

In the present day, however, the word **federalism** refers to the idea of democracy or republic itself, not necessarily the idea that the national government is superior to state and local governments. More to the point, federalism describes a government whose powers are divided between entities, so that no one part of that government is totally supreme over others. This is to be found in the famous "checks and balances" ideas of the Constitution itself. The three top branches of the U.S. Government have their various duties and responsibilities, and each can "check" or "balance" the other two, with the result being a three-headed whole that exists to protect and further the rights and defense of its citizens. Federalism is also used to describe the idea that power and authority is divided, not only between the three top branches of the federal government but also between the federal government as a whole and state and local governments. Citizens of such a society are expected to be sovereign to governments on all three levels, and the governments of those three levels are expected to legislate accordingly.

Skill 23.2: Examine the structure and operation of the federal government.

In the United States, the three branches of the federal government: the **Executive**, the **Legislative**, and the **Judicial** divide their powers thus:

Legislative - Article I of the Constitution established the legislative, or law-making branch of the government called the Congress. It is made up of two houses, the House of Representatives and the Senate. Voters in all states elect the members who serve in each respective house of Congress. The Legislative branch is responsible for making laws, raising and printing money, regulating trade, establishing the postal service and federal courts, approving the President's appointments, declaring war and supporting the armed forces. The Congress also has the power to change the Constitution itself and to impeach (bring charges against) the President. Charges for impeachment are brought by the House of Representatives and are tried in the Senate .

Executive – Article II of the Constitution created the Executive branch of the government, headed by the President, who leads the country, recommends new laws, and can veto bills passed by the Legislative branch. As the chief of state, the President is responsible for carrying out the laws of the country and the treaties and declarations of war passed by the Legislative branch. The President also appoints federal judges and is Commander in Chief of the military when it is called into service. Other members of the Executive branch include the Vice-President, also elected. Various cabinet members as he might appoint, ambassadors, presidential advisers, members of the armed forces, and other appointed and civil servants of government agencies, departments and bureaus. Though the President appoints them, they then must be approved by the legislative branch.

Judicial - Article III of the Constitution established the Judicial branch of government headed by the Supreme Court. The Supreme Court has the power to rule that a law passed by the Legislature, or an act of the Executive branch is illegal and unconstitutional (See *Judicial Review,* Section 1.2). In an appeal capacity, citizens, businesses, and government officials can also ask the Supreme Court to review a decision made in a lower court if someone believes that the ruling by a judge is unconstitutional. The Judicial branch also includes lower federal courts known as federal district courts that have been established by the Congress. The courts try lawbreakers and review cases refereed from other courts.

Skill 23.3: Compare the structure and functions of federal, state, and local governments

Powers delegated to the federal government

1. To tax.
2. To borrow and coin money
3. To establish postal service.
4. To grant patents and copyrights.
5. To regulate interstate & foreign commerce.
6. To establish courts.
7. To declare war.
8. To raise and support the armed forces.
9. To govern territories.
10. To define and punish felonies and piracy on the high seas.
11. To fix standards of weights and measures.
12. To conduct foreign affairs.

Powers reserved to the states:

1. To regulate intrastate trade.
2. To establish local governments.
3. To protect general welfare.
4. To protect life and property.
5. To ratify amendments.
6. To conduct elections.
7. To make state and local laws.

Concurrent powers of the federal government and states.

1. Both Congress and the states may tax.
2. Both may borrow money.
3. Both may charter banks and corporations.
4. Both may establish courts.
5. Both may make and enforce laws.
6. Both may take property for public purposes.
7. Both may spend money to provide for the public welfare.

Implied powers of the federal government.

1. To establish banks or other corporations implied from delegated powers to tax, borrow, and to regulate commerce.
2. To spend money for roads, schools, health, insurance, etc. implied from powers to establish post roads, to tax to provide for general welfare and defense, and to regulate commerce.
3. To create military academies, implied from powers to raise and support an armed force.
4. To locate and generate sources of power and sell surplus, implied from powers to dispose of government property, commerce, and war powers.
5. To assist and regulate agriculture, implied from power to tax and spend for general welfare and regulate commerce.

The Federal Court System - is provided for in the Constitution of the United States on the theory that the judicial power of the federal government could not be entrusted to the individual states, many of which had opposed the idea of a strong federal government in the first place. Thus Article III, Section 1, of the Constitution says: *"the judicial power of the United States shall be vested in one Supreme Court, and in such inferior courts as the Congress may from time to time ordain and establish".* In accordance with these provisions, Congress passed the

Judiciary Act in 1789, organizing the Supreme Court of the United States and establishing a system of federal courts of inferior jurisdiction. The states were left to establish their own judicial systems subject to the exclusive overall jurisdiction of the federal courts and to Article VI of the Constitution declaring the judges of the state courts to be bound to the Constitution and to the laws and treaties of the United States. This developed a dual system of judicial power and authority in the United States.

The jurisdiction of the federal courts is further defined in Article III, Section 2 of the Constitution as extending in law and in equity to all cases arising under the Constitution and through federal legislation to controversies in which the United States is a party, including those arising from treaties with other governments, to maritime cases on the high seas in areas under American control, to disagreements between the states, between a citizen and a state, between citizens in different states and between a citizen and a foreign nation. The federal courts were also originally empowered with jurisdiction over problems airing between citizens of one state and the government of another state.
The 11th Amendment to the Constitution (ratified 1795) however removed from federal jurisdiction those cases in which citizens of one state were the plaintiffs and the government of another state was the defendant. The amendment, though, did not disturb the jurisdiction of the federal courts in cases in which a state government is a plaintiff and a citizen of another state the defendant. The federal courts also have exclusive jurisdiction in all patent and copyright cases and by congressional law in 1898, the federal courts were empowered with original jurisdiction in all bankruptcy cases.

The courts established under the powers granted by Article III Section 1 & 2 of the Constitution are known as Constitutional Courts. Judges of the Constitutional courts are appointed for life by the President with the approval of the Senate. These courts are the ***district courts, lower courts of original jurisdiction,*** **the** ***courts of appeals*** (before 1948, known as the circuit court of appeals), exercising appellate jurisdiction over the district courts and the ***Supreme Court***. A district court functions in each of the more than ninety federal judicial districts and in the District of Columbia.

A court of appeals functions in each of the ten federal judicial circuits and also in the District of Columbia, (The federal district court and the circuit court of appeals of the District of Columbia performs all of the same functions discharged in the states by the state courts). All of the lower federal courts operate under the uniform rules of procedure promulgated by the Supreme Court.

The Supreme Court of the United States is the highest appellate court in the country and is a court of original jurisdiction according to the Constitution *"in all cases affecting ambassadors, other public ministers and consuls, and those in which a state shall be a party".* By virtue of its' power to declare legislation unconstitutional the Supreme Court is also the final arbitrator of all Constitutional questions.

Other federal courts, established by Congress under powers to be implied in other articles of the Constitution, are called legislative courts. These courts are the **Court of Claims, the Court of Customs and Patent Appeals, the Customs Court,** and the territorial courts established in the federally administered territories of the United States.

The special jurisdictions of these courts are defined by the Congress of the United States. (Except in the case of the territorial courts, which are courts of general jurisdiction), the specialized functions of these courts are suggested by their titles.

The State Courts - Each state has an independent system of courts operating under the laws and constitution of that particular individual state. Broadly speaking, the state courts are based on the English judicial system as it existed in colonial times, but as modified by succeeding statues. The character and names of the various courts differ from state to state, but the state courts as a whole have general jurisdiction, except in cases in which exclusive jurisdiction has by law been vested in the federal courts. In cases involving the United States Constitution or federal laws or treaties and such, the state courts are governed by the decisions of the Supreme Court of the United States and their decisions are subject to review by it.

Cases involving the federal Constitution, federal laws, or treaties and the like, may be brought to either the state courts, or the federal courts. Ordinary **civil suits** not involving any of the aforementioned elements can be brought only to the state courts, except in cases of different state citizenship between the parties, in which case the suit may be brought to a federal court. By an act of Congress, however, suits involving different federal questions or different state citizenship may be brought to a federal court only when it is a civil suit that involves $3,000 or more. All such cases that involve a smaller amount must be brought to a state court only. In accordance with a congressional law, a suit brought before a state court may be removed to a federal court at the option of the defendant.

Bearing in mind that any statements about state courts that is trying to give a typical explanation of all of them is subject to many exceptions. The following may be taken as a general comprehensive statement of their respective jurisdictions, functions, and organization.

County courts of general original jurisdiction exercise both criminal and civil jurisdictions in most states. A few states maintain separate courts of criminal and civil law inherited from the English judicial system. Between the lower courts and the supreme appellate courts of each state in a number of states, are intermediate appellate courts which, like the federal courts of appeals, provide faster justice for individuals by disposing of a large number of cases which would otherwise be added to the overcrowded calendars of the higher courts. Courts of last resort, the highest appellate courts for the states in criminal and civil cases are usually called **State Supreme Courts**.

The state court system also includes a number of minor, local courts with limited jurisdictions; these courts dispose of minor offenses and relatively small civil actions. Included in this classification are police and municipal courts in various cities and towns, and the courts presided over by justices of the peace in rural areas.

Skill 23.4: Recognize major features of governmental organization and political processes at the local, state, and tribal levels.

The various governments of the United States and of Native American tribes have many similarities and a few notable differences. They are more similar than not; and all in all, they reflect the tendency of their people to prefer a representative that has checks and balances that look after one another and the people that keep them in power.

The **United States Government** has three distinct branches: the Executive, the Legislative, and the Judicial. Each has its own function and its own "check" on the other two.

The Legislative Branch consists primarily of the House of Representatives and the Senate. Each house has a set number of members, the House having 435 apportioned according to national population trends and the Senate having 100 (two for each state). House members serve two-year terms; Senators serve six-year terms. Each house can initiate a bill, but that bill must be passed by a majority of both houses in order to become a law. The House is primarily responsible for initiating spending bills; the Senate is responsible for ratifying treaties that the President might sign with other countries.

The Executive Branch has the President and Vice-President as its two main figures. The President is the commander-in-chief of the armed forces and the person who can approve or veto all bills from Congress. (Vetoed bills can become law anyway if two-thirds of each house of Congress vote to pass it over the President's objections.) The President is elected to a four-year term by the Electoral College, which usually mirrors the popular will of the people. The President can serve a total of two terms. The Executive Branch also has several departments consisting of advisors to the President. These departments include State, Defense, Education, Treasury, and Commerce, among others. Members of these departments are appointed by the President and approved by Congress.

The Judicial Branch consists of a series of courts and related entities, with the top body being the Supreme Court. The Court decides whether laws of the land are constitutional; any law invalidated by the Supreme Court is no longer in effect. The Court also regulates the enforcement and constitutionality of the Amendments to the Constitution. The Supreme Court is the highest court in the land. Cases make their way to it from federal Appeals Courts, which hear appeals of decisions made by federal District Courts. These lower two levels of courts are found in regions around the country. Supreme Court Justices are appointed by the President and confirmed by the Senate. They serve for life. Lower-court judges are elected in popular votes within their states.

State governments are mirror images of the federal government, with a few important exceptions: Governors are not technically commanders in chief of armed forces; state supreme court decisions can be appealed to federal courts; terms of state representatives and senators vary; judges, even of the state supreme courts, are elected by popular vote; governors and legislators have term limits that vary by state.

Local governments vary widely across the country, although none of them has a judicial branch per se. Some local governments consist of a city council, of which the mayor is a member and has limited powers; in other cities, the mayor is the head of the government and the city council are the chief lawmakers. Local governments also have less strict requirements for people running for office than do the state and federal governments.

The format of the governments of the various **Native American tribes** varies as well. Most tribes have governments along the lines of the U.S. federal or state governments. An example is the Cherokee Nation, which has a 15-member Tribal Council as the head of the Legislative branch, a Principal Chief and Deputy Chief who head up the Executive branch and carry out the laws passed by the Tribal Council, and a Judicial branch made up of the Judicial Appeals Tribunal and the Cherokee Nation District Court. Members of the Tribunal are appointed by the Principal Chief. Members of the other two branches are elected by popular vote of the Cherokee Nation.

COMPETENCY 24: Understand the U.S. election process and the role of political parties and participatory citizenship in the U.S. political system.

Skill 24.1: Recognize components of the U.S. electoral process and analyze factors that influence political processes at the local, state, and national levels

The U.S. electoral process has many and varied elements, from simple voting to complex campaigning for office. Everything in between is complex and detailed.

First of all, American citizens vote. They vote for laws and statues and referenda and elected officials. They have to register in order to vote, and at that time they can declare their intended membership in a political party. America has a large list of political parties, which have varying degrees of membership. The Democratic and Republican Parties are the two with the most money and power, but other political parties abound. In some cases, people who are registered members of a political party are allowed to vote for only members of that political party. This takes place in many cases in primary elections, when, for example, a number of people are running to secure the nomination of one political party for a general election. If you are a registered Democrat, then in the primary election, you will be able to vote for only Democratic candidates; this restriction will be listed for the general election, in which the Democratic Party will expect you to vote for that party's candidate but in which you can also vote for whomever you want. A potential voter need not register for a political party, however.

Candidates affiliate themselves with political parties (or sometimes not—some candidates run unaffiliated, but they usually have trouble raising enough money to adequately campaign against their opponents). Candidates then go about the business of campaigning, which includes getting the word on out on their candidacy, what they believe in, and what they will do if elected. All of this costs money, of course, unless a candidate relies entirely on word-of-mouth or some sort of email campaign. Candidates sometimes get together for debates, to showcase their views on important issues of the day and how those views differ from those of their opponents. Candidates give public speeches, attend public functions, and spout their views to reporters, for coverage in newspapers and magazines and on radio and television. On Election Day, candidates cross their fingers and hope that what they've done is enough.

The results of elections are made known very quickly, sometimes instantly, thanks to computerized vote tallying. Once results are finalized, winning candidates give victory speeches and losing candidates give concession speeches. Losing candidates go back to the lives they were leading, and winning candidates get ready to take their places in the local, state, or national government.

Elections take place regularly, so voters know just how long it will be before the next election. Some candidates begin planning their next campaign the day after their victory or loss. Voters technically have the option to **recall** elected candidates; such a measure, however, is drastic and requires a large pile of signatures to get the motion on the ballot and then a large number of votes to have the measure approved. As such, recalls of elected candidates are relatively rare. One widely publicized recall in recent years was that of California Governor Gray Davis, who was replaced by movie star Arnold Schwarzenegger.

Another method of removing public officials from office is **impeachment**. This is also rare but still a possibility. Both houses of the state or federal government get involved, and both houses have to approve the impeachment measures by a large margin. In the case of the federal government, the House of Representatives votes to impeach a federal official and the Senate votes to convict or acquit. Conviction means that the official must leave office immediately; acquittal results in no penalties or fines.

All of these components of the U.S. electoral process are public and can be known by anyone who wishes to do a little digging.

The College of Electors—or the Electoral College, as it is more commonly known—has a long and distinguished history of mirroring the political will of the American voters. On some occasions, the results have not been entirely in sync with that political will.

Article II of the Constitution lists the specifics of the Electoral College. The Founding Fathers included the Electoral College as one of the famous "checks and balances" for two reasons: 1) to give states with small populations more of an equal weight in the presidential election, and 2) they didn't trust the common man (women couldn't vote then.) to be able to make an informed decision on which candidate would make the best president.

First of all, the same theory that created the U.S. Senate practice of giving two Senators to each state created the Electoral College. The large-population states had their populations reflected in the House of Representatives. New York and Pennsylvania, two of the states with the largest populations, had the highest number of members of the House of Representatives. But these two states still had only two senators, the exact same number that small-population states like Rhode Island and Delaware had. This was true as well in the Electoral College: Each state had just one vote, regardless of how many members of the House represented that state. So, the one vote that the state of New York cast would be decided by an initial vote of New York's Representatives. (If that initial vote was a tie, then that deadlock would have to be broken.)

Secondly, when the Constitution was being written, not many people knew a whole lot about government, politics, or presidential elections. A large number of people were farmers or lived in rural areas, where they were far more concerned with making a living and providing for their families than they were with who was running for which office. Many of these "common people" could not read or write, either, and wouldn't be able to read a ballot in any case. Like it or not, the Founding Fathers thought that even if these "common people" could vote, they wouldn't necessarily make the best decision for who would make the best president. So, the Electoral College was born.

Technically, the electors do not have to vote for anyone. The Constitution does not require them to do so. And throughout the history of presidential elections, some have indeed voted for someone else. But tradition holds that the electors vote for the candidate chosen by their state, and so the vast majority of electors do just that. The Electoral College meets a few weeks after the presidential election. Mostly, their meeting is a formality. When all the electoral votes are counted, the president with the most votes wins. In most cases, the candidate who wins the popular vote also wins in the Electoral College. However, this has not always been the case.

Most recently, in 2000 in Florida, the election was decided by the Supreme Court. The Democratic Party's nominee was Vice-President Al Gore. A presidential candidate himself back in 1988, Gore had served as vice-president for both of President Bill Clinton's terms. As such, he was both a champion of Clinton's successes and a reflection of his failures. The Republican Party's nominee was George W. Bush, governor of Texas and son of former President George Bush. He campaigned on a platform of a strong national defense and an end to questionable ethics in the White House. The election was hotly contested, and many states went down to the wire, being decided by only a handful of votes. The one state that seemed to be flip-flopping as Election Day turned into Election Night was Florida. In the end, Gore won the popular vote, by nearly 540,000 votes. But he didn't win the electoral vote. The vote was so close in Florida that a recount was necessary under federal law. Eventually, the Supreme Court weighed in and stopped all the recounts. The last count had Bush winning by less than a thousand votes. That gave him Florida and the White House.

Because of these irregularities, especially the last one, many have taken up the cry to eliminate the Electoral College, which they see as archaic and capable of distorting the will of the people. After all, they argue, elections these days come down to one or two key states, as if the votes of the people in all the other states don't matter. Proponents of the Electoral College point to the tradition of the entity and all of the other elections in which the electoral vote mirrored the popular vote. Eliminating the Electoral College would no doubt take a constitutional amendment, and those are certainly hard to come by. The debate crops up every four years; in the past decade, though, the debate has lasted longer in between elections.

Skill 24.2: Examine significant developments in the evolution of political parties in the United States.

Americans had good reason to fear the emergence of political parties. They had witnessed how parties worked in Great Britain. Parties, called "factions" in Britain, thus Washington's warning, were made up of a few people who schemed to win favors from the government. They were more interested in their own personal profit and advantage than in the public good. Thus, the new American leaders were very interested in keeping factions from forming. It was, ironically, disagreements between two of Washington's chief advisors, Thomas Jefferson and Alexander Hamilton that spurred the formation of the first political parties in the newly formed United States of America.

The two parties that developed through the early 1790s were led by Jefferson as the Secretary of State and Alexander Hamilton as the Secretary of the Treasury. Jefferson and Hamilton were different in many ways. Not the least was their views on what should be the proper form of government of the United States. This difference helped to shape the parties that formed around them.

By the time Washington retired from office in 1796, the new political parties would come to play an important role in choosing his successor. Each party would put up its own candidates for office. The election of 1796 was the first one in which political parties played a role. By the beginning of the 1800s, the Federalist Party, torn by internal divisions, began suffering a decline. The election in 1800 of Thomas Jefferson as President, Hamilton's bitter rival, and after its leader Alexander Hamilton was killed in 1804 in a duel with Aaron Burr, the Federalist Party began to collapse. By 1816, after losing a string of important elections, (Jefferson was reelected in 1804, and James Madison, a Democratic-Republican was elected in 1808), the Federalist party ceased to be an effective political force, and soon passed off the national stage.

By the late 1820s, new political parties had grown up. The **Democratic-Republican** Party, or simply the **Republican** Party, had been the major party for many years, but differences within it about the direction the country was headed in caused a split after 1824. Those who favored strong national growth took the name **Whigs** after a similar party in Great Britain and united around then President John Quincy Adams. Many business people in the Northeast as well as some wealthy planters in the South supported it.

Those who favored slower growth and were more worker and small farmer oriented went on to form the new **Democratic Party**, with Andrew Jackson being its first leader as well as becoming the first President from it. It is the forerunner of today's present party of the same name.

Other political parties came and went in the post-Civil War era. The Liberal Republican Party formed in 1872 to oppose Ulysses S. Grant. They thought that Grant and his administration were corrupt and sought to displace them. The Anti-Monopoly Party of 1789 was more short-lived than the previous one. It billed itself as progressive and supported things like a graduated income tax system, the direct election of senators, etc. The Greenback Party was formed in 1878 and advocated the use of paper money. The Populist Party was a party consisting mostly of farmers who opposed the gold-standard.

The process of political parties with short life spans continued in the twentieth century. Most of this is due to the fact that these parties come into existence in opposition to some policy or politician. Once the "problem" is gone, so is the party that opposed it. The Farmer-Labor Party was a Minnesota based political party. It supported farmers and labor and social security. It had moderate success in electing officials in Minnesota and merged with the Democratic Party in 1944.The Progressive Party was formed in 1912 due to a rift in the Republican Party that occurred when Theodore Roosevelt lost the nomination. This is not the same as the Progressive Party formed in 1924 to back LaFollette of Wisconsin. The Social Democratic Party was an outgrowth of a social movement and didn't have much political success.

There have also been other parties that have had a short termed life in the years following the Great Depression. The **American Labor Party** was a socialist party that existed in New York for a while. The **American Workers Party** was another socialist party based on Marxism. They also were short-lived. The Progressive Party came into being in 1948 to run candidates for President and Vice-President. The Dixicrats or **States Rights Democratic Party** also formed in 1948. They were a splinter group from the Democrats who supported Strom Thurmond. They also supported Wallace 1968. There have been various Workers' Parties that have come and gone. Most of these have had left-wing tendencies.

There are other political parties but they are not as strong as the Republicans and the Democrats. The **Libertarian** Party represents belief in the free rights of individuals to do as they wish without the interference of government. They favor a small government so propose a much lower level of government spending and services. The Libertarians are the third largest political party in America. The Socialist Party is also a political party. They run candidates in the elections. They favor the establishment of a radical democracy in which people control production and communities for all, not for the benefit of a few. The Communist Party is also a political party advocating very radical changes in American society. They are concerned with the revolutionary struggle and moving through Marx's stages of history. There are many other parties. The American First Party is a conservative party as is the American Party. The American Nazi Party is also active in politics. Preaching fascism, they run candidates for elections and occasionally win. The Constitution Party is also representative of conservative views. The Reform Party was founded by Ross Perot after his bid for President as an independent.

Skill 24.3: Analyze factors that influence political elections at the local, state, and national levels.

If there's one thing that drives American politics more than any other, it's **money**. Much more often than not, the candidate who has the most money at his or her disposal has the best chance of getting or keeping political office. Money can buy so many things that are necessary to a successful campaign that it is entirely indispensable. Money drives the utilization of every other factor in the running of a campaign.

First and foremost, money is needed to pay the people who will run a candidate's campaign. A candidate cannot expect people to give up, in some cases, years of their lives without monetary compensation. Volunteers on a political campaign are plentiful, but they are not at the top levels. The faithful lieutenants of a campaign are paid performers. Money is also needed to buy or rent all of the tangible and intangible *things* that are needed to power a political campaign: office supplies, meeting places, transportation vehicles, and many more. The inventory of these items can add up frighteningly quickly, and money can appear to disappear like water down a drain.

Of course, the expense that gets the most exposure these days is **media** advertising, specifically television advertising. This is the most expensive kind of advertising, but it also has the potential to reach the widest audience. TV ad prices can run into the hundreds of thousands of dollars, depending on when they run; but they have the potential to reach perhaps millions of viewers. Here, too, money can disappear quickly. A political campaign is also a fashion show and candidates cannot afford to go without showing their friendly faces to as wide an audience as possible on a regular basis. Other forms of advertising include radio and Web ads, signs and billboards, and good old-fashioned flyers.

The sources of all this money that is needed to run a successful political campaign are varied. A candidate might have a significant amount of money in his or her own personal coffers. In rare cases, the candidate finances the entire campaign. However, the most prevalent source of money is outside donations. A candidate's friends and family might donate funds to the campaign, as well as the campaign workers themselves. State and federal governments will also contribute to most regional or national campaigns, provided that the candidate can prove that he or she can raise a certain amount of money first. The largest source of campaign finance money, however, comes from so-called "special interests." A large company such as an oil company or a manufacturer of electronic goods will want to keep prices or tariffs down and so will want to make sure that laws lifting those prices or tariffs aren't passed.

To this end, the company will contribute money to the campaigns of candidates who are likely to vote to keep those prices or tariffs down. A candidate is not obligated to accept such a donation, of course, and further is not obligated to vote in favor of the interests of the special interest; however, doing the former might create a shortage of money and doing the latter might ensure that no further donations come from that or any other special interest. An oil company wants to protect its interests, and its leaders don't very much care which political candidate is doing that for them as long as it is being done.

Another powerful source of support for a political campaign is **special interest groups** of a political nature. These are not necessarily economic powers but rather groups whose people want to effect political change (or make sure that such change doesn't take place, depending on the status of the laws at the time). A good example of a special interest group is an anti-abortion group or a pro-choice group. The abortion issue is still a divisive one in American politics, and many groups will want to protect or defend or ban—depending on which side they're on—certain rights and practices. An anti-abortion group, for example, might pay big money to candidates who pledge to work against laws that protect the right for women to have abortions. As long as these candidates continue to assure their supporters that they will keep on fighting the fight, the money will continue to flow. This kind of social group usually has a large number of dedicated individuals who do much more than vote: They organize themselves into political action committees attend meetings and rallies, and work to make sure that their message gets out to a wide audience. Methods of spreading the word often include media advertising on behalf of their chosen candidates. This kind of expenditure is no doubt welcomed by the candidates, who will get the benefit of the exposure but won't have to spend that money because someone else is signing the checks.

Most recently, the question has revolved around the issue of what is called "**Gerrymandering**", which involves the adjustment of various electoral districts in order to achieve a predetermined goal. Usually this is used in regards to the problem of minority political representation. The fact that gerrymandering sometimes creates odd and unusual looking districts (this is where the practice gets its name) and most often the sole basis of the adjustments is racial. This has led to the questioning of this practice being a fair, let alone constitutional, way for society to achieve its desired goals. This promises to be the major issue in national electoral politics for some time to come. The debate has centered on those of the "left" (**Liberals**), who favor such methods, and the "right" (**Conservatives**), who oppose them. Overall, most Americans would consider themselves in the "middle" (**Moderates**).

Newspapers, then as now, influenced the growth of political parties. Newspaper publishers and editors took sides on the issues. Thus, from the very beginning, American newspapers and each new branch of the media have played an important role in helping to shape public opinion.

Skill 24.4: Identify skills and attitudes necessary for effective participatory citizenship in a democratic society and recognize forms of discussion and participation consistent with the ideals of U.S. citizens.

The most basic way for citizens to participate in the political process is to **vote**. Since the passing of the 23rd Amendment in 1965, US citizens who are at least 18 years old are eligible to vote. Elections are held at regular intervals at all levels of government, allowing citizens to weigh in on local matters as well as those of national scope.

The reality for Americans is that they don't play a large role in governmental decision-making, except perhaps at the local level. Only there, in the towns and cities in which they live, can they afford the time and money to personally lobby their lawmakers in the name of passage or defeat of laws. At the state and the national level, the country is just too big for one poor person to have much of a difference individually. Where people make a difference at the higher levels is in joining political parties and, more importantly, citizen action groups or political action committees. Only in the larger numbers that make up these groups can individual people make a difference in government. In such cases, however, people tend to lose their individual voices and are more easily swayed by the will of their peers.

Citizens wishing to engage in the political process to a greater degree have several paths open, such as participating in local government. Counties, states, and sometimes neighborhoods are governed by locally elected boards or councils, which meet publicly. Citizens are usually able to address these boards, bringing their concerns and expressing their opinions on matters being considered. Citizens may even wish to stand for local election and join a governing board, or seek support for higher office.

This is not to say that the avenues of lobbying lawmakers are closed to the average American. Letters are still read, phone calls are still taken, and donations are still appreciated. More cutting-edge methods of communication include e-mail, FAX, and SMS. Personal office visits are definitely appreciated as well. If enough people write or call or visit their lawmakers and say the same thing, those lawmakers will listen. That's why it's still important for people to speak out, not only to their neighbors but also their elected officials. And of course, the ultimate way of expressing one's political views is to elect or oust a lawmaker through the power of the ballot.
This kind of open access and potentially direct role in the political decision-making of the country has not always been with us, though. In the early days of the American colonies, the British settlers could disagree all they wanted with the kind of policies, laws, and taxes that were being impressed on them by the Parliament across the Atlantic. The settlers also couldn't very well decide who their colonial governors were. The British Government appointed those officials.

Supporting a political party is another means by which citizens can participate in the political process. Political parties endorse certain platforms that express general social and political goals, and support member candidates in election campaigns. Political parties make use of much volunteer labor, with supporters making telephone calls, distributing printed material and campaigning for the party's causes and candidates. Political parties solicit donations to support their efforts as well. Contributing money to a political party is another form of participation citizens can undertake.

Another form of political activity is to support an issue-related political group. Several political groups work actively to sway public opinion on various issues or on behalf of a segment of American society. These groups may have representatives who meet with state and federal legislators to "lobby" them - to provide them with information on an issue and persuade them to take favorable action.

A person who lives in a democratic society theoretically has an entire laundry list guaranteed to him or her by the government. In the United States, this is the Constitution and its Amendments. Among these very important rights are:

- the right to speak out in public;
- the right to pursue any religion;
- the right for a group of people to gather in public for *any* reason that doesn't fall under a national security cloud;
- the right *not* to have soldiers stationed in your home;
- the right *not* to be forced to testify against yourself in a court of law;
- the right to a speedy and public trial by a jury of your peers;
- the right *not* to the victim of cruel and unusual punishment;
- and the right to avoid unreasonable search and seizure of your person, your house, and your vehicle.

The average citizen of an authoritarian country has little if any of these rights and must watch his or her words, actions, and even magazine subscriptions and Internet visits in order to avoid *the appearance* of disobeying one of the many oppressive laws that help the government govern its people.

Both the democratic-society and the authoritarian-society citizens can serve in government. They can even run for election and can be voted in by their peers. One large difference exists, however: In an authoritarian society, the members of government will most likely be of the same political party. A country with this setup, like China, will have a government that includes representatives elected by the Chinese people, but all of those elected representatives will belong to the Communist Party, which runs the government and the country. When the voters vote they see only Communist Party members on the ballot. In fact, in many cases, only one candidate is on the ballot for each office. China, in fact, chooses its head of government through a meeting of the Party leaders. In effect, the Party is higher in the governmental hierarchy than the leader of the country. Efforts to change this governmental structure and practice are clamped down and discouraged.

On the other side of this spectrum is the citizen of the democratic society, who can vote for whomever he or she wants to and can run for any office he or she wants to. On those ballots will appear names and political parties that run the spectrum, including the Communist Party. Theoretically, *any* political party can get its candidates on ballots locally, statewide, or nationwide; varying degrees of effort have to be put in to do this, of course. Building on the First Amendment freedom to peacefully assembly, American citizens can have political party meetings, fund-raisers, and even conventions without fearing reprisals from the Government.

Skill 24.5: Examine the influence of public opinion and various forms of civic action on public policy and recognize ways in which public policies and citizen behaviors reflect the ideals of a democratic republican form of government.

From the earliest days of political expression in America, efforts were a collaborative affair. One of the first of the democratic movements was the Sons of Liberty, an organization that made its actions known but kept the identity of its members a secret. Famous members of this group included John and Samuel Adams. Other patriotic movements sprang up after the success of the Sons of Liberty was assured, and the overall struggle against British oppression was a collaborative effort involving thousands of people throughout the American colonies.

American political discussion built on the example of the British Parliament, which had two houses of its legislative branch of government containing representatives who had great debates on public policy before making laws. Although this process isn't anywhere near as wide open and public and spirited as it is today, the lawmakers nonetheless had their chance to make their views known on the issues of the day. Some laws, like those implementing the infamous taxes following the British and American victory in the French and Indian War, required relatively little debate, since they were so popular and were obviously wanted by the Prime Minister and other heads of the government. Other laws enjoyed spirited debate and took months to pass.

The Assemblies of the American colonies inherited this tradition and enjoyed spirited debate as well, even though they met just one or a few times a year. One of the most famous examples of both collaboration and deliberation was the Stamp Act Congress, a gathering of fed-up Americans who drafted resolutions demanding that Great Britain repeal the unpopular tax on paper and documents. The Americans who met at both of the Continental Congresses and the Constitutional Convention built on this tradition as well.

Thanks to the voluminous notes taken diligently by James Madison, we have a clear record of just how contentious at times the debate over the shape and scope of the American federal government was. Still, every interest was advanced, every argument put forward, and every chance given to repeal the main points of the government document. The result was a blueprint for government approved by the vast majority of the delegates and eventually approved by people in all of the American colonies. This ratification process has continued throughout the history of the country, through passage by both houses of Congress to ratification by state legislatures and finally to approval by a majority of the people of a majority of states.

With this sometimes spirited and sometimes virulent debate have come countless opportunities to influence that debate. Even in the earliest times, people having special interests were trying to influence political debates in their favor. Plenty of people who favored a strong central government or its opposite, a weak central government, could be found who were not delegates to the Constitutional Convention. No doubt these people were in communication with the delegates.

Refer to Skills in Competency 24.0

SUBAREA V—SOCIAL STUDIES SKILLS

COMPETENCY 25: Understand how to locate, gather, and organize primary and secondary information using standard historical and social science resources and research methodologies.

Skill 25.1: Recognize characteristics and uses of historical, geographic, and social science reference materials.

Libraries of all sorts are valuable when conducting research and nowadays almost all have digitized search systems to assist in finding information on almost any subject. Even so, the Internet with powerful search engines like Google readily available can retrieve information that doesn't exist in libraries or if it does exist, is much more difficult to retrieve.

Conducting a research project once involved the use of punch cards, microfiche and other manual means of storing the data in a retrievable fashion. No more. With high-powered computers available to anyone who chooses to conduct research, the organizing of the data in a retrievable fashion has been revolutionized and rendering classic forms of research such as encyclopedias obsolete since most information can be found on the Internet. Creating multi-level folders, copying and pasting into the folders, making ongoing additions to the bibliography at the very time that a source is consulted, and using search-and find functions make this stage of the research process go much faster with less frustration and a decrease in the likelihood that important data might be overlooked.

Serious research requires high-level analytical skills when it comes to processing and interpreting data. A degree in statistics or at least a graduate-level concentration is very useful. However, a team approach to a research project will include a statistician in addition to those members who are knowledgeable in the social sciences.

Skill 25.2: Apply research procedures in history and the social sciences.

The scientific method is the process by which researchers over time endeavor to construct an accurate (that is, reliable, consistent and non-arbitrary) representation of the world. Recognizing that personal and cultural beliefs influence both our perceptions and our interpretations of natural phenomena, standard procedures and criteria minimize those influences when developing a theory.

The scientific method has four steps:

1. Observation and description of a phenomenon or group of phenomena.
2. Formulation of a hypothesis to explain the phenomena.
3. Use of the hypothesis to predict the existence of other phenomena or to predict quantitatively the results of new observations.
4. Performance of experimental tests of the predictions by several independent experimenters and properly performed experiments.

While the researcher may bring certain biases to the study, it's important that bias not be permitted to enter into the interpretation. It's also important that data that doesn't fit the hypothesis not be ruled out. This is unlikely to happen if the researcher is open to the possibility that the hypothesis might turn out to be null. Another important caution is to be certain that the methods for analyzing and interpreting are flawless. Abiding by these mandates is important if the discovery is to make a contribution to human understanding.

Skill 25.3: Demonstrate knowledge of appropriate methods and techniques for collecting information in the social sciences.

Helping students become critical thinkers is an important objective of the social studies curriculum. The history, geography, and political science classes provide many opportunities to teach students to recognize and understand reasoning errors. Errors tend to fall into two categories: a) inadequate reasons; and b) misleading reasoning. Following are examples of each:

Inadequate reasons:

1. Faulty analogies: The two things being compared must be similar in all significant aspects if the reasoning is to be relied upon. If there is a major difference between the two, then the argument falls apart.
2. False cause (*Post Hoc Ergo Propter Hoc)*: after this, therefore because of this. There must be a factual tie between the effect and its declared cause.
3. *Ad Hominen*: Attacking the person instead of addressing the issues.
4. Slippery Slope: The domino effect. This is usually prophetic in nature—predicting what will follow if a certain event occurs. This is only reliable

when it is used in hindsight—not in predicting the future because no one is wise enough to know the future.

5. Hasty Conclusions: Leaping to conclusions when not enough evidence has been collected. A good example is the accusations made in the 1996 bombing at the summer Olympics in Atlanta. Not enough evidence had been collected and the wrong man was arrested.

Misleading reasoning:

1. The Red Herring: comes from a smoked fish being dragged across a trail to distract hunting dogs. Often used in politics—getting your opponent on the defensive about a different issue than the one under discussion.
2. *Ad Populum* or Jumping on the Bandwagon: "Everybody's doing it, so it must be right." Biggest is not necessarily best when it comes to following a crowd.
3. Appeal to Tradition: "We've always done it this way." Often used to squelch innovation.
4. The False Dilemma or the Either/Or Fallacy: No other alternative is possible except the extremes at each end. Used in politics a lot. The creative statesman finds other alternatives.

Skill 25.4: Apply procedures for retrieving information using traditional sources and current technologies.

See Skill 25.1.

Skill 25.5: Demonstrate knowledge of appropriate documentation of source and authorship

The resources used in the study of history can be divided into two major groups: primary sources and secondary sources.

Primary sources are works, records, etc. that were created during the period being studied or immediately after it. Secondary sources are works written significantly after the period being studied and based upon primary sources. "Primary sources are the basic materials that provide the raw data and information for the historian. Secondary sources are the works that contain the explications of, and judgments on, this primary material." [Source: Norman F Cantor & Richard I. Schneider. HOW TO STUDY HISTORY, Harlan Davidson, Inc., 1967, pp. 23-24.]

Primary sources include the following kinds of materials:

- Documents that reflect the immediate, everyday concerns of people: memoranda, bills, deeds, charters, newspaper reports, pamphlets, graffiti, popular writings, journals or diaries, records of decision-making bodies, letters, receipts, snapshots, etc.
- Theoretical writings which reflect care and consideration in composition and an attempt to convince or persuade. The topic will generally be deeper and more pervasive values than is the case with "immediate" documents. These may include newspaper or magazine editorials, sermons, political speeches, philosophical writings, etc.
- Narrative accounts of events, ideas, trends, etc. written with intentionality by someone contemporary with the events described.
- Statistical data, although statistics may be misleading.
- Literature and nonverbal materials, novels, stories, poetry and essays from the period, as well as coins, archaeological artifacts, and art produced during the period.

Guidelines for the use of primary resources:

1. Be certain that you understand how language was used at the time of writing and that you understand the context in which it was produced.
2. Do not read history blindly; but be certain that you understand both explicit and implicit referenced in the material.
3. Read the entire text you are reviewing; do not simply extract a few sentences to read.
4. Although anthologies of materials may help you identify primary source materials, the full original text should be consulted.

Secondary sources include the following kinds of materials:

- Books written on the basis of primary materials about the period of time.
- Books written on the basis of primary materials about persons who played a major role in the events under consideration.
- Books and articles written on the basis of primary materials about the culture, the social norms, the language, and the values of the period.
- Quotations from primary sources.
- Statistical data on the period.
- The conclusions and inferences of other historians.
- Multiple interpretations of the ethos of the time.

Guidelines for the use of secondary sources:

1. Do not rely upon only a single secondary source.
2. Check facts and interpretations against primary sources whenever possible.
3. Do not accept the conclusions of other historians uncritically.
4. Place greatest reliance on secondary sources created by the best and most respected scholars.
5. Do not use the inferences of other scholars as if they were facts.
6. Ensure that you recognize any bias the writer brings to his/her interpretation of history.
7. Understand the primary point of the book as a basis for evaluating the value of the material presented in it to your questions.

COMPETENCY 26: Understand and apply methods for evaluating and interpreting sources of social studies information.

Skill 26.1: Compare primary and secondary sources and analyze their advantages and limitations

The world of social science research has never been so open to new possibilities. Where our predecessors were unable to tread for fear of exceeding the limits of the available data, data access and data transfer, analytic routines, or computing power, today's social scientists can advance with confidence. Where once social scientists of empirical bent struggled with punch cards, chattering computer terminals, and jobs disappearing into the black hole of remote mainframe processors, often never reappearing, we now enjoy massive arrays of data, powerful personal computers on our desks, online access to data, and suites of sophisticated analytic packages. Never before has the social scientist come so well armed. Advances in technology can free social scientists from the tyranny of simplification that has often hampered attempts to grasp the complexity of the world.

Refer to the content under **Skill 25.5** for a thorough discussion of primary and secondary sources. Primary sources for a study in social sciences may be obtained one-on-one: the children in the school where you are a teacher or via electronic means. For example, government sources contain much data for social sciences research such as census statistics, employment statistics, health statistics, etc., that can be readily accessed and manipulated.

Secondary sources may also be obtained in a hands-on fashion: interviews of people who had first-hand knowledge; books, journals, etc., that record primary statistics or analyses of primary statistics. However, the best source for obtaining that information is the Internet. An excellent resource for social science information is MOST (Management of Social Transformations) at http://portal. unesco.org/shs/en/ev.php-URL_ID=3511&URL_DO=DO_TOPIC&URL_ SECTION=201.html.

Skill 26.2: Analyze factors affecting the reliability and validity of social studies information sources.

The sky is blue", "the sky looks like rain", one a fact and the other an opinion. This is because one is **readily provable by objective empirical data**, while the other is a **subjective evaluation based upon personal bias**. This means that facts are things that can be proved by the usual means of study and experimentation. We can look and see the color of the sky. Since the shade we are observing is expressed as the color blue and is an accepted norm, the observation that the sky is blue is therefore a fact. (Of course, this depends on other external factors such as time and weather conditions).

This brings us to our next idea: that it looks like rain. This is a subjective observation in that an individual's perception will differ from another. What looks like rain to one person will not necessarily look like that to another.

This is an important concept to understand since much of what actually is studied in political science is, in reality, simply the opinions of various political theorists and philosophers. The truth of their individual philosophies is demonstrated by how well they, (when they have been tried), work in the so called "real world."

The question thus remains as to how to differentiate fact from opinion. The best and only way is to ask oneself if what is being stated can be proved from other sources, by other methods, or by the simple process of **reasoning**.

Historians use primary sources from the actual time they are studying whenever possible. Ancient Greek records of interaction with Egypt, letters from an Egyptian ruler to regional governors, and inscriptions from the Fourteenth Egyptian Dynasty are all primary sources created at or near the actual time being studied. Letters from a nineteenth century Egyptologist would not be considered primary sources, as they were created thousands of years after the fact and may not actually be about the subject being studied.

The resources used in the study of history can be divided into two major groups: **primary sources** and **secondary sources**.

Primary sources are works, records, etc. that were created during the period being studied or immediately after it. Secondary sources are works written significantly after the period being studied and based upon primary sources. "Primary sources are the basic materials that provide the raw data and information for the historian. Secondary sources are the works that contain the explications of, and judgments on, this primary material." [Source: Norman F Cantor & Richard I. Schneider. "HOW TO STUDY HISTORY," Harlan Davidson, Inc., 1967, pp. 23-24.].

Also Refer to Skill 25.5 and 26.4.

Skill 26.3: Apply knowledge of the benefits and limitations of various standard map projections.

Refer to Skill 10.3

Skill 26.4: Interpret social studies information presented in various formats.

Posters. The power of the political poster in the 21st century seems trivial considering the barrage of electronic campaigning, mudslinging, and reporting that seems to have taken over the video and audio media in election season. Even so, the political poster has been a powerful propaganda tool, and it has been around for a long time. For example, in the 1st century AD, a poster that calls for the election of a Satrius as quinquennial has survived to this day. Nowhere have political posters been used more powerfully or effectively than in Russia in the 1920s in the campaign to promote communism. Many of the greatest Russian writers of that era were the poster writers. Those posters would not be understood at all except in the light of what was going on in the country at the time.

However, today we see them primarily at rallies and protests where they are usually hand-lettered and hand-drawn. The message is rarely subtle. Understanding the messages of posters requires little thought as a rule. However, they are usually meaningless unless the context is clearly understood. For example, a poster reading "Camp Democracy" can only be understood in the context of the protests of the Iraq War near President George W. Bush's home near Crawford, Texas. "Impeach" posters are understood in 2006 to be directed at President Bush, not a local mayor or representative.

Cartoons. The political cartoon (aka editorial) presents a message or point of view concerning people, events, or situations using caricature and symbolism to convey the cartoonist's ideas, sometimes subtly, sometimes brashly, but always quickly. A good political cartoon will have wit and humor, which is usually obtained by exaggeration that is slick and not used merely for comic effect. It will also have a foundation in truth; that is, the characters must be recognizable to the viewer and the point of the drawing must have some basis in fact even if it has a philosophical bias. The third requirement is a moral purpose.

Using political cartoons as a teaching tool enlivens lectures, prompts classroom discussion, promotes critical thinking, develops multiple talents and learning styles, and helps prepare students for standardized tests. It also provides humor. However, it may be the most difficult form of literature to teach. Many teachers who choose to include them in their social studies curricula caution that, while students may enjoy them, it's doubtful whether they are actually getting the cartoonists' messages.

The best strategy for teaching such a unit is through a subskills approach that leads students step-by-step to higher orders of critical thinking. For example, the teacher can introduce caricature and use cartoons to illustrate the principles. Students are able to identify and interpret symbols if they are given the principles for doing so and get plenty of practice, and cartoons are excellent for this. It can cut down the time it takes for students to develop these skills, and many of the students who might lose the struggle to learn to identify symbols may overcome the roadblocks through the analysis of political cartoons. Many political cartoons exist for the teacher to use in the classroom and they are more readily available than ever before.

A popular example of an editorial cartoon that provides a way to analyze current events in politics is the popular comic strip "Doonesbury" by Gary Trudeau. For example, in the time period prior to the 2004 presidential election, Alex, the media savvy teenager does her best for political participation. In January she rallies her middle school classmates to the phones for a Deanathon and by August she is luring Ralph Nader supporters into discussions on Internet chat rooms. Knowledgeable about government, active in the political process, and willing to enlist others, Alex has many traits sought by the proponents of civics education.

COMPETENCY 27: Understand how to formulate issues or frame questions, analyze and synthesize information, and communicate social studies information.

Skill 27.1: Evaluate alternative formulations of a research problem

There are many different ways to find ideas for **research problems**. One of the most common ways is through experiencing and assessing relevant problems in a specific field. Researchers are often involved in the fields in which they choose to study, and thus encounter practical problems related to their areas of expertise on a daily basis. The can use their knowledge, expertise and research ability to examine their selected research problem. This technique is not limited to qualified researchers engaged in specific fields; it can also be used by students. For students, all that this entails is being curious about the world around them. Research ideas can come from one's background, culture, education, experiences etc.

Another way to get research ideas is by exploring literature in a specific field and coming up with a question that extends or refines previous research.

Once a **topic** is decided, a research question must be formulated. A research question is a relevant, researchable, feasible statement that identifies the information to be studied. Once this initial question is formulated, it is a good idea to think of specific issues related to the topic. This will help to create a hypothesis. A research **hypothesis** is a statement of the researcher's expectations for the outcome of the research problem. It is a summary statement of the problem to be addressed in any research document. A good hypothesis states, clearly and concisely, the researchers expected relationship between the variables which they are investigating.

Once a hypothesis is decided, the rest of the research paper should focus on analyzing a set of information or arguing a specific point. Thus, there are two types of research papers: analytical and argumentative.

Analytical papers focus on examining and understanding the various parts of a research topic and reformulating them in a new way to support your initial statement. In this type of research paper, the research question is used as both a basis for investigation as well as a topic for the paper. Once a variety of information is collected on the given topic, it is coalesced into a clear discussion

Argumentative papers focus on supporting the question or claim with evidence or reasoning. Instead of presenting research to provide information, an argumentative paper presents research in order to prove a debatable statement and interpretation.

Skill 27.2: Analyze information in social studies materials.

Suppose you are preparing for a presentation on the Civil War and you intend to focus on causes, an issue that has often been debated. If you are examining the matter of slavery as a cause, a graph of the increase in the number of slaves by area of the country for the previous 100 years would be very useful in the discussion. If you are focusing on the economic conditions that were driving the politics of the age, graphs of GDP, distribution of wealth geographically and individually, and relationship of wealth to ownership of slaves would be useful.

If you are discussing the war in Iraq, detailed maps with geopolitical elements would help clarify not only the day-to-day happenings but also the historical features that led up to it. A map showing the number of oil fields and where they are situated with regard to the various political factions and charts showing output of those fields historically would be useful.

If you are teaching the history of space travel, photos of the most famous astronauts will add interest to the discussion. Graphs showing the growth of the industry and charts showing discoveries and their relationship to the lives of everyday Americans would be helpful.

Geography and history classes are notoriously labeled by students as dull. With all the visual resources available nowadays, those classes have the potential for being the most exciting courses in the curriculum.

Varying perspectives on the study of history may be summarized by one of three definitions:

1. History is the study of what persons have done and said and thought in the past.
2. History is a creative attempt to reconstruct the lives and thoughts of particular persons who lived at specific times (biography).
3. History is the study of the social aspects of humans, both past and present.

The first definition essentially applies to the *narrative school of history.* This approach attempts to provide a general account of the most important things people have said, done, written, etc. in the past. Several schools fall within this category:

- The political-institutional school believes that what has occurred in government and law is the most important.
- The school of intellectual history (the history of ideas) finds greatest importance in the emergence of higher thought and feeling (including philosophy, art, science, literature).
- Economic historians are most concerned with the way humans have controlled the environment and made a living.
- Cultural historians focus on the development of ideas within the total context of a social, economic, and political situation.

The second definition above understands history as biography of important persons. These historians fall into one of two schools:

- Psychologizing approaches – historians who believe the motivations and actions of people in the past can be understood and explained in terms of modern psychological theories.
- Non-psychologizing approaches – historians who believe it is impossible to psychoanalyze people who are dead and that people of the past must be understood in terms of the theories of personality and motivation that were accepted at the time.

The third definition above essentially equates history with sociology. This approach believes it is possible to study history to observe forms of social change that are relevant to current social problems. This group is also divided:

- One group uses the Marxist doctrine of dialectical materialism to explain social change.
- Another group believes that each society is unique and distinctive.
- Comparative sociological historians study history to identify consistent patterns that run through all or several societies.

For further discussion, also refer to Skill 26.2.

Skill 27.3: Determine whether specific conclusions or generalizations are supported by verifiable evidence

Helping students become critical thinkers is an important objective of the social studies curriculum. The history, geography, and political science classes provide many opportunities to teach students to recognize and understand reasoning errors. Errors tend to fall into two categories: a) inadequate reasons; and b) misleading reasoning. Following are examples of each:

Inadequate reasons:

6. Faulty analogies: The two things being compared must be similar in all significant aspects if the reasoning is to be relied upon. If there is a major difference between the two, then the argument falls apart.
7. False cause (*Post Hoc Ergo Propter Hoc)*: after this, therefore because of this. There must be a factual tie between the effect and its declared cause.
8. *Ad Hominen*: Attacking the person instead of addressing the issues.
9. Slippery Slope: The domino effect. This is usually prophetic in nature—predicting what will follow if a certain event occurs. This is only reliable when it is used in hindsight—not in predicting the future because no one is wise enough to know the future.
10. Hasty Conclusions: Leaping to conclusions when not enough evidence has been collected. A good example is the accusations made in the 1996 bombing at the summer Olympics in Atlanta. Not enough evidence had been collected and the wrong man was arrested.

Misleading reasoning:

5. The Red Herring: comes from a smoked fish being dragged across a trail to distract hunting dogs. Often used in politics—getting your opponent on the defensive about a different issue than the one under discussion.
6. *Ad Populum* or Jumping on the Bandwagon: "Everybody's doing it, so it must be right." Biggest is not necessarily best when it comes to following a crowd.
7. Appeal to Tradition: "We've always done it this way." Often used to squelch innovation.
8. The False Dilemma or the Either/Or Fallacy: No other alternative is possible except the extremes at each end. Used in politics a lot. The creative statesman finds other alternatives.

Also refer to Skill 25.3.

Skill 27.4: Demonstrate how to communicate social studies information using various formats and how to translate information from one format to another

Again, the Internet has transformed all kinds of communications all over the world. Very few people write letters in the 21st century that will be delivered physically to an individual's mailbox. However, there are still important reasons for writing letters. For one thing, they are more personal and convey a quite different message from an e-mail, especially if they are handwritten. For another, not everybody has and uses e-mail regularly.

An electronic mailbox will retain what has been sent and received, sometimes to the writer's regret; even so, those messages and exchanges will not endure in the way that paper letters sometimes do over long periods. A husband and wife who married in 1954 always corresponded with his parents by mail approximately once a week in the first thirty years of their marriage. The three children often included a note of their own. It was before the long-distance call became routine and affordable. After the grandmother and grandfather had died, the family discovered that they had kept all of those letters. It's a priceless record of a period in the family's life. If that correspondence had occurred via e-mail, it would be lost to history.

Sometimes there's a business reason for a paper letter. It may contain a receipt or legal information that needs to be retained. For those people who do not yet have a computer or access to e-mail, paper letters are necessary. Sometimes a company or organization wishes to advertise a product or even issue invitations to an event when not all e-mail addresses are known. Mass-mailings can be sent quite easily to make sure that everyone on the list can be reached. Advertisers, of course, use mass-mail more than anyone else because they do not even need to know the addresses to get their literature into all the mailboxes in a zip code.

Sometimes courtesy requires a personally written letter either typed or handwritten. If a person in high office has taken the time to do something for an individual, certainly a handwritten letter of thanks would be in order. In the U.S., the form of the letter can be full block (all lines blocked at the left margin); modified block (all lines blocked at the left margin except the date and closing lines, which begin at the center point); and semi-block (same as modified block except that the first lines of paragraphs are indented by five points). Microsoft Word's letter wizard will automatically format a business letter according to these three styles.

Social notes should be handwritten on note paper, which varies in size but is smaller than letter-sized paper. They should be courteous and brief and should be specific about what is intended. For example, if the note is to say thank you, then the gift or favor should be specifically acknowledged in the note. If the note is an invitation, the same rule applies: the language should be courteous, the place and time specified, and any useful information such as "casual dress" or parking recommendations should be included.

A high percentage of communications between individuals, groups, and businesses is conducted nowadays over the Internet. It has even replaced many telephone calls. Internet language should be courteous, free of words that might be offensive, and clear. In the early days of e-mail, a writer was censured for using bold or capital letters. That has relaxed somewhat. Nowadays, almost anything goes although it's generally accepted that restrained language is assumed for business people and personal communications. The blog, where a person has his/her own website and uses it to send messages, is a new wrinkle. Chat is available on most blogs as well as other Internet sites. The language and the messages tend to be unrestrained there.

Some people use the same styles for letters via e-mail that are recommended for paper letters; however, the formatting has tended to become less and less formal. It is not uncommon for thank-you letters and invitations to be sent via e-mail. One important feature of the Internet that makes it so valuable is that it reaches everywhere—to small communities, all the way across the country, and overseas. It's possible to dash off an e-mail note to a person or business or several persons or businesses in Europe as quickly as to a person in the next office, and it costs no extra money beyond the cost of equipment and Internet services.

The fax machine is yet another dimension of electronic communications. At first, it was used primarily by businesses, but it has become so affordable that many people have them in their homes. The fax makes possible an actual picture of a document. This may be preferable to retyping it or sending it by paper mail because it can go immediately. Sometimes people who are exchanging contracts will use the fax to cut down on the time it takes to get them signed and sent back and forth. The scanner will do the same thing but will produce a document that can be e-mailed.

Bibliography

Adams, James Truslow. (2006). "The March of Democracy," Vol 1. "The Rise of the Union". New York: Charles Scribner's Sons, Publisher.

Barbini, John & Warshaw, Steven. (2006). "The World Past and Present." New York: Harcourt, Brace, Jovanovich, Publishers.

Berthon, Simon & Robinson, Andrew. (2006. "The Shape of the World." Chicago: Rand McNally, Publisher.

Bice, David A. (2006). "A Panorama of Florida II". (Second Edition). Marceline, Missouri: Walsworth Publishing Co., Inc.

Bram, Leon (Vice-President and Editorial Director). (2006). "Funk and Wagnalls New Encyclopedia." United States of America.

Burns, Edward McNall & Ralph, Philip Lee. (2006. "World Civilizations Their History and Culture" (5th ed.). New York: W.W. Norton & Company, Inc., Publishers.

Dauben, Joseph W. (2006). "The World Book Encyclopedia." Chicago: World Book Inc. A Scott Fetzer Company, Publisher.

De Blij, H.J. & Muller, Peter O. (2006). "Geography Regions and Concepts" (Sixth Edition). New York: John Wiley & Sons, Inc., Publisher.

Encyclopedia Americana. (2006). Danbury, Connecticut: Grolier Inc, Publisher.

Heigh, Christopher (Editor). (2006). "The Cambridge Historical Encyclopedia of Great Britain and Ireland." Cambridge: Cambridge University Press, Publisher.

Hunkins, Francis P. & Armstrong, David G. (2006). "World Geography People and Places." Columbus, Ohio: Charles E. Merrill Publishing Co. A Bell & Howell Company, Publishers.

Jarolimek, John; Anderson, J. Hubert & Durand, Loyal, Jr. (2006). "World Neighbors." New York: Macmillan Publishing Company. London: Collier Macmillan Publishers.

McConnell, Campbell R. (2006). "Economics-Principles, Problems, and Policies" (Tenth Edition). New York: McGraw-Hill Book Company, Publisher.

Millard, Dr. Anne & Vanags, Patricia. (2006). "The Usborne Book of World History." London: Usborne Publishing Ltd., Publisher.

Novosad, Charles (Executive Editor). (2006). "The Nystrom Desk Atlas." Chicago:Nystrom Division of Herff Jones, Inc., Publisher.

Patton, Clyde P.; Rengert, Arlene C.; Saveland, Robert N.; Cooper, Kenneth S. & Cam, Patricia T. (2006). "A World View." Morristown, N.J.: Silver Burdette Companion, Publisher.

Schwartz, Melvin & O'Connor, John R. (2006). "Exploring A Changing World." New York: Globe Book Company, Publisher.

"The Annals of America: Selected Readings on Great Issues in American History 1620-1968." (2006). United States of America: William Benton, Publisher.

Tindall, George Brown & Shi, David E. (2006). "America-A Narrative History" (Fourth Edition). New York: W.W. Norton & Company, Publisher.

Todd, Lewis Paul & Curti, Merle. (2006). "Rise of the American Nation" (Third Edition). New York: Harcourt, Brace, Jovanovich, Inc., Publishers.

Tyler, Jenny; Watts, Lisa; Bowyer, Carol; Trundle, Roma & Warrender, Annabelle (2006) 'The Usbome Book of World Geography." London: Usbome Publishing Ltd., Publisher.

Willson, David H. (2006). "A History of England." Hinsdale, Illinois: The Dryder Press, inc., Publisher

Sample Test

1. **Which one of the following is not a reason why Europeans came to the New World?**

   A. To find resources in order to increase wealth

   B. To establish trade

   C. To increase a ruler's power and importance

   D. To spread Christianity

2. **The study of human origins has been a major contribution of:**

   A. Evans

   B. Schliemann

   C. Margaret Mead

   D. The Leakeys

3. **Downstream for the flow of the Yangtze River is primarily:**

   A. North

   B. South

C. East

D. West

4. The results of the Renaissance, Enlightenment, Commercial and Industrial Revolutions were more unfortunate for the people of:

A. Asia

B. Latin America

C. Africa

D. Middle East

5. Government regulation of economic activities for favorable balance of trade was the first major economic theory. It was called:

A. Laissez-faire

B. Globalism

C. Mercantilism

D. Syndicalism

6. The first ancient civilization to introduce and practice monotheism was the:

A. Sumerians

B. Minoans

C. Phoenicians

D. Hebrews

7. **Which one of the following does not affect climate?**

   A. Elevation or altitude

   B. Ocean currents

   C. Latitude

   D. Longitude

8. **The foundation of modern constitutionalism is embodied in the idea that government is limited by law. This was stated by:**

   A. John Locke

   B. Rousseau

   C. St. Thomas Aquinas

   D. Montesquieu

9. **The only colony not founded and settled for religious, political or business reasons was:**

   A. Delaware

   B. Virginia

   C. Georgia

   D. New York

10. **The "father of political science" is considered to be:**

    A. Aristotle

    B. John Locke

    C. Plato

    D. Thomas Hobbes

11. **Bathtubs, hot and cold running water, and sewage systems with flush toilets were developed by the:**

    A. Minoans

    B. Mycenaeans

    C. Phoenicians

    D. Greeks

12. In Western Europe, the achievements of the Renaissance were unsurpassed and made these countries outstanding cultural centers on the continent. All of the following were accomplishments except:

A. Investment of the printing press

B. A rekindling of interest in the learning of classical Greece and Rome

C. Growth in literature, philosophy and art

D. Better military tactics

13. Of the thirteen English colonies, the greatest degree of religious toleration was found in:

A. Archaeology

B. Geography

C. Sociology

D. Anthropology

14. The chemical process of radiocarbon dating would be most useful and beneficial in the field of:

A. Archaeology

B. Geography

C. Sociology

D. Anthropology

15. Which one of the following is not an important legacy of the Byzantine Empire?

A. It protected Western Europe from various attacks from the East by such groups as the Persians, Ottoman Turks, and Barbarians

B. It played a part in preserving the literature, philosophy, and language of ancient Greece

C. Its military organization was the foundation for modern armies

D. It kept the legal traditions of Roman government, collecting and organizing many ancient Roman laws

16. **In the United States, federal investigations into business activities are handled by the:**

A. Department of Treasury

B. Security & Exchange Commission

C. Government Accounting Office

D. Federal Trade Commission

17. **The makeup of today's modern newspapers including comics, puzzles, sports, and columnists was a technique first used by:**

A. William Randolph Hearst

B. Edward W. Scripps

C. Joseph Pulitzer

D. Charles A. Dana

18. **Which French Renaissance writer wrote about the dangers of absolute powers and later examined himself in an effort to make inquiries into humankind and nature?**

A. Francois Rabelais

B. Desiderius Erasmus

C. Michel de Montaigne

D. Sir Francis Bacon

19. **Which of the following contributed to the severity of the Great Depression in California?**

A. An influx of Chinese immigrants.

B. The dust bowl drove People out of the cities.

C. An influx of Mexican immigrants.

D. An influx of Oakies.

20. **Downstream for the flow of the Nile River is:**

A. North

B. South

C. East

D. West

21. The year 1619 was a memorable for the colony of Virginia. Three important events occurred resulting in lasting effects on US history. Which one of the following is not one of the events?

A. Twenty African slaves arrived.

B. The London Company granted the colony a charter making it independent.

C. The colonists were given the right by the London Company to govern themselves through representative government in the Virginia House of Burgesses

D. The London Company sent to the colony 60 women who were quickly married, establishing families and stability in the colony.

22. Of all the major causes of both World Wars I and II, the most significant one is considered to be:

A. Extreme nationalism

B. Military buildup and aggression

C. Political unrest

D. Agreements and alliances

23. The end to hunting, gathering, and fishing of prehistoric people was due to:

A. Domestication of animals

B. Building crude huts and houses

C. Development of agriculture

D. Organized government in villages

24. In the United States government, power or control over public education, marriage, and divorce is:

A. Implied or suggested

B. Concurrent or shared

C. Delegated or expressed

D. Reserved

25. The principle of "popular sovereignty" allowing people in any territory to make their own decision concerning slavery was stated by;

A. Henry Clay

B. Daniel Webster

C. John C. Calhoun

D. Stephen A. Douglas

26. Under the brand new Constitution, the most urgent of the many problems facing the new federal government was that of:

A. Maintaining a strong army and navy

B. Establishing a strong foreign policy

C. Raising money to pay salaries and war debts

D. Setting up courts, passing federal laws, and providing for law enforcement officers

27. Which one of the following was not a reason why the United States went to war with Great Britain in 1812?

A. Resentment by Spain over the sale exploration, and settlement of the Louisiana Territory

B. The westward movement of farmers because of the need for more land

C. Canadian fur traders were agitating the northwestern Indians to fight American expansion

D. Britain continued to seize American ships on the high seas and force American seamen to serve aboard British ships

28. "Participant observation" is a method of study most closely associated with and used in:

A. Anthropology

B. Archaeology

C. Sociology

D. Political Science

29. The early ancient civilizations developed systems of government:

A. To provide for defense against attack

B. To regulate trade

C. To regulate and direct the economic activities of the people as they worked together in groups

D. To decide on the boundaries of the different fields during planting seasons

30. The "divine right" of kings was the key political characteristic of:

A. The Age of Absolutism

B. The Age of Reason

C. The Age of Feudalism

D. The Age of Despotism

31. The principle of zero in mathematics is the discovery of the ancient civilization found in:

A. Egypt

B. Persia

C. India

D. Babylon

32. The Ganges River empties into the:

A. Bay of Bengal

B. Arabian Sea

C. Red Sea

D. Arafura Sea

33. One South American country quickly and easily gained independence in the 19th century from European control; was noted for the uniqueness of its political stability and gradual orderly changes. This most unusual Latin American country is:

A. Chile

B. Argentina

C. Venezuela

D. Brazil

34. In which of the following disciplines would the study of physical mapping, modern or ancient, and the plotting of points and boundaries be least useful?

A. Sociology

B. Geography

C. Archaeology

D. History

35. US foreign minister Robert R. Livingstone said, "From this day the United States takes their place among the greatest powers." He was referring to the action taken by President Thomas Jefferson:

A. Who had authorized the purchase of the Louisiana Purchase

B. Who sent the US Marines and naval ships to fight the Barbary pirates

C. Who had commissioned the Lewis and Clark expedition

D. Who repealed the Embargo Act

36. **The only Central American country with no standing army, a freely elected government, and considered the oldest democracy in the region is:**

A. Costa Rica

B. Belize

C. Honduras

D. Guatemala

37. **During the 1920s, the United States almost completely stopped all immigration. One of the reasons was:**

A. Plentiful cheap unskilled labor was no longer needed by industrialists

B. War debts from World War I made it difficult to render financial assistance

C. European nations were reluctant to allow people to leave since there was a need to rebuild populations and economic stability

D. The United States did not become a member of the League of Nations

38. **Seventeen sixty-three was the year of Great Britain's total victory over her European rivals and the establishment of a global empire. Of the American colonies, a European statesman accurately prophesied that these colonies no longer needed English protection and would soon gain independence. He was:**

A. Edmund Burke

B. Comte de Rochambeau

C. Count Vergennes

D. William Pitt

39. **Colonial expansion by Western European powers in the 18th and 19th centuries was due primarily to:**

A. Building and opening the Suez Canal

B. The Industrial Revolution

C. Marked improvements in transportation

D. Complete independence of all the Americas and loss of European domination and influence

40. America's weak foreign policy and lack of adequate diplomacy during the 1870s and 1880s led to the comment that "a special Providence takes care of fools, drunkards, and the United States" is attributed to:

A. Otto von Bismarck

B. Benjamin Disraeli

C. William Gladstone

D. Paul von Hindenburg

41. It can be reasonably stated that the change in the United States from primarily an agricultural country into an industrial power was due to all of the following except:

A. Tariffs on foreign imports

B. Millions of hardworking immigrants

C. An increase in technological developments

D. The change from steam to electricity for powering industrial machinery

42. Many American authors were noted for "local Color" writings about the way of life in certain regions. Which one of the following was not associated with the other three in writing about life in the mining camps of the West?

A. Hamlin Garland

B. Joaquin Miller

C. Bret Harte

D. Mark Twain

43. There is no doubt of the vast improvement of the US Constitution over the weak Articles of Confederation. Which one of the four accurate statements below is a unique yet eloquent description of the document?

A. The establishment of a strong central government in no way lessened or weakened the individual states.

B. Individual rights were protected and secured.

C. The Constitution is the best representation of the results of the American genius for compromise.

D. Its flexibility and adaptation to change gives it a sense of timelessness.

44. The study of a people's language and writing would be part of all of the following except:

A. Sociology

B. Archaeology

C. History

D. Geography

45. The changing focus during the Renaissance when artists and scholars were less concerned with religion but centered their efforts on a better understanding of people and the world was called:

A. Realism

B. Humanism

C. Individualism

D. Intellectualism

46. The "father of anatomy" is considered to be:

A. Vesalius

B. Servetus

C. Galen

D. Harvey

47. In the US government, the power of coining money is:

A. Implied or suggested

B. Concurrent or shared

C. Delegated or expressed

D. Reserved

48. The source of authority for national, state, and local governments in the US is:

A. The will of the people

B. The US Constitution

C. Written laws

D. The Bill of Rights

49. India's greatest ruler is considered to be:

A. Akbar

B. Asoka

C. Babur

D. Jahan

50. "Poverty is the parent of revolution and crime" was from the writings of:

A. Plato

B. Aristotle

C. Cicero

D. Gaius

51. Geography was first studied in an organized manner by:

A. The Egyptians

B. The Greeks

C. The Romans

D. The Arabs

52. From about 1870 to 1900 the settlement of America's "last frontier", the West, was completed. One attraction for settlers was free land but it would have been to no avail without:

A. Better farming methods and technology

B. Surveying to set boundaries

C. Immigrants and others to seek new land

D. The railroad to get them there

53. Meridians, or lines of longitude, not only help in pinpointing locations but are also used for:

A. Measuring distance from the Poles

B. Determining direction of ocean currents

C. Determining the time around the world

D. Measuring distance on the equator

54. Historians state that the West helped to speed up the Industrial Revolution. Which one of the following statements was not a reason for this?

A. Food supplies for the ever increasing urban populations came from farms in the West

B. A tremendous supply of gold and silver from western mines provided the capital needed to built industries

C. Descendants of western settlers, educated as engineers, geologists, and metallurgists in the East, returned to the West to mine the mineral resources needed for industry

D. Iron, copper, and other minerals from western mines were important resources in manufacturing products

55. In the United States government, the power of taxation and borrowing is:

A. Implied or suggested

B. Concurrent or shared

C. Delegated or expressed

D. Reserved

56. The post-Civil War years were a time of low public morality, a time of greed, graft, and dishonesty. Which one of the reasons listed would not be accurate?

A. The war itself because of the money and materials needed to carry on the War

B. The very rapid growth of industry and big business after the War

C. The personal example set by President Grant

D. Unscrupulous heads of large impersonal corporations

57. Studies in astronomy, skills in mapping, and other contributions to geographic knowledge came from:

A. Galileo

B. Columbus

C. Eratosthenes

D. Ptolemy

58. Which one of the following would not be considered a result of World War II?

A. Economic depressions and slow resumption of trade and financial aid

B. Western Europe was no longer the center of world power

C. The beginnings of new power struggles not only in Europe but in Asia as well

D. Territorial and boundary changes for many nations, especially in Europe

59. The study of the ways in which different societies around the world deal with the problems of limited resources and unlimited needs and wants is in the area of:

A. Economics

B. Sociology

C. Anthropology

D. Political Science

60. Nineteenth century imperialism by Western European nations had important and far-reaching effects on the colonial peoples they ruled. All four of the following are the result of this. Which one was most important and had lasting effects on key 20th century events?

A. Local wars were ended

B. Living standards were raised

C. Demands for self government and feelings of nationalism surfaced

D. Economic developments occurred

61. After the War of 1812, Henry Clay and others proposed economic measures, including raising tariffs to protect American farmers and manufacturers from foreign competition. These measures were proposed in the period known as:

A. Era of Nationalism

B. American Expansion

C. Era of Good Feeling

D. American System

62. "These are the times that try men's souls" were words penned by:

A. Thomas Jefferson

B. Samuel Adams

C. Benjamin Franklin

D. Thomas Paine

63. The Age of Exploration begun in the 1400s was led by:

A. The Portuguese

B. The Spanish

C. The English

D. The Dutch

64. Which one of the following is not a function or responsibility of the US political parties?

A. Conducting elections or the voting process

B. Obtaining funds needed for election campaigns

C. Choosing candidates to run for public office

D. Making voters aware of issues and other public affairs information

65. The economist who disagreed with the idea that free markets lead to full employment and prosperity and suggested that increasing government spending would end depressions was:

A. Keynes

B. Malthus

C. Smith

D. Friedman

66. The study of social behavior of minority groups would be in the area of:

A. Anthropology

B. Psychology

C. Sociology

D. Cultural Geography

67. An extensive knowledge of surgery and medicine as well as principles of irrigation, fertilization and terrace farming was unique to:

A. The Mayans

B. The Atacamas

C. The Incas

D. The Tarapacas

68. The idea of universal peace through world organization was a philosophy of:

A. Rousseau

B. Immanuel Kant

C. Montesquieu

D. John Locke

69. Which ancient civilization is credited with being the first to develop irrigation techniques through the use of canals, dikes, and devices for raising water?

A. The Sumerians

B. The Egyptians

C. The Babylonians

D. The Akkadians

70. The study of past human cultures based on physical artifacts is:

A. History

B. Anthropology

C. Cultural Geography

D. Archaeology

71. The "father" of modern economics is considered by most economists to be:

A. Thomas Robert Malthus

B. John Stuart Mill

C. Adam Smith

D. John Maynard Keynes

72. The ideas and innovations of the period of the Renaissance were spread throughout Europe mainly because of:

A. Extensive exploration

B. Craft workers and their guilds

C. The invention of the printing press

D. Increased travel and trade

73. The American labor union movement started gaining new momentum:

A. During the building of the railroads

B. After 1865 with the growth of cities

C. With the rise of industrial giants such as Carnegie and Vanderbilt

D. During the war years of 1861-1865

74. Soil erosion is most likely to occur in large amounts in:

A. Mountain ranges

B. Deserts

C. Tropical rainforests

D. River valleys

75. Who is considered to be the most important figure in the spread of Protestantism across Switzerland?

A. Calvin

B. Zwingli

C. Munzer

D. Leyden

76. The principle that "men entrusted with power tend to abuse it" is attributed to:

A. Locke

B. Rousseau

C. Aristotle

D. Montesquieu

77. After 1783, the largest "land owner" in the Americas was:

A. Britain

B. Spain

C. France

D. United States

78. The purchase of goods or services on one market for immediate resale on another market is:

A. Output

B. Enterprise

C. Arbitrage

D. Mercantile

79. After the Civil War, the US adapted an attitude of isolation from foreign affairs. But the turning point marking the beginning of the US becoming a world power was:

A. World War I

B. Expansion of business and trade overseas

C. The Spanish-American War

D. The building and financial of the Panama Canal

80. The programs such as unemployment insurance and health insurance for the elderly are the responsibility of:

A. Federal government

B. Local government

C. State government

D. Communal government

81. The English explorer who gave England its claim to North American was:

A. Raleigh

B. Hawkins

C. Drake

D. Cabot

82. The three day Battle of Gettysburg was the turning point of the Civil War for the North leading to ultimate victory. The battle in the West reinforcing the North's victory and sealing the South's defeat was the day after Gettysburg at:

A. Perryville

B. Vicksburg

C. Stones River

D. Shiloh

83. The study of the exercise of power and political behavior in human society today would be conducted by experts in:

A. History

B. Sociology

C. Political Science

D. Anthropology

84. During the period of Spanish colonialism, which of the following was not a key to the goal of exploiting, transforming and including the native people?

A. Missions

B. Ranchos

C. Presidios

D. Pueblos

85. Potential customers for any product or service are not only called consumers but can also be called a:

A. Resource

B. Base

C. Commodity

D. Market

86. An early cultural group was so skillful in navigating on the seas that they were able to sail at night guided by stars. They were the:

A. Greeks

B. Persians

C. Minoans

D. Phoenicians

87. One method of trade restriction used by some nations is:

A. Limited treaties

B. Floating exchange rate

C. Bill of exchange

D. Import quotas

88. A political system in which the laws and traditions put limits on the powers of government is:

A. Federalism

B. Constitutionalism

C. Parliamentary system

D. Presidential system

89. Which one of the following did not contribute to the early medieval European civilization?

A. The heritage from the classical cultures

B. The Christian religion

C. The influence of the German Barbarians

D. The spread of ideas through trade and commerce

90. The Roman Empire gave so much to the world, especially the Western world. Of the legacies below, the most influential, effective and lasting is:

A. The language of Latin

B. Roman law, justice, and political system

C. Engineering and building

D. The writings of its poets an historians

91. Charlemagne's most important influence on Western civilization is seen today in:

A. Relationship of church and state

B. Strong military for defense

C. The criminal justice system

D. Education of women

92. Public administration, such as public officials in the areas of budget, accounting, distribution of public funds, and personnel management, would be part of the field of:

A. Anthropology

B. Sociology

C. Law and Taxation

D. Political Science and Economics

93. "Marbury vs. Madison (1803)" was an important Supreme Court case which set the precedent for:

A. The elastic clause

B. Judicial review

C. The supreme law of the land

D. Popular sovereignty in the territories

94. Which one of the following is not a use for a region's wetlands?

A. Produces fresh clean water

B. Provides habitat for wildlife

C. Provides water for hydroelectric power

D. Controls floods

95. The philosopher who coined the term "sociology" also stated that social behavior and events could be measured scientifically. He is identified as:

A. Auguste Comte

B. Herbert Spencer

C. Rousseau

D. Kant

96. The belief that the United States should control all of North America was called:

A. Westward Expansion

B. Pan Americanism

C. Manifest Destiny

D. Nationalism

97. A well-known World War II figure who said that "democracy was like a rotting corpse that had to be replaced by a superior way of life and more efficient government" was:

A. Hitler

B. Stalin

C. Tojo

D. Mussolini

98. The Radical Republicans who pushed the harsh Reconstruction measures through Congress after Lincoln's death lost public and moderate Republican support when they went too far:

A. In their efforts to impeach the President

B. By dividing ten southern states into military-controlled districts

C. By making the ten southern states give freed African Americans the right to vote

D. Sending carpetbaggers into the South to build up support for Congressional legislation

99. The economic system promoting individual ownership of land, capital, and businesses with minimal governmental regulations is called:

A. Macro-economy

B. Micro-economy

C. Laissez-faire

D. Free enterprise

100. A political philosophy favoring or supporting rapid social changes in order to correct social and economic inequalities is called:

A. Nationalism

B. Liberalism

C. Conservatism

D. Federalism

101. China's last imperial ruling dynasty was one of its most stable and successful and, under its rule, Chinese culture made an outstanding impression on Western nations. This dynasty was:

A. Min

B. Manchu

C. Han

D. Chou

102. Development of a solar calendar, invention of the decimal system, and contributions to the development of geometry and astronomy are all the legacy of:

A. The Babylonians

B. The Persians

C. The Sumerians

D. The Egyptians

103. The study of "spatial relationships and interaction" would be done by people in the field of:

A. Political Science

B. Anthropology

C. Geography

D. Sociology

104. The circumference of the earth, which greatly contributed to geographic knowledge was calculated by:

A. Ptolemy

B. Eratosthenes

C. Galileo

D. Strabo

105. The first European to see Florida and sail along its coast was:

A. Cabot

B. Columbus

C. Ponce de Leon

D. Narvaez

106. Which one of the following events did not occur during the period known as the "Era of Good Feeling?"

A. President Monroe issued the Monroe Doctrine

B. Spain ceded Florida to the United States

C. The building of the National Road

D. The charter of the second Bank of the United States

107. Native communities in early California are commonly divided into several cultural areas. How many cultural areas?

A. 4

B. 5

C. 6

D. 7

108. The world religion which includes a caste system is:

A. Buddhism

B. Hinduism

C. Sikhism

D. Jainism

109. The idea that continued population growth would, in future years, seriously affect a nation's productive capabilities was stated by:

A. Keynes

B. Mill

C. Malthus

D. Friedman

110. After World War II, the United States:

A. Limited its involvement in European affairs

B. Shifted foreign policy emphasis from Europe to Asia

C. Passed significant legislation pertaining to aid to farmers and tariffs on imports

D. Entered the greatest period of economic growth in its history

111. France decided in 1777 to help the American colonies in their war against Britain. This decision was based on:

A. The naval victory of John Paul Jones over the British ship Serapis"

B. The survival of the terrible winter at Valley Forge

C. The success of colonial guerilla fighters in the South

D. The defeat of the British at Saratoga

112. What event sparked a great migration of people from all over the world to California?

A. The birth of Labor Unions

B. California statehood

C. The invention of the automobile

D. The gold rush

113. Which of the following does not differentiate provisions of the California constitution from the U.S. Constitution?

A. The governor of California has the pocket veto

B. In California representation in both houses of the legislature is based on population

C. The Governor and Lt. Governor are elected separately

D. The equivalent of cabinet positions are elected rather than appointed.

114. A number of women worked hard in the first half of the 19th century for women's rights but decisive gains did not come until after 1850. The earliest accomplishments were in:

A. Medicine

B. Education

C. Writing

D. Temperance

115. Nineteenth century German unification was the result of the hard work of:

A. Otto von Bismarck

B. Kaiser William II

C. Von Moltke

D. Hindenburg

116. The geographical drought stricken region of Africa south of the Sahara and extending east and west from Senegal to Somalia is:

A. The Kalahari

B. The Namib

C. The Great Rift Valley

D. The Sahel

117. The idea or proposal for more equal division of profits among employers and workers was put forth by:

A. Karl Marx

B. Thomas Malthus

C. Adam Smith

D. John Stuart Mill

118. The term that best describes how the Supreme Court can block laws that may be unconstitutional from being enacted is:

A. Jurisprudence

B. Judicial Review

C. Exclusionary Rule

D. Right of Petition

119. On the spectrum of American politics, the label that most accurately describes voters to the "right of center" is:

A. Moderates

B. Liberals

C. Conservatives

D. Socialists

120. Marxism believes which two groups are in continual conflict?

A. Farmers and landowners

B. Kings and the nobility

C. Workers and owners

D. Structure and superstructure

121. The United States legislature is bi-cameral, this means:

A. It consists of several houses

B. It consists of two houses

C. The Vice-President is in charge of the legislature when in session

D. It has an upper and lower house

122. What Supreme Court ruling established the principal of judicial review?

A. Jefferson vs. Madison

B. Lincoln vs. Douglas

C. Marbury vs. Madison

D. Marbury vs. Jefferson

123. To be eligible to be elected President one must:

A. Be a citizen for at least five years

B. Be a citizen for seven years

C. Have been born a citizen

D. Be a naturalized citizen

124. The international organization established to work for world peace at the end of the Second World War is the:

A. League of Nations

B. United Federation of Nations

C. United Nations

D. United World League

125. Which of the following is an example of a direct democracy?

A. Elected representatives

B. Greek city-states

C. The United States Senate

D. The United States House of Representative

Sample Essay

For example: **Discuss the emergence, expansion, and evolution of Islam**

Islam is a monotheistic faith that traces its traditions to Abraham and considers the Jewish patriarchs and prophets, especially Moses, King Solomon and Jesus Christ as earlier "Prophets of God".

Mohammed was born in 570 CE in a small Arabian town. Around 610, **Mohammed** came to some prominence through a new religion called **Islam** or submission to the will of God and his followers were called **Moslems.** His first converts were members of his family and his friends. As the new faith began to grow, it remained a secret society. But when they began to make their faith public, they met with opposition and persecution from the pagan Arabians who feared the loss of profitable trade with the pilgrims who came to the Kaaba every year. In 622, Mohammed and his close followers fled persecution in Mecca and found refuge in **Medina.** His flight is called the **Hegira**. Mohammed took advantage of feuds between Jews and Arabs and became the ruler, making it the capital of a rapidly growing state.

Islam changed significantly. It became a fighting religion and Mohammed became a political leader. The group survived by raiding caravans on the road to Mecca and plundering nearby Jewish tribes. It attracted many converts from Bedouin tribes. By 630, Mohammed conquered Mecca and made it the religious center of Islam, toward which all Moslems turned to pray. By taking over the sacred city, Mohammed made it easier for converts to join the religion. By the time of his death in 632, most of the people of Arabia had become adherents of Islam.

Mohammed left behind a collection of revelations (**surahs**) he believed were delivered by the angel Gabriel. The **Quran** was reputedly dictated to Muhammad as the Word of God and published in a book called the **Koran.** The revelations were never dated or kept in any kind of order. After Mohammed's death they were organized by length in diminishing order. The Koran contains Mohammed's teachings on moral and theological questions, his legislation on political matters, and his comments on current events. Five basic principles of Islam are: Allah, Pray five times a day facing Mecca, Charity, Fasting during Ramadan and Pilgrimage to Mecca.

The Islamic armies spread their faith by conquering the Arabian Peninsula, Mesopotamia, Egypt, Syria and Persia by 650 CE and expanding to North Africa and most of the Iberian Peninsula by 750 CE. During this period of expansion, the Muslim conquerors established great centers of learning in the Middle East.

Answer Key

1. B
2. D
3. C
4. C
5. C
6. D
7. D
8. C
9. C
10. A
11. A
12. D
13. B
14. A
15. C
16. D
17. C
18. C
19. D
20. A
21. B
22. A
23. C
24. D
25. D
26. C
27. A
28. A
29. C
30. A
31. C
32. A
33. D
34. A
35. A
36. A
37. A
38. C
39. B
40. A
41. A
42. A
43. C
44. A
45. B
46. A
47. C
48. A
49. A
50. B
51. B
52. D
53. C
54. C
55. B
56. C
57. D
58. A
59. A
60. C
61. D
62. D
63. A
64. A
65. A
66. C
67. C
68. B
69. A
70. D
71. C
72. C
73. B
74. C
75. A
76. D
77. B
78. C
79. C
80. C
81. D
82. B
83. C
84. B
85. D
86. D
87. D
88. B
89. D
90. B
91. A
92. D
93. B
94. C
95. A
96. C
97. D
98. A
99. D
100. B
101. B
102. D
103. C
104. B
105. A
106. A
107. C
108. B
109. C
110. D
111. D
112. D
113. A
114. B
115. A
116. D
117. D
118. B
119. C
120. C
121. B
122. C
123. C
124. C
125. B

Rationales for Sample Questions

1. Which one of the following is not a reason why Europeans came to the New World?

A. To find resources in order to increase wealth

B. To establish trade

C. To increase a ruler's power and importance

D. To spread Christianity

Answer:

B. To establish trade

The Europeans came to the New World for a number of reasons; often they came to find new natural resources to extract for manufacturing. The Portuguese, Spanish and English were sent over to increase the monarch's power and spread influences such as religion (Christianity) and culture. Therefore, the only reason given that Europeans didn't come to the New World was to establish trade.

2. The study of human origins has been a major contribution of:

A. Evans

B. Schliemann

C. Margaret Mead

D. The Leakeys

Answer:

D. The Leakeys

Although each of the above-mentioned people made significant contributions to the study of human history, (A) English archeologist Sir Arthur Evans (1851-1941) has been primarily associated with the excavation of the Knossos on the island of Crete. (B) Heinrich Schliemann (1922-1890) was the German archeologist most well known for the excavation of the ruins of Troy. (C) Margaret Mead (1901-1978) was a cultural anthropologist most acclaimed for her 1928 book *Coming of Age in Samoa.* Besides authoring numerous books, she was also the curator of ethnology at the American Museum of Natural History in New York City. (D) The Leakeys, Louis (1903-1972), Mary (1913-1976) and son Richard (1944-), discovered fossils in East Africa that changed the world consensus about the age of humans and also discovered ancient fossils in Olduvai Gorge, Tanzania. The Leakeys, however, were most concerned with the study of early human origins.

3. Downstream for the flow of the Yangtze River is primarily:

A. North

B. South

C. East

D. West

Answer:

C. East

The Yangtze River runs from Tibet through China and flows eastward to the Pacific Ocean. The Yangtze River is an important travel and trade route through China and meets the Pacific at Shanghai.

4. The results of the Renaissance, Enlightenment, Commercial and the Industrial Revolutions were more unfortunate for the people of:

A. Asia

B. Latin America

C. Africa

D. Middle East

Answer:

C. Africa

The results of the Renaissance, Enlightenment, Commercial and Industrial Revolutions were quite beneficial for many people in much of the world. New ideas of humanism, religious tolerance, and secularism were spreading. Increased trade and manufacturing were surging economies in much of the world. The people of Africa, however, suffered during these times as they became largely left out of the developments. Also, the people of Africa were stolen, traded, and sold into slavery to provide a cheap labor force for the growing industries of Europe and the New World.

5. Government regulation of economic activities for favorable balance of trade was the first major economic theory. It was called:

A. Laissez-faire

B. Globalism

C. Mercantilism

D. Syndicalism

Answer:

C. Mercantilism

(A) Laissez-faire is the doctrine that calls for no government interference in economic and political policy. (B) Globalism is not an economic or political theory, nor is it an actual word in the English language. Globalization is the idea that we are all increasingly connected in a worldwide system. (D) Syndicalism is similar to anarchism claiming that workers should control and govern economic policies and regulations as opposed to state control. Therefore, (C) mercantilism is the best regulation of economic activities for a favorable balance of trade.

6. The first ancient civilization to introduce and practice monotheism was the:

A. Sumerians

B. Minoans

C. Phoenicians

D. Hebrews

Answer:

D. Hebrews

The (A) Sumerians and (C) Phoenicians both practiced religions in which many gods and goddesses were worshipped. Often these gods/goddesses were based on a feature of nature such as a sun, moon, weather, rocks, water, etc. The (B) Minoan culture shared many religious practices with the Ancient Egyptians. It seems that the king was somewhat of a god figure and the queen, a goddess. Much of the Minoan art point to worship of multiple gods. Therefore, only the (D) Hebrews introduced and fully practiced monotheism, or the belief in one God.

7. Which one of the following does not affect climate?

A. Elevation and altitude

B. Ocean currents

C. Latitude

D. Longitude

Answer:

D. Longitude

Latitude is the primary influence of earth's climate as it determines the climatic region in which an area lies. Elevation or altitude and ocean currents are considered to be secondary influences on climate. Longitude is considered to have no important influence over climate.

8. The foundation of modern constitutionalism is embodied in the idea that government is limited by law. This law was stated by:

A. John Locke

B. Rousseau

C. St. Thomas Aquinas

D. Montesquieu

Answer:

C. St. Thomas Aquinas

(A) John Locke (1632-1704), whose book *Two Treatises of Government* has long been considered a founding document on the rights of people to rebel against an unjust government, was an important figure in the founding of the US Constitution and on general politics of the American Colonies. (D) Montesquieu (1689-1755) and (B) Rousseau (1712-1778) were political philosophers who explored the idea of what has come to be known as liberalism. They pushed the idea that through understanding the interconnectedness of economics, geography, climate and psychology, that changes could be made to improve life. Therefore, it was St. Thomas Aquinas (1225-1274) who merged Aristotelian ideas with Christianity, who helped lay the ideas of modern constitutionalism and the limiting of government by law.

9. The only colony not founded and settled for religious, political, or business reasons was:

A. Delaware

B. Virginia

C. Georgia

D. New York

Answer:

C. Georgia

The Swedish and the Dutch established Delaware and New York as Middle Colonies. They were established with the intention of growth by economic prosperity from farming across the countryside. The English, with the intention of generating a strong farming economy settled Virginia, a Southern Colony. Georgia was the only one of these colonies not settled for religious, political or business reasons as it was started as a place for debtors from English prisons.

10. The "father of political science" is considered to be:

A. Aristotle

B. John Locke

C. Plato

D. Thomas Hobbes

Answer:

A. Aristotle

(D) Thomas Hobbes (1588-1679) wrote the important work *Leviathan* in which he pointed out that people are by all means selfish, individualistic animals that will always look out for themselves and therefore, the state must combat this nature desire. (B) John Locke (1632-1704) whose book *Two Treatises of Government* has long been considered a founding document on the rights of people to rebel against an unjust government was an important figure in the founding of the US Constitution and on general politics of the American Colonies. (C) Plato (427-347 B.C.) and Aristotle (384-322 B.C.) both contributed to the field of political science. Both believed that political order would result in the greatest stability. In fact, Aristotle studied under Plato. Both Plato and Aristotle studied the ideas of causality and the Prime Mover, but their conclusions were different. Aristotle, however, is considered to be "the father of political science" because of his development of systems of political order the true development, a scientific system to study justice and political order.

11. Bathtubs, hot and cold running water, and sewage systems with flush toilets were developed by the:

A. Minoans

B. Mycenaeans

C. Phoenicians

D. Greeks

Answer:

A. Minoans

The (A) Minoans were one of the earliest Greek cultures and existed on the island of Crete and flourished from about 1600 B.C. to about 1400 B.C. During this time, the (B) Mycenaean were flourishing on the mainland of what is now Greece. However, it was the Minoans on Crete that are best known for their advanced ancient civilization in which such advances as bathtubs, hot and cold running water, sewage systems and flush toilets were developed. The (C) Phoenicians also flourished around 1250 B.C., however, their primary development was in language and arts. The Phoenicians created an alphabet that has still considerable influence in the world today. The great developments of the (D) Greeks were primarily in the fields of philosophy, political science, and early ideas of democracy.

12. In Western Europe, the achievements of the Renaissance were unsurpassed and made these countries outstanding cultural centers on the continent. All of the following were accomplishments except:

A. Invention of the printing press

B. A rekindling of interest in the learning of classical Greece & Rome

C. Growth in literature, philosophy, and art

D. Better military tactics

Answer:

D. Better military tactics

The Renaissance in Western Europe produced many important achievements that helped push immense progress among European civilization. Some of the most important developments during the Renaissance were Gutenberg's invention of the printing press in Germany and a reexamination of the ideas and philosophies of classical Greece and Rome that eventually helped Renaissance thinkers to approach more modern ideas. Also important during the Renaissance was the growth in literature (Petrarch, Boccaccio, Erasmus), philosophy (Machiavelli, More, Bacon) and art (Van Eyck, Giotto, da Vinci). Therefore, improved military tactics is the only possible answer as it was clearly not a characteristic of the Renaissance in Western Europe.

13. Of the thirteen English colonies, the greatest degree of religious toleration was found in:

A. Maryland

B. Rhode Island

C. Pennsylvania

D. Delaware

Answer:

B. Rhode Island

Roger Williams, founder of Providence and Rhode Island, had objected to the Massachusetts colonial seizure of Indian lands and settlements and the relationship between these seizures and the Church of England. Williams was banished from Massachusetts and purposely set up Rhode Island as the first colony with a true separation of church and state.

14. The chemical process of radiocarbon dating would be most useful and beneficial in the field of:

A. Archaeology

B. Geography

C. Sociology

D. Anthropology

Answer:

A. Archaeology

Radiocarbon dating is a chemical process that helps generate a more absolute method for dating artifacts and remains by measuring the radioactive materials present in them today and calculating how long it takes for certain materials to decay. Since geographers mainly study locations and special properties of earth's living things and physical features, sociologists mostly study human society and social conditions and anthropologists generally study human culture and humanity, the answer is archaeology because archeologists study past human cultures by studying their remains.

15. Which one of the following is not an important legacy of the Byzantine Empire?

A. It protected Western Europe from various attacks from the East by such groups as the Persians, Ottoman Turks, and Barbarians

B. It played a part in preserving the literature, philosophy, and language of ancient Greece

C. Its' military organization was the foundation for modern armies

D. It kept the legal traditions of Roman government, collecting and organizing many ancient Roman laws.

Answer:

C. Its' military organization was the foundation for modern armies

The Byzantine Empire (1353-1453) was the successor to the Roman Empire in the East and protected Western Europe from invaders such as the Persians and Ottomans. The Byzantine Empire was a Christian incorporation of Greek philosophy, language, and literature along with Roman government and law. Therefore, although regarded as having a strong infantry, cavalry, and engineering corps along with excellent morale amongst its soldiers, the Byzantine Empire is not particularly considered a foundation for modern armies.

16. In the United States, federal investigations into business activities are handled by the:

A. Department of Treasury

B. Security and Exchange Commission

C. Government Accounting Office

D. Federal Trade Commission

Answer:
D. Federal Trade Commission
The Department of Treasury (A), established in 1789, is an executive government agency that is responsible for advising the president on fiscal policy. There is no such thing as a Government Accounting Office. In the United States, Federal Trade Commission or FTC handles federal investigations into business activities. The establishment of the FTC in 1915 as an independent government agency was done so as to assure fair and free competition among businesses.

17. The makeup of today's modern newspapers – including comics, puzzles, sports, and columnists – was a technique first used by:

A. William Randolph Hearst

B. Edward W. Scripps

C. Joseph Pulitzer

D. Charles A. Dana

Answer:
C. Joseph Pulitzer

(A) William Randolph Hearst (1863-1951) was better known for his vast "empire" of publications, mostly newspapers and magazines. (B) Edward W. Scripps (1854-1926) set up the first chain of newspapers in the United States called the Scripps-McRae League and later set up the Scripps-Howard chain. (D) Charles A. Dana (1819-1897) was a newspaper editor most well known for his strong stance on the Civil War and his relentless pursuit of exposing corruption in the post-Civil War administration of Grant. The answer is, therefore, Joseph Pulitzer (1847-1911). His papers, *New York World* and *Evening World*, were the first to include such modern techniques as comics, puzzles, columnists, illustrations, and sports.

18. Which French Renaissance writer wrote about the dangers of absolute powers and later examined himself in an effort to make inquiries into humankind and nature?

A. Francois Rabelais

B. Desiderius Erasmus

C. Michel de Montaigne

D. Sir Francis Bacon

Answer:

C. Michel de Montaigne

(A) Francois Rabelais (1490-1553) was a French writer and physician who was both a practicing monk (first Franciscan then later Benedictine) and a respected humanist thinker of the Renaissance. (B) Desiderius Erasmus (1466-1536) was a Dutch humanist who was very critical of the Catholic Church but was equally conflicted with Luther's Protestant Reformation. Although Luther had once considered him an ally, Erasmus opposed Luther's break from the church and favored a more internal reform to corruption, he never left the Catholic Church. (D) Sir Francis Bacon (1561-1626) was an English philosopher and writer who pushed the idea that knowledge must come from thorough scientific knowledge and experiment, and insufficient data must not be used in reaching conclusions. (C) Michel de Montaigne (1533-1592), a French essayist from a mixed background, half Catholic and half Jewish, did write some about the dangers of absolute powers, primarily monarchs but also of the Church. His attitude changed as his examination of his own life developed into a study of mankind and nature.

19. Which of the following contributed to the severity of the Great Depression in California?

A. An influx of Chinese immigrants.

B. The dust bowl drove people out of the cities.

C. An influx of Mexican immigrants.

D. An influx of Oakies.

Answer:

D. An influx of Oakies

The answer is "An influx of Oakies" (D). The Dust Bowl of the Great Plains destroyed agriculture in the area. People living in the plains areas lost their livelihood and many lost their homes and possessions in the great dust storms that resulted from a period of extended drought. People from all of the states affected by the Dust Bowl made their way to California in search of a better life. Because the majority of the people were from Oklahoma, they were all referred to as "Oakies." These migrants brought with them their distinctive plains culture. The great influx of people seeking jobs exacerbated the effects of the Great Depression in California.

20. Downstream for the flow of the Nile River is:

A. North

B. South

C. East

D. West

Answer:

A. North

The Nile River flows from Central Africa, north to the Mediterranean Sea. The Nile River Delta is in Egypt.

21. The year 1619 was a memorable year for the colony of Virginia. Three important events occurred resulting in lasting effects on US history. Which one of the following was not one of the events?

A. Twenty African slaves arrived.

B. The London Company granted the colony a charter making it independent.

C. The colonists were given the right by the London Company to govern themselves through representative government in the Virginia House of Burgesses.

D. The London Company sent to the colony 60 women who were quickly married, establishing families and stability in the colony.

Answer:

B. The London Company granted the colony a charter making it independent.

In the year 1619, the Southern colony of Virginia had an eventful year including the first arrival of twenty African slaves, the right to self-governance through representative government in the Virginia House of Burgesses (their own legislative body), and the arrival of sixty women sent to marry and establish families in the colony. The London Company did not, however, grant the colony a charter in 1619.

22. Of all the major causes of both World Wars I and II, the most significant one is considered to be:

A. Extreme nationalism

B. Military buildup and aggression

C. Political unrest

D. Agreements and alliances

Answer:

A. Extreme nationalism

Although military buildup and aggression, political unrest, and agreements and alliances were all characteristic of the world climate before and during World War I and World War II, the most significant cause of both wars was extreme nationalism. Nationalism is the idea that the interests and needs of a particular nation are of the utmost and primary importance above all else. Some nationalist movements could be liberation movements while others were oppressive regimes, much depends on their degree of nationalism. The nationalism that sparked WWI included a rejection of German, Austro-Hungarian, and Ottoman imperialism by Serbs, Slavs and others culminating in the assassination of Archduke Ferdinand by a Serb nationalist in 1914. Following WWI and the Treaty of Versailles, many Germans and others in the Central Alliance Nations, malcontent at the concessions and reparations of the treaty started a new form of nationalism. Adolf Hitler and the Nazi regime led this extreme nationalism. Hitler's ideas were an example of extreme, oppressive nationalism combined with political, social and economic scapegoating and was the primary cause of WWII.

23. The end to hunting, gathering, and fishing of prehistoric people was due to:

A. Domestication of animals

B. Building crude huts and houses

C. Development of agriculture

D. Organized government in villages

Answer:

C. Development of agriculture

Although the domestication of animals, the building of huts and houses and the first organized governments were all very important steps made by early civilizations, it was the development of agriculture that ended the once dominant practices of hunting, gathering, and fishing among prehistoric people. The development of agriculture provided a more efficient use of time and for the first time a surplus of food. This greatly improved the quality of life and contributed to early population growth.

24. In the United States government, power or control over public education, marriage, and divorce is:

A. Implied or suggested

B. Concurrent or shared

C. Delegated or expressed

D. Reserved

Answer:

D. Reserved

In the United States government, power or control over public education, marriage, and divorce is reserved. This is to say that these powers are reserved for the people of the states to decide for themselves.

25. The principle of "popular sovereignty", allowing people in any Territory to make their own decision concerning slavery was stated by:

A. Henry Clay

B. Daniel Webster

C. John C. Calhoun

D. Stephen A. Douglas

Answer:

D. Stephen A. Douglas

(A) Henry Clay (1777-1852) and (B) Daniel Webster (1782-1852) were prominent Whigs whose main concern was keeping the United States one nation. They opposed Andrew Jackson and his Democratic party around the 1830s in favor of promoting what Clay called "the American System". (C) John C. Calhoun (1782-1850) served as Vice-President under John Quincy Adams and Andrew Jackson, and then as a state senator from South Carolina. He was very pro-slavery and a champion of states' rights. The principle of "popular sovereignty", in which people in each territory could make their own decisions concerning slavery, was the doctrine of (D) Stephen A. Douglas (1813-1861). Douglas was looking for a middle ground between the abolitionists of the North and the pro-slavery Democrats of the South. However, as the polarization of pro- and anti-slavery sentiments grew, he lost the presidential election to Republican Abraham Lincoln, who later abolished slavery.

26. Under the brand new Constitution, the most urgent of the many problems facing the new federal government was that of:

A. Maintaining a strong army and navy

B. Establishing a strong foreign policy

C. Raising money to pay salaries and war debts

E. Setting up courts, passing federal laws, and providing for law enforcement officers

Answer:

C. Raising money to pay salaries and war debts

Maintaining strong military forces, establishment of a strong foreign policy, and setting up a justice system were important problems facing the United States under the newly ratified Constitution. However, the most important and pressing issue was how to raise money to pay salaries and war debts from the Revolutionary War. Alexander Hamilton (1755-1804) then Secretary of the Treasury proposed increased tariffs and taxes on products such as liquor. This money would be used to pay off war debts and to pay for internal programs. Hamilton also proposed the idea of a National Bank.

27. Which one of the following was not a reason why the United States went to war with Great Britain in 1812?

A. Resentment by Spain over the sale, exploration, and settlement of the Louisiana Territory

B. The westward movement of farmers because of the need for more land

C. Canadian fur traders were agitating the northwestern Indians to fight American expansion

D. Britain continued to seize American ships on the high seas and force American seamen to serve aboard British ships

Answer:

A. Resentment by Spain over the sale, exploration, and settlement of the Louisiana Territory

The United States went to war with Great Britain in 1812 for a number of reasons including the expansion of settlers westward and the need for more land, the agitation of Indians by Canadian fur traders in eastern Canada, and the continued seizures of American ships by the British on the high seas. Therefore, the only statement given that was not a reason for the War of 1812 was the resentment by Spain over the sale, exploration and settlement of the Louisiana Territory. In fact, the Spanish continually held more hostility towards the British than towards the United States. The War of 1812 is often considered to be the second American war for independence.

28. "Participant observation" is a method of study most closely associated with and used in:

A. Anthropology

B. Archaeology

C. Sociology

D. Political science

Answer:

A. Anthropology

"Participant observation" is a method of study most closely associated with and used in (A) anthropology or the study of current human cultures. (B) Archaeologists typically the study of the remains of people, animals or other physical things. (C) Sociology is the study of human society and usually consists of surveys, controlled experiments, and field studies. (D) Political science is the study of political life including justice, freedom, power and equality in a variety of methods.

29. The early ancient civilizations developed systems of government:

A. To provide for defense against attack

B. To regulate trade

C. To regulate and direct the economic activities of the people as they worked together in groups

D. To decide on the boundaries of the different fields during Planting seasons

Answer:

C. To regulate and direct the economic activities of the people as they worked together in groups

Although ancient civilizations were concerned with defense, trade regulation and the maintenance of boundaries in their fields, they could not have done any of them without first regulating and directing the economic activities of the people as they worked in groups. This provided for a stable economic base from which they could trade and actually had something worth providing defense for.

30. The "divine right" of kings was the key political characteristic of:

A. The Age of Absolutism

B. The Age of Reason

C. The Age of Feudalism

D. The Age of Despotism

Answer:

A. The Age of Absolutism

The "divine right" of kings was the key political characteristic of The Age of Absolutism and was most visible in the reign of King Louis XIV of France, as well as during the times of King James I and his son, Charles I. The divine right doctrine claims that kings and absolute leaders derive their right to rule by virtue of their birth alone. They see this both as a law of God and of nature.

31. The principle of zero in mathematics is the discovery of the ancient civilization found in:

A. Egypt

B. Persia

C. India

D. Babylon

Answer:

C. India

Although the Egyptians practiced algebra and geometry, the Persians developed an alphabet, and the Babylonians developed Hammurabi's Code, which would come to be considered among the most important contributions of the Mesopotamian civilization, it was the Indians that created the idea of zero in mathematics changing drastically our ideas about numbers.

32. The Ganges River empties into the:

A. Bay of Bengal

B. Arabian Sea

C. Red Sea

D. Arafura Sea

Answer:

A. Bay of Bengal

The Ganges River runs 1,560 miles, northeast through India across the plains to the Bay of Bengal in Bangladesh. The Ganges is considered to be the most sacred river in India according to the Hindus.

33. One South American country quickly and easily gained independence in the 19th century from European control; was noted for the uniqueness of its political stability and gradual orderly changes. This most unusual Latin American country is:

A. Chile

B. Argentina

C. Venezuela

D. Brazil

Answer:

D. Brazil

While Chile, Argentina, and Venezuela all have had histories marred by civil wars, dictatorships, and numerous violent coups during their quests for independence, Brazil experienced a more rapid independence. Independence was gained quickly and more easily than the other countries due to a bloodless revolution in 1889 that officially made Brazil a republic and the economic stability they had in place from a strong coffee and rubber based economy.

34. In which of the following disciplines would the study of physical mapping, modern or ancient, and the plotting of points and boundaries be least useful?

A. Sociology

B. Geography

C. Archaeology

D. History

Answer:

A. Sociology

In geography, archaeology, and history, the study of maps and plotting of points and boundaries is very important as all three of these disciplines hold value in understanding the spatial relations and regional characteristics of people and places. Sociology, however, mostly focuses on the social interactions of people and while location is important, the physical location is not as important as the social location such as the differences between studying people in groups or as individuals.

35. U.S. foreign minister Robert R. Livingstone said, "From this day the United States take their place among the greatest powers." He was referring to the action taken by President Thomas Jefferson:

A. Who had authorized the purchase of the Louisiana Territory

B. Who sent the US Marines and naval ships to fight the Barbary pirates

C. Who had commissioned the Lewis and Clark expedition

D. Who repealed the Embargo Act

Answer:

A. Who had authorized the purchase of the Louisiana Territory

Livingstone's claim that "from this day, the United States takes their place among the greatest powers" was a reference to Jefferson's authorization and acquisition of the Louisiana Territory. What he meant was that now the United States was beginning to fulfill what would later become known as "Manifest Destiny", and it would be this growth of physical size and political power that put the United States on course to be a world super power.

36. The only Central American country with no standing army, a freely elected government, and considered the oldest democracy in the region is:

A. Costa Rica

B. Belize

C. Honduras

D. Guatemala

Answer:

A. Costa Rica

Belize, Guatemala, and Honduras have all struggled over the past few hundred years. Efforts for independence from colonial powers such as Spain and Great Britain proved difficult and brought up many difficult issues such as the violent border disputes between Guatemala and Belize as late as the 1980s and 1990s that created strong tensions and almost all out war. Honduras experienced many bloody civil wars since its quest for independence began in the early nineteenth century. Even today, Honduras struggles as one of the poorest nations in the world and has continued to experience serious exploitation and abuses of workers by first world multinational corporations. Since the late eighteenth century, Costa Rica on the other hand, has experienced longstanding democracy and stability. They have no army and despite a couple of breakdowns in the political system, most notably in 1917 and 1948, it is considered the longest standing democracy in Central America.

37. During the 1920s, the United States almost completely stopped all immigration. One of the reasons was:

A. Plentiful cheap, unskilled labor was no longer needed by industrialists

B. War debts from World War I made it difficult to render financial assistance

C. European nations were reluctant to allow people to leave since there was a need to rebuild populations and economic stability

D. The United States did not become a member of the League of Nations

Answer:

A. Plentiful cheap, unskilled labor was no longer needed by industrialists

The primary reason that the United States almost completely stopped all immigration during the 1920s was because their once, much needed, cheap, unskilled labor jobs, made available by the once booming industrial economy, were no longer needed. This has much to do with the increased use of machines to do the work once done by cheap, unskilled laborers.

38. In the year 1763, Great Britain's total victory over her European rivals and the establishment of a global empire. Of the American colonies, a European statesman accurately prophesied that these colonies no longer needed English protection and would soon gain independence. He was:

A. Edmund Burke

B. Comte de Rochambeau

C. Count Vergennes

D. William Pitt

Answer:

C. Count Vergennes

Edmund Burke (1729-1797) was a British statesman that did believe in some political reforms in Great Britain's dealing with the American colonies but still believed in the needed guidance and power of the crown in maintaining order. He supported the Declaratory Acts that reasserted Great Britain's control over the colonies in 1766. Burke was important in both the American and French Revolutions. Comte de Rochambeau (1725-1807) was a French marshal who helped George Washington during the American Revolution. William Pitt (1759-1806) was a British statesman who was also a liberal in terms of his ideas for change in economic policy but he never speculated about the future independence of the American colonies. Count Vergennes or Charles Gravier Vergennes (1717-1787) was the French statesman who made the accurate prophecy that the American Colonies would soon be independent from Great Britain. Vergennes not only supported the American Revolution but also helped negotiate the Treaty of Paris in 1783 that secured independence for the colonies.

39. Colonial expansion by Western European powers in the 18th and 19th centuries was due primarily to:

A. Building and opening the Suez Canal

B. The Industrial Revolution

C. Marked improvements in transportation

D. Complete independence of all the Americas and loss of European domination and influence

Answer:

B. The Industrial Revolution

Colonial expansion by Western European powers in the late eighteenth and nineteenth centuries was due primarily to the Industrial Revolution in Great Britain that spread across Europe and needed new natural resources and therefore, new locations from which to extract the raw materials needed to feed the new industries.

40. America's weak foreign policy and lack of adequate diplomacy during the 1870s and 1880s led to the comment that "a special Providence takes care of fools, drunkards, and the United States" is attributed to:

A. Otto von Bismarck

B. Benjamin Disraeli

C. William Gladstone

D. Paul von Hindenburg

Answer:

A. Otto Von Bismarck

Benjamin Disraeli (1804-1881), a conservative, and William Gladstone (1809-1898), a liberal, were political rivals in Great Britain. Gladstone was greatly disliked by both his rival Disraeli and his Queen for being such a staunch political and economic reformer. Paul von Hindenberg (1847-1934) was a German field marshal and president (1925-1934) who fought against the Americans in World War I.

However, it was Otto von Bismarck (1815-1898), the German statesman who came to be known as the Iron Chancellor, who once said "a special Providence takes care of fools, drunkards, and the United States". Bismarck was saying that despite the United States' shortcomings in foreign policy, leadership and military strength, they continued to grow and gained power in the face of much better run governments, armies and foreign policy makers.

41. It can be reasonably stated that the change in the United States from primarily an agricultural country into an industrial power was due to all of the following except:

A. Tariffs on foreign imports

B. Millions of hardworking immigrants

C. An increase in technological developments

D. The change from steam to electricity for powering industrial machinery

Answer:

A. Tariffs on foreign imports

It can be reasonably stated that the change in the United States from primarily an agricultural country into an industrial power was due to a great degree of three of the reasons listed above. It was a combination of millions of hard-working immigrants, an increase in technological developments, and the change from steam to electricity for powering industrial machinery. The only reason given that really had little effect was the tariffs on foreign imports.

42. Many American authors were noted for "local color" writings about the way of life in certain regions. Which one of the following was not associated with the other three in writing about life in the mining camps of the West?

A. Hamlin Garland

B. Joaquin Miller

C. Bret Harte

D. Mark Twain

Answer:

A. Hamlin Garland

Hamlin Garland (1860-1940), unlike the other three authors mentioned, grew up in the mid-western farmlands and wrote stories that were bitter pictures of the difficulties of farm life. He also wrote political critiques. Joaquin Miller (1839-1913), an American poet, moved in 1852 to the Oregon frontier where he wrote about life in gold-mining camps, experiences with Native Americans, and painted an overall energetic and pleasant picture of frontier life. Bret Harte (1836-1902) moved to California at age 19 and wrote local-color short stories of life in mining camps and on the western frontiers of California. Mark Twain (1835-1910), however, was perhaps the most well known and celebrated novelist of early American. Twain, also known as Samuel Langhorne Clemens, was born in Missouri and lived in a variety of places before making it out West, first to Carson City, Nevada, and then later to Sacramento. Twain would return to Hartford, Connecticut, where he spent his later years and wrote *Roughing It* in 1887, about the difficult lives he saw lived on the Western frontier. Twain is best known for his books *The Adventures* of *Huckleberry Finn* and *The Adventures of Tom Sawyer*, the former of which is considered by many to be the first truly great American novel.

43. There is no doubt of the vast improvement of the U.S. Constitution over the weak Articles of Confederation. Which one of the four statements below is not a description of the document?

A. The establishment of a strong central government in no way lessened or weakened the individual states

B. Individual rights were protected and secured

C. The Constitution demands unquestioned respect and subservience to the federal government by all states and citizens

D. Its flexibility and adaptation to change gives it a sense of timelessness

Answer:

C. The Constitution demands unquestioned respect and subservience to the federal government by all states and citizens.

The U.S. Constitution was indeed a vast improvement over the Articles of Confederation and the authors of the document took great care to assure longevity. It clearly stated that the establishment of a strong central government in no way lessened or weakened the individual states. In the Bill of Rights, citizens were assured that individual rights were protected and secured. Possibly the most important feature of the new Constitution was its flexibility and adaptation to change which assured longevity.

Therefore, the only statement made that doesn't describe some facet of the Constitution is "The Constitution demands unquestioned respect and subservience to the federal government by all states and citizens". On the contrary, the Constitution made sure that citizens could critique and make changes to their government and encourages such critiques and changes as necessary for the preservation of democracy.

44. The study of a people's language and writing would be part of all of the following except:

A. Sociology

B. Archaeology

C. History

D. Geography

Answer:

A. Sociology

The study of a people's language and writing would be a part of studies in the disciplines of sociology (study of social interaction and organization), archaeology, (study of ancient artifacts including written works), and history (the study of the past). Language and writing would be less important to geography that tends to focus more on locations and spatial relations than on the people in those regions and their languages or writings.

45. The changing focus during the Renaissance when artists and scholars were less concerned with religion but centered their efforts on a better understanding of people and the world was called:

A. Realism

B. Humanism

C. Individualism

D. Intellectualism

Answer:

B. Humanism

Realism is a medieval philosophy that contemplated independence of existence of the body, the mind, and God. The idea of individualism is usually either a reference to an economic or political theory. Intellectualism is the placing of great importance and devotion to the exploring of the intellect. Therefore, the changing focus during the Renaissance when artists and scholars were less concerned with religion but centered their efforts on a better understanding of people and the world was called humanism.

46. The "father of anatomy" is considered to be:

A. Vesalius

B. Servetus

C. Galen

D. Harvey

Answer:

A. Vesalius

Andreas Vesalius (1514-1564) is considered to be the "father of anatomy" as a result of his revolutionary work on the human anatomy based on dissections of human cadavers. Prior to Vesalius, men such as Galen, (130-200) had done work in the field of anatomy, but they had based the majority of their work on animal studies.

47. In the United States government, the power of coining money is:

A. Implied or suggested

B. Concurrent or shared

C. Delegated or expressed

D. Reserved

Answer:

C. Delegated or expressed

In the United States government, the power of coining money is delegated or expressed. Therefore, only the United States government may coin money, the states may not coin money for themselves.

48. The source of authority for national, state, and local governments in the United States is:

A. The will of the people

B. The United States Constitution

C. Written laws

D. The Bill of Rights

Answer:

A. The will of the people

The source of authority for national, state, and local governments in the United States is the will of the people. Although the United States Constitution, the Bill of Rights, and the other written laws of the land are important guidelines for authority, they may ultimately be altered or changed by the will of the people.

49. India's greatest ruler is considered to be:

A. Akbar

B. Asoka

C. Babur

D. Jahan

Answer:

A. Akbar

Akbar (1556-1605) is considered to be India's greatest ruler. He combined a drive for conquest with a magnetic personality and went so far as to invent his own religion, Dinillahi, a combination of Islam, Christianity, Zoroastrianism, and Hinduism. Asoka (273 B.C.-232 B.C.) was also an important ruler as he was the first to bring together a fully united India. Babur (1483-1540) was both considered to be a failure as he struggled to maintain any power early in his reign, but later to be somewhat successful in his quest to reunite Northern India. Jahan's (1592-1666) rule of India is considered to be the golden age of art and literature in the region.

50. "Poverty is the parent of revolution and crime" was from the writings of:

A. Plato

B. Aristotle

C. Cicero

D. Gaius

Answer:

B. Aristotle

Aristotle once wrote "Poverty is the parent of revolution and crime", a comment that is probably as relevant today as it was in Aristotle's day. It showed his true insight as one of the great political and social commentators and philosophers of all time.

51. Geography was first studied in an organized manner by the:

A. Egyptians

B. Greeks

C. Romans

D. Arabs

Answer:

B. Greeks

The Greeks were the first to study geography, possibly because of the difficulties they faced as a result of geographic conditions. Greece had difficulty uniting early on as their steep, treacherous, mountainous terrain made it difficult for the city-states to be united. As the Greeks studied their geography, it became possible to defeat more powerful armies on their home turf, such as the great victory over the Persians at Marathon.

52. From about 1870 to 1900, the last settlement of America's "last frontier", the West, was completed. One attraction for settlers was free land but it would have been to no avail without:

A. Better farming methods and technology

B. Surveying to set boundaries

C. Immigrants and others to see new lands

D. The railroad to get them there

Answer:

D. The railroad to get them there

From about 1870 to 1900, the settlement for America's "last frontier" in the West was made possible by the building of the railroad. Without the railroad, the settlers never could have traveled such distances in an efficient manner.

53. Meridians, or lines of longitude, not only help in pinpointing locations, but are also used for:

A. Measuring distance from the Poles

B. Determining direction of ocean currents

C. Determining the time around the world

D. Measuring distance on the Equator

Answer:

C. Determining the time around the world

Meridians, or lines of longitude, are the determining factor in separating time zones and determining time around the world.

54. Historians state that the West helped to speed up the Industrial Revolution. Which one of the following statements was not a reason for this?

A. Food supplies for the ever-increasing urban populations came from farms in the West.

B. A tremendous supply of gold and silver from western mines provided the capital needed to build industries.

C. Descendants of western settlers, educated as engineers, geologists, and metallurgists in the East, returned to the West to mine the mineral resources needed for industry.

D. Iron, copper, and other minerals from western mines were important resources in manufacturing products.

Answer:

C. Descendants of western settlers, educated as engineers, geologists, and metallurgists in the East, returned to the West to mine the mineral resources needed for industry.

The West helped to speed up the Industrial Revolution in a number of important and significant ways. First, the land yielded crops for the growing urban populations. Second, the gold and silver supplies coming out of the Western mines provided the capital needed to build industries. Also, resources such as iron and copper were extracted from the mines in the West and provided natural resources for manufacturing. The descendants of western settlers typically didn't become educated and then returned to the West as miners. The miners were typically working class with little or no education.

55. In the United States government, the power of taxation and borrowing is:

A. Implied or suggested

B. Concurrent or shared

C. Delegated or expressed

D. Reserved

Answer:

B. Concurrent or shared

In the United States government, the power of taxation is concurrent or shared with the states. An example of this is the separation of state and federal income tax and the separate filings of tax returns for each.

56. The post-Civil War years were a time of low public morality, a time of greed, graft, and dishonesty. Which one of the reasons listed would not be accurate?

A. The war itself because of the money and materials needed to carry on war

B. The very rapid growth of industry and big business after the war

C. The personal example set by President Grant

D. Unscrupulous heads of large impersonal corporations

Answer:

C. The personal example set by President Grant

The post-Civil War years were a particularly difficult time for the nation and public morale was especially low. The war had plunged the country into debt and ultimately into a recession by the 1890s. Racism was rampant throughout the South and the North where freed Blacks were taking jobs for low wages. The rapid growth of industry and big business caused a polarization of rich and poor, workers and owners. Many people moved into the urban centers to find work in the new industrial sector, jobs were typically low-wage, long hours, and poor working conditions. The heads of large impersonal corporations were arrogant in treating their workers inhumanely and letting morale drop to a record low. The heads of corporations showed their greed and malice towards the workingman by trying to prevent and disband labor unions.

57. Studies in astronomy, skills in mapping, and other contributions to geographic knowledge came from:

A. Galileo

B. Columbus

C. Eratosthenes

D. Ptolemy

Answer:

D. Ptolemy

Ptolemy (2nd century AD) was important in the fields of astronomy and geography. His theory stated that the earth was the center of the universe and all the other planets rotated around it, a theory that was later proven false. Ptolemy, however, was important for his contributions to the fields of mapping, mathematics, and geography. Galileo (1564-1642) was also important in the field of astronomy but did not make the mapping and geographic contributions of Ptolemy. He invented and used the world's first telescope and advanced Copernicus' theory that the earth revolved around the sun, much to the dismay of the Church.

58. Which one of the following would not be considered a result of World War II?

A. Economic depressions and slow resumption of trade and financial aid

B. Western Europe was no longer the center of world power

C. The beginnings of new power struggles not only in Europe but in Asia as well

D. Territorial and boundary changes for many nations, especially in Europe

Answer:

A. Economic depressions and slow resumption of trade and financial aid

Following World War II, the economy was vibrant and flourished from the stimulant of war and an increased dependence of the world on United States industries. Therefore, World War II didn't result in economic depressions and slow resumption of trade and financial aid. Western Europe was no longer the center of world power. New power struggles arose in Europe and Asia and many European nations underwent changing territories and boundaries.

59. The study of ways in which different societies around the world deal with the problems of limited resources and unlimited needs and wants is in the area of:

A. Economics

B. Sociology

C. Anthropology

D. Political Science

Answer:

A. Economics

The study of the ways in which different societies around the world deal with the problems of limited resources and unlimited needs and wants is a study of Economics. Economists consider the law of supply and demand as fundamental to the study of the economy. However, Sociology and Political Science also consider the study of economics and its importance in understanding social and political systems.

60. Nineteenth century imperialism by Western Europe nations had important and far-reaching effects on the colonial peoples they ruled. All four of the following are the results of this. Which one was the most important and had lasting effects on key 20th century events?

A. Local wars were ended

B. Living standards were raised

C. Demands for self-government and feelings of nationalism surfaced

D. Economic developments occurred

Answer:

C. Demands for self-government and feelings of nationalism surfaced

The nineteenth century imperialism by Western European nations had some very serious and far-reaching effects. The most important and lasting effect on events of the twentieth century were the demands for self-government and the rise of nationalism. Both World War I and World War II were caused to a large degree by the rise of nationalist sentiment across Europe and Asia. Nationalism has also fueled numerous liberation movements and revolutionary movements across the globe from Central and South America to the South Pacific to Africa and Asia.

61. After the War of 1812, Henry Clay and others proposed economic measures, including raising tariffs to protect American farmers and manufacturers from foreign competition. These measures were proposed in the period known as:

A. Era of Nationalism

B. American Expansion

C. Era of Good Feeling

D. American System

Answer:

D. American System

Although there is no official (A) "Era of Nationalism", it could be used to describe the time leading up to and including the First and Second World Wars, as nationalism was on the rise. (B) American Expansion describes the movement of American settlers across the frontier towards the West. The so-called (C) "Era of Good Feeling" is the period after the War of 1812 but doesn't describe the policies proposed by Clay. The economic measures, including raising tariffs to protect American farmers and manufacturers from foreign competition, was known as the (D) American System.

62. "These are the times that try men's souls" were words penned by:

A. Thomas Jefferson

B. Samuel Adams

C. Benjamin Franklin

D. Thomas Paine

Answer:

D. Thomas Paine

Thomas Paine (1737-1809), the great American political theorist, wrote "these are the times that try men's souls" in his 16 part pamphlet *The Crisis*. Paine's authoring of *Common Sense* was an important step in spreading information to the American colonists about their need for independence from Great Britain.

63. The Age of Exploration begun in the 1400s was led by:

A. The Portuguese

B. The Spanish

C. The English

D. The Dutch

Answer:

A. The Portuguese

Although the Age of Exploration had many important players among them, the Dutch, Spanish and English, it was the Portuguese who sent the first explorers to the New World.

64. Which one of the following is not a function or responsibility of the US political parties?

A. Conducting elections or the voting process

B. Obtaining funds needed for election campaigns

C. Choosing candidates to run for public office

D. Making voters aware of issues and other public affairs information

Answer:

A. Conducting elections or the voting process

The US political parties have numerous functions and responsibilities. Among them are obtaining funds needed for election campaigns, choosing the candidates to run for office, and making voters aware of the issues. The political parties, however, do not conduct elections or the voting process, as that would be an obvious conflict of interest.

65. The economist who disagreed with the idea that free markets lead to full employment and prosperity and suggested that increasing government spending would end depressions was:

A. Keynes

B. Malthus

C. Smith

D. Friedman

Answer:

A. Keynes

John Maynard Keynes (1883-1946) advocated an economic system in which government regulations and spending on public works would stimulate the economy and lead to full employment. This broke from the classical idea that free markets would lead to full employment and prosperity. He was still a firm believer in capitalism, but in a less classical sense than Adam Smith (1723-1790), whose *Wealth of Nations* advocated for little or no government interference in the economy.

Smith claimed that an individual's self-interest would bring about the public's welfare. It is important to note that Smith was firmly against the free market systems of monopoly power and warned that the private sector, particularly large manufacturers, if left unregulated could potentially stand in opposition to the public welfare.

66. The study of the social behavior of minority groups would be in the area of:

A. Anthropology

B. Psychology

C. Sociology

D. Cultural Geography

Answer:

C. Sociology

The study of social behavior in minority groups would be primarily in the area of Sociology, as it is the discipline most concerned with social interaction and being. However, it could be argued that Anthropology, Psychology, and Cultural Geography could have some interest in the study as well.

67. An extensive knowledge of surgery and medicine as well as principles of irrigation, fertilization and terrace farming was unique to:

A. The Mayans

B. The Atacamas

C. The Incas

D. The Tarapacas

Answer:

C. The Incas

The Incas of Peru had an extensive knowledge of surgery and medicine as well as principles of irrigation, fertilization, and terrace farming. These were unique achievements for an ancient civilization.

68. The idea of universal peace through world organization was a philosophy of:

A. Rousseau

B. Immanuel Kant

C. Montesquieu

D. John Locke

Answer:

B. Immanuel Kant

Immanuel Kant (1724-1804) was the German metaphysician and philosopher, who was a founding proponent of the idea that world organization was the means for achieving universal peace. Kant's ideas helped to found such world peace organizations as the League of Nations in the wake of World War I.

69. Which ancient civilization is credited with being the first to develop irrigation techniques through the use of canals, dikes, and devices for raising water?

A. The Sumerians

B. The Egyptians

C. The Babylonians

D. The Akkadians

Answer:

A. The Sumerians

The ancient (A) Sumerians of the Fertile Crescent of Mesopotamia are credited with being the first to develop irrigation techniques through the use of canals, dikes, and devices for raising water. The (B) Egyptians also practiced controlled irrigation but that was primarily through the use of the Nile's predictable flooding schedule. The (C) Babylonians were more noted for their revolutionary systems of law than their irrigation systems.

70. The study of past human cultures based on physical artifacts is:

A. History

B. Anthropology

C. Cultural Geography

D. Archaeology

Answer:

D. Archaeology

Archaeology is the study of past human cultures based on physical artifacts such as fossils, carvings, paintings, and engraved writings.

71. The "father" of modern economics is considered by most economists today to be:

A. Thomas Robert Malthus

B. John Stuart Mill

C. Adam Smith

D. John Maynard Keynes

Answer:

C. Adam Smith

Adam Smith (1723-1790) is considered by many to be the "father" of modern economics. In the *Wealth of Nations,* Smith advocated for little or no government interference in the economy. Smith claimed that individuals' self-interest would bring about the public's welfare. It is important to note that Smith was firmly against the free market systems of monopoly power and warned that the private sector, particularly large manufacturers, if left unregulated could potentially stand in opposition to the public welfare. John Maynard Keynes 1883-1946) was also an important economist. He advocated an economic system in which government regulations and spending on public works would stimulate the economy and lead to full employment. John Stuart Mill (1806-1873) was a progressive British philosopher and economist, whose ideas came closer to socialism than to the classical capitalist ideas of Adam Smith. Mill constantly advocated for political and social reforms, including emancipation for women, labor organizations, and farming cooperatives. Thomas Malthus (1766-1834) was a British economist who introduced the study of population and early on considered famine, war, and disease to be the primary checks on world population. He later modified his views and recognized his early theoretical shortcomings and shifted his focus to the causes of unemployment.

72. The ideas and innovations of the period of the Renaissance were spread throughout Europe mainly because of:

A. Extensive exploration

B. Craft workers and their guilds

C. The invention of the printing press

D. Increased travel and trade

Answer:

C. The invention of the printing press

The ideas and innovations of the Renaissance were spread throughout Europe for a number of reasons. While exploration, increased travel, and spread of craft may have aided the spread of the Renaissance to small degrees, nothing was as important to the spread of ideas as Gutenberg's invention of the printing press in Germany.

73. The American labor union movement started gaining new momentum:

A. During the building of the railroads

B. After 1865 with the growth of cities

C. With the rise of industrial giants such as Carnegie and Vanderbilt

D. During the war years of 1861-1865

Answer:

B. After 1865 with the growth of cities

The American Labor Union movement had been around since the late eighteenth and early nineteenth centuries. The Labor movement began to first experience persecution by employers in the early 1800s. The American Labor Movement remained relatively ineffective until after the Civil War. In 1866, the National Labor Union was formed, pushing such issues as the eight-hour workday and new policies of immigration. This gave rise to the Knights of Labor and eventually the American Federation of Labor (AFL) in the 1890s and the Industrial Workers of the World (1905). Therefore, it was the period following the Civil War that empowered the labor movement in terms of numbers, militancy, and effectiveness.

74. Soil erosion is most likely to occur in large amounts in:

A. Mountain ranges

B. Deserts

C. Tropical rainforests

D. River valleys

Answer:
C. Tropical rainforests

Soil erosion is most likely to occur in tropical rainforests as the large amount of constant rainfall moves the soil at a greater rate across a greater area. Mountain ranges and river valleys experience some soil erosion but don't have the levels of precipitation found in a tropical rainforest. Deserts have virtually no soil erosion due to their climate.

75. Who is considered to be the most important figure in the spread of Protestantism across Switzerland?

A. Calvin

B. Zwingli

C. Munzer

D. Leyden

Answer:

A. Calvin

While Huldreich Zwingli (1484-1531) was the first to spread the Protestant Reformation in Switzerland around 1519, it was John Calvin (1509-1564), whose less radical approach to Protestantism who really made the most impact in Switzerland. Calvin's ideas separated from the Lutherans over the "Lord's Supper" debate over the sacrament, and his branch of Protestants became known as Calvinism. Calvin certainly built on Zwingli's early influence but really made the religion widespread throughout Switzerland. Thomas Munzer (1489-1525) was a German Protestant reformer whose radical and revolutionary ideas about God's will to overthrow the ruling classes and his siding with the peasantry got him beheaded. Munzer has since been studied and admired by Marxists for his views on class. Leyden (or Leiden) was a founder of the University of Leyden, a Protestant place for study in the Netherlands.

76. The principle that "men entrusted with power tend to abuse it" is attributed to:

A. Locke

B. Rousseau

C. Aristotle

D. Montesquieu

Answer:

D. Montesquieu

The principle that "men entrusted with power tend to abuse it" is attributed to Montesquieu (1689-1755), the great French philosopher whose ideas based much on Locke's ideas, along with Rousseau, had a strong influence on the French Revolution of 1789. Although it would be reasonable to assume that Locke, Rousseau, and Aristotle would probably agree with the statement, all four of these men had profound impacts on the ideas of the Enlightenment, from humanism to constitutionals.

77. After 1783, the largest "land owner" in the Americas was:

A. Britain

B. Spain

C. France

D. United States

Answer:

B. Spain

Despite the emergence of the United States as an independent nation in control of the colonies over the British, and the French control of Canada, Spain remained the largest "land owner" in the Americas controlling much of the southwest as well as much of Central and South America.

78. The purchase of goods or services on one market for immediate resale on another market is:

A. Output

B. Enterprise

C. Arbitrage

D. Mercantile

Answer:

C. Arbitrage

(A) Output is an amount produced or manufactured by an industry. (B) Enterprise is simply any business organization. (D) Mercantile is one of the first systems of economics in which goods were exchanged. Therefore, arbitrage (C) is an item or service that an industry produces. The dictionary definition of arbitrage is the purchase of securities on one market for immediate resale on another market in order to profit from a price discrepancy.

79. After the Civil War, the United States adapted an attitude of isolation from foreign affairs. But the turning point marking the beginning of the US becoming a world power was:

A. World War I

B. Expansion of business and trade overseas

C. The Spanish-American War

D. The building and financing of the Panama Canal

Answer:

C. The Spanish-American War

The turning point marking the beginning of the United States becoming a super power was the Spanish-American War. This was seen as an extension of the Monroe doctrine, calling for United States dominance in the Western Hemisphere and removal of European powers in the region. The United States' relatively easy defeat of Spain in the Spanish-American War marked the beginning of a continuing era of dominance for the United States. In addition, in the post-Civil War era, Spain was the largest land owner in the Americas. Their easy defeat at the hands of the United States in Cuba, the Philippines, and elsewhere showed the strength of the United States across the globe.

80. The programs such as unemployment insurance and health insurance for the elderly are the responsibility of:

A. Federal Government

B. Local Government

C. State Government

D. Communal Government

Answer:

C. State Government

Assistance programs, such as unemployment insurance and free health insurance for the elderly is the responsibility of state governments.

81. The English explorer who gave England its claim to North America was:

A. Raleigh

B. Hawkins

C. Drake

D. Cabot

Answer:

D. Cabot

Sir Walter Raleigh (1554-1618) was an English explorer and navigator, who was sent to the New World in search of riches. He founded the lost colony at Roanoke, Virginia, and was later imprisoned for a supposed plot to kill the King for which he was later released. Sir John Hawkins (1532-1595) and Sir Francis Drake (1540-1596) were both navigators who worked in the slave trade, made some voyages to the New World, and commanded ships against and defeated the Spanish Armada in 1588. John Cabot (1450-1498) was the English explorer who gave England claim to North America.

82. The three-day Battle of Gettysburg was the turning point of the Civil War for the North leading to ultimate victory. The battle in the West reinforcing the North's victory and sealing the South's defeat was the day after Gettysburg at:

A. Perryville

B. Vicksburg

C. Stones River

D. Shiloh

Answer:

B. Vicksburg

The Battle of Vicksburg was crucial in reinforcing the North's victory and sealing the South's defeat for a couple of reasons. First, the Battle of Vicksburg potentially gave the Union full control of the Mississippi River. More importantly, the battle split the Confederate Army and allowed General Grant to reach his goal of restoring commerce to the important northwest area.

83. The study of the exercise of power and political behavior in human society today would be conducted by experts in:

A. History

B. Sociology

C. Political Science

D. Anthropology

Answer:

C. Political Science

Experts in the field of political science today would likely conduct the study of exercise of power and political behavior in human society. However, it is also reasonable to suggest that such studies would be important to historians (study of the past, often in an effort to understand the present), sociologists (often concerned with power structure in the social and political worlds), and even some anthropologists (study of culture and their behaviors).

84. During the period of Spanish colonialism in California, which of the following was not a key to the goal of exploiting, transforming and including the native people?

A. Missions

B. Ranchos

C. Presidios

D. Pueblos

Answer:

B. Ranchos

The answer is "Ranchos" (b). The goal of Spanish colonialism was to exploit, transform and include the native people of California. The Spanish empire sought to do this first by gathering the native people into communities where they could both be taught Spanish culture and be converted to Roman Catholicism and its value system. The social institutions by which this was accomplished was the encouragement of the Mission System, which established a number of Catholic missions a day's journey apart. Once the native people were brought to the missions, they were incorporated into a mission society and indoctrinated in the teachings of Catholicism. The Presidios were fortresses that were constructed to protect Spanish interests and the communities from invaders. The Pueblos were small civilian communities that attracted settlers with the gift of land, seed, and farming equipment. The function of the Pueblos was to produce food for the missions and for the presidios.

85. Potential customers for any product or service are not only called consumers but can also be called a:

A. Resource

B. Base

C. Commodity

D. Market

Answer:

D. Market

Potential customers for any product or service are not only customers but can also be called a market. A resource is a source of wealth; natural resources are the basis for manufacturing goods and services. A commodity is anything that is bought or sold, any product.

86. An early cultural group was so skillful in navigating on the sea that they were able to sail at night guided by stars. They were the:

A. Greeks

B. Persians

C. Minoans

D. Phoenicians

Answer:

D. Phoenicians

Although the Greeks were quite able sailors and developed a strong navy in their defeat of the Persians at sea in the Battle of Marathon, it was the Eastern Mediterranean culture of the Phoenicians that had first developed the astronomical skill of sailing at night with the stars as their guide. The Minoans were an advanced early civilization off the Greek coast on Crete more noted for their innovations in terms of sewage systems, toilets, and running water.

87. One method of trade restriction used by some nations is:

A. Limited treaties

B. Floating exchange rate

C. Bill of exchange

D. Import quotas

Answer:

D. Import quotas

One method of trade restriction used by some nations is import quotas. The amount of goods imported are regulated in an effort to protect domestic enterprise and limit foreign competition. Both the United States and Japan, two of the world's most industrialized nations have import quotas to protect domestic industries.

88. A political system in which the laws and traditions put limits on the powers of government is:

A. Federalism

B. Constitutionalism

C. Parliamentary system

D. Presidential system

Answer:

B. Constitutionalism

Constitutionalism is a political system in which laws and traditions put limits on the powers of government. Federalism is the idea of a strong, centralized national government to hold together the nation. The parliamentary system, such as the governments of Great Britain and Israel, are systems in which a group of representatives are led by a prime minister contrasting with a presidential system which is run by a head of state, the elected (or sometimes self-appointed) president.

89. Which one of the following did not contribute to the early medieval European civilization?

A. The heritage from the classical cultures

B. The Christian religion

C. The influence of the German Barbarians

D. The spread of ideas through trade and commerce

Answer:

D. The spread of ideas through trade and commerce

The heritage of the classical cultures such as Greece, the Christian religion which became dominant, and the influence of the Germanic Barbarians (Visigoths, Saxons, Ostrogoths, Vandals and Franks) were all contributions to early medieval Europe and its plunge into feudalism. During this period, lives were often difficult and lived out on one single manor, with very little travel or spread of ideas through trade or commerce. Civilization seems to have halted progress during these years.

90. The Roman Empire gave so much to the world, especially the Western world. Of the legacies below, the most influential, effective and lasting is:

A. The language of Latin

B. Roman law, justice, and political system

C. Engineering and building

D. The writings of its poets and historians

Answer:

B. Roman law, justice, and political system

Of the lasting legacies of the Roman Empire, it is their law, justice, and political system that has been the most effective and influential on our Western world today. The idea of a Senate and different houses is still maintained by our United States government and their legal justice system is also the foundation of our own. We still use many Latin words in our justice system, terms such as *habeas corpus* and *voir dire*. English, Spanish, Italian, French, and others are all based on Latin. The Roman language, Latin itself has died out. Roman engineering and building and their writings and poetry have also been influential but not nearly to the degree that their government and justice systems have been.

91. Charlemagne's most important influence on Western civilization is seen today in:

A. Relationship of church and state

B. Strong military for defense

C. The criminal justice system

D. Education of women

Answer:

A. Relationship of church and state

Charlemagne was the leader of the Germanic Franks responsible for the promotion of the Holy Roman Empire across Europe. Although he unified governments and aided the Pope, he re-crowned himself in 802 A.D. to demonstrate that his power and right to rule was not a grant from the Pope, but rather a secular achievement. Therefore, although he used much of the Church's power in his rise to power, the Pope in turn used Charlemagne to ascend the Church to new heights. Thus, Charlemagne had an influence on the issues between Church and state.

92. Public administration, such as public officials in the areas of budgets, accounting, distribution of public funds, and personnel management, would be a part of the field of:

A. Anthropology

B. Sociology

C. Law and Taxation

D. Political Science and Economics

Answer:

D. Political Science and Economics

Public administration, such as public officials in the areas of budgets, accounting, distribution of public funds, and personnel management, would be parts of the fields of Economics and Political Science. While political scientists would be concerned with public administration, economists would also be concerned with the distribution of public funds, budgets, and accounting and their effects on the economy.

93. "Marbury vs. Madison (1803)" was an important Supreme Court case which set the precedent for:

A. The elastic clause

B. Judicial review

C. The supreme law of the land

D. Popular sovereignty in the territories

Answer:

B. Judicial review

Marbury vs. Madison (1803) was an important case for the Supreme Court as it established judicial review (B). In that case, the Supreme Court set precedence to declare laws passed by Congress as unconstitutional. Popular sovereignty (D) in the territories was a failed plan pushed by Stephen Davis to allow states to decide the slavery question for themselves. In his attempt to appeal to the masses in the pre-Civil War elections. The supreme law of the land (C) is just that, the law that rules. (A) The elastic clause is not a real term.

94. Which one of the following is not a use for a region's wetlands?

A. Produces fresh clean water

B. Provides habitat for wildlife

C. Provides water for hydroelectric power

D. Controls floods

Answer:

C. Provides water for hydroelectric power

A region's wetlands provide a number of uses and services not limited to but including production of fresh water, habitat and natural preserve of wildlife, and flood control. Wetlands are not used in the production of hydroelectric power the way dams or other power structures do.

95. The philosopher who coined the term "sociology" also stated that social behavior and events could be measured scientifically. He is identified as:

A. Auguste Comte

B. Herbert Spencer

C. Rousseau

D. Immanuel Kant

Answer:

A. Auguste Comte

Auguste Comte (1798-1857) was a French philosopher and social reformer who founded the school of positivism. Comte identified the uses of different scientific applications as dependent on the preceding science in the order of mathematics, astronomy, physics, chemistry, biology, and finally his coined term, sociology. Herbert Spencer (1820-1903) also helped spread sociology, although his evolutionary theory was more practical and popular than it was scientific. Rousseau (1712-1778) was a political philosopher who explored the idea of what has come to be known as liberalism. Immanuel Kant (1724-1804) was the German metaphysician and philosopher who was a founding proponent of the idea that world organization was the means for achieving universal peace.

96. The belief that the United States should control all of North America was called:

A. Westward Expansion

B. Pan Americanism

C. Manifest Destiny

D. Nationalism

Answer:

C. Manifest Destiny

The belief that the United States should control all of North America was called (B) Manifest Destiny. This idea fueled much of the violence and aggression towards those already occupying the lands such as the Native Americans. Manifest Destiny was certainly driven by sentiments of (D) nationalism and gave rise to (A) westward expansion.

97. A well known World War II figure who said that "democracy was like a rotting corpse that had to be replaced by a superior way of life and more efficient government" was:

A. Hitler

B. Stalin

C. Tojo

D. Mussolini

Answer:

D. Mussolini

(A) Adolf Hitler (1889-1945), the Nazi leader of Germany, and (C) Hideki Tojo (1884-1948), the Japanese General and Prime Minister, were well known World War II figures who led Axis forces into war on a quest of spreading fascism. (B) Joseph Stalin (1879-1953) was the Communist Russian head of state during World War II. Although all three were repressive in their actions, it was (D) Benito Mussolini (1883-1945), the Fascist and widely-considered incompetent leader of Italy during World War II, who once said "democracy was like a rotting corpse that had to be replaced by a superior way of life and more efficient government".

98. The Radical Republicans who pushed the harsh Reconstruction measures through Congress after Lincoln's death lost public and moderate Republican support when they went too far:

A. In their efforts to impeach the President

B. By dividing ten southern states into military-controlled districts

C. By making the ten southern states give freed African-Americans the right to vote

D. Sending carpetbaggers into the South to build up support for Congressional legislation

Answer:

A. In their efforts to impeach the President

The public support and the moderate Republicans were actually being drawn towards the more radical end of the Republican spectrum following Lincoln's death during Reconstruction. Because many felt as though Andrew Johnson's policies towards the South were too soft and were running the risk of rebuilding the old system of white power and slavery. Even moderate Republicans in the North felt as though it was essential to rebuild the South but with the understanding that they must be abide by the Fourteenth and Fifteenth Amendment assuring Blacks freedom and the right to vote. The radical Republicans were so frustrated that the President would make concessions to the old Southerners that they attempted to impeach him. This turned back the support that they had received from the public and from moderates.

99. The economic system promoting individual ownership of land, capital, and businesses with minimal governmental regulations is called:

A. Macro-economy

B. Micro-economy

C. Laissez-faire

D. Free enterprise

Answer:

D. Free Enterprise

(D) Free enterprise or capitalism is the economic system that promotes private ownership of land, capital, and business with minimal government interference. (C) Laissez-faire is the idea that an “invisible hand” will guide the free enterprise system to the maximum potential efficiency.

100. A political philosophy favoring or supporting rapid social changes in order to correct social and economic inequalities is called:

A. Nationalism

B. Liberalism

C. Conservatism

D. Federalism

Answer:

B. Liberalism

A political philosophy favoring rapid social changes in order to correct social and economic inequalities are called Liberalism. Liberalism was a theory that could be said to have started with the great French philosophers Montesquieu (1689-1755) and Rousseau (1712-1778). It is important to understand the difference between political, economic, and social liberalism, as they are different and how they sometimes contrast one another in the modern world.

101. China's last imperial ruling dynasty was one of its most stable and successful and under its rule, Chinese culture made an outstanding impression on Western nations. This dynasty was:

A. Ming

B. Manchu

C. Han

D. Chou

Answer:

B. Manchu

The (A) Ming Dynasty lasted from 1368-1644 and was among the more successful dynasties but focused attention towards foreign trade and encouraged growth in the arts. Therefore, it was the (B) Manchu Dynasty, the last imperial ruling dynasty, which came to power in the 1600s and expanded China's power in Asia greatly that was and still is considered to be among the most important, most stable, and most successful of the Chinese dynasties. The (C) Han and (D) Chou Dynasties were part of the "ancient" dynasties of China and while important in Chinese History, their influence did not hold impression on Western nations as the Manchu.

102. Development of a solar calendar, invention of the decimal system, and contributions to the development of geometry and astronomy are all the legacy of:

A. The Babylonians

B. The Persians

C. The Sumerians

D. The Egyptians

Answer:

D. The Egyptians

The (A) Babylonians of ancient Mesopotamia flourished for a time under their great contribution of organized law and code, called Hammurabi's Code (1750 B.C.), after the ruler Hammurabi. The fall of the Babylonians to the Persians in 539 B.C. made way for the warrior-driver Persian Empire that expanded from Pakistan to the Mediterranean Sea until the conquest of Alexander the Great in 331 B.C. The Sumerians of ancient Mesopotamia were most noted for their early advancements as one of the first civilizations and their contributions towards written language known as cuneiform. It was the (D) Egyptians who were the first true developers of a solar calendar, the decimal system, and made significant contributions to the development of geometry and astronomy.

103. The Study of "spatial relationships and interaction" would be done by people in the field of:

A. Political Science

B. Anthropology

C. Geography

D. Sociology

Answer:

C. Geography

Geography is the discipline within Social Science that most concerns itself with the study of "spatial relationships and interaction".

104. The circumference of the earth, which greatly contributed to geographic knowledge, was calculated by:

A. Ptolemy

B. Eratosthenes

C. Galileo

D. Strabo

Answer:

B. Eratosthenes

There is no doubt to Ptolemy and Galileo's influence as astronomers. (A) Ptolemy as an earlier theorist and (C) Galileo as a founder of modern scientific knowledge of astronomy and our place in the galaxy. However, it was (B) Eratosthenes (275 B.C. – 195 B.C.), the Greek writer, philosopher, and astronomer, who is credited with measuring the earth's circumference as well as the distances between Earth, sun, and moon. (D) Strabo was more concerned with geography and history than astronomy.

105. The first European to see Florida and sail along its coast was:

A. Cabot

B. Columbus

C. Ponce de Leon

D. Narvaez

Answer:

A. Cabot

(A) John Cabot (1450-1498) was the English explorer who gave England claim to North America and the first European to see Florida and sail along its coast. (B) Columbus (1451-1506) was sent by the Spanish to the New World and has received false credit for "discovering America" in 1492, although he did open up the New World to European expansion, exploitation, and Christianity. (C) Ponce de Leon (1460-1521), the Spanish explorer, was the first European to actually land on Florida. (D) Panfilo de Narvaez (1470-1528) was also a Spanish conquistador, but he was sent to Mexico to force Cortes into submission. He failed and was captured.

106. Which one of the following events did not occur during the period known as the "Era of Good Feeling"?

A. President Monroe issued the Monroe Doctrine

B. Spain ceded Florida to the United States

C. The building of the National Road

D. The charter of the second Bank of the United States

Answer:

A. President Monroe issued the Monroe Doctrine

The so-called "Era of Good Feeling" describes the period following the War of 1812. This was during the Presidency of James Madison and focused the nation on internal national improvements such as the building of the second national bank (Charter for Bank of United States), construction of new roads (National Road), and the Treaty of Ghent, which ended the War of 1812 by forcing Spain to cede Florida to the United States. Of the possible answers, only the Monroe Doctrine (1823), which called for an end to any European occupation and colonization in the Americas, was not a part of the "Era of Good Feeling", it came a bit after.

107. Native communities in early California are commonly divided into several cultural areas. How many cultural areas?

A. 4

B. 5

C. 6

D. 7

Answer:

C. 6

The answer is 6 (C). Due to the great diversity of the native communities, the state is generally divided into six "culture areas." The culture areas are: (1) the Southern Culture Area, (2) the Central Culture Area, (3) the Northwestern Culture Area, (4) the Northeastern Culture Area, (5) the Great Basin Culture Area, and (6) the Colorado River Culture Area. These areas are geographically distinct and supported different sorts of cultures depending upon the availability of an adequate water supply, the ability to cultivate the land, and the availability of game.

108. The world religion, which includes a caste system, is:

A. Buddhism

B. Hinduism

C. Sikhism

D. Jainism

Answer:

B. Hinduism

Buddhism, Sikhism, and Jainism all rose out of protest against Hinduism and its practices of sacrifice and the caste system. The caste system, in which people were born into castes, would determine their class for life including who they could marry, what jobs they could perform, and their overall quality of life.

109. The idea that continued population growth would, in future years, seriously affect a nation's productive capabilities was stated by:

A. Keynes

B. Mill

C. Malthus

D. Friedman

Answer:

C. Malthus

(C) John Maynard Keynes (1883-1946) advocated an economic system in which government regulations and spending on public works would stimulate the economy and lead to full employment. (C) Thomas Malthus (1766-1834) was the English economist who had the idea that population growth would seriously affect a nation's productive capabilities. Malthus' ideas also included predictions about running out of food and a natural selection-like process brought about by population that would maintain balance. His theory was proven wrong long ago. (B) Mill (1806 -1973), an English economist and (D) Friedman (1912-) an American economist contrasted one another greatly. Mill was almost a Socialist and wrote the early work in Political Economy while Friedman was a financial advisor in the arch conservative government of President Ronald Reagan.

110. After World War II, the United States:

A. Limited its involvement in European affairs

B. Shifted foreign policy emphasis from Europe to Asia

C. Passed significant legislation pertaining to aid to farmers and tariffs on imports

D. Entered the greatest period of economic growth in its history

Answer:

D. Entered the greatest period of economic growth in its history

After World War II, the United States did not limit or shift its involvement in European affairs. In fact, it escalated the Cold War with the Soviet Union at a swift pace and attempted to contain Communism to prevent its spread across Europe. There was no significant legislation pertaining to aid to farmers and tariffs on imports. In fact, since World War II, trade has become more liberal than ever. Free trade, no matter how risky or harmful to the people of the United States or other countries, has become the economic policy of the United States called neo-liberalism. Due to this, the United States after World War II entered the greatest period of economic growth in its history and remains a world superpower.

111. France decided in 1777 to help the American colonies in their war against Britain. This decision was based on:

A. The naval victory of John Paul Jones over the British ship "Serapis"

B. The survival of the terrible winter at Valley Forge

C. The success of colonial guerilla fighters in the South

D. The defeat of the British at Saratoga

Answer:

D. The defeat of the British at Saratoga

The defeat of the British at Saratoga was the overwhelming factor in the Franco-American alliance of 1777 that helped the American colonies defeat the British. Some historians believe that without the Franco-American alliance, the American Colonies would not have been able to defeat the British and American would have remained a British colony.

112. What event sparked a great migration of people from all over the world to California?

A. The birth of Labor Unions

B. California statehood

C. The invention of the automobile

D. The gold rush

Answer:

D. The gold rush

The discovery of gold in California created a lust for gold that quickly brought immigrants from the eastern United States and many parts of the world. To be sure, there were struggles and conflicts, as well as the rise of nativism. Yet this vast migration of people from all parts of the world began the process that has created California's uniquely diverse culture.

113. Which of the following does not differentiate provisions of the California constitution from the U.S. Constitution?

A. The governor of California has the pocket veto

B. In California representation in both houses of the legislature is based on population

C. The Governor and Lt. Governor are elected separately

D. The equivalent of cabinet positions are elected rather than appointed.

Answer:

A. The governor of California has the pocket veto.

The answer is (A) "The governor of California has the pocket veto." One of the differences between the California constitution and the U.S. Constitution concerns the executive power to veto and nullify legislation enacted by the legislature. The pocket veto, a policy that permits the President of the United States to nullify an act of Congress by simply withholding signature on a bill, is not shared by the Governor of California. Although the Governor of California does not have this particular power, the Governor holds a power that has not been extended to the President of the United States. This is the "Line-Item Veto" which permits the Governor to veto individual items that are part of a piece of legislation without nullifying the entire piece of legislation.

114. A number of women worked hard in the first half of the 19th century for women's rights but decisive gains did not come until after 1850. The earliest accomplishments were in:

A. Medicine

B. Education

C. Writing

D. Temperance

Answer:

B. Education

Although women worked hard in the early nineteenth century to make gains in medicine, writing, and temperance movements, the most prestigious accomplishments of the early women's movement was in the field of education. Women such as Mary Wollstonecraft (1759-1797), Alice Palmer(1855-1902), and of course Elizabeth Blackwell (1821-1910), led the way for women, particularly in the area of higher education.

115. Nineteenth century German unification was the result of the hard work of:

A. Otto von Bismarck

B. Kaiser William II

C. von Moltke

D. Hindenburg

Answer:

A. Otto von Bismarck

(A) Otto von Bismarck is the man most often credited with the unification of Germany. Bismarck became the first Chancellor of a unified Germany. He ultimately lost power to his successor Kaiser William II, who ultimately led Germany into World War I, when nationalist sentiment proved too strong for the united Germany. Ultimately, Germany's concessions in the Treaty of Versailles to end World War I, and Adolf Hitler's Nazi regime's defeat at the hands of Allied forces in World War II had destroyed the unified Germany that Bismarck had achieved in the mid to late 1800s.

116. The geographical drought-stricken region of Africa south of the Sahara and extending east and west from Senegal to Somalia is:

A. The Kalahari

B. The Namib

C. The Great Rift Valley

D. The Sahel

Answer:

D. The Sahel

The (A) Kalahari is located between the Orange and Zambezi Rivers and has an annual rainfall of about 5 to 20 inches. The (B) Namib is a desert, rocky plateau along the coast of Namibia in Southwest Africa that receives less than .5 inches of rainfall annually. The (C) Great Rift Valley is a fault system that runs 3000 miles from Syria to Mozambique and has great variations in elevation. Therefore, it is the (D) Sahel, the region of Africa South of the Sahara and extending East and West from Senegal to Somalia. The Sahel experienced a serious drought in the 1960s and then again in the 1980s and 1990s. International relief efforts have been focused there in an effort to keep the region alive.

117. The idea or proposal for more equal division of profits among employers and workers was put forth by:

A. Karl Marx

B. Thomas Malthus

C. Adam Smith

D. John Stuart Mill

Answer:

D. John Stuart Mill

(A) Karl Marx (1818-1883) was the German social philosopher and economist who wrote *The Communist Manifesto* and numerous other landmark works in his goal to help the world understand the inability of capitalism to provide for the workers, the idea of class struggle, and the central role of economy. (B) Thomas Malthus (1766-1834) was a British economist who introduced the study of population and early on considered famine, war, and disease to be the primary checks on world population. He later modified his views and recognized his early theoretical shortcoming and shifted his focus to the causes of unemployment. (C) Adam Smith (1723-1790) is considered by many to be the "father" of modern capitalist economics. In the *Wealth of Nations*, Smith advocated for little or no government interference in the economy. Smith claimed that an individual's self-interest would bring about the public's welfare.

It is important to note that Smith was firmly against the free market systems of monopoly power and warned that the private sector, particularly large manufacturers, if left unregulated could potentially stand in opposition to the public welfare. (D) John Stuart Mill (1806-1873) was the progressive British philosopher and economist whose ideas came closer to socialism than to the classical capitalist ideas of Adam Smith. Mill constantly advocated for political and social reforms, including emancipation for women, labor organizations, farming cooperatives, and most importantly a more equal division of profits among employers and workers.

118. The term that best describes how the Supreme Court can block laws that may be unconstitutional from being enacted is:

A. Jurisprudence

B. Judicial Review

C. Exclusionary Rule

D. Right of Petition

Answer:

B. Judicial Review

(A) Jurisprudence is the study of the development and origin of law. (B) Judicial review is the term that best describes how the Supreme Court can block laws that they deem as unconstitutional as set forth in Marbury vs. Madison. The (C) "exclusionary rule" is a reference to the Fourth Amendment of the Constitution and says that evidence gathered in an illegal manner or search must be thrown out and excluded from evidence. There is nothing called the (D) "Right of Petition", however the Petition of Right is a reference to a statement of civil liberties sent by the English Parliament to Charles I in 1628.

119. On the spectrum of American politics the label that most accurately describes voters to the "right of center" is:

A. Moderates

B. Liberals

C. Conservatives

D. Socialists

Answer:

C. Conservatives

(A) Moderates are considered voters who teeter on the line of political centrality or drift slightly to the left or right. (B) Liberals are voters who stand on the left of center. (C) Conservative voters are those who are "right of center". (D) Socialists would land far to the left on the political spectrum of America.

120. Marxism believes which two groups are in continual conflict:

A. Farmers and landowners

B. Kings and the nobility

C. Workers and owners

D. Structure and superstructure

Answer:

C. Workers and owners

Marxism believes that the workers and owners are in continual conflict. Marxists refer to these two groups as the proletariat and the bourgeoisie. The proletariat is exploited by the bourgeoisie and will, according to Marxism, rise up over the bourgeoisie in class warfare in an effort to end private control over the means of production.

121. The United States legislature is bi-cameral, this means:

A. It consists of several houses

B. It consists of two houses

C. The Vice-President is in charge of the legislature when in session

D. It has an upper house and a lower house

Answer:

B. It consists of two houses

The bi-cameral nature of the United States legislature means that it has two houses, the Senate and the House of Representatives, that make up the Congress. The Vice-President is part of the Executive branch of government but presides over the Senate and may act as a tiebreaker. An upper and lower house would be parts of a Parliamentary system of government such as the governments of Great Britain and Israel.

122. What Supreme Court ruling established the principal of Judicial Review?

A. Jefferson vs. Madison

B. Lincoln vs. Douglas

C. Marbury vs. Madison

D. Marbury vs. Jefferson

Answer:

C. Marbury vs. Madison

Marbury vs. Madison established the principal of judicial review. The Supreme Court ruled that it held no authority in making the decision (regarding Marbury's commission as Justice of the Peace in District of Columbia) as the Supreme Court's jurisdiction (or lack thereof) in the case, was conflicted with Article III of the Constitution.

123. To be eligible to be elected President one must:

A. Be a citizen for at least five years

B. Be a citizen for seven years

C. Have been born a citizen

D. Be a naturalized citizen

Answer:

C. Have been born a citizen

Article II, Section 1 of the United States Constitution clearly states, "No person except a natural-born citizen, or citizen of the United States at the time of the adoption of this Constitution, shall be eligible to the office of President, neither shall any person be eligible to that office who shall not have attained to the age of thirty-five years, and been fourteen years a resident within the United States."

124. The international organization established to work for world peace at the end of the Second World War is the :

A. League of Nations

B. United Federation of Nations

C. United Nations

D. United World League

Answer:

C. United Nations

The international organization established to work for world peace at the end of the Second World War was the United Nations. From the ashes of the failed League of Nations, established following World War I, the United Nations continues to be a major player in world affairs today.

125. Which of the following is an example of a direct democracy?

A. Elected representatives

B. Greek city-states

C. The Constitution

D. The Confederate States

Answer:

B. Greek city-states

The Greek city-states are an example of a direct democracy as their leaders were elected directly by the citizens and the citizens themselves were given voice in government. (A) Elected representatives in the United States as in the case of the presidential elections are actually elected by an electoral college that is supposed to be representative of the citizens. As we have learned from the elections of 2000, this is a flawed system. The United States Congress, the Senate, and the House of Representatives are also examples of indirect democracy as they represent the citizens in the legislature as opposed to having citizens represent themselves.

XAMonline, INC. 21 Orient Ave. Melrose, MA 02176
Toll Free number 800-301-4647

TO ORDER Fax 781-662-9268 OR www.XAMonline.com

NEW MEXICO TEACHER ASSESSMENT - NMTA - 2007

P0# Store/School:

Address 1:

Address 2 (Ship to other):

City, State Zip

Credit card number_______-________-_________-________ **expiration**_______

EMAIL ______________________________

PHONE **FAX**

13# ISBN 2007	TITLE	Qty	Retail	Total
978-1-58197-750-9	NMTA New Mexico Assessment of Teacher Basic Skills 01			
978-1-58197-751-6	NMTA New Mexico Assessment of Teacher Competency 03, 04 , 05			
978-1-58197-752-3	NMTA Elementary Education 11			
978-1-58197-753-0	NMTA French Sample Test 18			
978-1-58197-754-7	NMTA Language Arts 12			
978-1-58197-755-4	NMTA Mathematics 14			
978-1-58197-756-1	NMTA Middle Level Language Arts 23			
978-1-58197-757-8	NMTA Middle Level Mathematics 24			
978-1-58197-758-5	NMTA Middle Level Science 25			
978-1-58197-759-2	NMTA Middle Level Social Studies 26			
978-1-58197-760-8	NMTA Reading 13			
978-1-58197-761-5	NMTA Science 15			
978-1-58197-762-2	NMTA History, Geography, Civics, and Government 16			
978-1-58197-763-9	NMTA Spanish 20			
978-1-58197-764-6	NMTA Visual Arts Sample Test 22			
			SUBTOTAL	
	FOR PRODUCT PRICES GO TO WWW.XAMONLINE.COM		Ship	$8.25
			TOTAL	

CPSIA information can be obtained at www.ICGtesting.com
Printed in the USA
240098LV00001B/5/A

9 781581 977622